# DYNAMICS
# AND
# INDETERMINISM IN
# DEVELOPMENTAL AND
# SOCIAL PROCESSES

# DYNAMICS AND INDETERMINISM IN DEVELOPMENTAL AND SOCIAL PROCESSES

Edited by

**Alan Fogel**
*University of Utah*

**Maria C. D. P. Lyra**
*Federal University of Pernambuco, Brazil*

**Jaan Valsiner**
*University of North Carolina at Chapel Hill*

**LEA** LAWRENCE ERLBAUM ASSOCIATES, PUBLISHERS
1997   Mahwah, New Jersey

Lawrence Erlbaum Associates, Inc., Publishers
10 Industrial Avenue
Mahwah, New Jersey 07430

**Library of Congress Cataloging-in-Publication Data**

Dynamics and indeterminism in developmental and social processes/ Alan
   Fogel, Maria C. D. P. Lyra, Jaan Valsiner.
      p.    cm.
   Includes bibliographical references and indexes.
   ISBN 0-8058-1805-7 (cloth : alk. paper). — ISBN 0-8058-1806-5
(pbk. : alk. paper).
   1. Free will and determinism—Congresses.  2. Developmental
psychology—Congresses.  I. Fogel, Alan.  II. Lyra, Maria C. D. P.
III. Valsiner, Jaan.
BF621.D86  1997
123'.5—dc20                                                96-34678
                                                             CIP

Books published by Lawrence Erlbaum Associates are printed on acid-free paper,
and their bindings are chosen for strength and durability.

Printed in the United States of America
10  9  8  7  6  5  4  3  2  1

# CONTENTS

# Introduction: Perspectives on Indeterminism and Development

Alan Fogel
University of Utah

Maria C. D. P. Lyra
Federal University of Pernambuco, Brazil

Jaan Valsiner
University of North Carolina at Chapel Hill

*All scientists are determinists. It is difficult to imagine what not being a determinist could mean ... There is no magical force (no vitalist spirit or melded interaction) that shapes development, apart from genetic/biological systems that propel and guide development and environments that are necessary and provide opportunities for its expression.*

—Scarr, 1993, pp. 1342–1343

*We have not sufficiently taken into account that we need the laboratory with its incisive restrictions in order to demonstrate the invariable validity of natural law. If we leave things to nature, we see a very different picture: every process is partially or totally interfered with by chance, so much so that under natural circumstances a course of events absolutely conforming to specific laws is almost an exception.*

—Jung, 1950, p. xxii

*Webs and chains of historical events are so intricate, so imbued with random and chaotic elements, so unrepeatable in encompassing such a multitude of unique (and uniquely interacting) objects, that standard models of simple prediction and replication do not apply.*

—Gould, 1994, p. 85

I

Perhaps there are two kinds of behavioral scientists: those who view development as a lawful and determined process, and those who believe that there are indeterministic shadows cast by those laws. Or, perhaps there are three kinds of behavioral scientists represented by the themes from the opening quotes: the strict determinism of Scarr, the contextual determinism of Jung, and the historical indeterminism of Gould. Or, what is more likely, there is only one kind of behavioral scientist: one who is inquisitive about people and their development and who struggles with an inner dialogue between these positions on determinism vs. indeterminism.

## THE SCENE AND CHARACTERS

In a way, this volume reveals such dialogues for a diverse group of developmentalists who participated in a workshop on the topic of "Determinism and Indeterminism in Development" held in July 1993. The workshop took place in a resort hotel in the village of Serrambi, in the state of Pernambuco, Brazil, following the meetings of the International Society for the Study of Behavioral Development, Recife, July, 1993. The workshop was supported by the Brazilian National Science Foundation (Conselho Nacional de Desenvolvimento Cientifico e Tecnologico–CNPq), the Fundacao de Amparo a Ciencia e Tecnologia do Estado de Pernambuco (Facepe), and the Banco Nacional do Norte (Banorte). It was co-organized by the editors of this book. Participants included 27 developmental psychologists from 11 national origins (Belgium, Brazil, Canada, Estonia, Finland, Japan, the Netherlands, Turkey, England, the United States, and Yugoslavia) representing some of the most innovative scholars in theoretical developmental psychology from a diversity of points of view.

Each participant had a unique perspective on the issue of determinism vs. indeterminism. Most of the contributors had never been asked to ponder the issue, and were often surprised by all that they had to say about it. It was clear that the basic human questions of destiny and fate vs. free will and creativity were present in all the participants but we differed in how much we had made explicit these issues in the context of our professional work.

To raise the issue of indeterminism in development is potentially risky. If scientific approaches require a deterministic stance, as suggested by the Scarr quote, then contributors might either feel constrained to mask indeterministic intuitions or they may have already decided that indeterminism cannot exist in principle. The organizers of the conference took two deliberate steps to enhance the probability for participants to address the issue of indeterminism. First, we invited scholars who we thought would be willing to enter into public dialogues about the issue. Second, we chose to hold the conference in Brazil at a beach resort which we hoped would facilitate the flow of ideas.

Brazil is a country in which psychology is a relatively new field of scholar-ship and in which there is a newly emerging group of developmental psychologists who have been willing to enter into the international arena of scholarship with nontraditional ideas. In Brazil people live with uncertainty and indeterminism on a daily basis. This is expressed, in part, by economic and political instabilities. But those processes are embedded in a culture in which life is lived more spontaneously and opportunistically; in which the present moment is alive and shares an equal status with the past and the future in the flow of everyday activity; in which contradictions are not reduced to logical impossibilities but accepted as part of life. This cultural process of living yields a different way of thinking about human development than the traditional Western European and North American approaches. It is a perspective that we editors value and trust is a principled alternative to those traditional views and we encourage readers from North America and Western Europe to recognize the possibilities and limits of their own cultural grounding as they read and evaluate the work presented in this book.

It is a mistake for scholars in the traditional intellectual centers of the West to interpret work from Brazil, Japan, and Eastern Europe, for example, as cross-cultural data; as just another population to be reduced to the same traditional forms of analysis. Rather, the work of senior scholars from these countries should be understood as an alternative world view, foundationally different, with important implications for the theoretical and philosophical basis for understanding human development.

## THE INTELLECTUAL CONTEXT

During the past several years, a radical change in world view has begun to take hold in the traditional social sciences. This new world view is based on concepts such as complexity and chaos that underlie a more general perspective referred to most commonly as the study of dynamic self-organizing systems. The concepts and methods underlying the study of dynamic systems emerged in the physical sciences and have gradually begun to find a niche in the social sciences. Papers and books, both theoretical and empirical, have appeared in social science fields as diverse as psychology, sociology, anthropology, economics, geography, linguistics, and education. The dynamic systems model appears to have important implications for the understanding of functioning of social and psychological systems.

One of the more important aspects of dynamic systems thinking is all living systems are inherently developmental. Living systems are not rigid structures, but dynamically stable processes. Systems de-stabilize through phase transitions in systematic ways that can be modelled by the dynamic systems perspective. The application of dynamic systems thinking to developmental phenomena, however, has only been applied to a limited number of developmental phenomena and the theoretical implications of the perspective have only begun to be articulated.

One of the most profound insights of the dynamic systems perspective is that the new structures resulting from the developmental process do not need to be planned in advance, nor is it necessary to have these structures represented in a genetic or neurological template prior to their emergence. Rather, new structure can emerge as components of the individual and the environment self-organize, that is, as they mutually constrain each other's actions.

This theoretical possibility brings into developmental theory the important concept of indeterminism: the possibility that developmental outcomes may not be predictable in any simple linear causal way from their antecedents. What is the source of this indeterminism? What is it's role in developmental change? Is it merely the result of incomplete observational data or error in measurement?

## OUTLINE OF THE BOOK

This is the first volume to take a critical and serious look at the role of indeterminism in psychological and behavioral development. We begin with a series of opening chapters in which the concepts of indeterminism and determinism are reviewed and discussed in their historical, philosophical, and theoretical perspectives, particularly in relation to dynamic systems thinking.

The chapters in Part I raise issues regarding how to deal with the emergence of novelty versus predictability in developmental change. Van Geert presents an insightful and elegant computer modeling of developmental change. Dealing with what he calls process determinism, he proposes that taking into account the dynamics of change through time we can have different causal–historical explanations for differences in developmental trajectories. These explanations range from truly indeterministic toward deterministic ones, dependent on the reduction or creation of degrees of freedom unfolding through time. So, Van Geert's model proposes that indeterministic developmental change can be understood through the analysis of its dynamics. An analysis of how novelty emerges the dynamics of early communication is presented in the chapters by Fogel and Branco and by Lyra and Winegar. These authors assume that communicative dynamics and hence developmental change have an inherent degree of indeterminacy and unpredictability. Both chapters examine the micro-processes of developmental change in the system of early communication.

Fogel and Branco suggest that indeterminacy is inherent to the process of creation of novelty in the dynamics of the communication system. In their chapter, the processes of meta-communication are discussed as a source of creation of novelty which is reelaborated at the level of actual communication. Communication and meta-communication function as dialectical counterparts to maintain the stability and change, determinacy and indeterminacy, of the system of communication.

Lyra and Winegar, exploring the microprocesses of communication at the beginning of life, propose that the dynamics of the partners' negotiations unfold meaning as an emergent characteristic. The authors propose how determinacy and indeterminacy come to be inscribed in the history of dyadic constructions leading to the abbreviation of these created meanings. But, as the abbreviated meaning carries a historical determinacy, it also carries unpredictability inherent to the dynamics of the communicative context in which it occurs and to the process of possibilities intrinsic to meaning making.

Gulerce proposes a broad and integrative model which aims to integrate the biological, the social, and the cultural dimensions of developmental change. She argues in favor of separating predictability from determinacy, suggesting that at some levels—for instance, the ones which call for survival values—the predictability of developmental change can be high. However, at the cultural–symbolic level the characteristics of unpredictability and indeterminacy dominate.

The commentary by Butterworth makes two main points for research. Point one is an argument for applying mathematical models that can be tested, allowing identification of cause, and the use of predictions. Point two is the question about discovering what processes in natural life give rise to novelty. This commentary raises a dilemma that is related to the epistemology which frames the kind of questions we are asking.

What kind of questions do we want to answer? The possibility of using formal mathematical models that can be applied to the dynamics of developmental change, yielding more precision and testability are promising. However, for grasping the question of how novelty emerges in human developmental systems we should not discard a phenomenological analysis of the micro-processes of meaning making. As a consequence, the possibility of approaching the question of "how" developmental change occurs can be done through phenomenological-verbal models which do not carry the exactitude and predictability claimed by the present dominant scientific community. Nevertheless, phenomenological-verbal models are well suited to capture nuances of meaning making, historical relatedness, and human creativity that are the sources of indeterminism. The question remains, however, of how do use such methods in a scientifically credible manner.

In a similar way, when the inclusive model proposed by Gulerce refers to cultural–symbolic dimensions, which claims for careful analysis of the micro-processes of change, the possibility of achieving precise predictability is ruled out. The challenge seems to be placed in the question of how to articulate different epistemological levels of our research questions. In other words, at one level the possibility of predictability needs to rely on the limits of using a dynamic systems approach to deal with a variability resolvable into quantifiable variables and parameters. However, the comprehension of the process of emergence of this variability, the process through which novelty emerges, seems to be only graspable through models that describe the micro-processes of change in real life which, at the present the moment, are still verbal–conceptual models.

The second part of the book stresses the indeterminacy inherent to symbols and meaning making in social systems. The chapter by Oliveira and Valsiner exhibits the power of imagination in creating indeterminacy in developmental change using examples from children's peer interactions and the internal dialogues in early adulthood. The determinate side is present in this chapter through the boundaries imposed by the conservative aspects of language and social rules.

Smolka, Goes, and Pino's chapter approaches indeterminacy through highlighting the pluridimensionality of voices present in the symbolic dialogues which constitute developmental change. For these authors who stress the indeterminate side of development, the question of determinacy seems, in some sense, irrelevant. The chapter is more an example of the immense possibilities we face when we take seriously the plasticity (and indeterminacy) of our symbolic system.

The chapter by Pedrosa, Carvalho, and Hamburger is an excellent exhibition of how meaning emerges from the dynamics of an apparently chaotic system formed by preschool children in a play situation. These indeterminate systems acquire a determinate side through the dynamics of what they call emergent correlations through time. The intricate nature of indeterminacy and determinacy are traced through the use of the concept of attractors. However, the place of indeterminacy is highlighted through the recognition of the constant development of this system, amplified by the temporal dimension in which meaning emerges.

Both commentaries, by Lightfoot and by Litvinovic, point out the power of symbols to entail the indeterminate side of developmental change. However, they differ in their interpretation of the chapters in this section. Lightfoot sees a dichotomy at the level of intra- and interindividual symbolic functioning, arguing that the chapter by Oliveira and Valsiner and the one by Smolka, Goes, and Pino cover these two sides but the chapter done by Pedrosa, Carvalho, and Hamburger does not. Litvinovic, reads both intra- and interindividual levels as present in the three chapters. Both commentators point out the necessity to consider symbolic functioning as structured by the normative rules of society, which would constitute the determinate side of developmental change. Nevertheless, even placing the source of novelty at the level of the indeterminate symbolic functioning and considering inter- and intraindividual functioning as instances of the indeterminate side of symbols, these commentators fluctuate in balancing the individual and the social-relational aspects of this process, stressing, in some moments, the individual as the major source of developmental change.

Part III addresses processes within the individual related to emotional, social, and cognitive development. The chapter by Lewis exhibits an important extension of the dynamic system perspective to understanding personality development. His proposition of a cascade model of personality change conceptualizes the interconnections that allow, through time, the emergence of both novel–indeterminate and more stable–therefore determinate–instances of personality characteristics. However, even integrating novelty and indeterminacy in his model, Lewis argues for increasing stability–determinism and less openness for novelty and indeterminacy as the individual gets older.

The chapter by Legerstee shows one interesting attempt to make a compromise between the causal, preadapted, tendencies of early life to cope with social and nonsocial stimuli, and the insertion of the dynamic system approach to the development of the social side of development. One of the interesting questions that her chapter raises is about determinacy/causality. In other words, how do the dynamics of the developing system integrate preadapted biological–perceptual endowment into the relatively indeterminate flow of social discourse?

Finally, the chapter by Roazzi and Souza, represents a more traditional and individual perspective on the issue of indeterminism in development. Using correlational analysis, this chapter does not exhibit clearly the role of determinacy and indeterminacy. They assume the perspective that indeterminacy is not a characteristic of developmental change but rather a problem of incomplete measurement.

The commentaries by Kojima and Hurme exhibit very different perspectives. Hurme calls for a consensus in the use of terminology/metaphors and asks for a model that would integrate the individual and the relational in the functioning of determinacy and indeterminacy. Kojima analyzes the chapters from a point of view both deeply dynamic and cultural relativistic. His comment is very sensitive to the identification of mechanical–causal aspects of the models used in all chapters. He takes a broad view of the historical–contextual and moral frames that underlie all scientific enterprise. He argues that the scientific demand for causality specification and/or the directionality and determinism of change in developmental models is a relativistic social construction. As he points out, "In a sense, these scientific models reflect cultural ways of story-telling."

As a whole, this book illustrates not only the dialogue between different perspectives on development but also the dialogue between different "cultural ways of story-telling" using Kojima's expression. Because the book puts together scholars from different parts of the world, it is interesting for the reader to evaluate and think about the implicit—not only the explicit—ways of conceiving development shown in the different chapters and comments. The reader should pay particular attention to the commentaries. They are especially interesting from the perspective of the culture of scientific discourse mentioned earlier in this introduction. Each of the commentators is from a different intellectual and cultural tradition: Western Europe (Butterworth, Hurme), Eastern Europe (Litvinovic), the United States (Lightfoot), and Japan (Kojima). Notice how their reactions to the chapters are framed, both explicitly and implicitly, within their scientific culture. For instance, Butterworth and Hurme call for more specificity, clearer measures, and better mathematical models. Alternatively, Kojima raises the issue of relativistic sociocultural ways of conceiving developmental change. The reference lists for their chapters are also telling of the cultural literature on which they have drawn. No less is true, of course, for the authors of the chapters themselves. In the chapters we can also see the emergence of dialogues between traditions by the ways in which the articles of joint authorship resolved their different points of view and integrated their different backgrounds (Fogel & Branco, Lyra & Winegar, Oliveira & Valsiner). The fact that one of the authors of each of these chapters is an editor of this book and organizer of the Serrambi conference reflects, we hope, our commitment to bring together different intellectual traditions. We believe that it is the tensions inherent to such dialogues that remains the core of the dynamics from which emerges creativity and novelty in the scientific field. However, we never know from which size of sand grain will result a small or a big avalanche, even knowing (or believing?) that it is always no more than a grain dropping onto the pile.

## THE DEVELOPMENT OF THIS BOOK

From the outset, the planning and development of this volume was illustrative of a balance between determinism and indeterminism in social developmental processes. The question of indeterminacy of developmental change emerged indeterministically from the work of each of the editors on the processes of social developmental change. There was also a set of complex and often unplanned circumstances that led to the acquaintenship and developing relationship of the coeditors and their decision to propose the conference at Serrambi.

The next step on was a search for concrete possibilities of financial support, the choice of including scholars from different cultural backgrounds, and the waiting for the acceptance of those scholars to attend the meeting and funding agencies to support it. It was only weeks before the conference that we heard a positive reply from the funding agencies. By then another conference had been scheduled at the resort where we had originally intended to hold the meeting, so the site at Serrambi was selected at the last minute.

It is fair to say that the element of indeterminism was present at virtually all times in the concrete organization of the workshop from which this book came. Besides the dialogues and work done during the discussion at the workshop, new relationships developed between the participants gave us the feeling of doing science as an alive and relational enterprise.

Perhaps the tone of the workshop was set by an entirely unexpected event. The transportation by bus from Recife to the small town on the coast—Serrambi—where the workshop took place was interrupted when the bus got stuck on a muddy road in the middle of the sugar cane plantations under a completely clear starry night. The driver had taken a wrong turn, apparently. After trying to free the bus on his own, the driver asked participants, dressed in their conference clothing, to step into the mud and help push the bus. When this failed, we began to believe that we would spend the night in the bus. Several of the Brazilian participants set out on foot toward the nearest town. Others found some bits of wood to place under the tires and with some effort, the driver finally succeeded in freeing the bus. As we drove into the town, we unexpectedly found those who had walked. We arrived late in the evening at the hotel, greeting the palm trees and the dark sea with gratitude.

The two-day workshop was planned in the following way. The organizers created a list of questions about the problem of determinism and indeterminism in development and we hoped discussion at the workshop would focus around these questions. We decided not to ask participants to present papers at the workshop, but rather to participate in an open discussion of the issues. What happened instead was an extended discussion of the participants' assumptions about the theme "processes of development: determinacy and indeterminacy." Most of the time was spent with each participant giving his or her own views of what is meant by determinism and indeterminism. Although we attempted to reach a consensus, it proved impossible after two days of discussion. In the final afternoon we discussed whether we should edit a book and what kind of book it should be. We decided that some of the participants would write chapters about their own field of research, discussing the question of dynamics of developmental change and the place of determinacy and indeterminacy in their work. Other participants would write comments about groups of chapters.

We sent the book proposal to 20 academic publishers. A most positive response came from Judi Amsel at Erlbaum and we are grateful for her continued support in the development of the project. Our discussions with

Judi and the outside reviewers added further changes and introduced indeterministic novelty as the plan of the book emerged from the editorial fire.

Much was learned by the editors during the exchange of chapters written for the book. We divided the task so that at least two of us read each chapter and gave comments to the authors. This often inspired discussions between the editors and between the editors and the authors. We strived to balance our critiques with our respect for the authors assumptions and ways of conceiving their contributions, and for the cultural differences mentioned earlier. These dialogues exhibited the relational pluridimensionality of linguistic meanings in communication as well as the diversity of cultural and individual readings of the texts. It is hard to accept different perspectives, and as editors we struggled with conflicting emotions. But we also realized that this struggle, full of uncertainty, is the way knowledge develops and communication deepens.

Perhaps the best metaphor for the work presented here is suggested by Hideo Kojima in his commentary. As a story teller, each participant, or group of participants, reflects their cultural background in the way they see the dynamics of developmental change and the role of indeterminacy in it. We hope this book, and the story of its development, can reflect that meaning making in science is an alive, dynamic, plurivocal, indeterministic process that is realized through the history of its own development.

## REFERENCES

Gould, S. J. (1994, October). The evolution of life on the earth. *Scientific American*, 85–91.

Jung, C. G. (1950). Forward to *The I Ching: Book of changes*. New Jersey: Princeton University Press.

Scarr, S. (1993). Biological and cultural diversity: The legacy of Darwin for development. *Child Development, 64*, 1333–1353.

# DETERMINACY AND INDETERMINACY: THEORETICAL AND PHILOSOPHICAL PERSPECTIVES

# 1

# QUE SERÁ, SERÁ: DETERMINISM AND NONLINEAR DYNAMIC MODEL BUILDING IN DEVELOPMENT

Paul van Geert
University of Groningen

The most forceful fighters of developmental determinism are probably found among parents of kids in the sweet age of adolescence. Whatever determines the behavior of adolescents, it certainly is not the parents' good advice and lessons that they teach. It's true, there is a certain form of determinism, in that adolescents are in general very determined to do what is stupid and inadvisable, and the only form of determinism they themselves seem to support is that of self-determinism, if any such philosophical concept exists. Of course, the preceding comments are nothing but the lamentations of a developmental psychologist who has gone through the purifying experience of parenthood. The trouble with educating kids is that parents are almost forced to believe in some form of determinism, preferably environmental determinism, which teaches that what children do and the kind of people they become is, to a considerable extent, a consequence of what their parents and schoolmasters taught them, but very often kids grow up in a way that strays so markedly from the life course that parents had in mind. Que será, será.

In its original form, *determinism* is the philosophical doctrine that every event, act, and decision, is the inevitable consequence of antecedents that are independent of the human will (The American Heritage Dictionary of the English Language, 1992). Nobody, with the exception of a few weirdos maybe, will seriously endorse philosophical determinism in this particular form. However, there exist forms of physical and statistical determinism that still color the scientific discussion about how human development comes about, and to what extent development is determined by either natural or nurtural factors.

The verb *determine* comes from the Latin *determinare*, which means *to limit*. In view of its etymology, determinism boils down to the doctrine that antecedents limit the range and properties of consequent events, or that events are constrained by their past. It is hard to imagine that anyone would seriously object to this particular form of determinism.

In summary, there is a form of determinism that no one would endorse, and there is a form of determinism that no one would seriously reject. The fight over developmental determinism must take place somewhere between these two poles. In this chapter, I begin by exploring some potential sources of the determinism debate in physics, and then proceed to (developmental) psychology and dynamic systems theory. My aim is to show that nonlinear dynamics provides a view of development that sheds a new and interesting light on the determinism issue.

## SOURCES OF THE DETERMINISM DEBATE IN PHYSICS

### Physical Determinism in Celestial Mechanics

Whereas determinism as applied to human acts and free will has never found widespread acceptance, it has been strongly endorsed in classical physics. The best known formulation of physical determinism is as follows: If an imaginary being would know the position and speed of all particles in the universe, this being would, in principle, be capable of computing the fate of the universe into an infinitely distant future (Smith, 1989; Stewart, 1989). The "invention" of physical determinism is often attributed to Pierre Simon, Marquis de Laplace (1749–1827). Employing Newton's equations, Laplace computed the orbits of comets and planets and published his results in the five volumes of his *Mécanique céleste* (1799–1825). The fact that the orbits of heavenly bodies so distant from the world of man could be inferred from mathematic theories that the human mind could not only grasp but also discover, marked a turning point in scientific thinking. One could say that the normal relationship between reality and model was turned upside down. The model was no longer considered a representation of reality, but rather reality was seen as the instantiation of a (mathematical) model. This view expressed the triumph of Platonism, in a sense, because, with the discovery of Newton's laws, mankind was supposed to have found the eternal Ideas that underlay the structure of the Universe.

## The Epistemological Character of Physical Determinism

It is important to note that physical determinism was basically an episte-mological issue. It referred not to causality per se, but to a state of knowl-edge: If I know the present, I can foresee the future. This epistemological stance is based on an ontological one, which claims that if exactly the same antecedents hold, exactly the same consequents must follow. The general objection against physical determinism is that it is, in principle, impossible to have a complete knowledge of the properties of particles or objects, that is, a knowledge of infinite accuracy. An infinitesimally small error will soon diverge into a macroscopic error that is of the same magnitude as the events that one intends to predict. Imagine seven perfect billiard balls aligned on a perfect table, and a perfect player wants to make a seven ball carom. An initial error no bigger than the radius of a single atom suffices to make the sixth ball miss the seventh (Smith, 1989). If similar reasoning is applied to atoms in a gas, for instance, two gaseous states that are similar except for an infinitesimally small factor will have evolved into two massively different states after only $1^{-11}$ seconds.

The impossibility of knowing the future is mirrored in the impossibility of knowing the past, given an almost perfectly accurate knowledge of the present. The reason for this fact lies not only in the previously mentioned exponential increase of error, but also in the fact that the arrow of time is not symmetrical. In addition to celestial mechanics, during the late 18th and early 19th centuries, physicists were highly interested in heat and in ma-chines that turned heat into mechanical energy (given that mechanical energy was so easily turned into money). Nicolas Léonard Sadi Carnot (1796–1832) discovered that the transformation of heat into energy was asymmetrical. Because of this asymmetry, events flow in only one direction, namely, that of increasing entropy. *Entropy*, loosely defined, is a state of disorder, or loss of information. Put differently, the inevitable course of time corresponds with a decreasing possibility of reconstructing the past, given knowledge of the present.

## Ontological Determinism and Uncertainty in Quantum Physics

The confutation of the epistemological version of physical determinism does not affect the potential truth of ontological determinism. However, it is still possible to think of two identical states of affairs, or more simply, to think of the same state of affairs twice, and then to ask oneself whether or not identical antecedents must lead to identical consequents.

Physics, however, is far from a monolithic discipline. It deals with a variety of subjects, each of which requires its own particular assumptions and models. Quantum physics, for instance, deals with an entirely different world than classic Newtonian physics does. At the beginning of the 20th century, quantum mechanical principles were discovered that shed an entirely different light on the issue of definite and determined properties in physical states. Heisenberg's *uncertainty principle*, introduced in 1927, raises doubts about the possibility that events at the level of elementary particles have definite properties and are thus, in principle, replicable. Or, more precisely, the principle shows that it makes no sense to conceive of events as if all their relevant properties (momentum and position) can be accurately known or measured simultaneously. So, there is no meaning in the statement that events can, in principle, be replicated and should, therefore, have exactly the same consequences. Exit determinism?

All this talk about unknowable futures and pasts should not make us forget that physics is about the only scientific discipline where truly amazing predictions of past and present events are possible. Mathematical models that account for uncertainty and lack of accuracy are actually very well suited to overcome these problems as far as the limits of computation allow us to go. Actual quantum mechanical predictions are extremely accurate. We have seen that gases, for instance, lose track of their past, so to speak, after unimaginably small amounts of time. But as a whole, gases behave very neatly and predictably. The reason is that indeterminism at the level of small particles is definitely outweighed by their large numbers. The large numbers of particles allow for a statistical treatment that reintroduces determinism at the practical scale of macroscopic events. This brings us to a second view on determinism, namely, statistical determinism, which is not only reigning in certain branches of physics, but also in the life and social sciences. Although statistical determinism sounds like a *contradictio in terminis*, it makes perfect sense and there's even a law that accounts for it: the *law of large numbers*.

### Statistical Determinism

We are all familiar with the imaginary pinball machine from statistics class: a perfect upright surface, with perfectly aligned nails set in triangular form. Perfectly round marbles are put into the pinball machine, through a slot on the top exactly in the middle. Although it is impossible to predict the course of any individual marble, even given arbitrarily high accuracy of initial-state knowledge, a great number of marbles will produce a highly predictable pattern, namely, a bell-shaped distribution at the bottom of the machine. As the number of marbles approaches infinity, the bell shape will approach absolute geometric accuracy. This is an illustration of the so-called *central limit theorem*, an essential theorem of probability theory.

Ludwig Boltzmann's kinetic-molecular theory of gases infers macroscopic determinacies, such as the gases' pressure and temperature, from the indeterminate interactions among the masses of gas particles. It seems that, in order to understand the behavior of phenomena such as gases, the microscopic level is the wrong level of aggregation; laws and determinacies reign at the macroscopic level. In the physical universe, determinism comes about. Just as Venus, the goddess of beauty, was born out of the ephemeral foam of the ocean, determinism comes about as the result of indeterminacies at a lower level of aggregation, namely, the level of particles. But the law of large numbers does set a few restrictions. First, the events or objects at the lower level should be treated as a homogeneous class; that is, they should lose their proper identity and become exactly similar to one another. In addition to homogeneity at the object level, time should become a mere rank ordering dimension. Different occurrences of similar events are completely independent of one another.[1]

## Summary

What can we learn from this small and probably also extremely selective excursion into the field of physical determinism? One conclusion that I find interesting is that determinism in its traditional, absolute sense, turned out to be an epistemological issue. It is not about the fact that causality per se is deterministic, but rather about whether or not causal chains can be predicted to an infinite degree of accuracy. First, it is, in principle, impossible to achieve an infinite degree of accuracy in the measurement of physical conditions. Second, even infinitesimally small inaccuracies turn into major errors after surprisingly small amounts of time (small in comparison to the error). It follows, then, that there is no support for the determinist claim.

A second interesting conclusion is that determinism (or rather, the impossibility of determinism) is a two-sided phenomenon. Not only can the future not be predicted, but the past can be known only to a limited extent. Events lose information about their past, and eventually all information about the past will be lost in a state of maximal entropy.

Third, if the problems are lifted to the macroscopic level, determinism, in the sense of predictability and knowableness, has demonstrated its viability very persuasively in the form of highly accurate physical predictions.

Finally, microscopic indeterminacy turns into macroscopic order, simplicity, and predictability, basically because of one iron law: the law of big numbers. It is interesting to see that time, taken separately and acting on the microscopic particle level, acts to increase the physical degrees of

---

[1] I owe this and several other clarifying remarks to Jaan Valsiner.

freedom, whereas space greatly reduces the degrees of freedom and creates a regular, greatly deterministic macroscopic world, provided the homogeneity and independence principles hold.

## SOURCES OF THE DETERMINISM DEBATE IN NONLINEAR DYNAMICS

### From Mechanics to Dynamics

The motions of planets and heavenly bodies were the showpiece of classical physical determinism. The wonderfully accurate application of Newton's laws to the motions of these huge and distant objects can be attributed to the fact that the problem of their motions reduced reasonably well to an analytically solvable problem, basically to the problem of how two large masses affect one another. But at the end of the 19th century, mathematicians, Poincaré in particular, discovered that this reduction turned out to be a fortuitous hit, an exception rather than the rule: Three bodies attracting each other yielded a problem that could no longer be solved by straightforward analytical means, and three bodies are only one more than two, but also a lot fewer than the numbers statistical mechanics worked with (Stewart, 1989). A new mathematical discipline—dynamics—had to be invented in order to account for processes of change and motion that occurred in relatively small sets of interacting objects. In those sets, the law of large numbers and the central limit theorem could not be invoked to bypass the problems of indeterminacy.

### Dynamics, Order, and Indeterminacy

*Dynamics* is the study of how variables affect each other over time. It studies transactions of the form: "If variable A affects B, and B affects A, how will A and B evolve, given a particular way in which that transaction occurs?" Transactions of this kind have a wealth of interesting properties, but two are worth mentioning. The first is that they usually cause a massive reduction in the degrees of freedom. Because A and B are variables, the transaction could, in principle, result in any possible combination of a value of A and a value of B. In that case, there would be an infinite number of possible states. Classical determinism claimed that any of those possible states could be predicted given perfectly accurate knowledge of the initial conditions of A and B, but in many dynamic systems, the result of the transaction is that A and B evolve toward one out of only very few potential states. Those are the so-called *attractor states* of the dynamic system. All states that fall within a relatively wide range of initial values home in on one particular attractor state. That is, one needs only very crude information about the initial state in order to correctly predict a final state. However, the fact that initial-state regions border on each other means that the more an initial state approaches a border, the more accurate must be the information to make a correct prediction. And for initial states that lie exactly on the border of regions, it is impossible to predict which end state will result.

Dynamic systems theory combines several elements from determinism and indeterminism: prediction, information, and uncertainty. It shows that the universe is not uniformly structured, as far as determinacy and accuracy are concerned. For some regions of the "universe" consisting of variables A and B, only very little information suffices to make very accurate predictions, whereas for other regions an extremely high level of accuracy of measurement is just about as good as throwing dice.

Another interesting property of nonlinear dynamic systems is that they produce their own irregularity, their own noise, so to speak. In classical systems, noise comes from outside the system under consideration. Variables that fall outside the limited scope of theory building or measurement still continue to affect the actual system described by that theory or measurement, and the effect of those variables appears in the form of unpredictable noise. The fact that many dynamic systems home in on a small number of fixed attractors implies that at least some display another kind of behavior. There is a vast domain of dynamics that lead to so-called *chaotic attractors*. A chaotic attractor is characterized by the fact that its effective predictability is limited by a relatively short range, a *prediction horizon*. Within that horizon, the prediction error[2] is approximately proportional to the accuracy of the measurement on which the prediction is based. Immediately across that horizon, however, error increases exponentially and becomes about as big as the predicted phenomenon itself.

It is interesting to note that the theory of chaotic dynamics is based on perfectly deterministic systems, that is, systems that are deterministic in the ontological sense. A computer operating on limited numbers (with a limited number of digits before or after the decimal point) using basic fixed algorithms, is a reasonable example of such a deterministic system. Figure 1.1 shows the results of three simple computer models: a linear model, a chaotic model, and a point-attractor model. The linear model is a mere addition or multiplication of an initial level by a constant. The chaotic and point-attractor models are based on a simple logistic growth equation. The magnitude of the growth parameter determines whether the produced growth curve homes in on a stable state or falls into an infinite chaotic oscillation. The error term is computed by comparing two versions of each model: one that is the control

---

[2]Note that, for the sake of simplicity, I deal with the notion of *prediction error* in a simple quantitative way: Prediction error is the difference between a predicted measurement at some later time and the actual value of that later measurement.

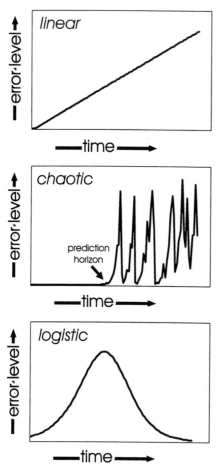

FIG. 1.1. Changes in the magnitude of error across time in three different models: linear, chaotic, and logistic; initial level is about zero; in the chaotic model, error increases suddenly and explosively (the prediction horizon); in the logistic model, error increases during the process of growth, but decreases as growth settles into a steady state level.

model and one that is the error model and differs from the former only in the initial state value. The difference between the initial-state values is then defined as an initial measurement error. In the linear model the error, that is, the difference between initial levels, increases linearly across time; in the point-attractor model, the error increases and then decreases again as the system approaches its end point; in the chaotic model, the error (which is extremely small) suddenly explodes into a magnitude of approximately the size of the dynamic process itself. This point of error explosion is the prediction horizon beyond which increases in measurement accuracy no longer make sense.

The universe we live in is far from the entropy death predicted by classical thermodynamics. This is not to say that this prediction is wrong. It is just that we see so many signs to the contrary in that little part of the cosmos where we can sustain our lives. We see living beings emerging out of relatively simple beginnings and evolving toward great complexity. We see cultures and societies evolve and prosper. All that lives must die in the end, and that's the way we pay our tribute to entropy, so to speak. But in the meantime, we witness the constant creation of order and structure. It is interesting to note that this physical order, which occurs mostly in that part of the physical we call *biological*, requires a certain amount of indeterminacy and fluctuation in order to emerge and maintain itself (Nicolis & Prigogine, 1989). This is another example of how determinism (i.e., the reduction of the degrees of freedom) is based on or requires a certain amount of indeterminacy. Indeterminacy, which takes the form of random fluctuations is, in turn, the eventual product of deterministic chaotic dynamics.

## Summary: A Dynamic View of Determinism

Let me try to summarize what this journey into dynamics has taught us about determinism. It seems that the notion of determinism is replaced by another concept, which acts more or less as the synthesis of determinism on the one hand and its antithesis, indeterminism, on the other. Determinism and indeterminism are antithetic concepts in that they both stand for a "dead" universe. A deterministic universe is dead because it has no degrees of freedom: Everything is predestined, and no information is created because all information is contained in the initial state (whatever that may be). An indeterministic universe is lifeless because it contains an infinite number of degrees of freedom. No information is created because every event has a similar probability. However, where the two principles meet, information and order are created in the form of highly reduced degrees of freedom, in which differences between events become meaningful and informative. The new synthetic concept that unites determinism and indeterminism is the concept of *complex order*, emerging out of self-organization. In order for complex order to emerge, both determinism and indeterminism are needed.

Complex order is what one typically finds in the realm of the biological, the sociocultural, and the psychological. Self-organization means that we don't need the nearly infinite knowledge of Laplace to compute and predict the future of the universe. It suffices that we find fingerprints of self-organization, signs that some processes of self-organization and the creation of dynamic order are at work. Those fingerprints will lead us, more or less automatically, to solving the problem of where the future will bring us. However, having said this, we should realize that the reduction of the degrees of freedom in physical self-organizing systems does not make the problem easier. Just look at the variation among people and you will see that the number of possibilities is still enormous. It is true that in the physical sense, human differences are only a minute subset of the differences that are possible, but such reduction is hardly consoling. As developmental psychologists, for instance, we want to know under which conditions a certain child will develop a certain personality or acquire specific knowledge or skills. Let us look at how psychology deals with the problem of determinism.

## SOURCES OF THE DETERMINISM DEBATE IN PSYCHOLOGY

### Determinism and Probability

Determinism is directly related to predicting the future, and prediction relates directly to probability. Probability shares its originally Latin stem with the verb *prove*, implying that one tries out whether something is good or whether a prediction comes true. Probability, in the sense of truth, therefore, is by its very nature dichotomous: Some things come true and some do not. The concept of probability, however, makes sense only if it can be applied to generalized statements, that is, statements about a class of similar occurrences. The problem is that if something is tried out, it is no longer available for a next, identical try, unless one falls back on the homogeneity assumption. Jaan Valsiner (1995) made a distinction among three views on statistical probability. One is *frequentistic*, and deals with the proportion between the occurrence and the nonoccurrence of an event in a class of homogeneous events. I discuss this form of probability in the next section, because it is the form that dominates most of the empirical work in psychology.

The second form of probability is *Bayesian*, and concentrates on the epistemological aspect of (in)determinacy (see also the section on *The epistemological character of physical determinism*). Bayesian statistics deals with the question of whether and how added knowledge reduces uncertainty. Maximal uncertainty is the number that averages the possible occurrences of an event (an event occurs, i.e., $p = 1$; an event does not occur, i.e., $p = 0$; therefore maximal uncertainty is $(1 + 0)/2$). In the Bayesian tradition, probability is defined as a psychological state of a "predictor," not as a property of an object world whose events one wants to know.

The third form of probability is of the *propensity* type. Probability is viewed as that property of an object, person, or event that relates to a future property, to becoming. For instance, if a person has the propensity of becoming president of the Communal Goat Breeders Society, that person (in his or her environment) must have a certain property that corresponds with this propensity, irrespective of whether he or she actually becomes president. That propensity can, of course, be present to a variable extent, that is, occur with different magnitudes that relate to the probability that the person will someday occupy the predicted position. A statistical theory of probability should therefore take the form of a developmental model. I discuss this form of probability in a later section, because it is basic to the view on (in)determinism that I want to present in this chapter.

## Determinism and Generalization

How do psychologists predict the future? (It goes without saying that this future pertains only to the level or quality of future psychological properties, such as a person's intelligence, knowledge, or personality traits.) They do so basically by applying empirically established *generalizations*. For instance, because we have so often observed the empirical relationship between parents' socioeconomic status and the level of schooling that their offspring get, we may predict a young person's future scholastic level by a generalized probability. For instance, we may say that this person has a 60% chance of finishing a university degree, whereas another person may have only a 45% chance. A similar generalization becomes rather ludicrous if applied to language development, for instance. The only thing I have to know is that a 1-year-old child has no serious handicaps, and that suffices to predict with, say, 98% accuracy, that this child will have developed a complex language skill by the age of 4.

I hesitate to call such an empirical generalization a prediction. In its original meaning, that word means "to foretell something." We would be highly surprised if the prophets from the Bible had shouted prophecies such as, "Oh ye Israelites! Thou hast a 65% chance of falling into the hands of evil sinners!" Foretelling means that out of a vast array of possibilities, one is chosen that will come true. If one cannot see into the future, as fortune-tellers or prophets are supposed to do, one should rely on the Laplacian skill of computation. Laplace's superbeing knows the laws of nature, which is not too difficult because these laws are surprisingly simple. By measuring the properties of the current state of affairs and through a laborious process of computation, the superbeing deductively infers the future in a step-by-step fashion. The problem with psychology, however, is that it hardly has any laws that act over small stretches of time. Psychology has a lot of probabilistic generalizations that relate events separated by considerable intervals, such as the social and cultural environment early in life and later achievements in adulthood. A person's life course is believed to be governed by massively stochastic processes, which are basically of the same kind as the probabilistic generalizations discussed previously.

In order to demonstrate some of the ways the determinism debate is conducted in psychology, I present a concrete case, namely, the current discussion about the way genes are supposed to determine psychological properties. The genes debate provides such a nice example, not only because it is an old and well-established issue, but more so because it comes and goes in waves of heated debates in which opposite stands are taken. I use this particular example to introduce a new concept, that of *factor determinism*, which I think plays an important role in much of our current psychological thinking, and which is highly contradictory to the kind of propensity thinking that I introduced in the preceding section.

## For Whom the Bell (Curve) Tolls

Folk wisdom ascribes a person's traits, properties or life course by referring either to that person's descent or milieu, or directly to the person. For instance, if a person shows certain characteristics that the neighborhood still remembers from the person's granduncle, those characteristics are likely to be explained on the grounds of what in modern terminology would be called genes. If youngsters deviate from the common moral path, the deviation may be attributed to their having had bad friends, that is, by explaining their behavior as a consequence of the milieu. An explanation by descent, however, does not always distinguish among nature and nurture: It seems that folk wisdom knows intuitively that one inherits not only genes but also a family environment from one's parents. Finally, if there's no apparent similarity between the person's course of life and that of his biological and familial environment, the likely thing is to vindicate this fact by referring to the person's own initiative and effort, or lack thereof. A person may be called a self-made man, for instance, or someone who is a good-for-nothing. Of course, any combination of explanatory factors is also likely to occur. For instance, a person may be seen as someone who comes from a good family and who also used these opportunities well by working hard. Put differently, if three factors—genes (G), environment (E), and self (S)—can, potentially, explain the life course of an individual, then any combination of them (G; E; S; GE; GS; ES; GES) is possible. How do psychology and behavioral genetics deal with this issue? Note that it is not my aim to discuss behavioral genetics nor to criticize the empirical and theoretical claims that are made on its behalf. My point is that, taken in isolation, those claims are characteristic of a form of determinism that is widespread in psychology.

   Scientific psychology (or whatever has been taken for that in the past) has always been suspect of the notion that some combination of explanatory factors is possible and likely to occur under its own specific set of circumstances. Instead, many great historical names in psychology are associated with the belief that one factor always overrules the others. The struggle has concentrated on either genes (nature) or environment (nurture), and because the wrestlers seem to be about equally strong, the fight goes up and down in waves. It is no surprise, therefore, that we currently witness a revival of the genetic explanation of human traits and behavior.

Recently, the influential journal *Science* published several papers under a special topic, *Genes & Behavior*. The subtitle of the opening paper stated, "A mass of evidence—animal and human—shows that genes influence behavior" (Mann, 1994, p. 1684). Put differently, genes determine behavior in the original sense of the word *determine*, namely, "to limit" or "confine." In that same issue, Bouchard wrote, "about two-thirds of the reliable variance in measured personality traits are due to genetic influence" (Bouchard, 1994, p. 1700), and "The similarity we see in personality between biological relatives is almost entirely genetic in origin" (p. 1701). The final paper in the series is by Plomin, Owen, and McGuffin. These authors claimed that "For cognitive ability, genetic factors become increasingly important for general intelligence throughout the life span, reaching heritabilities as high as 80% later in life" (Plomin, Owen, & McGuffin, 1994, p. 1734).

Although I hesitate to discuss quotes out of their context, I nevertheless want to focus on some of the terminology that is used. Just assume that *Science* opens a special issue with the statement that, "A mass of evidence shows that the weather influences behavior." No one would really be surprised by that. And, in fact, no one should be surprised by the fact that genes influence behavior. The problem is, however, that *influence* seems to have a different meaning in the lexical context of *genes* than it has in the context of *weather*. If it occurs with *genes*, we are inclined to read *influence* as "has a deep, direct, causal effect on what we do and think irrespective of what occurs in our environment or has happened during our life span." But this reading makes sense only because *influence* as such has a nearly empty meaning. The same conclusion holds true for more technically stated claims, for instance, that variance is due to genetic influence. The problem is that the technical meaning of this and similar statements is very different from the intuitive meaning, attributed on the basis of lexical contexts.

Behavioral genetics is about how genes determine behavior. The form of determinism that speaks from the genetics literature has three striking characteristics. To begin with, it states determinacy in terms of a determining factor. In this particular case, the determining factor is the genetic endowment, but in other times and places it has been the environment or the will of God. Second, it claims that a particular factor is the determiner of a certain outcome because it significantly outweighs the contributions of other factors. Third, it is a form of statistical determinism, which claims that the said relationship holds for a population. From this last, it follows that the relationship is random in the case of single individuals. Basically, it is a form of determinism that says, "Here's a factor A that limits the expression of a property B to such-and-such an extent." This particular form of determinism is usually associated with a strong belief in a particular determining factor, for instance, either genetic or environmental influences. Let me call it *factor determinism*, that is, a form of determinism that projects a determining or limiting relationship from one factor onto another. The point is, however, that the nature of this limiting or determining relationship only rarely is made clear. It is easy to fall into the trap of a simple two-node metaphor, one being the genes, the other the behavior, and to conceive of the influence as some kind of string or pulley that directly transmits causality from one node (genes) to the other. Meanwhile, almost everybody knows that the causal chain is incredibly more complicated than that. The causal chain is often obscured by that old workhorse of social science statistics, the correlation.

Whereas classical physical determinism expressed the nature of its determinacy in the particular mathematical format of calculus, psychological factor determinism has its canonic mathematical format in the computation of group association, better known as *correlation*. Correlation is about how the variation of one variable around the overall mean of a group relates to the variation of another variable around its mean. Correlation accounts for neither the value of a mean nor for why means differ across populations. The problem, however, is that correlation does not appeal to any simple and intuitive notion. Even for those who have had statistics training and who know very well that correlation does not mean causation, statements like those about heritability and genetic influences are confusing. If you read about heritability of general intelligence that reaches a magnitude of 80% during adulthood, you will find it difficult to avoid the intuitive conclusion that genes contain a sort of rough building plan for a person's intelligence, specifying about 80% of the later properties in advance. I regularly hear people with academic training in psychology conclude that behavioral genetics has reduced education to a marginal endeavor. They forget that there exists a basic difference between what one can and has to do to bring a child to a certain knowledge and intelligence *level* and what one can do to make a child more (or less) smart than another child.

The heritability measure has a technical meaning that goes far beyond its intuitive causal interpretation (or, more precisely, is far less complex and encompassing than the intuitive notion). A classic estimation of heritability consists of taking twice the difference between correlations obtained for monozygotic twins and those obtained for dizygotic twins (Bouchard, 1994; Plomin, 1994). Although recent behavioral genetics studies work with considerably more complex estimations than just doubling the difference, the results of heritability research are still primarily based on differences between monozygotic and dizygotic twins.

## Factor and Process: Dynamic Models and the Determinism Question

I am not accusing any of the behavioral geneticists of misinforming their readership about the statistical techniques they use. Claims about how much of the variance of a particular property is accounted for by genetic factors have well-defined technical meanings. In the serious scientific literature, one seldom finds explicit simplifications that turn those technical statements into claims about simple and direct causality. My point is that the notion of determinism that underlies psychological research into the effects of genetic or environmental factors is a form of factor determinism, a particular form of statistical determinism. Statements about heritability, for instance, specify the probability of a distribution of properties (such as IQ), given a distribution of genetic properties. That is, they specify how a given genetic property, for instance the 100% similarity between monozygotic twins, limits the statistical degrees of freedom of a later behavioral or cognitive property, such as IQ.

Unfortunately, factor determinism has little to do with the intuitive notion of determinism, that of a straightforward and direct causal process. It is at this point that (nonlinear) dynamic models might be helpful. They are among the scientific and mathematical models that come closest to the intuitive notion of causative determinism. Dynamic models describe causal or conditional chains in a step-like manner, a previous state directly causing or affecting the next one, with or without the added effects of coincidental fluctuations or chaotic variability. I call the determinism that underlies dynamic models process determinism, to distinguish it from the factor determinism that we are used to in the social sciences. Factor determinism is probably the best bet if process determinism is, for instance, unreachable because the process takes too long, or goes too fast, or is simply too complicated. The problem is, however, that although the meaning of a particular factor determinism is clearly defined, it is difficult to avoid confusion with a process determinism, simply because factor determinisms don't directly appeal to people's intuitive and colloquial thinking. This difficulty is responsible for the recurrent fights in the media and in the public forum about the eventual biological determinacy of IQ or male versus female characteristics. The difference between factor and process determinism also explains the difficulties that people have with findings of empirical research that pertain to "significant differences" between groups or probabilities relating an early developmental condition, such as child abuse, to later problems.

Factor determinism poses difficulties not only to the mind of the psychological layperson. Measures of association, such as correlation, depend entirely on the sources of variation that are operative. Correlations between genetic similarity and later behavioral outcome depend entirely on the variation in the environmental conditions. It is obvious that, if environmental variation is extremely low, whatever variance remains must be to the account of nonenvironmental factors, which are sheer coincidence on the one hand and genetic variation on the other hand. Genetic variation is so much easier to determine than environmental variation. We know, for instance, that the average genetic similarity between siblings is 50%, simply because of the way genetic transmission works. But we have no way to determine environmental similarities, because there exist no objective standards by which environments can be compared on an absolute scale. Consequently, statements about heritability *percentages* make no sense, because we have no comparable estimation of the associated environmental variance. The only thing those figures say is that under the present *unknown* environmental variability, a certain percentage of the variance is due to genetic variance.

In the next section, I argue that developmental psychology can profit from a return to a form of process determinism that explains not only how degrees of freedom are reduced, but also how they are created.

## PROCESS DETERMINISM IN DEVELOPMENTAL PSYCHOLOGY

### The Quest for Formal Models and the Exploration of the Developmental Universe

The great theoreticians of developmental psychology—Piaget, Vygotsky, and Werner—were basically interested in the process of development. How does development come about as a result of an individual's personal and social activities? What are the mechanisms that determine the kind of change that we call "development"? However, as soon as those questions were subjected to "real" scientific research, they turned into matters of differences between groups, ages, or contexts. The main reason was that the mathematical formalism underscoring the empirical research was one of factor determinism. The jump from the classic verbal-conceptual theories to formal models was hampered by the lack of appropriate process formalisms and technical means for testing and elaborating those models. Piaget, the only one in this illustrious triad who actually accomplished a considerable amount of formalization, had to turn to predicate and group logic, and paid only verbal tribute to the basically homeostasis-oriented systems theory of the 1960s. The problem with these formalisms, especially logic, is that they fail to capture the basic property of development, namely, the process of change.

Today, developmentalists can rely on another mathematical formalism, that of dynamic systems theory—and a technical tool that is now often associated with it, the computer—to turn at least part of their verbal-conceptual models into deductive structures that allow them to formally explore the range of possibilities that the conceptual models entail. I am not saying that formalism and mathematics are the true signs of science, and that mere verbal models are unscientific. My stance is purely instrumental, in that I see formalisms (and computers, note pads, videos, and university labs for that matter) as technical tools that help us clarify and extend our models, our theories, and our empirical knowledge of the world.

The use of computers in present-day psychology provides a nice illustration of both a Wernerian and a Vygotskian principle. Computers are a new tool for thought, but currently they are mostly used to satisfy an old function, namely, that of computing factor determinisms in the form of correlations, LISREL models, and so forth. But computers are particularly suited for simple repetitive, combinatorial, and algorithmic operations. Their new function lies exactly in the opportunity they offer for exploring models that rely on such operations. This brings me to the Vygotskian theme, that a culturally developed external tool offers new opportunities for thought, which may be interiorized and turned into new psychological functions (or, more modestly, subfunctions or parts of subfunctions). It is true that tools do not automatically provide the right affordances that lead to further development; they have to be made that way. However, it is my firm belief that computers, notwithstanding their limitations and inherent dangers (such as eventual intellectual imperialism and the likelihood of a mentally absorbing *funktionslust*), allow us to explore an important domain of classical developmental thought that has remained largely untouched so far: the domain of simple repetitive (i.e., iterative) functions across time. I must explain why I think this is so important to developmental psychology.

## Simple Mechanisms, Complicated Patterns

The classical theories explain development by referring to relatively simple mechanisms. Examples are Piaget's assimilation and accommodation, Vygotsky's actual and proximal development and interiorization, and Werner's differentiation and integration. Whatever corresponds to these mechanisms might, of course, be extremely complicated, but the concepts, as such, have never been specified in the form of intricate models. Put differently, these concepts can be employed as relatively simple and straightforward building blocks in models that investigate whether or not these dynamic concepts indeed produce patterns and trajectories that are considered typical of developmental processes. At a later stage, they can be used to build more comprehensive models in an attempt to explain the actual developmental variety and patterns found among subjects.

An interesting property of these mechanisms is that they are supposed to operate in a repetitive—or, more precisely, an *iterative*—way. For instance, a particular experience is assimilated to an existing cognitive scheme, but also leads to an accommodation of that scheme. The slightly altered (i.e., accommodated) scheme forms a starting point for a new assimilation, leading to another accommodation, and so on. The iterative nature of these basic mechanisms has been explicitly described by Piaget (1975). The problem with iterative mechanisms is that, although they are basic to development, they lend themselves only very reluctantly to mental, verbally represented, model building.

Take, for instance, a highly simplified assimilation and accommodation model. Assume the model defines a developmental step as any event in which a child encounters some piece of information that he or she then assimilates (i.e., reduces to what he or she already understands). Part of the information, however, remains unassimilable and requires a slight accommodation of the knowledge base. This mechanism can be applied in an iterative way: An event occurs, which leads to assimilation, but also to an alteration of the knowledge base, which is then ready for a new assimilatory event, *ad infinitum.* Perhaps one can perform a few of such assimilation and accommodation rounds in one's mind or on paper, but it is very difficult to do a mental exercise with hundreds of such repetitive steps, even with the help of lots of paper and lots of pencils. The human brain is simply not built to do that kind of rather stupid, repetitive exercise.

But, because it is so hard to do the step-by-step exercise, developmentalists tend to think that they can get around the difficulty by applying linear extrapolation. That is, because a few assimilation–accommodation rounds lead to a certain degree of adaptation of a cognitive scheme, it seems natural to assume that many such rounds lead to an adaptation proportional to the number of rounds. For instance, if a week of study leads to an increase in knowledge of 1% (whatever that may mean; this is just for the sake of illustrating the argumentation), it is assumed that a year of study should lead to an increase of approximately 50%. Of course, hardly anyone would be so naive as to defend this type of quantitative extrapolation. Nevertheless, the principle, as such, either explicitly or implicitly underlies a great deal of developmental thinking.

## Dynamic Models and the Nature of Development

The problem with linear extrapolation is that many natural mechanisms contain a nonlinear aspect. Examples of such aspects are the existence of equilibrium levels, either one or several, or the existence of increasing or decreasing rates of change. Such nonlinearities are usually hardly observable if only a few iterative steps are taken into account, but they show up rather dramatically if the number of iterations reaches a certain level. Thus, the only way to see what a model will get you is to let it do its iterative job long enough, and the only way you can make it do so is by putting it into a computer (unless you are prepared to do a lot of boring manual calculation).

But before making the computer run, you have to turn the verbal, conceptual model into a formal model. That is, you have to make choices about which formal operations correspond to the mechanisms specified in the model and which variables and parameters are needed to describe what the model does. This exercise in formalization can lead to interesting alterations to the conceptual model, for instance, when it turns out that the conceptual model lacks operative components necessary to get the model off the ground. Formalization in terms of growth models may lead to putting more emphasis on general resource limitations in processes of cognitive and language development, which is a good way to explain the occurrence of equilibrium levels, but also the occurrence of fluctuations or temporary regressions. Growth models also lead to an abandonment of the strong distinction between independent and dependent variables. Variables that actually affect development are conceived of as mutually dependent: They influence one another. Dependency is just a local and temporal property of a particular variable. The learning of a new skill, for instance, depends, among other things, on the instruction provided, but the properties of the instruction will, in turn, be dependent on the properties of the learning process and the eventual progress made (van Geert, 1991, 1994a, b).

What will running your model buy you other than what you already knew? A lot, sometimes. First, simulations will show whether the model actually leads to the predicted results. If it leads to an exponential explosion, or to a lack of distinction among potential individuals, the model is clearly insufficient and needs further conceptual and formal refinements. Second, simulation will eventually show potential developmental paths that are logically entailed in the structure of the formal model, but not explicitly accounted for in the verbal-conceptual form of the model. For instance, a simulation of a Vygotskyan model of learning leads to the discovery of threshold values under which learning and teaching do not get off the ground (van Geert, 1994b). These new possibilities are sometimes in line with empirical findings or established general intuitions about development. On other occasions, they cannot be reconciled with what is known about the developmental process at issue and should therefore lead to either conceptual or formal adaptations of the model. Third, simulation is a way of deductively inferring testable hypotheses from a model. For instance, if the model yields descriptions of unexpected developmental patterns, those patterns may be tested empirically.

Before proceeding to the discussion of dynamic model building and determinism, I must emphasize that dynamic model building concerns more than just a methodological issue. More than anything else, it entails a new and fascinating conceptual approach to development. Principles of nonlinear dynamics, self-organization, and complexity may be used in a qualitative way and applied to various domains. Examples are work in social relationships (Fogel, 1993), emotion development (Lewis, 1995), and motor and cognitive development (Thelen & Smith, 1994). The fact that I emphasize the mathematical model building aspect in this chapter is explained by my own fascination for this particular aspect, and by the fact that I see it as an interesting approach to the determinism problem.

## (In)Determinism and Degrees of Freedom
## in Development

To a certain extent, dynamic model building in developmental psychology restores Laplacian determinism. Dynamic model building allows us to at least *pretend* we are like Laplace's practically omniscient being who knows the laws of Nature (or of Development, in our case) and who is able to compute the future course of events. By so doing, we can test if or to what extent a particular developmental model makes a justifiable claim about how developmental degrees of freedom are reduced, and how the present eventually limits the future. We can also test to what extent we need true randomness (indeterminacy with regard to the present model domain) in order to explain the developmental phenomena we are interested in. Put differently, our determinism is purely *instrumental*, in that it yields particular hypotheses about the future and about potential explanations of how development comes about.

Furthermore, dynamic model building is similar to Laplacian determinism in two additional senses. First, it is basically epistemological, not ontological. It is a technique allowing us to obtain mental access to some aspects of the future in the form of an explicit deductive method or calculus. Second, it is a form of process determinism: Dynamic systems reconstruct processes in a step-by-step fashion, not by projecting factorial relationships over long stretches of time.

So far, I have emphasized the limiting aspect of dynamic models. That is, I have presented them as ways to select the more likely out of an endless sea of possible futures. If a dynamic model provides a valid description of the way development works, it shows how conditions at some previous state (and preferably an initial state) constrain the set of possible outcomes. If the dynamic developmental model works strictly deterministically (in the mathematical sense), the determinism may boil down to a severe limitation in the possible outcomes (e.g., to one final state or to just a few attractors). If the deterministic model contains chaotic dynamics, the range of possible outcomes almost literally explodes: A primary characteristic of chaotic dynamics is that arbitrarily small differences between initial states will cause major differences in resulting trajectories, and all trajectories are different. It is possible, however, that another part of the dynamics binds the new degrees of freedom caused by a chaos-producing mechanism into a much more restricted range. And finally, if the model works with random components, it usually turns out that those components can have major consequences around certain points or states of the dynamics, making a truly nondeterministic choice for one developmental direction or another. However, for the major part of the dynamics, randomness undergoes two transformations. The first is that its variation is greatly reduced. For instance, random variation in the parameters of a simple growth dynamics results in a macroscopic oscillation with a frequency that is much smaller than the frequency of changes in the random components. The second is that variation is amplified (in addition to the reduction). For instance, a transitional growth dynamics shows only one major jump at one particular (random) moment although it is continuously affected by small random influences.

## Creating New Degrees of Freedom

There is still another sense in which dynamic models explain how degrees of freedom are affected. The standard way is to explain how degrees of freedom are reduced, that is, how development picks a very limited set of plausible outcomes out of an innumerable range of possible futures. But there exists another way in which development—and the dynamic models that attempt to explain development—affects the future degrees of freedom: by creating new possibilities for change, new structures, and new ranges of potential variation. The creation of new degrees of freedom is an old and central problem in development, known, among others, as the *novelty* or *epigenesis* problem. Piaget, for instance, believed strongly in the creation of new cognitive structures through processes of adaptation and equilibration. The new nativists, such as Chomsky and Fodor, on the other hand, claim that the structures that emerge during development are innately given (see, e.g., Chomsky, 1980; Piatelli-Palmarini, 1980). In the Chomskyan model of language development, the child starts with a rich but highly restricted structure, "Universal Grammar." The function of experience is to further reduce the already highly limited degrees of freedom by a process called *parameter setting*. Languages differ with respect to certain linguistic parameters (such as *head-final* versus *head-initial*), and language–learning children have to decide which value of certain parameters their language accords with.

The discussion about novelty focuses on the problem of whether the mechanisms put forward to explain cognitive growth and learning are logically capable of explaining the eventual emergence of truly new structures, that is, structures that are not already present, in the form of initial formats that are richer than the ones that result as a consequence of development. The problem of whether a dynamic model can explain the emergence of structures richer than those present at the beginning is not easy to solve. There exist several possible approaches. One seeks to describe the general processes of sudden shifts toward qualitatively new levels or states. This is usually done with the help of the catastrophe theory, a branch of mathematics that categorizes the set of possible forms and properties that sudden qualitative changes can take, whatever their exact nature. Examples in developmental psychology are the explanation of sudden jumps, for instance, in conservation understanding (van der Maas, 1993; van der Maas & Molenaar, 1992). A basic advantage of the catastrophe theory is that it provides a set of empirically testable criteria for when a jump to a new qualitative plane occurs. A disadvantage is that it does not specify a model of how a particular dynamic system actually accomplishes the creation of a new level. A second approach to novelty is to build a dynamic model that increases its degrees of freedom in a nontrivial and nonexplosive way. By *nonexplosive* I mean that the new degrees of freedom must be limited to a specified region of possibilities, in order to maintain the structural integrity of the system that has to exploit these new possibilities. This particular approach has been shown to be productive in the field of evolutionary biology and in the explanation of biological (somatic) growth (Kauffman, 1993; Langton, Taylor, Farmer, & Rasmussen, 1992). In psychology, it has been applied in the form of so-called *connectionist* networks, which create new patterns of excitation and representation in the form of a self-organizing process.

A third approach to the novelty issue is to employ so-called *symbol dynamics*. Symbol dynamics are highly reduced descriptions in the form of discrete states and sets of states of more complicated, underlying dynamics (Farmer, 1990; Nicolis & Prigogine, 1989). It is possible to transform existing, as well as potential, stage theories of arbitrary complexity into graphs and then apply a simple iterative dynamics to the graph to reconstruct the pattern of qualitative state changes (van Geert, 1995). So far, however, it is not yet clear whether symbol dynamics can be applied to the explanation (instead of mere description) of qualitative jumps in development. The point, however, is that dynamic systems models not only explain how degrees of freedom are reduced; they have the possibility to explain how degrees of freedom are created.

## DETERMINISM AND DEVELOPMENTAL MODEL BUILDING

### Determinism and Necessity

Many years ago, Doris Day, the chaste maiden of the silver screen, taught her admirers a wonderful lesson: "Whatever will be, will be; The future's not ours to see. . . ." Whether Miss Day actually intended to contribute to the present debate on determinism is not clear (but certainly highly dubious), but her timeless lines point to two important aspects of the problem. First, they refer to the issue of *logical necessity* (that she, rather tautologically, referred to by claiming that "whatever will be, will be. . . ."). Logical necessity is a necessary prerequisite of any form of deterministic model building. We believe that we live in a world that conforms to our logical and mathematical principles. That is, we believe that it makes sense to build models of the world, operate on them in accordance with those logical principles, and then project the results of those operations onto reality. Our projections take the form of predictions, anticipations, and any form of activity intended to make wanted phenomena come true. For instance, we predict that poverty or abuse will lead to deviant or delayed development because we have a model that reconstructs the relevant causal steps in the chain that leads from the conditions to the expected results (or more precisely, that's how that model is supposed to work). Logical necessity, in the sense of causal and conditional connections modeled by logical and mathematical relationships, is a central issue here. It is very different from empirical generalizations of the form we referred to as factor determinism. For instance, an empirically established relationship associating childhood poverty with later social and economic deprivation is generalized and turned into a prediction about childhood poverty in general. But that prediction is not based on a process of logical necessity in the form of a deterministic causal chain. Lacking such a model, it is hardly possible to infer the conditions under which logical necessity takes the form of possible choices, driven either by randomness or by deliberate intention.

The second major issue relates to the extent to which the future can be foretold. And here, Miss Day has warned us that "The future's not ours to see." We have seen that determinism is an epistemological issue. Is it possible to foresee the future, by applying the best of our knowledge to the conditions and mechanisms that drive development and shape the future of individual human beings? Knowledge is, by definition, limited, but this fact has no bearing on the extent to which the future can indeed be foretold. Sometimes we can base our predictions and expectations on very little knowledge, simply because the developmental processes are attracted toward a single outcome. In other cases, there is no knowledge precise enough to prevent us from making serious errors, because the mechanisms that drive development there are extremely sensitive to initial conditions, or to conditions in the vicinity of threshold or switch points. Put differently, there is a nonlinear and context-dependent relationship between our knowledge of the present (and the past, eventually) and the degree to which the future can be predicted. Note that by *prediction* I mean a step-by-step construction of a developmental process as it unfolds in time. I am not referring to a prediction based on an empirical generalization over a group (such as, "Given the socio-ecomomic status of this girl's family, she has a 60% chance of entering adulthood with an educational level lower than $x$").

### Prediction and Postdiction

Often, dynamic models of development, especially the ones that try to fit a mathematical model onto available data, make predictions of a very particular kind. They do not *pre*dict, in the sense of foretelling the future, but they *post*dict. That is, they use knowledge of developmental trajectories, mostly in the form of time series, to reconstruct those trajectories by applying a dynamic model and parameter values estimated on the basis of all available knowledge, including knowledge about the trajectories.

It seems a bit trivial that one should try to predict a developmental process whose outcome is already known, but by *prediction* I mean a *process prediction*, that is, a reconstruction of a developmental process in a stepwise fashion, based on a model that runs in a deterministic fashion. This, as it turns out, is not easy to accomplish. Of course, one could eventually adapt the mechanisms and the parameters involved in each step in the process based on the ex post facto knowledge one has about each and every one of those steps, but that would trivialize the whole postdiction endeavor.

The fact that it is possible to build ex post facto models that fit the time series data very well, suggests that the developmental mechanisms behind those data are reasonably covered by the simple deterministic operations of the models (e.g., van Geert, 1991, 1994; Ruhland, Cats, & van Geert, 1994), but it also suggests that our present knowledge and measurement of developmental mechanisms do not suffice to estimate necessary parameters and variables. We hope, of course, that as our ex post models increase in power and generality our ability to estimate necessary variables and parameters based on present-state knowledge alone will increase accordingly and will allow us to make real process predictions, but it is likely that the knowledge necessary to build a process model of a developmental trajectory cannot be extracted from single developmental states (e.g., initial states), even if the process as such is, to a considerable extent, deterministic in nature. If the information needed to build a deterministic model is not completely accessible through observation of short stretches of time series alone, determinism will remain a matter of reconstruction, of retelling a developmental story, instead of predicting and foretelling the future.

## Determinism in Developmental Model Building: The Happy Marriage Between Pierre Simon and Doris

In this chapter, I have argued that determinism is an epistemological issue. It is about the possibility of predicting the future, given knowledge of the present. Physics, the field where incredibly accurate predictions are made and confirmed, is also the field providing evidence for the principled inaccuracy of observation. It has demonstrated the basic limits on how much information can be extracted from a given state of affairs and retained long enough to make predictions of the kind that Laplace wanted. A new form of determinism arose based on the law of large numbers, which turned microscopic indeterminacy into macroscopic determinism. The law of large numbers has been used in the social sciences, too, where it led to a new form of determinism (or indeterminism, depending on which side you look at it). I called this new form of determinism *factor determinism* and argued that it is not the kind of determinism we need in developmental psychology. Developmental explanation and model building are concerned with processes that unfold across time. Explaining such processes requires dynamic models. The classic developmental theories contained such dynamic models of iterative mechanisms, but the models were cast in a verbal-conceptual format. The difficulty with these models is that they are hardly suitable for long-range process prediction. The availability of mathematical dynamic models allows developmentalists, maybe for the first time in the history of their discipline, to turn their verbal models into formal models that deductively infer developmental trajectories. Although our attempts toward formal dynamic model building are still very modest, they have already brought us a new view onto the old problem of determinism. Nonlinearities in our models are responsible for different kinds of relationships between antecedents and consequents, and between knowledge of a present state and prediction of future states. It is the synthesis of determinacy and indeterminacy; the reduction, as well as the creation, of degrees of freedom; and the existence of chaos next to order that make the determinism issue a fascinating starting point for a new kind of developmental thinking.

## REFERENCES

Bouchard, T. J. (1994). Genes, environment and personality. *Science, 264*, 1700–1701.

Chomsky, N. (1980). *Rules and representations*. Oxford: Blackwell.

Farmer, J. D. (1990). A Rosetta stone for connectionism. *Physica D, 42*, 153–187.

Fogel, A. (1993). *Developing through relationships. Origins of communication, self and culture.* New York: Harvester Wheatsheaf.

Kauffman, S. A. (1993). *The origins of order. Self-organization and selection in evolution.* New York: Oxford University Press.

Langton, C. G., Taylor, C., Farmer, J. D., & Rasmussen, S. (1992). *Artificial Life II.* Redwood City, CA: Addison-Wesley.

Lewis, M. D. (1995). Cognition-emotion feedback and the self-organization of developmental paths. *Human Development, 38*, 71–102.

Mann, C. C. (1994). Behavioral genetics in transition. *Science, 264*, 1686–1689.

Nicolis, G., & Prigogine, I. (1989). *Exploring complexity. An introduction.* New York: Freeman.

Piaget, J. (1975). *L'equilibration des structures cognitives. Problème central du développement.* Paris: Presses Universitaires de France.

Piatelli-Palmarini, M. (1980). *Language and learning: The debate between Jean Piaget and Noam Chomsky.* London: Routledge.

Plomin, R. (1994). *Genetics and experience. The interplay between nature and nurture.* Newbury Park, CA: Sage.

Plomin, R., Owen, M. J., & McGuffin, P. (1994). The genetic basis of complex human behaviors. *Science, 264*, 1733–1739.

Ruhland, R., Cats, M., & van Geert, P. (1994). *A dynamic growth model of early syntactic development.* Unpublished manuscript, University of Groningen.

Smith, P. B. (1989). *Determinisme en de Onzekerheidsrelatie [Determinism and the uncertainty relation]*. University of Groningen: Valedictory address.

Stewart, I. (1989). *Does God play dice? The mathematics of chaos*. London: Basil Blackwell.

*The American Heritage Dictionary of the English Language* (3rd ed.). New York: Houghton Mifflin.

Thelen, E., & Smith, L. B. (1994). *A dynamic systems approach to the development of cognition and action*. Cambridge, MA: MIT Press.

Valsiner, J. (1995). Comments upon an earlier version of P. van Geert (1996), *Que será, será: Determinism and non-linear dynamic model building in development*. Personal communication.

van der Maas, H. (1993). *Catastrophe analysis of stage-wise cognitive development: Model, method and applications*. Unpublished doctoral dissertation, University of Amsterdam.

van der Maas, H., & Molenaar, P. (1992). A catastrophe-theoretical approach to cognitive development. *Psychological Review, 99*, 395–417.

van Geert, P. (1991). A dynamic systems model of cognitive and language growth. *Psychological Review, 98*, 3–53.

van Geert, P. (1994a). *Dynamic systems of development. Change between complexity and chaos*. New York: Harvester.

van Geert, P. (1994b). Vygotskian dynamics of development. *Human Development, 37*(6), 346–365.

van Geert, P. (1995). *The dynamics of developmental sequences: Toward a calculus for developmental theory*. Unpublished manuscript.

# CHANGE IN THE PROCESS OF CHANGE: COPING WITH INDETERMINISM

Aydan Gulerce
Bogazici University

On a more general and abstract level than that taken by van Geert (this volume, chap. 1), I would like to discuss an apparently recent change in science's view of order and change, that is, the (re)occurrence of metaphysical commitment in a disorderly and dynamic universe. Very briefly, I try to place the issue within a philosophical and sociohistorical context first, and look at the contemporary fields of mathematics, physics, biology, and communication in this regard and at their reflections into psychology. By doing so, I expect to contour various meanings and connotations that the notion of determinism/indeterminism has gained (or lost) in time, and are still in use, in various scientific circles.

Once the terminological and the conceptual stage is set, I turn to developmental, social, and cultural processes in psychology in relation to change and order. Thus, on a more specific and local level, I discuss the variations among, but also within, the so-called "invariant" processes and "mechanisms" of change and the issue of "introduction of novelty" that have been advocated by various theoretical programs and for different units of analysis. I conclude the discussion with a proposal of a possibility for, and utility of, the coexistence of these multiple ways of seeing reality, or multiple realities, through transformational thinking. I posit, for example, that dialectical and systemic aspects of three major realms that have been constructed by various developmental theories can be exclusively used for better understanding of coevolutionary transformations of our units of analysis in coherence within their contexts. These realms are the ones that simultaneously form and are formed by the natural reality (ecology/biology) and organism, social reality (society/individual) and identity, and cultural reality (collective/private culture) and self pairs. Hence, as different degrees of determinism and indeterminism for different subject matters and/or epistemologies are admitted to this coordination, a call for a "new" future agenda for human studies will be made from here.

## THE TROUBLESOME ISSUE
## OF DETERMINISM/INDETERMINISM

Science-making is a joint human production. Thus, like any other human by-product, science is subject to various religious, philosophical, political, cultural, and personal influences (see, e.g., Feyarabend, 1976; Gergen, 1994). It is not surprising, however, that we gain this self-reflexivity in retrospect, and through various reevaluations of scientific events. With an awareness that these examinations themselves cannot escape aims and biases of similar sorts, in what follows next, I selectively review various meanings and functions that the issue of order has carried in Western science. I expect to demonstrate that determinism in no way entails necessary pairings with the notions of causality, free will, prediction, and control, which have all been needed to make any academic intelligibility more scientific. Determinism is simply a human-made assumption, be it a metaphysical kind on a more general level or a theoretical one on a local level.

Myths, for example, reflect the earliest and most powerful signs of human construction of order over the world, as Giambattista Vico (1725/1948; Verene, 1981) suggested. According to Vico, accounts of life and nature were primarily expressed by supernatural and mystical metaphors. These "primitive" beliefs were then to turn into organized religions or philosophical reasonings.

Indeed, an important historical predecessor of determinism in Western science that was formed and clarified between the times of Galileo and Laplace was an anthropomorphic force: Rooted in ancient Greek thought, the concept of *moira* (meaning fate or necessity) was believed to govern events, especially the destiny of those who violated moral injunctions. Other cultures, too, have some concept that corresponds more or less to the notion of fate. However, it is in Christian thinking, particularly in notions about the creation of the world and about all human activity as the unraveling of God's essence and its necessity that appears to provide a more sophisticated precursor of modern determinism (Berofsky, 1966).

Furthermore, the Christian view that God has foreknowledge of everything that happens, and that whatever happens happens necessarily, is to say that the world is knowable in advance (predictable) and is governed (lawful). In other words, the world is (pre)determined. This very idea has been influenced by neo-Platonism, and was later supported by Spinoza in a purely pantheistic fashion. In the 17th and 18th centuries, deists took a position that even if God created a deterministic world, its deterministic character may not necessarily require reference to God or God's nature. Other thinkers based their notion of determinism on the science of mechanics, which took God to be the First Cause. Newton was the first to posit what came to be known as *scientific determinism*, which eventually gave way to Laplace's modern formulation of universal lawfulness.

Laplace's determinism relied on a scientific theory (particle mechanics), instead of on theological or animistic thinking. He contended that knowledge about the state of all mechanical particles, and of all the forces acting in nature at any given time, would sufficiently lead to knowledge about all the past and future states of the world. His world was not limited to mechanics, but also included the chemical, electromagnetic, psychological, and so forth.

Laplace's notion of determinism, therefore, further prescribed that classical (Newtonian) mechanics would turn out to be a universal science of nature. In effect, not surprisingly perhaps, various leading theories in psychological science relied on mechanistic models and metaphors of linear mechanics. As we know, however, the replacement of classical mechanics with quantum mechanics in physics ended an era. This also brought about an erosion of science's view of the traditional determinism principle, for it was grounded on that very scientific theory. Nevertheless, and despite a logical awareness of the need for paradigmatic change, most of the traditional assumptions (e.g., linear causality) are still prevalent, even in developmental psychology.

On the other hand, although Laplace had deemphasized the powerful role of God in the universe, the intelligence he had imagined was perfectly capable of measuring all the fundamental particles and, departing from these, of inferring their future states in the world. So, not only did determinism mean that future states necessitate present states, as an epistemological doctrine, but it also suggested prediction, in principle.

## Determinism and Prediction

Predictability requires not only the determination of future states by present states, but the ascertainability of the present state with sufficient accuracy and a mathematically tractable link between the present and future states, as well. Yet, these two preconditions of prediction (precision and the particular mode of logic being sought) have been proved to produce an impasse, by Heisenberg's theory of turbulence in physics. Because the studies of complicated, irregular, and erratic motion of fluids and the later theory of chaos have shown that predictability and determinism are compatible, what is now called *chaos* (in physics) is a time evolution with sensitive dependence on the initial condition.

At the heart of the matter, it has been shown that, in fully deterministic mathematical functions, the values of variables at time $t_1$ perfectly determine the values at time $t_2$. However, a time evolution with many periodic orbits does not show sensitive dependence to initial conditions (at time $t_1$), and often their presence is not relevant to the long-term time evolution of the system (Li & Yorke, 1975). In other words, the precise prediction of future states from any exact value given to a parameter at the present time is possible.

Paradoxically, chaos theory strengthened, rather than threatened, a commitment to determinism, for the central functions of the theory are quite deterministic. Indeed, in a chaotically behaving system, one speaks of *deterministic noise* when irregular oscillations that are observed appear noisy, for example, because the mechanism which produces them is deterministic (Ruelle, 1991). As Dupre (1993) phrased it, chaos theory serves only "to show that it was a mistake to assume that, in a deterministic universe, even Laplace's demon could predict the evolution of events" (p. 3), and is not sufficient by itself to abandon determinism.

We can conclude, perhaps, that in today's scientific climate, prediction has been divorced from determinism. This suggests not only that deterministic systems can be unpredictable, but also that predictions can be made without needing a determined world and/or a theory that is based on redundancy. In psychology, many theoretical predictions rely on post hoc understandings, such as the *repetition compulsion* principle in psychoanalytic theory. That is, if there is a repetitive order, then behavior A, for instance, is predicted to lead to outcome B in the future. In the empirist and positivist tradition, prediction is demanded as the scientific guesswork for a specific outcome. Because prediction is a scientific task too important to give up, in a changing world understanding, new meanings and/or forms of prediction, are needed. For instance, commitment to indeterminism does not exclude predictions, say, of the means and the trajectories, if not the ends and the destinations. Although immensely difficult and complex, progressive (not regressive), future-oriented (not past-determined) and change- (not redundancy-) based theories would be of value in new predictive formulas.

### Determinism and Causality

Another common understanding in modern science has been that *causality*, the notion that something directly produces a certain effect, has been placed within the context of determinism. Hume (1748/1902), for example, defined *cause* to be "an object, followed by another, and where all the objects, similar to the first, are followed by objects similar to the second" (p. 51). This

**43**

Enlightenment philosopher and great skeptic questioned traditional notions of causality and induction. However, what he had doubts about was not the doctrine of necessity (meaning that every event has a cause, and that regularity is not accidental, but necessary), but rather its knowability. Whereas necessity was a construction of the human mind for Kant, Hume gave an empirical status to the causal relationship, and treated determinism as beyond human powers to know or question. By saying that a cause (or antecedent) must be followed by its same effect (or consequent) in every instance, he took a lawful universe for granted.

In effect, many of his followers viewed determinism as a necessary and a priori truth about the world, rather than, or based on, a scientific theory (e.g., Laplace, 1814/1951). This way, they also saved it from refutation on the basis of disconfirming theoretical evidence, so that, some positions (regardless of human capacities to have knowledge about, predict, or explain an event) simply considered the event to have been determined if it was lawful or caused.

Yet, and expectedly perhaps, this traditional approach to determinism (that whenever the cause, the event) proved to be problematic. For one, because an event takes time to evolve and because it changes, strict determinists extended the definition in such a way as to involve lack of change as determined, as well. A major difficulty, however, stemmed from lawless or chosen causes and unique events. Eventually, the bond between lawfulness and causality has been weakened in time. The first departures from the extreme form of causal regularity maintained a causal nexus, but included the idea of free will or chance.

## Determinism and Free Will

In psychological science, a distinction, such as that between physical and psychological determinism, is made (i.e., Lawry, 1981). Whereas the first one refers to mechanism, and was originally attributed to Newton, the latter has a philosophical connotation, referring to the opposite of voluntarism and freedom as posited by Spinoza. Classical understanding has suggested the incompatibility of determinism and free will. It was thought that if an action was determined, then the person was not acting with free will, and doing anything otherwise was outside the person's power. This also suggested, of course, that the person was not morally responsible for having done a predetermined action. However, transformations in both philosophy and physics have weakened the link between determinism and free will.

Philosophically, for instance, because people felt guilt or remorse and held themselves responsible for not having acted differently, the belief that all acts were determined was challenged. This meant that the belief in free will should remain, but it must be illusory. Yet, if the feeling that one could have done otherwise is true, then the incompatibility of determinism and the free will hypothesis should be false. If determinism and free will are truly incompatible, then human action could not be determined, and, hence, determinism should be false. Along similar lines, human experiences, such as making decisions, choosing among alternatives, and making an effort to accomplish something, all become seen as essentially undetermined activities, by most philosophers.

In the realm of physics, Schrodinger (1936), one of the founders of quantum mechanics, opened science's door to randomness, yet he noted that, although this new mechanics had built some hopes up for free will, it would be a mistake to think that quantum mechanics would agree with free will better than Laplace's determinism. In that paper, he clearly stated that by choosing one possibility of many, one engages one's responsibility. Freedom of choice is often illusory.

James (1884) called the radical position that argues against human freedom (as it has been best crystallized in Spinoza) *hard determinism*. *Soft determinists*, or *reconciliationists*, on the other hand, like Hume, Hobbes, and Locke, found no compelling reason to reject determinism while still believing in conscious choice. For them, some choices were made freely, and yet those alternatives themselves were determined. Hence, they were interested in studying the content of the law that accounts for the action taken, to decide if the person could have done otherwise. The *libertarian* position, as advocated by Aristotle, Kant, Campbell, Stuart Mill, and Sartre, gave the total power of making choices and causing one's own behavior to the person. People were seen as active agents, who may be challenged by external constraints. Thus, free will was not a pseudoproblem at all. They accepted that some actions are not determined, and considered the incompatibility of free will and determinism to be true. Freedom of choice was possible, then, only when behavior was not governed by any deterministic law. So, they rejected outright the idea that deterministic accounts could be possible for all actions.

In short, the old problem of free will versus determinism seemed to reach a satiety level without finding a solution. Eventually, little by little, it will disappear and be forgotten. In a way, it is like Godel's *incompleteness theorem*, where consideration of the paradox proves that some assertions cannot possibly be falsified. This is not only because of the mere complexity of the task, but also because it is not logically falsifiable. As Godel demonstrated, any formal line drawn between scientific and nonscientific is meaningless by its own criterion and self-contradictory as well. In other terms, the formal system of axiomatic logic created by the free will versus determinism issue is necessarily incomplete. Further, it is inconsistent, in that it presumes its own derivation without logical justification. To conclude, to hold one responsible for one's actions is a different matter and cannot be solved with the issue of determinism.

## Determinism and Chance

Not surprisingly, determining what role could be given to chance in a deterministic world has also been a struggle. Aristotle had suggested that chance is the result of intersecting, but causal, paths, a mere "seeming." For some, *chance* was mere word, considered "atheistical" (De Moivre, 1738/1978) or "vulgar" (Hume, 1739/1888). That is perhaps because chance was given a positive connotation, such as good luck and fortune.

Nietzsche (1982), however, believed in a chancy world. He viewed necessity and chance as an inseparable couple, in that one was necessary to explain the other. He described two realms, chance and purpose, the latter being derived from an apparently ordered world, like reason and irrationality, but by accident: "Those iron hands of necessity shake the dice box of chance play this game for an infinite length of time: so that there have to be throws which exactly resemble purposiveness and rationality of every degree" (p. 17).

Although Leibniz, in the 17th century, talked about the emergence of probability in science, and also about mutation and rapid radical change, it was C. S. Pierce who first believed in absolute chance. Pierce (1972) had the courage to shift to indeterminism and thus reverse Hume's dictum. He forcefully argued that "chance, when strictly examined, is a mere negative word, and means not any real power which has anywhere a being in nature" (Pierce, 1972, p. 11).

Pierce (1961) had given chance the first place, law the second, and the tendency to make habits, the third. Pierce (1972) then saw the world as probabilistic and totally denied deterministic causality. He defended the idea that the laws of nature should be seen as statistical regularities.

Undoubtedly, advancements in mathematics, physics, biology, and cybernetics, have made noticeable room in science for chance, uncertainty, and blind fortune. The scientific study of chance started with the analysis of games of chance in mathematics. As the calculus of probabilities demonstrated, tossing a coin a large number of times, the probability of one side coming up was close to 50%. In physics, statistical mechanics devoted itself to measuring randomness or chance in molecular chaos, that is, to large numbers of molecules flying in all directions at great speed in a liter of air, for example. These efforts led to measuring *entropy* (the amount of chance) with precision. In biology, on the other hand, studies of genetic transmission have shown that errors (i.e., mutations) take place on the basis of chance during the coding of the hereditary information via DNA messages. And, speaking of messages and information, information theory was also concerned with measuring the amount of randomness that is present in the variety of messages one considers until one destroys it by choosing a particular message.

In a more recent account, Hacking (1992) traced in detail how the erosion of determinism was subverted by statistical regularities as a gradual transformation. He called it "an incredible [and quadruple] success story of probability" (p. 4): First, in metaphysics, Cartesian causation was displaced by the probabilities of quantum mechanics. Second, in epistemology, data were analyzed, experiments were designed, and credibility was assessed in terms of probabilities. Third, in logic, statistical inferences were used. Fourth, in ethics, although probability could not dictate human values, public decisions, risk analyses, military strategies, and so on were all based on decision theory. "By covering opinion with a veneer of objectivity, we replace judgement by computation" (p. 4).

Some disciplines, among them psychology, resisted indeterminism more than others (see Gigerenzer et al., 1989). This defensiveness has not been so much against the use of descriptive statistics, because numerization and quantification still fall within the mainstream agenda. Gergen (1977), for instance, proposed an aleatory orientation that demanded a radical reframing of traditional positivist psychology.

In sum, it is already too late, nowadays, to be content with an invariant truth position. It has been shown empirically by various disciplines that the prevalence of metaphysical order is much lower in actual life than is often presupposed. Earlier presumptions of an orderly universe may be seen as reflections or projections of historically meaningful philosophical, sociocultural, and even scientific "needs," which, I believe, do not seem to be relevant in today's climate.

On the other hand, however, to hold on to determinism only as a theoretical assumption may be practical and pragmatic in some ways, because most theories and practices in use (and common sense, too) are based on deterministic models, definitely including (developmental) psychology. Prior to further engaging into these issues, it may be useful to reconsider the notion of change within the present context of determism/indeterminism debate.

## THE CHANGING NATURE OF CHANGE

Through Einstein's demonstrating the relativity of time, perspective, and space, and Heisenberg's argument of observation as a posture of choices, the nature of reality, and, hence, of change, were recast at the turn of the 20th century. Nearing the end of the present century, psychology still struggles with their implications, such as that epistemology is no longer distinct from ontology, and that there are alternative ways of thinking about thinking that are acceptable.

Interestingly, however, diverse views of change were present even among early Greek philosophers. Parmenides (510–450 B.C.), for example, was known for denying change and asserting a fixed and timeless reality. His contemporary, Heraclitus (535–475 B.C.), however, had declared the famous lines: "Into the same river, one cannot step twice" and "All is flux." He defended the primacy of opposing tensions in leading and maintaining dynamic stabilities. Nevertheless, along with determinism, Western philosophy valued stability, mere being, absolutism, and independence. Hence, change, becoming, relativity, and relatedness, were devalued.

According to Aristotle, for example, if anything (say God) was stable, absolute, and independent from other things that change, then it was superior to them. Because, for Aristotle, knowing was closely tied to what is known, therefore, God could not have knowledge of the contingent and changing world. Yet, for religious obligations, Christian, Jewish, and most Muslim theists affirmed God's knowledge of the changing things. "Only a few Mohammedans dared even to hint that this must mean change in God. The result was a glaring inconsistency which troubled many" (Hartshorne, 1965, p. vi).

To deal with this conflict perhaps, Spinoza totally rejected change and contingency, not only in God, but also in the world. This saved the ultimate truth, the reality, which is eternally there (before us to be discovered), because novel reality would demand novel truth. Later on, when change could not be denied any longer, it was seen as replacing one set of qualities with another, in an enduring substance or subject of change. Because the reality consisted essentially of beings, not happenings or events, this position became known as the *philosophy of being*.

On the other side, however, Buddhism and Taoism were known to be the earliest *philosophies of becoming* or *process philosophies*. As these names suggest, and as opposed to philosophies of being, the emphasis was on becoming, process, relations, and relativity. *The Book of Changes* (I Ching), a classic on Confucian thought, Taoism, and Buddism, focused on change as essential, and as the creation of a dynamic and devoloping whole (the Tao) through two opposite and co-dependent forces (the passive Yin and the active Yang).

This very idea of the unity of opposites, which had been also implicit in Heraclitus, later constituted Hegelian dialectics. The philosophical notion of process was further developed in the writings of Bergson (1910, 1946), Dewey (1940), James (1884, 1892, 1911), Mead (1932), and Whitehead (1919, 1922, 1929), and was carried to developmental psychology via Freud's and Piaget's models of dynamic equilibrium. However, as they adopted metaphors from physics (mechanistic) and biology (organismic), the flavors of becoming and process got lost along the way. Hence, views of development have not been developmental in essence, nor sufficiently historical (see Valsiner, 1987, 1994).

Yet, it is still the achievements in the hard sciences, such as the shift from linear dynamics to nonlinear dynamics (see van Geert, this volume, chap. 1), that continue to help significantly to capture a dynamic world in today's psychology. In "From Being to Becoming: Time and Complexity in the Physical Sciences," Prigogine (1980), for instance, stated that Western science could hardly maintain the traditional belief in the simplicity of the microscopic models, such as atoms, molecules, and so on. Simplicity was not to be found in the elementary particles, but rather in idealized macroscopic representations. He introduced the concept of *dissipative structures*, and discussed relations between time and complexity.

In sum, process philosophers made an attempt to replace substance with process, and causality with creativity. They sought *being* in *becoming* (note that none of them denied being, but defined it through becoming), and *stability* in the *novel*. This was completely the reverse of the philosophy of being that sought becoming in being and novelty in the stable, and dominated mainstream science. The importance of a dynamic and process understanding for us lies in its significant influence on the "true" (and ongoing) transformation of our understanding of change in psychology, be it revolutionary or evolutionary.

### Change Metaphors in Development

Uninfluenced by process philosophies, the earliest theories of development in psychology were confined to metaphors such as *hypertrophy* (physical enlargement), *duplication* (as in mass production), or others signifying an alteration in matter over space/time (see Mahoney, 1989). The essence of these theories was a view of development that involved a series of fixed, successive changes, a pattern determined by natural laws and, hence, the stable substance assumption. Associationist and vertical stage theories softened this posture. They gave way to the notion of complexity and differentiation, and, more recently, to continuities and discontinuities in development. Nevertheless, all classical stage theories commonly used in developmental psychology reflect a philosophy of being and ordered change. Change is seen as discontinuous, and development is the connection of successive changes and new structures in time. Although the time frame was expanded into the life span, automatic unfolding left its place to the active agent, and continuities were also accepted; the developmental sequence remained fixed, unidirectional, and linear, for the most part.

The physicist Prigogine's (1969) concept of *evolutionary feedback* (a nonequilibrium ordering principle that governs the system at many levels) emphasized not stability and homeostasis, but the idea of discontinuous change. In this view, change was associated with disequilibrium: When moved away from equilibrium, all living forms seem vulnerable to change, the form of which was not predictable. His notion of *order through fluctuation* referred to the idea that a movement that may appear as fluctuation at one time may transform suddenly into an entirely novel organization of the system at another time. The system spontaneously evolves toward less probable situations.

These ideas took place in current attempts to unify theoretical determinism/indeterminism in developmental psychology with an understanding of time-evolving, self-organizing systems that participate in their own development. New accounts have shown growing interest in the newborn's skills, preparedness, human interaction, and in the cognitive, emotional, and communication activity contexts, as part of recognizing process dynamics (see, e.g., Bornstein, 1985; Fischer, 1987; Fogel & Thelen, 1987; Gibson, 1987; Sroufe, 1979).

Jantsch and Waddington (1976) defined some basic principles and characteristics of time-evolving, self-organizing systems. For example, such a system exhibits a state of dynamic nonequilibrium within itself and with its environment. In effect, the system's resilience is closely and positively linked with its variability and heterogeneity. An inherent capacity is described as qualitative and ordered successive changes between dynamically stable states. Complementarity between deterministic and indeterministic processes and between system's structure and functions are necessary. A time-evolving system is inherently open; furthermore, the system's openness is provided with its imperfectness. It can be thought of as moving toward perfection to compensate for its incompleteness.

More recently, then, with the recognition of process dynamics, stage and structure understanding shifted to a systems and processes orientation and its related metaphors. Evolutionary, systemic, self-organizing, dialectical, hermeneutic, autopoietic, constructivist, and holistic paradigms have been most instrumental in this regard (Bateson, 1985; Butterworth, Rutkowska, & Scaife, 1985; Dell, 1983; Mischel, 1971). As a result, instead of stable entities or equilibrium states of closed (mechanistic) systems, evolving and self-organizing systems were generally made the focus of scientific study. Because they actively participated in their own development, the idea of change has been drastically altered for this self-changing (becoming) unit.

## Transformation as a Change Metaphor

I have suggested and discussed the use of transformation as a metaphor of human change elsewhere (Gulerce, 1987, 1991, 1993a), and have pointed to change in motion through dialectical fluctuations and difference. Although the transformational process is commonly understood as a dramatic metamorphosis occurring through transient regression or a system's vulnerability (see, e.g., Mahoney, 1989), that is not necessarily or exclusively so in my suggested use of the concept. Transformations can be both deterministic and indeterminate, slow and rapid, continuous and discontinuous, evolutionary and revolutionary. Also, although the term *transformation* may read as a change in form (not substance) at first sight, it refers to qualitative change (formation) through the quantitative, and vice versa.

I offer here the essential meanings of the term *transformation*, with the help of some other current terminology in present-day developmental psychology. It does not, for example, give any clue about the direction of change, as does regression, progression, or *adaptation*. Nor does it suggest the route of development to be taken, unlike the concept of hierarchical stages. Similarly, desired end-, or initial-states are not stated, leaving room for multiplicity, whereas this is not true for *growth*. Whereas causality and type of determination are implied in *maturation*, intentionality in *action*, and primary actor in *construction, transformation* is free from these preset suggestions. Further, the primacy of structure, as in *co-construction*; of the social/historical over the natural or the cultural, as in *social construction*; of the external over the internal, as in *appropriation*; and so forth, are not inherent in the notion of transformation. In short, because it is almost a generic or agnostic term, it is less value-laden and demands the careful and unique analysis of developmental phenomena. It is distinct from various other alternatives that employ certain restrictions, and its meaning can be acquired or seen in its *use* (Wittgenstein, 1953).

## THE TRANSFORMATIONAL VIEW
## OF ORDER AND MEANS OF CHANGE

The transformational view is an orientation to knowledge and an ontology of psychological development; having its own methodological and practical considerations, it adopts a particular position on determinism/indeterminism and change. That is what I briefly focus on here. My thinking is consistent with a general time-evolving systems understanding, in principle, perhaps with a less constructivist and more hermeneutic emphasis, particularly when studying the individual as the unit of analysis and human developmental change. Therefore, in what follows, I only point at what seems to be a deviation from, or expansion of, the time-evolving systems approach.

Whereas a time-evolving systems approach excludes some important phenomena with its fundamental commitments, a transformational view has a larger scope. I underline several advantages that my position offers for the challenges such a time-evolving model faces, particularly when it uses a different unit of analysis than the individual, or must deal with a nondevelopmental change. It must first be understood, however, as a metatheoretical commitment, and as being in a similar line with various poststructuralist movements toward convergence and recursivity of all knowing.

## The Coexistence of Multiple Realms

As a metatheoretical position, transformational thinking leaves room for the coexistence of different modes and processes of change, which is also necessary for its own existence and sustenance. Thus, it is not a compromising or unified theory, in contrast to the self-evolving systems model. Rather, it views change as an ongoing by-product of *coherence* of different realms and/or of accounts about them. Thus, whether these realms are representations of reality or are human constructions is not a major concern for a transformationalist, because, for practical purposes, no such distinction is made between the two. Those multiple subepistemologies and/or subontologies, then, serve as coordinates of transformations, and can, in principle, be numerous. Nevertheless, I limit myself to the three major ones here. It is crucial to note that all paradigms brought into the discussion here have acknowledged a dynamic (dialectical) reciprocity between their living systems and their environments (i.e., they are ecosystemic and communicational), and form a paradigmatic embeddedness and interdependence, like realms within realms (see Gulerce, 1991, 1992).

The first realm is called the ecological/biological world (axis EB, defining Area 1, in Fig. 2.1), because it serves as the meeting realm that most organismic models in developmental psychology (or in epistemology) seem to describe. It can be thought of in the same terms as Wundt's *Naturwissenshaft* or Bateson's *Natura*. The sociobiological, constructivist approaches to cognitive development (in which the organism is an active agent in its own development; e.g., Piaget, 1967/1971, 1970/1972), ego psychology (e.g., Hartmann, 1958) and the epistemology of Maturana and Varela (1973) fit here best.

The second realm (axis IS, defining Area 2, in Fig. 2.1) is the realm of individual/societal relations and is the counterpart of historical aspects of Wundt's *Geisteswissenshaft* and societal aspects of Bateson's *Cretura*. Object-

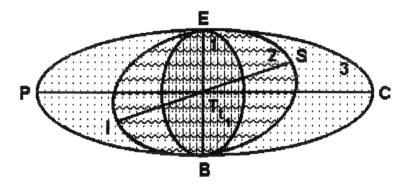

FIG. 2.1. The three coordinating realms of the transformational unit (1. organism, 2. identity, 3. self).

relations theory (e.g., Grotstein, 1977; Mahler, 1968, 1972; Slipp, 1984) and sociogenetic theories (e.g., Baldwin, 1911) are illustrative examples.

The third realm (axis PC, defining Area 3, in Fig. 2.1) is the cultural/spiritual world. It may be considered as the cultural aspects in Wundt's *Geisteswissenshaft* and symbolic aspects of Bateson's *Cretura*. Various aspects of hermeneutics, symbolic anthropology, psychoanalysis, depth psychology, some cultural psychology theories, and the like would fall into this realm, with their approaches to human development through its meaning contexts.

I now turn to describing how a transformationalist constructs relations between these three major realms and coordinates them. Thus, possible diversions in description (my deconstructions and reconstructions) from the "pure" forms of the examples mentioned become necessary for the purpose of coherence. Again, I limit my discussion to the issues concerning, directly or indirectly, determinism and change only.

## Multiplicity of Degrees of Determinism

Although the metaphysical commitment of this position is necessarily indeterministic, each of its *coordinating realms* has the theoretical presumption of order, each of a different degree. The first realm, for instance, is highly deterministic, reductionistic, and essentialistic. Pathways in this realm are highly structured, and can be thought, analogically, as if they were designed like railroads, highways, and so on. What I have said about hard determinism would apply to this domain.

In the second realm, causal relations are not deterministic but probabilistic. Keeping the same analogy, pathways are like seaways. This semistructured realm aims at organization and maintanence via regulations (*structuration*, as I call it) of time, bound to past, present, and future; context, bound to meaning, information, material, and situation; texture, bound to object, self, and subject; and the joint relations between the members.

That is the world of what Dupre (1993) called *probabilistic uniformitarianism* "where the reign of law is as universal as under determinism; it is just that the laws decree only the range of possible events and the (precise) probabilities of their occurrence" (p. 172). Thus, as the connections between states of the universe, say, between early childhood and later adult experiences, become more diffuse with increases in the time interval and allows other contingencies, most events cannot be necessitated (determined). However, mechanistic models (such as Skinner's) can also be represented here as a special case when the probabilty is maximum, that is, 1.

Although the events occur randomly and indeterministically in the third realm, meanings may emerge into an order over longer periods of time. Pathways are constructed analogous to airways. They are undifferentiated, but they are available for meaning attributions and symbol making.

## Codeterminants of the Transformational Unit

Our unit of analysis is a transformational system that can be imagined almost as a three-legged creature—a *triopus*, as Valsiner (1995) named it. However, this creature cannot exist independently of its symbiotically bonded *inner* and *outer contexts*, and is nothing but the reciprocal negotiations with and between the three realms. As it moves, each leg is jointly coordinated and constructed by and within one of the realms described. Analogically, and consequently, I think of their material structure as solid, liquid, and gas forms of matter. Thus, each has a distinct mode of interaction, fitting its realms' structured (or differentiated), semi-structured and unstructured coordinates. That is, what is predetermined (conceptually inherent) in my (a priori) position is these legs' capacities to move in certain ways. They follow certain guiding rules, norms, or signifiers of the coordinating realms in which they move. In a sense, these codeterminates of the unit share the same methodical language with the realms they belong to. Again, the metaphysical commitment is to indeterminism, coexisting with various degrees of theoretical determinism.

The first leg (or codeterminant), for example, can be called the *organism*. It is assigned to move in the first realm (in the way a train is meant for a railway) and toward survival of the ecosystem. Thus, it is coordinated by the ecological/biological messages. That is, what moves this leg feeds and coordinates the system through this codeterminant; it is matter-energy within the first realm that is used for survival. Both the realm and the leg are open only to external *matter-energy*. Just as a train cannot sail or fly, this leg cannot function with *information* and *meaning*.

The second leg is *identity* (as in personality, gender identity, social identity, etc.). It moves in the second, sociorelational, realm. This leg has aspects in common with the other two realms: It is both material (the overlap of Area 1 and Area 2 in Fig. 2.1), and meaning/symbolic (the overlap of Area 2 and Area 3, but not Area 1, in Fig. 2.1). It feeds the system back and forth with information for organizational and regulatory purposes. It is predeterministically assigned for *objectification* and for *construction* (of meaning, through construction of matter-energy), as in making cultural tools, such as art, language, and technology. However, it also accomplishes deobjectification and deconstruction (of meaning, through demolition of matter-energy), as in destroying cultural tools or the natural environment.

I call the third leg *self*. It is navigated by the cultural/spiritual messages from within the third realm that are not (and cannot be) fully coded with *objectification*, but also the meaning messages themselves. Thus, it feeds the unit with meaning for coordination toward (spiritual) connection. Unstructured or undifferentiated alternatives of meaning-making are too many for this leg. Also, because the decodings of the messages (which are carried with the cultural tools) do not necessarily translate into the same meaning across societies—or across individuals within same societies, communities, families, and so on—variability is maximal in this realm of culture.

## Means of Change and Novelty

It may be useful to stress here that the unit's legs, although moving simultaneously, follow different tracks, while pulling the unit toward its own direction at its own pace. The legs move as different dance steps that together serve as the means of change of the entire unit. Nevertheless, all of these *mechanisms/processes* bring about the paradigmatic (metatheoretical, content-free, formal) consistency that is needed by the transformational unit. They are all compatible with the very nature of the *system/structure* of the transformational unit, because they are all dialectical (see Gulerce, 1987), ecosystemic (see Keeney, 1979; Wilden, 1977), bidirectional (see Valsiner, 1993) and multicommunicational (or multilingual) (see Gulerce, 1993a).

For instance, accommodation/assimilation, as in Piaget (1970/1972), best describes the first leg's developmental process that the organism adapts. The type of ecosystemic communication between this leg and its realm is asemiotic (see Gulerce, 1996b). Because the mode is digital (either/or, absence/presence), as in binary logic, the steps appear as numerous microgenetic hops. The messages flow in the form of discontinuous transmissions, so that the motion is very rapid and revolutionary and, again, deterministic. Hence, future states depend strongly on the initial conditions, such as the biological birth of the organism. Development would proceed as the unfolding of biological determinism if the unit were carried only on this leg, without the influence of the other two.

The second leg's mechanism of change is internalization/externalization, as in Vygotsky (see Valsiner, 1992; Valsiner & Lawrence, 1993). The messages are both digital and analog. Change offered by this coordinate can be both rapid and slow. They can be analogical to twist steps, I think. Transformations are both deterministically indeterminate and indeterministically deterministic. Hence, future states are less dependent on initial conditions, such as psychosocial status at birth: For example, a male infant can grow up, transform his gender-related identity, and define himself as gay.

The transformatory mechanism for the third leg is projective identification, as in Kline (see Grotstein, 1977; Slipp, 1984). The mode of the transformatory communication is analog: images, icons, fantasms, dreams, ideas, and so on. The flow of messages and, hence, the change are continuous. Although the ideas and meanings float freely, the leg's steps appear to me as swings. Change in this realm is macrogenetic and very slow, and is in form (not in substance) if it ever takes place. It is also theoretically indeterministic and unknowable. As expected, then, the dependence of future states on initial conditions (e.g., cultural birth of the self) is nil. For example, an American person can form a Buddhist self at some point in time. Similarly, an 18th-century individual's self (private culture) can join in a collective cultural form of the 21st century.

## Deterministically Indeterminate and Indeterministically Deterministic Transformations

Although the overall path for a time-evolving system (be it through successive, hierarchical stages or not) is predetermined, it is absolutely indeterminate for the transformational unit. The unit transforms as its legs "move" simultaneously. At any given point in time, the unit is always situated at the intersection of its three realms (point $T_{t_i}$ in Fig. 2.1), and moves to the next point in time $(T_{t_{i+1}})$ as a function of its three coordinates so that whether there is a pattern in the "developmental path" and/or nicely coordinated (i.e., harmonious or well-balanced) action of the system's moves are only seen via retrospective or existential analyses and as empirical or self-reflexive attributes. Again, it is not the end points, but the possible trajectories of the three legs, that are predictable.

For example, there are pulls toward morphostasis, and the organism is always oriented to reproduction. Hence, the feedback mechanism of the first leg is deviation-correcting, so that any diversion from the rule is corrected before it occurs: The railway and the train predefine the path for the train, and predictability is maximal. Novelty, then, is extraordinary and error-based, as in mutation. An extra chromosome, for instance, is not a regular (normal) thing to happen following the biological rules, and such a novelty is atypical (and abnormal). The regulatory messages are lost as the matter-energy diminishes: The railway and the train get old or damaged, and then an accident happens.

The second leg, however, is open to both information and matter-energy, and is semi-structured for relevant identity formation. It paradoxically pulls the unit toward both homeostasis (matter-energy) and heterostasis (symbolic aspects) on different levels. Therefore, it simultaneously aims at both maintenance (of the matter-energy) and dialectical action and communicational interchange (of the meaning). Thus, feedback mechanisms can be both deviation-correcting and deviation-amplifying. That is how identity crises can occur, particularly if the messages are double-binding. Novelty, however, is always considered in the form of compensation (see, e.g., Adler, 1931) as a pragmatic solution to an acknowledged problem or "lack" in a societal community. Some normative (digital) messages are lost as the law or rule systems change in the societal realm, and some messages (analog) are kept. An adolescent, or a "hippie," for example, may change the dress code of a particular community, but keep the social values.

The third leg, *self*, flows in the the ocean of culture. The messages are never lost here (see, e.g., Gulerce, 1993a; Kojima, 1993), but are restyled in time: at any time, in any place, in any form (see, e.g., Jung, 1956; Obeyese-kere, 1990). Because this realm is rich in terms of intersubjectivity, self is pulled toward heterostasis and is always growth-activating, so that the feedback mechanism is deviation-amplifying to such an extent that creativity is not only desired, but actually facilitated within this realm. Creativity (see Kris, 1952), in my thinking, is fostered mainly by this leg as novelty. It is proactively reflected onto the third realm as self-expression, say, in the form of art or scientific innovation.

## The Issue of Coherence

The three legs, moving in the three realms and on their strictly, moderately, and loosely defined coordinates, are in charge of holding the transforma-tional system coherently together and codetermining its motion. There is no general recipe for maximum coordination and coherence independent of the unit. Thus, *coherence* does not mean harmony or equilibrium. Rather, it is a byproduct of ongoing negotiations between the legs. It is unique to the transformational unit, because it is defined in a relative way by the system or structure itself (also see Gulerce, 1993a, 1996a).

Let us consider mother–infant interaction during breast-feeding as an example for our analysis here. The nutritious quality of mother's milk op-erates in the first realm and is utilized for the development of the infant's body (i.e., the organism). That is why it is not a surprise that malnourished Third World infants have higher mortality rates and show psychological developmental delays in comparison to their Western peers. The absence or presence of the mother (and the milk), on the other hand, the feeding schedule and continuity pattern, the familiarity, consistency, and sameness of experience, all function in the second realm. They help with identity formations (see Erikson, 1963; Hartmann & Kriss, 1945). The psychological quality of the relationship, as communicated via mostly nonverbal and diffused messages across time, constructs the self (private culture) in the third realm (see Kohut, 1971; Mahler, 1972; Winnicott, 1965). Obviously, the needed time span subsequently increases for the three legs, and serves as the invisible and irreversible 4th dimension in the coordination.

Also, although there is no predefined attainable and knowable equilib-rium state, we can talk about disequilibrium to understand change. At times of maximum conflict, when all the legs pull the system equally in their own directions, when differences cannot be mediated ("translated") and so can-not be negotiated, maximum disequilibrium (i.e., ambivalence) is experi-enced by the unit. For example, a schizophrenic mother may exhibit loving behaviors and cuddle her crying infant in her arms to comfort her, and yet, she may not be sensitive and responsive to the infant's cues for hunger (say, because she is not hungry herself at that moment) and may not think of nursing and, hence, frustrates the child.

These are the exact times when the unit is faced with the unknown: uncertainty and crisis. That is another way of saying that the unit temporarily gets stuck, as the dynamic movement stems from the difference in motivation among the legs. Although, the directions provided by the coordinates are different (which seemingly should create necessary conflict for motion), the impetus of the motivations are said to be equal. It would be a state (though hypothetical) of maximum equilibrium if all the directions (with equal impetus) were in agreement. In my thinking, maximum harmony (though only a theoretical possibility) also puts the transformational unit into a momentarily fixed, motionless state, which would demand change.

Far from being malfunctional, the states of both disequilibrium (which I call *developmental arrest*), and equilibrium (which I call *developmental rest*), both give way to novelty. In other words, my transformational position (also see Gulerce, 1991) views both goodness-of-fit and goodness-of-misfit models of development (van Geert, 1988) sensible and as describing different forms of change in the unit. This change of the system or structure as a whole is a major transformation, which I call *restructuration*. As I suggested before, if this restructuration is primarily guided by the first leg and its coordinates, it appears as metamorphosis. If the resolution of conflict is canalized primarily by the second leg and represented in the second realm with societal (interpersonal) concerns, it appears as compensation (see, e.g., Adler, 1931) and is reproductive.

## Primacy and Hierarchy of the Realms

Although in a self-organizing systems model, social and symbolic influences are said to outweigh genetic ones, in my developmental transformations model, there is no such predetermined hierarchical ordering independent of the unit and time span of analysis. I would argue, however, that the first realm described here is more suitable for microgenetic, the second for mezzogenetic (ontogenetic, dyadic, small-group), and the third for macrogenetic (cultural/historical) units of analysis. In addition, the second ontology is a mediator between the first and third ontologies. It provides a metacommunicative context (see Fogel & Branco, this volume, chap. 3, for a relevant discussion) at a higher logical level (see Bateson, 1972; Whitehead & Russell, 1910) for the first realm, and it is punctuated by metacommunications by the third realm.

Reversibility and replicability of events, and thus generalization or universality of developmental processes, are more probable for the first realm, although the outcomes of development are still very much context-specific.

The context in question here is the sociocultural, as in the use of cultural tools, and language. Let us think of cultural variations among Piagetian task accomplishments (e.g., Cole, 1975; Cole & Bruner, 1971; Dasen, 1972).

The opposite can be said, however, for the third realm, because it is indeterministic with irreversible events, so that developmental processes here are highly singular and context-bound, and yet the outcome (i.e., the meanings that emerge) can be quite common (even universal) across the world and over time. The context in question here is primarily matter-energy based, provided by the natural/physical setting and, hence, constraining the cultural activity of tool or symbol making. In other words, cultural units may apply their own unique grammars to the available raw material in order to make novel cultural tools, signs, and signifiers, which may have equivalence of meaning and/or function across units (also see Gulerce, 1992).

## Fluidity of Transformations

This kind of understanding inevitably makes all the realms *symbiotically interdependent* (and, thus, mutually beneficial), without placing primacy of one over another. Also, in the transformational view, and historically speaking, none of these realms emerges prior to any other, or is present before or after the transformational unit. It has been a common understanding in psychology that the individual is born into a highly structured world and is "constantly canalized by the goal-oriented 'social others,' directly or indirectly" (Valsiner, 1994, p. 38), even in the recent accounts where the irreversibility of time, fuzziness, and fluidity of developmental transformations are recognized. Also, the infant, in ego psychological theorizing, is presupposed to be born as an undifferentiated ego mass and to develop the capacity for autoplastic and alloplastic activities through, and for further reciprocal relations with, the environment (i.e., Blanck & Blanck, 1974; Hartmann, 1958).

All three of the realms (and also the three different ways of constructing reality or three different realities) I described here emerge simultaneously and coexist with the transformational unit of analysis. That is, there is no preassigned chronological order for these worlds. What may be time-dependent, however, is that the *visibility* of the paradigmatic elements and patterns to both the analyst and the unit itself for self-reflexive accounts. This is how the transformational system truly contributes to its own making, and how the overall path of development is indeterminate at the metaphysical level.

## COPING WITH INDETERMINISM

For whatever reasons, and through our transformational lenses, it seems clear that Western science has been dominated by its first leg, toward the positivist, empiricist, rationalist, and "real" reality for a long while. This bias is easy to link to the Western cultural, philosophical attributes of seeking control over a highly determined universe and, hence, the power to survive and escape from the anxiety of the ambiguous.

Paradoxically, introduction of the concepts of chance, chaos, uncertainty, unpredictability, probabilistic laws, freedom of choice, and so on in Western science further increased the desire to gain control over a disorderly universe. This enormous interest in order and systems of order, and in power and political economy of truth (Foucault, 1970), and in the meaning and purpose (Frankl, 1965) such order might carry, has dominated Western "male" science throughout the centuries. Knowledge is always seen as power, and power is understood as control over the single truth.

Tolerating ambiguity and the multiplicity of truths, living with ambivalence, knowing one's limits (scientist or not) before the dynamic world are non-Western cultural, philosophical qualities. Perhaps enough time has passed to make the other legs' demands recognizable for both self-reflexive acts, because many Western attempts have been self-critical of Western science, and epistemological variations in making science or other kinds of intelligibility. Hence, we can say, optimistically perhaps, that the transformational system of human intelligibility is soon to face confusion, created by further pulls toward the other two paradigms, by the other two legs. Examples are already evident in psychology, in individual (Mahoney, 1991) and familial (Hoffman, 1981) psychotherapeutic process, and in children's cognitive development (van Geert, 1994), where the system brings about its own resolution in a singular fashion.

## CONCLUDING REMARKS

I have shown here, first, that the notion of determinism has been divorced from its previously matched connotations for prediction, causality, scientific control, and free will in contemporary science. However, none of these conceptual partners has left determinism for indeterminism. Most likely, due to the deep-seated metaphysical (religous and philosophical) roots of determinism in Western science, there has been a resistance to an indeterminate world understanding. For example, evidence for the possibility of prediction without needing an orderly (knowable) reality, I think, further led to equating indeterminism with inaccuracy of measurement, along with an intensified need for control and power. It is unfortunate that many efforts have been invested in advancing technology, assessment devices, and so on. Increasing the preciseness of predictions by improving the sensitivity of the measures has been given priority, instead of addressing what I see as the real problem, the type of epistemology, the shortage of conceptual knowledge, and the scientific and cultural regulations and limitations. On the other hand, if today's irrelevant debate about determinism versus free will is the only way to keep our own (human) richness and complexity in mind, and to rehumanize the human subject and the human scientist after long-lasting mechanistic paradigms in psychology, then it is extremely functional to keep in the agenda.

Second, I pointed to the close ties between the notion of change and the commitment to order. Being methodologically bound to positivism (which is also deterministic, essentialistic, reductionistic, and empiricist), most scientific accounts of human development sacrificed the dynamic nature of human change and development. Current attempts, however, having recognized the necessity to study change in motion, are seeking reconciliation between determinism and indeterminism. The unified approach of dynamic and time-evolving systems is a good example. Keeping in mind the distinction I drew between determinism and indeterminism as metatheoretical and theoretical assumptions, however, I find this model only sufficient to deal with the issue on the theoretical level, while it is still under the influence of the Western sociocultural climate. In my opinion, this sort of unification or exclusivity (i.e., denying the unique nature of other different types of change) would be limited only, although not as constraining as in the case of unification psychology (Staats, 1991).

By introducing transformational thinking, which is indeterminate on the epistemological level, I have tried to address the indispensible coexistence of multiple ontologies, or multiple ways of seeing human reality. By definition, then, there is room for different degrees of (theoretical) determination and for their reciprocal interactions.

From this transformationalist stand, if we view the discipline as an intellectual unit, it seems to be moving so awkwardly (both pragmatically and aesthetically speaking), and yet not developing: It has been, and still is, heavily leaning on the numerous (empirical) repetitive hops on its first leg, and with some recent reproductions (of old theories) by its second leg's twists, apparently serving as a cane, compensating for the first whenever needed. In short, today's scientific-cultural zeitgeist can use some creative swings of the third leg, enabling the coherence of novelty, the nature of which cannot be foreseen.

## REFERENCES

Adler, A. (1931). *What life should mean to you.* Boston: Little, Brown.

Baldwin, J. M. (1911). *The individual and society.* Boston: Richard G. Badger.

Bateson, G. (1972). *Steps to an ecology of mind.* New York: Ballantine.

Bateson, P. (1985). Problems and possibilities in fusing developmental and evolutionary thought. In G. Butterworth, J. Rutkowska, & M. Scaife (Eds.), *Evolution and developmental psychology* (pp. 3–21). Sussex: Harvester Press.

Bergson, H. (1910). *Time and free will.* London: George Allen and Unwin.

Bergson, H. (1946). *The creative mind.* New York: The Philosophical Library.

Berofsky, B. (Ed.). (1966). *Free will and determinism.* New York: Harper and Row.

Blanck, G., & Blanck, R. (1974). *Ego psychology. Theory and practice.* New York: Columbia University Press.

Bornstein, M. H. (1985). How infant and mother jointly contribute to developing cognitive competence in the child. *Proceedings of the National Academy of Science, 1,* 7470–7473.

Browning, D. (Ed.). (1965). *Philosophers of process.* New York: Random House.

Butterworth, G., Rutkowska, J., & Scaife, M. (1985). *Evolution and developmental psychology.* Sussex: Harvester Press.

Cole, M. (1975). An ethnographic psychology of cognition. In R. W. Brislin, S. Bochner, & W. Lonner (Eds.), *Cross-cultural perspectives on learning* (pp. 157–175). New York: Wiley.

Cole, M., & Bruner, J. S. (1971). Cultural differences and inferences about psychological processes. *American Psychologist, 26,* 867–876.

Dasen, P. R. (1972). Cross-cultural Piagetian research: A summary. *Journal of Cross-Cultural Psychology, 3,* 23–40.

Dell, P. (1983). Beyond homeostasis: Toward a concept of coherence. *Family Process, 21,* 21–41.

De Moivre, A. (1738/1978). *The doctrine of chances.* London: Harper and Row.

Dewey, J. (1940). *Time and individuality.* New York: New York University Press.

Dupre, J. (1993). *The disorder of things: Metaphysical foundations of the disunity of science.* Cambridge, MA: Harvard University Press.

Erikson, E. (1963). *Childhood and society* (2nd ed.). New York: Norton.

Feyarabend, P. K. (1976). *Against method.* New York: Humanities Press.

Fischer, R. (1987). On fact and fiction: The structures of stories that the brain tells to itself about itself. *Journal of Social and Biological Structures, 10,* 343–351.

Fogel, A., & Thelen, E. (1987). Development of early expressive and communicative action: Reinterpreting the evidence from a dynamic systems perspective. *Developmental Psychology, 23,* 747–761.

Foucault, M. (1978). *The history of sexuality, Vol. I* (R. Hurley, Trans.). New York: Random House.

Frankl, V. E. (1965). *The doctor and the soul: From psychotherapy to logotherapy* (2nd ed.). New York: Knopf.

Gergen, K. J. (1977). Stability, change and chance in understanding human development. In N. Datan & H. Reese (Eds.), *Life-span developmental psychology: Dialectical perspectives on experimental research* (pp. 135–158). New York: Academic Press.

Gergen, K. J. (1994). *Realities and relationships.* Boston, MA: Harvard University Press.

Gibson, E. J. (1987). Introductory essay: What does infant perception tell about theories of perception? *Journal of Experimental Psychology: Human Perception and Performance, 13,* 515–523.

Gigerenzer, G., Swijtink, Z., Porter, T., Daston, L., Beatty, J., & Kruger, L. (1989). *The empire of chance.* Cambridge, England: Cambridge University Press.

Grotstein, J. S. (1977). *Splitting and projective identification.* New York: Jason Aronson.

Gulerce, A. (1987). *Transformational epistemology: A methodological synthesis of psychoanalysis and family systems thinking.* Unpublished doctoral dissertation. Denver: University of Denver.

Gulerce, A. (1991). The transformational approach: Basic assumptions for an alternative model for human sciences. *Bogazici University Journal, 8,* 60–69.

Gulerce, A. (1992, September). *Transformational epistemology.* Paper presented at the First Socio-Cultural Studies Conference, Madrid, Spain.

Gulerce, A. (1993a, July). *Transformational view of human development.* Paper presented at the Twelfth Biennial Meeting of the International Society for the Study of Human Development, Recife, Brazil.

Gulerce, A. (1993b, July). *Parental notions of child development*. Paper presented at the Twelfth Biennial Meeting of the International Society for the Study of Human Development, Recife, Brazil.

Gulerce, A. (1996a). A family structure assessment device for Turkey. In J. Pandey (Ed.), *Asian contributions to crosscultural psychology* (pp. ). London: Sage.

Gulerce, A. (1996b). On necessary transformations of Piaget's genetic epistemology. *Bogazici University Journal, 16,* 223–248.

Hacking, I. (1992). *The taming of chance*. Cambridge, England: Cambridge University Press.

Hartmann, H. (1958). *Ego psychology and the problem of adaptation*. New York: International Universities Press.

Hartshorne, C. (1965). Introduction: The development of process philosophy. In D. Browning (Ed.), *Philosophers of process* (pp. v–xxii). New York: Random House.

Hoffman, L. (1981). *Foundations of family therapy*. New York: Basic Books.

Hume, D. (1739/1888). *A treatise of human nature*. Oxford: Oxford University Press.

Hume, D. (1748/1902). *Enquiry concerning human understanding*. Oxford: Oxford University Press.

James, W. (1884). The dilemna of determinism. *The Uniterian Review, 22,* 193–224.

James, W. (1892/1965). The stream of consciousness. In D. Browning (Ed.), *Philosophers of process* (pp. 139–159). New York: Random House.

James, W. (1911). *Some problems of philosophy*. New York: Longmans, Green.

Jantsch, E., & Waddington, C. H. (1976). *Evolution and consciousness: Human systems in transition*. Reading, MA: Addison-Wesley.

Jung, C. G. (1956). *The archetypes and the collective unconscious*. New York: Pantheon.

Keeney, B. (1979). Ecosystemic epistemology: An alternative paradigm for diagnosis. *Family Process, 19,* 117–129.

Kohut, H. (1971). *The analysis of the self*. New York: International Universities Press.

Kojima, H. (1993, July). *Ethnopsychological pool of theories of child-rearing and human development: Its functions in cultural and historical perspectives*. Paper presented at Twelfth Biennial Meetings of the International Society for the Study of Human Development, Recife, Brazil.

Kris, E. (1952). *Psychoanalytic explorations in art*. New York: International Universities Press.

Laplace, P. S. de. (1814/1951). *A philosophical essay on probabilities* (F. W. Truscott & F. L. Emory, Trans.). New York: Harper and Row.

Lawry, J. D. (1981). *Guide to the history of psychology*. Totowa, NJ: Littlefield, Adams.

Li, T., & Yorke, J. A. (1975). Period three implies chaos. *American Mathematical Monthly, 82,* 985–992.

Mahler, M. S. (1968). *On human symbiosis and the vicissitudes of individuation*. New York: International Universities Press.

Mahler, M. S. (1972). On the first three subphases of the separation-individuation process. *International Journal of Psychoanalysis, 53,* 333–338.

Mahoney, M. J. (1989). Scientific psychology and radical behaviorism: Important distinctions based in scientism and objectivism. *American Psychologist, 44,* 1372–1377.

Mahoney, M. J. (1991). *Human change process*. New York: Basic Books.

Maturana, H. R., & Varela, F. J. (1973/1980). Autopoisesis: The organization of the living. In H. R. Maturana & F. J. Varela (Eds.), *Autopoiesis and cognition: The realization of the living*. Boston, MA: Reidel.

Mead, G. H. (1932). *The philosophy of the present (Carus lectures)*. La Salle, IL: Open Court.

Mischel, T. (Ed.). (1971). *Cognitive development and epistemology*. New York: Academic Press.

Nietzsche, F. (1982). *Daybreak thoughts on the origins of morality*. Cambridge, England: Cambridge University Press.

Obeyesekere, G. (1990). *The work of culture: Symbolic transformation in psychoanalysis and anthropology*. Chicago: University of Chicago Press.

Piaget, J. (1967/1971). *Biology and knowledge*. Chicago: The University of Chicago Press.

Piaget, J. (1970/1972). *The principles of genetic epistemology*. London: Routledge & Kegan Paul.

Pierce, C. S. (1891/1965). The architecture of theories, *Monist*, January. Reprinted In D. Browning (Ed.), *Philosophers of process*. New York: Random House.

Pierce, C. S. (1972). *The essential writings*. New York: Harper & Row.

Prigogine, I. (1969). Structure, dissipation and life. *Theoretical physics and biology* (pp. 57–70). Amsterdam: North Holland.

Prigogine, I. (1980). *From being to becoming*. San Francisco: Freeman.

Ruelle, D. (1991). *Chance and chaos*. Princeton, NJ: Princeton University Press.

Schrodinger, E. (1936). Indeterminism and freewill. *Nature, 4*, 13–14.

Slipp, S. (1984). *Object relations: A dynamic bridge between individual and family treatment*. New York: Jason Aronson.

Sroufe, L. (1979). The coherence of individual development: Early care, attachment, and subsequent developmental issues. *American Psychologist, 34*, 834–841.

Valsiner, J. (1987). *Culture and development of children's action*. Chichester: Wiley.

Valsiner, J. (1992). Social organization of cognitive development: Internalization and externalization of constraint systems. In A. Demetriou, M. Shayer, & A. Efklides (Eds.), *Neo-Piagetian theories of cognitive development* (pp. 65–78). London: Routledge & Kegan Paul.

Valsiner, J. (1994). Irreversibility of time and the construction of historical developmental psychology. *Mind, Culture and Activity, 1*(1&2), 25–42.

Valsiner, J. (1995). Personal communication.

Valsiner, J., & Lawrence, A. J. (1993). Social determinacy of human development: An analysis of the conceptual roots of the internalization process. *Human Development, 28*, 131–143.

van Geert, P. (1988). The concept of transition in developmental theories. In W. J. Baker, L. P. Mos, H. V. Rappard, & H. J. Stam (Eds.), *Recent trends in theoretical psychology* (pp. 225–235). New York: Springer.

van Geert, P. (1994). *Dynamics systems of development. Change between complexity and chaos*. New York: Harvester.

Verene, D. P. (1981). *Vico's science of imagination*. Ithaca, NY: Cornell University Press.

Vico, G. (1725/1948). *The new science* (T. G. Bergin & M. H. Fisch, Trans.). Ithaca, NY: Cornell University Press.

Whitehead, A. N. (1919). *An inquiry concerning the principles of natural knowledge*. Cambridge, England: Cambridge Universitry Press.

Whitehead, A. N. (1922). *The principle of relativity*. Cambridge, England: Cambridge University Press.

Whitehead, A. N. (1929). *Process and reality. An essay in cosmology*. New York: Macmillan.

Whitehead, A. N., & Russell, B. (1910). *Principia mathematica*. Cambridge, England: Cambridge University Press.

Wiener, P. P. (1974). *Dictionary of the history of ideas: Studies of pivotal ideas*. New York: Scribner.

Wilden, A. (1977). *System and structure*. London: Tavistock.

Winnicott, D. W. (1965). *The maturational process and the facilitating environment*. New York: International Universities Press.

Wittgenstein, L. (1953). *Philosophical investigations*. Oxford: Blackwell.

# 3

# METACOMMUNICATION AS A SOURCE OF INDETERMINISM IN RELATIONSHIP DEVELOPMENT

Alan Fogel
University of Utah

Angela Uchoa Branco
University of Brasilia

The premise of this chapter is that interpersonal relationships are developing systems of communication, systems that generate meaning in the form of emotion, commitment, and memories. Relationships construct their own life histories and move through developmental phases, such as getting acquainted, establishing trust and intimacy, maintenance, decline, and rejuvenation or termination. We take a dialectical perspective on relationship continuity and change, focusing on the everyday communication processes that constitute the direct contacts between participants.

One purpose of this chapter is to examine relationship development from the perspective of determinism and indeterminism. According to the dynamic systems theory that guides our work, organized patterns form because of the mutual constraints imposed by participants on each other within particular contexts. The emergence of new patterns is never strictly determined by prior conditions, because the local interactions create sources of indeterminacy. We review the literature on dynamic systems theory to suggest how indeterminacy can arise in a developing system and, in particular, how it may arise in relationship development.

A second purpose of this chapter is to explore the relative roles of communication and metacommunication in relationship development. *Communication* includes all forms of everyday coactions between participants, including sharing, cooperation, conflict, debate, social play, and conversation. In *metacommunication*, participants evaluate their own communication process. Metacommunication, therefore, is a reflexive process in which individuals communicate about the way in which they communicate, in the past, present, or future.

In order to explore the process of metacommunication, we review the literature on adult relationships and present data from our own work on parent–infant and preschool peer play. We hypothesize that metacommunication may be one source of indeterministic change in interpersonal relationships, primarily because it constrains the future course of a relationship by making explicit the connection of the future with the past and the present. Indeterminism can arise with respect to the timing of metacommunication, its topic and scope, and its impact on action.

## DIALECTICAL PROCESSES: HISTORY AND NOVELTY

We offer a dialectical perspective in which developmental change in a relationship arises from the process of communication between participants, that is, through their coaction. This approach does not deny the existence of individual feelings, ideas, and goals as important to what happens in a relationship. Rather, the dialectical approach suggests that individual experience is constituted, in part, by dialogical coaction. Individual experience is as much an outcome of dialogue as the content and form of the dialogue itself.

The dialectical perspective views relationships as inherently dynamic and as constituted by a continuous process in which multiple voices form momentary fusions in the midst of countervailing tendencies and tensions (Bahktin, 1988; Baxter, 1994; Rawlins, 1983; Werner, Altman, Brown, & Ginat, 1993). Effort has been devoted to articulate the types of oppositions that frame relational dialectical processes. The conflict between retaining one's independence, as contrasted with the necessary interdependence of a relationship, is an example of two dialogical poles (Baxter, 1994; Wilmot, 1994). Another example is the opposition between individuals with divergent experiences, such that intersubjectivity is created synthetically from the discourse between different positions (Linell, 1990; Rommetveit, 1990; Vygotsky, 1978).

One hypothesized dialogical opposition is directly relevant to the theme of this chapter. It is the contrast between the relative predictability and repeatability of relationship patterns (relationship stability) compared to the generation of novelty and indeterminacy (relationship change; Altman, Vinsel, & Brown, 1981; Baxter, 1994). Relationships that are too predictable are more likely to experience difficulties (Baxter, 1994; Cody, 1982; Cupach & Metts, 1986), as are relationships that are relatively chaotic and lack stability (Berger, 1988; Planalp, Rutherford, & Honeycutt, 1988).

This particular process—the emergence of novelty/indeterminism as part of a dialectical encounter—is our central theme. From a dialectical perspective, novelty is a spontaneous and partially indeterminate result of the encounter between multiple voices and different dialectical poles. Although repeating patterns occur in relationships, they have been likened more to a spiral of continuously evolving change rather than to a circle of repetition (Linell, 1990; Wilmot, 1994), to a fluidity of process, such that "relationships are indeterminate processes of ongoing flux" (Baxter, 1994, p. 233). Thus, acts in a dialogue are not only connected to the past history of actions, but are, simultaneously, partially novel actions that furnish a constant source of renewal of the dialogue.

How can indeterminacy arise in the context of a historically constrained relationship system? One answer can be found in the creativity of everyday dialogical processes. Markova (1990), for example, envisioned a three-step dialogical process as a minimal unit of analysis in the following way. A acts and B responds, but as B is composing the response, A is already changing, and perhaps the observed changes in A alter the response of B as it is unfolding in time. The passage of time in a dialogue, therefore, implies the emergence of novelty. Because that novelty is created in the moment, it cannot be entirely predicted on the basis of past actions and is thus partly indeterminate. Henri Bergson's concept of enduring (*durée*) as a characteristic of being suggests a continuous invention and creation of new forms. The historical process never precisely repeats, because the person is coordinated with contextual demands that are changing, partly because of outside forces, but also because the act of living provides a continuously updated local context of the person as part of a set of relationships (Bergson, 1910; Valsiner, 1994).

Narrative and dramaturgical approaches to human action also share a similar focus on the creativity of the unfolding story or narrative plot in the context of its historical embeddedness within the relationship. A narrative is a form of personal organization that brings experiences together into a set of episodes and accounts. Narratives are more, however, than telling and retelling a fixed personal story. They are creative activities in which the teller alters the tale to suit the listener, or in which two or more people creatively coconstruct a joint narrative by which they make up their future or recreate their past (Goffman, 1974; Harre, 1988; Hermans & Kempen, 1993; Knoespel, 1991; Sarbin, 1986).

The dialectical literature reviewed thus far focuses primarily on verbal dialogues and their self-sustaining and self-creating dimensions. One of us (Fogel, 1993, in press) has argued that the creative emergence of novelty in coaction also arises in nonverbal communication in both human and nonhuman species. Verbal exchanges in humans are embedded in an ongoing process of nonverbal coaction in which posture, gaze direction, facial expression, and body movements are mutually coordinated to create emergent social patterns. Examples include postural coorientation, kissing and other courtship behaviors, establishing and breaking mutual gaze, game playing, and fighting. Indeed, if one examines verbal action at a more microscopic level of analysis, words are themselves produced as continuous streams of sound in which a person is free to alter the intensity, pitch, and timing of the utterance to create social meanings that are both context-dependent and context-renewing. Infants and young children, also, are capable of entering into these forms of creative nonverbal communication (Fogel, 1993; Grammer, 1989; Heath, 1984; Kendon, 1975; Scherer, 1982).

These forms of nonverbal coaction have characteristics similar to those described for verbal dialogue, in that each succeeding coaction builds on the historical series of prior actions and at the same time contributes to the renewal of the dialogue through emergent novelty. Many nonverbal (and some verbal) social encounters are built on the coordination of participants' simultaneous coaction. Mutual postural adjustments, mutual gazing, certain forms of mutual play and conflict, cooperation, singing, dancing, and even conversation all depend on the simultaneous coordination between individuals. Fogel (1992, 1993) has referred to this simultaneous coordination as *coregulation*. Dialogue is coregulated if (a) there is a simultaneous mutual adjustment of action, and (b) the dialogue yields emergent novelty and mutual creativity; that is, the communication is more than the simple sum of its partners' input.

## DETERMINISM AND INDETERMINISM
## IN COMMUNICATIVE SYSTEMS

The theoretical problem in relationship development is to explain both stability and change. The dialectical perspective can be enhanced in this regard by application of a dynamic systems perspective on *self-organizing systems*. Indeed, a number of scholars of development of both individuals and interpersonal relationships have explicitly invoked this theoretical analogy (Fogel, 1992, 1993; Fogel & Thelen, 1987; Rogers & Millar, 1988; Thelen, 1989; Thelen & Ulrich, 1991; Valsiner, 1994). The concept of the self-organizing system originated in the physical sciences with the study of irreversible processes in which patterns were formed in physical and chemical systems (Prigogine & Stengers, 1984).

Deterministic processes are reversible and dependent primarily on the initial conditions. In other words, historical and contextual factors do not play a role in the development of the system: Its evolution would be the same regardless of changing conditions once the process begins. Also, a deterministic process can be reversed. A pendulum without friction is a good example. The amplitude and frequency of the swings are entirely dependent on where the pendulum begins in its cycle, and you could make it go in reverse or re-create the same movement on limitless occasions.

Indeterministic processes, on the other hand, are irreversible in the sense that they can't be repeated. Initial conditions are important, but so are changing conditions that occur during the evolution of the process. Chance events may occur that alter the subsequent course of the process. Stability can be created through indeterministic processes, but it is only relative to the maintenance of a set of systemic conditions. Relatively small fluctuations in those conditions may preserve the stability of the system, but larger fluctuations, as well as chance events, may create the conditions for system reorganization.

Dynamic systems may have a number of dynamically stable patterns of organization that are described by deterministic processes. Changes in the particular features of the system, including chance events, can push the system toward a transition point in which it can shift into two or more new stable modes of action, a process called a *bifurcation*. There can be indeterminacy in the time of occurrence of the bifurcation and in which of the resulting stable patterns the system will settle into at any given time (Davies, 1988; Gleick, 1987; Pattee, 1987).

Biological systems—including behavioral systems—are different from physical systems, because biological systems are partially under the control of a set of semiotic or informational symbols whose significance is based on the history of the system and whose action on the system is not directly reducible to physical forces. Semiotic meanings become especially important during periods of system bifurcation, and may add another source of indeterminism in the creation of change in the system, because a symbol that represents a system cannot contain all the information necessary to generate the complete dynamics of the system (Pattee, 1987).

The same word or gesture, for example, is likely to produce a variety of outcomes in communication depending on how it is interpreted and how that interpretation is played out in action. On the other hand, there is a partial determinism in the effect of a particular word or gesture, because it constrains action toward a subset of alternatives. Nevertheless, communicative actions, in particular, and semiotics, in general, are not mandatory commands, but partially indeterminate suggestions. When words and gestures are combined into complex narrative forms, new forms of determinism and indeterminism are introduced. Narratives and social discourses reveal and hide, communicate and confuse, stabilize and destabilize (Knoespel, 1991; Paulson, 1991). How can we understand this paradox of communicative systems: that they are both determinate and indeterminate?

The answer to this question lies in the assumptions a dialectical framework uses to interpret the behavior of living systems, where apparent opposites relate to each other in an inclusive rather than exclusive way. Therefore, the tension between determinism and indeterminism in human development derives from the simultaneous, coactive existence of a set of constraining factors allowing for the predictability of the system's development, together with the continuous generation of novelty coming from the multiple interactions in which the system participates. The dialectical interplay between both sources of development—stability/predictability versus change/novelty—can be conceptualized as a process of "bounded indeterminacy" (Valsiner, 1987, 1994).

When two people meet for the first time, there are many possible ways in which they can combine their actions into a coregulated communication system. This potentially very high indeterminacy is reduced rapidly by cultural constraints, such as role and partner relationship expectations; contextual factors, such as public or private sanctions; the cultural constraints on communication itself, such as appropriate forms of language and gesture; and by the past history of each individual with others and with each other.

Thus, in order to understand how relationships develop, we must conceptualize them as part of a system of communication, a system that works simultaneously at cultural, relational, and communicative levels. The next section describes our model of the communication system.

## THE COMMUNICATION SYSTEM

A relationship is a multimodal phenomenon occurring within the realm of a systemic organization linking together participating individuals. The communication modes involve the direct real-time dialogue between partners; the relationship involves the developmental historical domain and the sociocultural community—including scripts, roles, families, peer groups, and the like—in which the relationship is embedded. The traditional mechanical model consisting of sequential alternation of messages to be transmitted from an emitter to a receiver has been replaced by a systemic conceptualization where participants continuously coconstruct the meanings of what is being communicated between them (Fogel, 1993). Besides being multimodal, communication is also multifunctional; that is, it not only has a referential, denotative function, but also serves other purposes in the context of interaction (Jakobson, 1960; Rawlins, 1987). Multiple channels, reflecting all observable dimensions of human expression, work together in the coconstruction of a semiotic/informational dance that goes more or less smoothly.

Figure 3.1 outlines some of the main characteristics of human communication: the multiple channels, the metacommunication processes, the participation of both verbal and nonverbal modes of information, and the

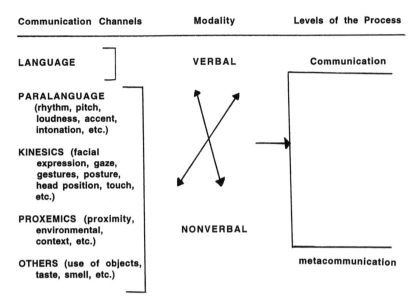

FIG. 3.1. Communication and metacommunication processes.

systemic quality of the phenomena. The crossed arrows represent the existence of different patterns of reciprocal influence within the system. Such patterns result from all possible combinations between the various communicative channels, which provide the system with a complex and intricate organization. In Fig. 3.1, human interactional phenomena are presented as a process encompassing two different coregulated pathways: (a) the communication of content, that is, the information coconstructed by the interactants; and (b) the evaluative and reflexive metacommunication about the communication process.

Via both communicative and metacommunicative processes, relationships create stable patterns of coaction called *frames*. The term *frame* was used by Bateson (1972) to refer to a kind of interpretative context in the communicative process, allowing for specific figure–ground differentiations made possible by metacommunication. According to Goffman (1974), frames are principles of organization used by people to structure social life. In this chapter, a frame is conceptualized as a relatively stable pattern of coaction (Fogel, 1993) that constrains the meanings that create repeating patterns of coactivity.

Frames and communication processes are not always creative and consensual; communication can be ritualized or imperfect. We conceptualize the diversity of intersubjectivity within a frame using the notions of convergence and divergence of goal orientations (Branco & Valsiner, 1992, 1995; London, 1949). The term *goal orientation* does not suggest a specific aim to be attained, but points, in a flexible way, toward a desired process or outcome (Cranach, 1982). As such, goal orientation is a relational motivational construct that preserves the dynamic feature of the systemic approach. It can be defined as an "internal constraining system, semiotically mediated, that, by projecting into the future, constrains actions, feelings, and thoughts in the present time" (Branco & Valsiner, 1995). Convergence and divergence, then, reflect the dyadic goal orientation either toward or away from consensual action.

Here, we propose to define relationships as communicative systems composed of three mutually embedded levels: (a) the level of communication occurring in the present moment, the direct dialogue that occurs between participants, (b) the level of the relationship, which involves a temporal domain of the history and future of the communication in the particular dyad or group of individuals, and (c) the sociocultural-contextual level in which communication and relationships are embedded within cultural scripts, roles, and expectations, and larger social-contextual systems, such as family, peer group, work group, church, community, or society (Bernal & Baker, 1979; Branco & Valsiner, 1992).

## METACOMMUNICATION
## AND RELATIONAL CHANGE

In this section, we explore the process of metacommunication from the perspective of the theory of relational dialectics outlined in the previous section. *Metacommunication* is an explicit strategy by which individuals reflexively call attention to a communication process, or to the relationship as a whole. Metacommunication, therefore, is an evaluative communication that is created in order to bring the quality of the relationship into direct focus. Thus, communication that is both reflexive and evaluative is metacommunication.

Participants in relationships seem to be sensitive to changes in the relationship process, and metacommunication is seen often during relational change periods. In romantic and courtship relationships, for example, individuals can detect *turning points* (Baxter & Bullis, 1986) or *social transitions* (Surra & Huston, 1987), at which the relationship changes in its level of intimacy or commitment. During the course of friendship formation, participants notice changes in the levels of mutual trust, attraction, and uncertainty (Baxter & Wilmot, 1985; Chovil, 1994; Goffman, 1974; Harre, 1988; Miell & Duck, 1982; O'Hair & Cody, 1994; VanLear & Trujillo, 1986). Individuals and families in psychotherapeutic relationships can recognize and reflect on a variety of change processes (Mitchell, 1988; Waller, 1938; Watzlawick, Weakland, & Fisch, 1974).

During such transitions, relationships may shift rapidly between convergence and divergence of goal orientations. The potential loss of stability of the relational frames, and the divergence engendered at such moments, may be part of the motivation to reflexively evaluate the relationship by using metacommunicative strategies. As relationships enter new periods of convergence, perhaps with the emergence of newly stabilized frames, metacommunication may serve as a positive evaluation to solidify and confirm the growing consensual feelings.

Figure 3.2 shows some alternative pathways for the course of social interactions that can emerge from metacommunicative processes. Through such evaluative processes, participants provide each other with information and feedback about certain dimensions of their interaction or relationship, leading to a negotiation over their current goal orientations. Depending on this evaluation, the relationship may move toward the maintenance of its previous characteristics, or it may lead to a total or a partial transformation in the quality of the communication process. In the former case, there is an adjustment of the communicative patterns to fit previous goal orientations held by the participants, in which case the effect of metacommunicative processes is basically conservative. When the evaluation process allows for the emergence of new goal orientations, however, the system experiences a substantive change, which entails an element of novelty that necessarily restructures the communication system as a whole. Some of the changes can be predictable from the knowledge of relevant deterministic factors; other transformations, however, cannot be predicted, due to the occurrence of uncertainty induced by the impact of the new information on the system. There is relatively little research, but a great deal of theoretical speculation,

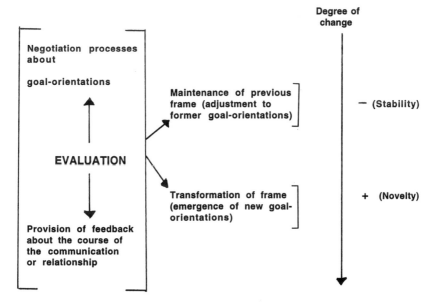

FIG. 3.2. Metacommunicative processes and predictability.

that metacommunication, like communication, can be both predictable and unpredictable from past encounters; that is, it can induce either stability or novelty.

As one kind of communication, metacommunication is created at the moment and is open to varying interpretations and future pathways. Research suggests that the frequency of metacommunication is not related to relationship stability or to relationship problems (Cissna, Cox, & Bochner, 1990; Wilmot, 1980). On the other hand, the content and timing of metacommunication may be extremely important for the relationship, suggesting that it is not how much partners metacommunicate, but rather the appropriateness and spontaneity of metacommunication that creates both stability and novelty in the relationship. Metacommunication can be used either to avoid issues or to address them. It can be timed in such a way as to create anxiety or increase a feeling of belonging or comfort. It can rejuvenate or stabilize a relationship or end it (Ayres, 1983; Canary & Stafford, 1993; Cissna et al., 1990; Dindia, 1994; Newman, 1982; Wilmot, 1994).

Metacommunication requires a symbolization of the relationship itself, the symbol referring to the memory of a relational history invoked to alter the course of future events. Recent studies of memory suggest that remembering is a creative activity. Memory is not a mere playing of a prerecorded tape, but a reconstruction of past events in the context of the present. When one narrates a story of a past experience, the narrative is not the same as the lived experience. It is selective, it enhances and diminishes, and it re-creates the experience in a way that is consistent with the narrative forms called for in the particular sociocultural setting. Thus, remembering, like communicating, is partially constrained by history and context and at the same time has elements of novelty and indeterminacy (Bransford, McCarrell, Franks, & Nitsch, 1977; Edelman, 1992; Merleau-Ponty, 1962; Ricoeur, 1983; Rogoff, 1990; Smirnoff & Zinchenco, 1969; Valsiner, 1987; Watzlawick, Beavin, & Jackson, 1967; Wertsch, 1985).

In psychotherapy, metacommunication is commonly used to regulate the transference and countertransference processes in the therapist–patient relationship. Metacommunication arises any time historical features of the therapist–client relationship is reflexively interpreted or made salient as part of the therapy process. In addition, the recapitulation of the patient's past history is made symbolically present and interpreted via metacommunication in the therapist–client relationship. Each time that is done, however, it is not a simple replay of a past experience, but a retelling and re-creation of it in the context of the particular theoretical context from which the therapist is working (Bernal & Baker, 1979; Cissna et al., 1990; Loewald, 1980; Modell, 1990).

There are different forms of metacommunication that correspond to each of the mutually embedded levels of a relationship, mentioned in the last section. *Episodic metacommunication* refers to an evaluation of specific events within a communication episode. Examples include saying "I'm only joking," "I'm sorry for what I just said," "Please don't interrupt," or "I'm not making myself clear." These types of statements suggest that the participants are attempting to reflexively evaluate the flow of communication, referring in some symbolic way to the immediate past in order to change the future (Bernal & Baker, 1979; Wilmot, 1980). In addition to verbal statements, nonverbal actions, such as smiles and frowns, may serve to evaluate the quality of previous communicative actions. *Relationship metacommunication* refers to communications about the relationship as a whole system. This might include references to relationship phases, such as saying "We are friends," or it could refer to past patterns that typify the relationship, such as "You always support me," or "You never pay attention to what I say" (Bernal & Baker, 1979; Wilmot, 1980). Again, these examples can be distinguished from ordinary communication by their reflexive and evaluative quality. Finally, there is *contextual metacommunication*, in which participants discuss their cultural and social orientations as it affects their relationship. This might include the role of a couple within a larger family system, family-of-origin issues, religious beliefs, the relationship between work and personal life, or the history and context of incidents that affect the relationship from the outside (Bernal & Baker, 1979). Metacommunication, therefore, serves to contextualize and/or evaluate the communicative action with respect to the participants' understanding of its role as a communicative event (Bateson, 1972; Watzlawick et al., 1967). The next sections turn to examples of metacommunication taken from our own research on relationships in infancy and early childhood.

## INFANT METACOMMUNICATION
## IN PARENT–INFANT INTERACTION

Very little is known about metacommunication in infancy and early childhood. There is some evidence that infants and young children are adept at using nonverbal means for episodic metacommunication, that is, communication about the process of ongoing interaction. Infants react to breakdowns of communication as early as 2 months of age. During experimental perturbations of mother–infant face-to-face interaction, such as simulated maternal depression or maternal cessation of action (still-face), infants are more likely to cease smiling and vocalizing and become sober. If the disturbance lasts more than several minutes, the infants will look away. Most interestingly from the perspective of metacommunication, infants begin to cry only after the mother resumes her normal interaction suggesting that the infants are communicating something to the mother about the immediately prior interactive break (Cohn & Tronick, 1983; Fogel, Diamond, Langhorst, & Demos, 1982; Toda & Fogel, 1993; Trevarthen & Hubley, 1978). In studies comparing infant responses to a variety of animate and inanimate objects, infants as young as 2 months could distinguish between objects and people and expected reciprocal interaction from people. If that was not forthcoming, the infants changed their behavior (Legerstee, 1991).

It may be that infant episodic metacommunication is primarily emotional in nature. Through emotional expression, the infant is making a reflexive evaluation of the immediate past history. The emotional expression is a way of referring to the immediate past as an evaluative comment, and thus could be interpreted as a metacommunication.

Emotional expression, however, is not the only possible form of infant metacommunication. In at least one case study, a 3-month-old infant was reported to actively avoid, by turning away, a mother whose bids for communication were overly intrusive (Beebe, Stern, & Jaffee, 1979; Stern, 1971), the infant's avoidance an apparent reflexive evaluation of the mother's prior intrusions. One of us found that among the subjects in the still-face research, most of whom increase looking away from the mother, there were two infants who looked more at the mother during the still-face period, and less at her during the subsequent normal interaction period. Examination of the videotapes showed these infants to have extremely intrusive mothers who overwhelmed the infant's ability to regulate the flow of interaction in the normal situation (Fogel et al., 1982). These infants may have been using gaze aversion as an evaluation of the communication.

Examples of both orienting/avoidance and positive/negative emotional expression can be seen during normally occurring face-to-face play. Three-month-old infants signal their willingness to engage in play by both gazing at mother and smiling, and they use gaze away and the cessation of smiling or the onset of crying to indicate their desire to end a bout of play. Before 3 months, infants do not have the ability to do this. They have little control over the direction of gazing, and once their gaze becomes captured by a moving object or the mother's face, they have difficulty turning away and may become distressed as a result (Beebe & Lachman, 1992; Brazelton, Koslowski, & Main, 1974; Stern, 1974).

Between 3 and 6 months, infants become more sophisticated in metacommunicatively regulating the flow of interactive engagement. During object play at 4 months, for example, they will refuse to accept an object offered by the mother or push offered objects away. Between 4 and 5 months, these refusals are often accompanied by an infant smile, as if to metacommunicate the importance of the relationship in spite of the current potentially negative action. Thus, the use of avoidance as a metacommunication is tempered by the inclusion of a metacommunicative smile. By 6 months, infants are more likely to allow the mother to take initiative and, by their attentive gazing and brief smiles, seem to metacommunicate to the mother that it is acceptable for her to take the initiative (Trevarthen, 1979).

At the current state of research on young infants' communicative action, it is not possible to clearly distinguish communicative from metacommunicative emotional expressions. Some smiles, for example, are embedded within play routines and do not appear to have an evaluative aspect. Other smiles occur at the end of a play sequence, during the transition to alternative frames, and these are more clearly evaluative comments on the prior action. Similarly, during ordinary play, infants alternate their gaze toward and away from the mother, as part of a nonreflexive communicative process. Apparently, deliberate gaze aversion or avoidant body movements, occurring at the ends of unpleasant sequences, are more clearly metacommunicative.

By the second half of the first year, instances of metacommunication increase in frequency and variety. Infants use a rich array of facial expressions, gestures, and vocalizations to metacommunicate about their evaluation of the flow of the interactive process. Again, these are observed more clearly at the transition points between frames. When the parents fail to understand the infant's intent, infants will maintain gaze or continue pointing at the desired object, emit "fake" cries and disgust expressions, alternate gaze between mother and object combined with pointing and reaching, or grab hold of the mother's arm or leg to direct her to the desired location or action (Golinkoff, 1983; Mosier & Rogoff, 1994; Robinson, 1989; Shatz & O'Reilly, 1990; Trevarthen, 1993). There is some evidence that infants who use more metacommunicative actions later in the first year have mothers who used more metacommunication with the infants earlier in the first year (Service, Lock, & Chandler, 1989).

In sum, the research suggests that the function of metacommunication is to reestablish normal modes of communication and thus to allow the relationship to develop according to both determinate and indeterminate dialogical processes. The inferential nature of the analysis of metacommunication does not allow the researcher to go beyond the level of the episode.

To the extent that the adult partner recognizes the infant's attempt to metacommunicate, this increases the probability of continued communication with its usual dose of indeterminacy. Should the adult consistently fail to recognize the metacommunication or ignore it, even young infants may be capable of relational metacommunication. Some forms of crying, acting out, depressive episodes, and inappropriate behavior may be symptoms of attachment or relational problems that could be interpreted as metacommunications. If even these relational metacommunications are ignored, the result becomes highly deterministic. Continuing breakdowns in communication lead predictably to disengagement, withdrawal, negative emotion, and estrangement (Gianino & Tronick, 1988). Should these conditions persist, infants are susceptible to pathologies of communication, attachment, and psychological well-being. There is a long history of research on this area of developmental psychopathology and its origins in the adult–infant communication system (Stern, 1985).

The research reported thus far has not been done from an explicit metacommunicative perspective, nor has work been done to explore the resulting discourse and its relative determinism or indeterminism as a result of the metacommunicative action. There is no reported evidence that infants can engage in contextual metacommunication. Most instances reported are episodic, and a few—probably pathological forms—may be relational.

The following illustrations of metacommunication are taken from a longitudinal study of mother–infant relationships during the first 2 years of life. Thirteen dyads were videotaped during weekly free-play interactions during the first year, and 11 continued biweekly sessions until the end of the second year. During the first year, instances of metacommunication are nonverbal on the part of the infant. During the second year, infants begin to use more verbal forms of metacommunication, but this is still compounded by nonverbal actions, as seen in the next section, on preschool peer play.

Mothers, on the other hand, frequently use both verbal and nonverbal forms of metacommunication with children of all ages. At the episodic level, mothers comment or act directly on the infant's action in an evaluative manner. Mothers make attempts at episodic metacommunication during caregiving and play, encouraging infants to initiate and maintain appropriate actions while discouraging inappropriate actions ("You're not looking at me." "Don't bite." "Do you want to play peekaboo?"). Mothers refer to their relationship with the baby and interpret the infant's actions with respect to feelings about the mother ("Are you angry with me?" "You love Mommy, right?"). Mothers also make cultural evaluations, such as not allowing infants to put toys in their mouths, discouraging too much excitement, or following particular infant care beliefs.

During a convergent doll play frame near the end of the first year, a mother tried to get her baby to cuddle a doll (with the communication, "You love the doll, don't you?"). The infant, apparently not wanting to play that game, pushed the doll away and cried with her eyes closed. The mother's response to this divergent metacommunication was to metacommunicate by offering to end the doll game and change to another toy ("Should we play with the telephone now?"). The mother also used nonverbal metacommunication, by ending her insistence on cuddling the doll, making an understanding facial expression to the infant, and touching the infant gently.

At 1 year, dyads can play convergently with a toy telephone as long as the infants are allowed to treat the telephone as a mechanical object, pushing the keys to hear the sound and banging the phone. If the mother introduces a divergent goal orientation (episodic metacommunication embedded within a cultural metacommunication), that of putting the phone to her ear and wanting to initiate pretend talking to an imaginary caller, infants typically resist. Infants' episodic metacommunication consists of pulling the phone away from the mother's ear, pushing the phone away if the mother holds it to their ear, making disgusted facial expressions, shaking their heads, and grabbing the phone away from the mother (Reinecke & Fogel, 1994). Mothers vary in their metacommunicative response, some insisting on the pretend play frame (thereby ending the phone play), others returning to a convergent mechanical play frame, and still others introducing another toy that the baby could play with in a more culturally appropriate manner. Eventually, however, all the infants in the sample developed a convergent pretend phone play frame with the mother.

Another variant of the telephone game occurred with a 1-year-old infant who had begun to pretend play with the telephone. As part of the communicative process, the baby put the phone to her ear and said, "Dada?" The mother, on another phone, said, "No, it's Grandma." The infant responded with, "Dada," and this exchange continued for five rounds, as a kind of mock divergence within convergent play. In the last round, however, the baby's tone of voice changed to sound more serious, perhaps indicating metacommunicatively that wanted the mother to enter into the "Dada" routine, rather than responding as "Grandma." The mother said, "Should we put the phone away?" (an episodic metacommunication). The baby, holding the phone and not looking at the mother, in a robot-like high pitch said, "Dadadada." The mother then took the phone away saying, "OK," showing that she understood the infant's change in paralanguage to mean an episodic metacommunication. This was confirmed, because after the mother removed the phone, the baby continued, "Dada, dada, dada," almost squealing the sounds and smiling at the mother. This particular infant developed a series of actions that had this same humorous or mocking quality, to which the mother typically responded as if they were indeed metacommunications: with a maternal laugh, showing her complicity in the coregulation of the infant's development of this form of metacommunication. The mother also used smiles and mock laughs to metacommunicate her requests for changes in the infant's actions.

In another example, the infant was playing divergently with a toy. The mother, in a metacommunicative attempt to establish a convergent frame, began tickling the infant with a toy puppet, making noises, and trying to establish a puppet play frame that they had shared on earlier occasions. At first, the baby ignored the mother and continued to play with his toy (not clearly a metacommunication). The mother persisted for a while with the puppet until the infant finally turned his body away from her, as if using his trunk to shield his toy from the mother's intrusions (a clear episodic metacommunication to be left alone). The episode ended as it had begun, with divergent play. This turning away to establish the desire for a divergent frame was a typical metacommunicative strategy for this baby during the entire second year of life.

Another mother developed a communicative style of teasing play with her 1-year-old in which she frequently held toys out of reach and taunted the infant or grabbed toys away from him. In one instance, the infant reached out to the mother to "ask" for the toy back as he had done many times before as part of the communicative process in this frame, but she refused to give back the toy. His metacommunication began at this point with a sad expression and opening his arms to be picked up. In response, the mother wiped his face (ignoring the infant's metacommunication?), and he violently shook his head (another metacommunication). A series of hostile metacommunicative actions followed as the mother said, "Hey," and the infant took another toy and threw it down, to which the mother responded, "No." In this example, an initially divergent frame continued to be divergent as the infant's apparent sadness turned to anger and frustration.

The infant's reaching out to be picked up, just at that moment in the sequence, could be interpreted as a relational metacommunication. It is similar to the infant response at 1 year during a reunion with the mother following separation in the Ainsworth Strange Situation Test. It could be that relational metacommunication does not appear at 1 year unless the infant's relationship to the mother is somehow stressed or perturbed. Because our study was meant to capture normal, spontaneous play, we saw relationship metacommunication only rarely.

These examples show evidence of both determinism and indeterminism. Because we observed these same infants and mothers weekly during the first year, we could easily recognize certain patterns of metacommunication that were stable within frames over several months or more. Thus, the relationship history of communication within a frame constrains the possible forms of communication and metacommunication. On the other hand, in any specific instance, the outcome of the negotiation could not always be predicted in advance. Whether the dyad made a transition from convergence to divergence, or vice versa, was relatively indeterminant. The indeterminism depended on the mother's and the infant's particular emotions at the moment, the creative features of the coregulated action, and the willingness of each partner to change goal orientations. What is clear is that metacommunication is an essential component of the transition between convergent and divergent phases of communication, both within and between frames. It is also clear that forms of metacommunication are established within particular frames and develop as stable components of those frames, as reflected by the negotiated history of communication within a dyad.

Repeated patterns of metacommunication within dyadic frames—such as grabbing, smiling while saying "no," or turning the body away from the partner—are semiotic devices that serve as abbreviated markers for the history of metacommunication within the particular frame (Branco & Valsiner, 1995; Lyra & Rossetti-Ferreira, 1994). Such semiotic devices symbolize the past and thereby constrain the future of the relationship. These constraints are not entirely deterministic, however. In the case of the mother not responding to the infant's reaching out for a toy she had taken from him, the semiotic device of reaching out failed to function. This led to metacommunicative appeals to the relationship, more rejection, and the eventual divergence and loss of harmony in the dyad. This indeterministic outcome resulted from a novel or chance event (the mother's failure to acknowledge the infant's reaching for the toy), which precipitated a dynamically emergent process of divergence.

## METACOMMUNICATION IN EARLY CHILDHOOD PEER INTERACTION

Bateson (1972) devised the concept of metacommunication after observing play-fighting between preschool children and between young animals. In these situations, individuals use all the gestures and actions in play that might be used in a serious fight, but rarely is anyone hurt. Bateson suggested that the lack of injury was the result of an episodic metacommunication—usually accomplished through laughs and smiles—indicating the pretend, rather than serious, nature of the encounter. Later studies showed that human children and young animals from a variety of species have the ability to signal when they, or their partners, are simulating (Mitchell, 1991). An opposite metacommunication is a cry, growl, or baring of the teeth to suggest that the play is becoming too aggressive (de Waal, 1989).

There are few studies that investigate the characteristics and role of metacommunication in peer interaction (e.g., McLoyd, Warren, & Thomas, 1984; Pratt & Kerig, 1986; Robinson & Robinson, 1983), the usual emphasis being a theoretical elaboration of the relevance of the concept—especially referring to pretend play—without any empirical approach to metacommunicative processes (Fein, 1991). Nonetheless, the study conducted by McLoyd et al. (1984) analyzed the amount of verbal metacommunication exhibited by 12 same-age, same-sex triads of 3½- to 5-year-old children participating in four different kinds of pretend role enactment (fantasy, domestic, occupational, and peripheral). Results showed that interactive behavior and metacommunication were more frequent among older boys, particularly during fantasy role enactment, when compared to other types of pretend play.

Observing young children at play in a natural preschool environment, Leeds-Hurwitz (1989) proposed the occurrence of five different metacommunicative strategies (three of which occur only occasionally), all of them referring to the construction of a play frame among participants: invitation, establishment, maintenance, breaking, and renegotiation (see Fig. 3.3).

| *Message* | *Message Function* |
|-----------|-------------------|
| "Shall we play?" | Invitation |
| "This is play"/"Is this play" | Establishment of play frame |
| "This is still play" | Maintenance of play frame |
| "This is no longer play" | Breaking of play frame |
| "That was/was not play" | Renegotiation of play frame |

FIG. 3.3. Metacommunicative messages observed during young children's free play. From Leeds-Hurwitz (1989).

Leeds-Hurwitz (1989) illustrated the occurrence of "This is play" messages with a dialogue between a 5-year-old boy and his 4-year-old friend: The older boy says, "Let's go fight in there!," and the other replies, "OK! I won't even cry because we're just playing and it won't hurt" (p. 144). "This is no longer play" messages can take place within the context of pretend play, for example, when the 4-year-old boy informs his playmate, "I'm not the bad guy anymore, so stop chasing me!" (p. 146).

Observing sequences of peer interactions in both natural and experimental contexts (Branco, 1994; Branco & Valsiner, 1992, 1993), one can identify numerous examples of metacommunication in 3-year-old children's play. The way they make use of multiple channels to metacommunicate, that is, to provide each other the interpretative cues to make sense of the particular frame, is complex and creative. As we proposed before, these cues, intertwined with the communicative flow, create the qualitative dimension of the frame, and interesting recurrent patterns of metacommunication unfold in different combinations of the various communicative channels referred to earlier (see Fig. 3.1). The use of nonverbal communicative channels, such as postures, gestures, facial expressions, and particularly paralinguistic components of verbal expression, continuously indicates the specific nature of the frame in terms of a range of convergence to divergence of goal orientations.

Many of the gestures and postures observed by Montagner (1978) in his investigation of the functional dimension of young children's social behavior could be identified in the play of the children (age range 2;3–2 years, 3 months–to 3;2 years) that participated in our study. We observed the "head leaning" position, emphasized by Montagner as a strategy conducive to affiliative interactions, as well as the tendency to move one's face in line with another's as a way to invite the other to convey a convergent mood or expectation. For example, in the same sequence of social interaction, a boy goes into a crouched position to talk to a playmate within a convergent frame, whereas the boy stays in a standing position while he talks to another boy within a divergent frame. Paralinguistic characteristics of verbal behavior were especially significant in expressing the affective quality of the communication frame: The voice pitch, for instance, usually indicated whether they were engaged in a convergent or divergent process.

Linguistic components played a significant metacommunicative role. Very often, when involved in convergent interactions, children would make "confirmation questions," such as "Don't you think so?," or "Is that OK for you?," or "Is that right?" By asking for confirmation, the child was manifesting to the peer his or her willingness to proceed in a convergent way with the other child's goal orientations. We also observed the use of conventional speech, such as asking for permission to approach the other's territory and a careful control of what kind of gesture (and gesture intensity) to perform in order to make clear one's respectful intentions and a convergent mood, despite the child's having verbally expressed the wish to get something that belonged to the other.

A very frequent convergent metacommunicative strategy employed by young children is imitation. The functional role of imitation has been investigated by many researchers (Eckerman, 1994; Nadel & Baudonniere, 1981; Stambak et al., 1982), and our own observation also suggests the fundamental metacommunicative role played by such a strategy. In many instances, imitation immediately precedes longer episodes of convergent play; in others, imitation is used after a divergence, as a means of reestablishing convergence between the interactants.

To illustrate the complexity of metacommunicative phenomena in peer relationships, we present data from two triads that participated in our study on cultural canalization of communication in young children (Branco & Valsiner, 1993); both triads were composed of two boys and one girl. Most cases of metacommunication can be classified as episodic metacommunication, but some relationship metacommunication instances could also be found. The use of *friend* and *not friend* seemed to fulfill, for this age group, a functional role in referring to the past quality of the relationship. For instance, William approaches Frederick, who's building a construction with wooden blocks and says, "Friend, friend, would you give one of those to me?" By invoking the status of a friendship relationship between them, William tries to influence Frederick's decision to give him the block. The use of the term *friend* could be observed on other occasions, such as when one child tried to invite the other into a new kind of play.

The following three examples represent segments of metacommunicative transitions (or possible transitions) between convergent and divergent frames.

*Example 1:* William, Frederick, and Paola are playing with a big paper box. Frederick and Paola cover William's body with the box. They are all laughing and emitting vocal sounds that resemble a cry of pain (e.g., "Ouch!"). The way the sounds are distorted indicates an episodic metacommunication in a make-believe situation. Then William changes his facial expression, starts to complain for real, cries and shouts at his peers, and moves away from them. Paola smiles at William and, while looking at him, goes under the box herself. William stops complaining and goes together with Frederick to put the box over Paola, and they start again with their playful communication using vocalizations of a pretend cry of pain, while laughing at each other.

This example illustrates three points we have discussed so far. First, the occurrence of laughter and the quality of the distorted "Ouch!" cry can be considered a metacommunication indicating the playful nature of their activity. Second, the transition from a convergent frame into a divergent one is signaled by William through metacommunicative cues. Finally, the active utilization of smile, gaze, and action (Paola's going under the box) acts as an invitation to return to the convergent playful frame. It represents a nice example of the effectiveness of metacommunicative signals in influencing the dynamic course of social interaction.

*Example 2:* Frederick and William are communicating by talking to each other within a convergent frame while playing with pieces of plasticine. William picks up another piece of plasticine that sticks to his fingers. Trying to get rid of the plasticine on his fingers, William starts abrupt movements with his arms straight in Frederick's direction. Frederick immediately interprets them as a possible form of attack and changes his whole facial and body expression. William notices his reaction and, while looking at him, starts laughing aloud, saying, "Uaoh!" Frederick slowly changes his stiff, tense expression into a more relaxed mood and cautiously approaches William to look at what he's doing. The uneasy expression vanishes and the conversation goes on.

The main point in this case is the "wrong" interpretation made by Frederick of a specific gesture performed by William. The abruptness, intensity, and direction of William's arm movements led Frederick to consider an attack possible, which would change the frame between them from convergence to divergence. The strategies employed by William, however, to metacommunicate to Frederick that they were still in a convergent frame (laughter, gaze, vocalizations) proved effective, and they moved back into a friendly conversation.

*Example 3:* William and Frederick run toward Frederick's construction, laughing loudly within a convergent frame. They throw themselves to the floor and William accidentally knocks down Frederick's construction. Frederick, very upset, screams, "NO!" William looks at Frederick and says with a nice intonation in his voice, while smiling to Fred: "I fell down!" Frederick is still upset and says, "You should not!" William leans his head, and still smiling he says again, "I fell down!" Then William adds, "Let's go, Fred, let's go to fall down?" Frederick finally says, "Let's go!" Both boys stand up, run toward William's construction and knock it down while laughing and rolling over each other.

In a certain way, this example is similar to the previous one, but it included an important new element of metacommunication: Because the outcome of William's act was a "serious" one (destroying the other child's construction), a verbal explanation was necessary to make clear the intention—or lack of intention—of this act. As he explains, he also expresses his convergent mood by looking and smiling at his peer. His final strategy—inviting Frederick to go on playing—seems to complete the work of bringing the child back into play, accomplishing a noteworthy backward transition from a potentially divergent situation.

These examples demonstrate that metacommunication is extensive and significant in the context of peer relationships, and it plays a central role in transitions between frames. In each of these cases, the metacommunication served to return the triad to a convergent play frame. At these transition points, there is both determinism and indeterminism. The transitions are deterministic to the extent that they are constrained within the existing play frame, which favors its own stability because it is enjoyable. Because children use relatively clear metacommunicative strategies (crying, laughing, smiling), they reduce the uncertainty in making the transition. Nevertheless, small changes in any of these situations could create indeterministic outcomes, leading to unresolved conflicts, or unexpected changes in the play frame (toward convergence or divergence).

The other triad in our study showed more evidence of indeterminism in its transitions. This was often because of the presence of ambiguous or conflicting metacommunications. One boy, in particular, exhibited such ambiguous behavioral patterns. For instance, he would hit his peer relatively hard on the head while laughing and emitting playful vocalizations. The way the other child responded to these conflicting messages—alternating convergent and divergent attitudes during the whole episode and finally withdrawing—demonstrates the difficulties met by these children to coconstruct a well-defined communication frame between them. This pattern has been defined as a *double bind* in human communication (Bateson, 1972; Rieber, 1989). A *double bind* occurs whenever two conflicting messages are created within the communicational system, making the interpretation of communicative and metacommunicative cues relatively indeterministic. Even though examples like these may suggest that a certain degree of individual social competence or communicative skill is implied in the establishment of successful relational systems (which may be partially correct), from our perspective the main factors contributing to the quality of the relationship should be found within the system itself, and not in each participating individual.

## CONCLUSIONS

Metacommunication appears to be a fundamental part of communication, and it develops from as early as the first year of life. Metacommunication serves to reflexively evaluate the quality of ongoing communication processes. It occurs primarily during transitions of communicative frames, from a pattern of divergent to convergent goal orientations, or vice versa. The form of metacommunication can be either verbal or nonverbal, depending on the history of communication in the context of the organized frames that develop in dyads and groups.

Dialectical and dynamic systems approaches to communication represent one way to understand this process of change. These approaches predict both determinism and indeterminism in the process of development. Deterministic change is patterned on the historical constraints of the communication system. Transitions occur along pathways that are well established, and even developmental change may seem relatively predictable from the history of the relationship. Indeterministic change is not entirely novel. It is rooted in the constraints of the historical frames of the relationship, yet all relationships are composed of dynamically emergent processes that cannot be predicted from the past. On the one hand, dynamic systems are inherently irreversible processes, such that chance events and small changes in initial and current conditions can lead to the sudden transition of the system into innovative patterns of coregulation. On the other hand, historical patterns within the frame take on semiotic characteristics that symbolize for the participants the meaning of their actions. Because semiotic markers cannot capture the richness of the past, they cannot prescribe the future. The semiotic marker is a "soft" constraint that regulates, but does not entirely determine, the emergence of novel action. Partners may not recognize or respond to shared markers or they may alter the meaning of the markers through chance discoveries that emerge in the dynamics of coactivity.

This chapter suggests that creativity and indeterminism are fundamental features of human communicative action and that development cannot be understood entirely by deterministic laws. The study of irreversible thermodynamic systems has led to the physics of dynamic systems that create order out of nonprescriptive relationships, patterns whose forms are emergent and not predicted by the properties of the component parts, and chaotic patterns that never exactly repeat themselves as the system evolves. In the humanities, postmodernism leaves room for the introduction of novelty in the system, for the indeterministic relationship of the past to the future. A relational or dialectical developmental theory would focus both on relationship processes (the coregulated emergence of novelty within historical frames) and bounded indeterminism as a way of understanding change. The methods appropriate to such a world view involve the careful description of communicative frames, metacommunicative transitions between frames, and the preservation of the history of the relationship as the unit of analysis.

## ACKNOWLEDGMENTS

This work was supported by grants to Alan Fogel from the National Institute of Health (R01 HD21036), the National Science Foundation (BNS9006756) and the National Institute of Mental Health (R01 MH48680), and to Angela U. Branco from the CNPq (Conselho Nacional de Pesquisa) of Brazil.

## REFERENCES

Altman, I., Vinsel, A., & Brown, B. B. (1981). Dialectic conceptions in social psychology: An application to social penetration and privacy regulation. *Advances In Experimental Social Psychology, 14*, 107–160.

Ayres, J. (1983). Strategies to maintain relationships: Their identification and perceived usage. *Communication Quarterly, 31*, 62–67.

Bahktin, M. M. (1988). Discourse in the novel. In N. Mercer (Ed.), *Language and literacy from an educational perspective, Vol. 1* (pp. 47–57). Philadelphia, PA: Open University Press.

Bateson, G. (1972). *Steps to an ecology of mind.* New York: Chandler.

Baxter, L. A. (1994). A dialogic approach to relationship maintenance. In D. J. Canary & L. Stafford (Eds.), *Communication and relational maintenance* (pp. 233–254). San Diego, CA: Academic Press.

Baxter, L. A., & Bullis, C. (1986). Turning points in developing romantic relationships. *Human Communication Research, 12*, 469–493.

Baxter, L. A., & Wilmot, W. W. (1985). Taboo topics in close relationships. *Journal of Social and Personal Relationships, 2*, 253–269.

Beebe, B., & Lachmann, F. M. (1992). The contribution of mother-infant mutual influence to the origins of self- and object representations. In N. J. Skolnick & S. C. Warshaw (Eds.), *Relational perspectives in psychoanalysis* (pp. 83–117). Hillsdale, NJ: The Analytic Press.

Beebe, B., Stern, D. N., & Jaffee, J. (1979). The kinesic rhythm of mother-infant interactions. In A. W. Siegman & S. Feldstein (Eds.), *Of speech and time: Temporal patterns in interpersonal contexts* (pp. 23–43). Hillsdale, NJ: Lawrence Erlbaum Associates.

Berger, C. R. (1988). Planning, affect, and social action generation. In L. Donohew, H. Sypher, & E. T. Higgins (Eds.), *Communication, social cognition, and affect* (pp. 99–116). Hillsdale, NJ: Lawrence Erlbaum Associates.

Bergson, H. (1910). *Time and free will.* London: George Allen & Unwin.

Bernal, G., & Baker, J. (1979). Toward a metacommunicational framework of couple interactions. *Family Processes, 18*, 293–303.

Branco, A. U. (1994, June). *An experimental study of the role of context structure in the development of cooperation among children.* Paper presented at the Thirteenth Biennial Meeting of the International Society for the Study of Behavioral Development, Amsterdam, The Netherlands.

Branco, A. U., & Valsiner, J. (1992, July). *Development of convergence and divergence in joint actions of preschool children within structured social contexts.* Paper presented at the 25th International Congress of Psychology, Brussels, Belgium.

Branco, A. U., & Valsiner, J. (1993, July). *Dynamics of social interaction strategies among young children: The emergence of cooperation and competition within structured contexts.* Paper presented at the Twelfth Biennial Meeting of the International Society for the Study of Behavioral Development, Recife, Brazil.

Branco, A. U., & Valsiner, J. (1995). *Changing methodologies: A co-constructivist study of goal orientations in social interactions.* In G. Misra (Ed.), *Cultural construction of social cognition.* Cambridge, England: Cambridge University Press.

Bransford, J. D., McCarrell, N. S., Franks, J. J., & Nitsch, K. E. (1977). Toward unexplaining memory. In R. Shaw & J. Bransford (Eds.), *Perceiving, acting, and knowing: Toward an ecological psychology* (pp. 431–466). Hillsdale, NJ: Lawrence Erlbaum Associates.

Brazelton, T. B., Koslowski, B., & Main, M. (1974). The origins of reciprocity. In M. Lewis & L. Rosenblum (Eds.), *The effect of the infant on its caregiver.* New York: Wiley.

Canary, D. J., & Stafford, L. (1993). Preservation of relational characteristics: Maintenance strategies, equity, and locus of control. In P. J. Kalbfleisch (Ed.), *Interpersonal communication: Evolving interpersonal relationships* (pp. 237–259). Hillsdale, NJ: Lawrence Erlbaum Associates.

Chovil, N. (1994). Equivocation as an interactional event. In W. R. Cupach & B. H. Spitzberg (Eds.), *The dark side of interpersonal communication* (pp. 105–123). Hillsdale, NJ: Lawrence Erlbaum Associates.

Cissna, K. N., Cox, D. E., & Bochner, A. P. (1990). The dialectic of marital and parental relationships within the stepfamily. *Communication Monographs, 57,* 44–61.

Cody, M. (1982). A typology of disengagement strategies and an examination of the role intimacy, reactions to inequity and relational problems play in strategy selection. *Communication Monographs, 49,* 148–170.

Cohn, J. F., & Tronick, E. Z. (1983). Three-month-old infants' reaction to simulated maternal depression. *Child Development, 54,* 185–193.

Cranach, M. von. (1982). The psychological study of goal-directed action: Basic issues. In M. von Cranach & R. Harre (Eds.), *The analysis of action: Recent theoretical and empirical advances.* Cambridge, England: Cambridge University Press.

Cupach, W., & Metts, S. (1986). Accounts of relational dissolution: A comparison of marital and non-marital relationships. *Communication Monographs, 53,* 311–334.

Davies, P. (1988). *The cosmic blueprint.* New York: Touchstone.

de Waal, F. (1989). *Chimpanzee politics: Power and sex among apes.* New York: Harper & Row.

Dindia, K. (1994). A multiphasic view of relationship maintenance strategies. In D. J. Canary & L. Stafford (Eds.), *Communication and relational maintenance* (pp. 91–112). San Diego, CA: Academic Press.

Eckerman, C. O. (1994). Toddlers' achievement of coordinated action with conspecifics: A dynamic systems perspective. In L. B. Smith & E. Thelen (Eds.), *Dynamical systems in development: Applications.* Cambridge, MA: MIT Press.

Edelman, G. M. (1992). *Bright air, brilliant fire: On the matter of the mind.* New York: Basic Books.

Fein, G. G. (1991). Bloodsuckers, blisters, cooked babies, and other curiosities: Affective themes in pretense. In F. S. Kessel, M. H. Bornstein, & A. J. Sameroff (Eds.), *Contemporary constructions of the child: Essays in honor of William Kessen.* Hillsdale, NJ: Lawrence Erlbaum Associates.

Fogel, A. (1992). Co-regulation, perception and action. *Human Movement Science, 11,* 505–523.

Fogel, A. (1993). *Developing through relationships.* London: Harvester Wheatsheaf and University of Chicago Press.

Fogel, A. (1996). Information, creativity, and culture. In C. Dent-Reed & P. Zukow-Goldring (Eds.), *Changing ecological approaches to development: Organism–environment mutualities*. Washington, DC: APA Publications.

Fogel, A., Diamond, G. R., Langhorst, B. H., & Demos, V. (1982). Affective and cognitive aspects of the two-month-old's participation in face-to-face interaction with its mother. In E. Tronick (Ed.), *Social interchange in infancy: Affect, cognition, and communication* (pp. 37–57). Baltimore, MD: University Park Press.

Fogel, A., & Thelen, E. (1987). Development of early expressive and communicative action: Reinterpreting the evidence from a dynamic systems perspective. *Developmental Psychology, 23*, 747–761.

Gianino, A., & Tronick, E. Z. (1988). The mutual regulation model: The infant's self and interactive regulation and coping and defensive strategies. In T. M. Field, P. M. McCabe, & N. Schneiderman (Eds.), *Stress and coping across development* (pp. 47–68). Hillsdale, NJ: Lawrence Erlbaum Associates.

Gleick, J. (1987). *Chaos: Making a new science*. New York: Viking.

Goffman, E. (1974). *Frame analysis: An essay on the organization of experience*. Cambridge, MA: Harvard University Press.

Golinkoff, R. M. (1983). The preverbal negotiation of failed messages: Insights into the transition period. In E. R. Golinkoff (Ed.), *The transition from prelinguistic to linguistic communication*. Hillsdale, NJ: Lawrence Erlbaum Associates.

Grammer, K. (1989). Human courtship behavior: Biological basis and cognitive processing. In A. E. Rasa, C. Vogel, & E. Voland (Eds.), *The sociobiology of sexual and reproductive strategies* (pp. 147–169). New York: Chapman and Hall.

Harre, R. (1988). *The social construction of emotions*. New York: Basil Blackwell.

Heath, C. (1984). Talk and recipiency: Sequential organization in speech and body movement. In J. M. Atkinson & J. Heritage (Eds.), *Structures of social action: Studies in conversation analysis* (pp. 247–265). New York: Cambridge University Press.

Hermans, H. J. M., & Kempen, H. J. G. (1993). *The dialogical self: Meaning as movement*. San Diego, CA: Academic Press.

Jakobson, R. (1960). Closing statement: Linguistics and poetics. In T. A. Sebeok (Ed.), *Style in language*. Cambridge, MA: MIT Press.

Kendon, A. (1975). Some functions of the face in a kissing round. *Journal of the International Association for Semiotic Studies, 15*(4), 99–134.

Knoespel, K. J. (1991). The emplotment of chaos: Instability and narrative order. In N. K. Hayles (Ed.), *Chaos and order: Complex dynamics in literature and science* (pp. 100–122). Chicago, IL: University of Chicago Press.

Legerstee, M. (1991). Changes in the quality of infant sounds as a function of social and nonsocial stimulation. *First Language, 11*, 327–343.

Leeds-Hurwitz, W. (1989). *Communication in everyday life: A social interpretation*. Norwood, NJ: Ablex.

Linell, P. (1990). The power of dialogue dynamics. In I. Markova & K. Foppa (Eds.), *The dynamics of dialogue* (pp. 147–177). New York: Springer-Verlag.

Loewald, H. W. (1980). *Papers on psychoanalysis*. New Haven, CT: Yale University Press.

London, I. D. (1949). The developing person as a joint function of convergence and divergence. *Journal of Social Psychology, 40*, 219–228.

Lyra, M., & Rossetti-Ferreira, M. C. (1994). Transformation and construction in social interaction: A new perspective on analysis of the mother-infant dyad. In J. Valsiner (Ed.), *Child development within culturally structured environments, Vol. 3: Comparative-cultural and co-constructionist perspectives*. Norwood, NJ: Ablex.

Markova, I. (1990). Why the dynamics of dialogue? In I. Markova & K. Foppa (Eds.), *The dynamics of dialogue* (pp. 1–22). New York: Springer-Verlag.

Merleau-Ponty, M. (1962). *Phenomenology of perception* (C. Smith, Trans.). London: Routledge & Kegan Paul.

McLoyd, V. C., Warren, D., & Thomas, E. A. C. (1984). Anticipatory and fantastic role enactment in preschool triads. *Developmental Psychology, 20,* 807–814.

Miell, D., & Duck, S. (1982). Strategies in developing friendships. In V. J. Derlega & B. A. Winstead (Eds.), *Friendship and social interaction* (pp. 129–143). New York: Springer-Verlag.

Mitchell, S. A. (1988). *Relational concepts in psychoanalysis: An integration.* Cambridge, MA: Harvard University Press.

Mitchell, R. W. (1991). Bateson's concept of "metacommunication" in play. *New Ideas in Psychology, 9,* 73–87.

Modell, A. H. (1990). *Other times, other realities: Toward a theory of psychoanalytic treatment.* Cambridge, MA: Harvard University Press.

Montagner, H. (1978). *L'enfant et la communication.* Paris: Stock.

Mosier, C., & Rogoff, B. (1994). Infants' instrumental use of their mothers to achieve their goals. *Child Development, 65,* 70–79.

Nadel, J., & Baudonniere, P. M. (1981). Imitacao, modo preponderante de intercambio entre pares, durante o terceiro ano de vida [Imitation as a primary mode of interchange between peers during the third year of life]. Sao Paulo: *Cadernos de Pesquisa da Fundacao Carlos Chagas, 39,* 26–31.

Newman, H. M. (1982). Talk about a past relationship partner: Metacommunicative implications. *The American Journal of Family Therapy, 10,* 25–32.

O'Hair, H. D., & Cody, M. J. (1994). Deception. In W. R. Cupach & B. H. Spitzberg (Eds.), *The dark side of interpersonal communication* (pp. 181–213). Hillsdale, NJ: Lawrence Erlbaum Associates.

Pattee, H. H. (1987). Instabilities and information in biological self-organization. In F. E. Yates (Ed.), *Self-organizing systems: The emergence of order.* New York: Plenum.

Paulson, W. (1991). Literature, complexity, interdisciplinarity. In N. K. Hayles (Ed.), *Chaos and order: Complex dynamics in literature and science* (pp. 37–53). Chicago, IL: University of Chicago Press.

Planalp, S., Rutherford, D., & Honeycutt, J. (1988). Events that increase uncertainty in personal relationships: II. Replication and extension. *Human Communication Research, 14,* 516–547.

Pratt, M. W., & Kerig, P. (1986). Knowing and telling: Type of rule and level of knowledge about messages in children's use of self-regulative communication training. *Canadian Journal of Behavioral Science, 18,* 294–307.

Prigogine, I., & Stengers, I. (1984). *Order out of chaos: Man's new dialogue with nature.* New York: Bantam.

Rawlins, W. K. (1983). Negotiating close friendships: The dialectic of conjunctive freedoms. *Human Communications Research, 9,* 255–266.

Rawlins, W. K. (1987). Gregory Bateson and the composition of human communication. *Research on Language and Social Interaction, 20,* 53–77.

Ricoeur, P. (1983). *Time and narrative Vol. 1.* [Translated by K. McLaughlin & D. Pellauer, 1984]. Chicago, IL: The University of Chicago Press.

Rieber, R. W. (1989). *The individual, communication and society: Essays in memory of Gregory Bateson.* Cambridge, England: Cambridge University Press.

Reinecke, M. A., & Fogel, A. (1994). The development of referential offering in the first year. *Early Development and Parenting, 3,* 181–186.

Robinson, E. J., & Robinson, W. P. (1983). Communication and metacommunication: Quality of children's instructions in relation to judgements about the adequacy of instructions and the locus of responsibility for communication failure. *Journal of Experimental Child Psychology, 36,* 305–320.

Robinson, J. A. (1989). "What we've got here is a failure to communicate": The cultural context of meaning. In J. Valsiner (Ed.), *Child development within culturally structured environments:*

*Social co-construction and environmental guidance in development* (pp. 137–198). Norwood, NJ: Ablex.

Rogers, L. E., & Millar, F. E. (1988). Relational communication. In S. W. Duck (Ed.), *Handbook of personal relationships* (pp. 289–303). New York: Wiley.

Rogoff, B. (1990). *Apprenticeship in thinking: Cognitive development in social context*. New York: Oxford University Press.

Rommetveit, R. (1990). On axiomatic features of a dialogical approach to language and mind. In I. Markova & K. Foppa (Eds.), *The dynamics of dialogue* (pp. 83–104). New York: Springer-Verlag.

Sarbin, T. R. (1986). *Narrative psychology: The storied nature of human conduct*. New York: Praeger.

Scherer, K. R. (1982). Methods of research on vocal communication: Paradigms and parameters. In K. Scherer & P. Ekman (Eds.), *Handbook of methods in non-verbal behavior research*. Cambridge, MA: Cambridge University Press.

Service, V., Lock, A., & Chandler, P. (1989). Individual differences in early communicative development: A social constructivist perspective. In S. von Tetzchner, L. S. Siegel, & L. Smith (Eds.), *The social and communicative aspects of normal and atypical language development* (pp. 23–49). New York: Springer-Verlag.

Shatz, M., & O'Reilly, A. W. (1990). Conversational or communicative skill? A reassessment of two-year-olds' behavior in miscommunication episodes. *Journal of Child Language, 17*, 131–146.

Smirnov, A. A., & Zinchenko, P. I. (1969). Problems in the psychology of memory. In M. Cole & I. Maltzman (Eds.), *A handbook of contemporary Soviet psychology* (pp. 452–502). New York: Basic Books.

Stambak, M., Barriere, M., Bonica, L., Maisonnet, R., Musatti, T., Rayana, S., & Verba, M. (1982). *Les bebes entre eux*. Paris: P.U.F.

Stern, D. N. (1971). A micro-analysis of mother-infant interaction: Behavior regulating the social contact between a mother and her 3½-month-old twins. *Journal of the Academy of Child Psychology, 10*, 501–517.

Stern, D. N. (1974). Mother and infant at play: The dyadic interaction involving gaze, facial and vocal behavior. In M. Lewis & L. Rosenblum (Eds.), *The effect of the infant on its caregiver* (pp. 187–214). New York: Wiley.

Stern, D. N. (1985). *The interpersonal world of the infant*. New York: Basic Books.

Surra, C. A., & Huston, T. L. (1987). Mate selection as a social transition. In D. Perlman & S. Duck (Eds.), *Intimate relationships: Development, dynamics, and deterioration* (pp. 88–120). Beverly Hills, CA: Sage.

Thelen, E. (1989). The (re)discovery of motor development: Learning new things from an old field. *Developmental Psychology, 25*(6), 946–949.

Thelen, E., & Ulrich, B. D. (1991). Hidden skills. *Monographs of the Society for Research in Child Development, 56*, 6–97.

Toda, S., & Fogel, A. (1993). Infant response to the still-face situation at 3 and 6 months. *Developmental Psychology, 29*, 532–538.

Trevarthen, C. (1979). Communication and cooperation in early infancy: A description of primary intersubjectivity. In M. Bullowa (Ed.), *Before speech: The beginning of interpersonal communication* (pp. 321–347). New York: Cambridge University Press.

Trevarthen, C. (1993). The function of emotions in early infant communication and development. In J. Nadel & L. Camaioni (Eds.), *New perspectives in early communicative development* (pp. 48–81). New York: Routledge.

Trevarthen, C., & Hubley, P. (1978). Secondary intersubjectivity: Confidence, confiding and acts of meaning in the first year. In A. Lock (Ed.), *Action, gesture and symbol: The emergence of language* (pp. 183–227). New York: Academic Press.

Valsiner, J. (1987). *Culture and the development of children's action*. Chichester: Wiley.

Valsiner, J. (1994). Culture and human development: A co-constructionist perspective. In P. van Geert & L. Mos (Eds.), *Annals of theoretical psychology* (Vol. 10). New York: Plenum.

VanLear, C. A., Jr., & Trujillo, N. (1986). On becoming acquainted: A longitudinal study of social judgement processes. *Journal of Social and Personal Relationships, 3,* 375–392.

Vygotsky, L. A. (1978). *Mind in society.* Cambridge, MA: Harvard University Press.

Waller, W. (1938). *The family: A dynamic interpretation* [revised by Reuben Hill, 1951]. New York: Dryden Press.

Watzlawick, P., Beavin, J. H., & Jackson, D. D. (1967). *Pragmatics of human communication: A study of interactional patterns, pathologies, and paradoxes.* New York: W. W. Norton.

Watzlawick, P., Weakland, J., & Fisch, R. (1974). *Change: Principles of problem formation & problem resolution.* New York: W. W. Norton.

Werner, C. M., Altman, I., Brown, B. B., & Ginat, J. (1993). Celebrations in personal relationships: A transactional/dialectical perspective. In S. Duck (Ed.), *Social context and relationships* (pp. 109–138). Newbury Park, CA: Sage.

Wertsch, J. V. (1985). *Vygotsky and the social formation of mind.* Cambridge, MA: Harvard University Press.

Wilmot, W. W. (1980). Metacommunication: A re-examination and extension. In D. Nimmo (Ed.), *Communication yearbook 4* (pp. 61–69). New York: Transaction Books.

Wilmot, W. W. (1994). Relationship rejuvenation. In D. J. Canary & L. Stafford (Eds.), *Communication and relational maintenance* (pp. 255–273). San Diego, CA: Academic Press.

# 4

# PROCESSUAL DYNAMICS OF INTERACTION THROUGH TIME: ADULT–CHILD INTERACTIONS AND PROCESS OF DEVELOPMENT

Maria C. D. P. Lyra
Federal University of Pernambuco
Recife, Brazil

Lucien T. Winegar
Randolph–Macon College

This chapter discusses the development of human subjects as relational outcome that is emerging from the history of social exchanges. We consider here the question of the social embeddedness of the subject as an emergent partner. We also consider the specificity and creative nature of processes of social exchanges, which, we argue, give rise to emergence of meaning. Meaning is thus conceptualized as a processual and relational outcome of interactive social exchanges. To emphasize the historical nature of development, we propose and develop three concepts that describe the changing form of such interactions through time: establishment, extension, and abbreviation. These concepts are illustrated through their application to mother–infant dyadic exchanges. The analysis of the development of communicative interactions using these concepts guides us in our examination of both deterministic and indeterministic characteristics of development.

## QUESTIONS OF DETERMINACY AND INDETERMINACY FOR DEVELOPMENTAL PHENOMENA

Positions on determinacy and indeterminacy are metatheoretical stances; they provide guiding assumptions for construction of theory through consideration of phenomena. In the physical sciences, determinacy and indeterminacy has become an epistemological question, because the ontological question of determinism is presumed to be answered. In short, and most simply, because physical events are presumed to be determined, any appearance of indeterminacy must result from a current lack of information or understanding (see van Geert, this volume, chap. 1, for a more detailed discussion of this and related issues). However, the status of questions of determinacy and indeterminacy is less clear in developmental science. In this area, where outcomes and even pathways may not be presumed to be established, it is much more difficult to make ontological assumptions of determinism in influences of antecedent conditions on later conditions. Thus, in the study of development, it is tempting to consider determinism and indeterminism as unanswered questions of ontology. Considered this way, such questions can lead to much unproductive debate by the champions of positions toward one or the other extreme.

The subjects studied by developmental scientists differ from the objects studied by physical scientists in fundamental ways. Perhaps the most important of these differences is that the objects of study for development are active, responsive, intentional agents who participate, with other active, responsive, intentional agents in their own development (and both of whom, in turn, are studied by other active, responsive, intentional agents undergoing development). Given this difference, it seems important to keep in mind that, at least in some important sense, it is participants *acting* as if some aspect of interactional or developmental outcome is determined that contributes to being established as determined. That is, because persons are active participants in their own development, the avenues they take in the coordination of their activity with others is both based on current conditions and influential on future conditions. Thus, acting *as if* a particular interactive routine has been established increases the likelihood of that routine being repeated and, so, in practice, being established. Acting as if a particular outcome cannot be achieved reduces efforts in that direction and, therefore, makes it, in practice, unreachable.

It would seem useful for participants in these processes to be able to make predictions from current conditions about the likelihood of future conditions. Such an ability might reduce uncertainty and, so, promote smoother interaction. At the same time, if development is to enable creativity and emergence of novelty, there must remain a level of unpredictability from current conditions to future conditions. Existence and assumption of both determinacy and indeterminacy are necessary for developmental processes. Starting with this assumption, we use the remainder of this chapter to stress how determinism and indeterminism, acting together in dynamic, social processes of face-to-face interaction, lead to the establishment and development of communication.

## SOCIAL EMBEDDEDNESS AND THE PROCESSUAL NATURE OF DEVELOPMENT: DEVELOPMENT AS PROCESS OF CHANGE IN ORGANISM–ENVIRONMENT RELATIONSHIPS

*Development* is a process of change in organism–environment relationships, a process that allows the emergence of new organizational levels. These new organizational levels appear through the transformation of novelty in meaning, *within the specific context where development occurs*. Such specific context is fundamentally social. We suggest that the process of change that occurs within the context of social interactions and relationships promotes meaning construction. In so doing, it gives rise to the emergence of both a historically derived process of communication and a social dialogical self from the characteristic dynamic required by social exchanges. This communication and this self are emergent, because they arise from, but are not reducible to, the dynamics of social exchange and meaning construction.

The inclusion of a time-based dimension as a requirement for understanding developmental change and, therefore, the description of interactive process as the object of study of all living systems has been pointed out by a number of theorists (e.g., Laszlo, 1972), and has found application in biology (e.g., Weiss, 1969), social psychology (e.g., Boulding, 1956), and developmental psychology (e.g., Sameroff, 1982). More recently, Fogel (1990) has highlighted two main points arising from a similar approach: (a) living systems, acting in a context, are dynamically self-organizing; and (b) these acting systems create regularities and patterns recognized as different from simple, random organizations. Therefore, we propose that it is the power of dynamic processes of exchange that gives rise to new organizational levels in development.

In the field of language acquisition, the study of early communicative development attracted great interest during the 1970s, very much as a consequence of the failure to understand the emergence of language from a more nativist point of view (e.g., Bates, 1979; Carter, 1975; Dore, 1975; Halliday, 1975; Howie, 1981; Snow & Ferguson, 1977). At the same time, as a consequence of in-depth investigations of the patterns of communication exchanges in early life, studies using small samples became respectable. However, many of these early studies were oriented primarily toward the role of the adult (usually the mother) as directing or facilitating infant communicative development through interactional exchanges.

On the other side, a growing understanding of the infant's capacities, particularly those capacities preadapted for social exchange, supported a changing perspective toward a consideration of more equal contributions of infant and adult within communicative interaction. The active role of the infant in altering the communication process and promoting his or her own development has been increasingly validated (e.g., Bruner, 1975, 1983; Bullowa, 1979; Ochs & Schieffelin, 1979; Schaffer, 1977). This recognition has led to research that considers interaction as the unit of analysis. This approach moves from attempts to combine adult and child data to understand development of communication toward attempts that begin with assumptions of the interdependence of adult and child during communicative exchanges. Thus, interaction and its history, the sequence of partners' exchanges through time, has become the focus of contemporary research on early communication and its development (e.g., Fogel, 1990, 1993; Lyra, 1987; Lyra & Rossetti-Ferreira, 1987, 1995; Papousek & Papousek, 1984; Tronick, Als, & Brazelton, 1980; Trevarthen, 1977; van Wulfften Palthe & Hopkins, 1984).

The change in emphasis from partners' discrete actions toward the dynamics of social exchange has gained further momentum through the influence of the ideas of J. J. Gibson (1966, 1979), particularly his notion of the infant's capacities as part of a perceptual-action system. This ecological perspective claims that the origins of perceptual capacities are embedded in the dynamics of an embodied self, and that physical and social realities are situated in context. Two implications of this position are that the focus of analysis should be dynamic, unitary patterns of perceiving and acting, and that our understanding of the physical and social worlds emerges directly from those relationships.

One challenge in applying theoretical and methodological implications of these approaches is to consider adequately the uniqueness of developmental phenomena. Perhaps the most distinctive characteristics of development are that it is creative and irreversible. The processual perspective we apply to the development of communication considers these distinctive characteristics in arguing that the unit of analysis is simultaneously the relationship and the subjects interacting through time. It is the dialogue established through time, including the dialogue itself and the participating selves, that is the focus of analysis (e.g., Fogel, 1993, in press; Lyra & Rossetti-Ferreira, 1995; Lyra, Pantoja, Cabral, Souza, & Moutinho, 1995). Through time, the mutual and interdependent dynamic that characterizes dialogue creates both new understanding and changed dialogical partners.

## THE SOCIAL CONTEXT OF DEVELOPMENT
## AND DISTINCTIVENESS OF SOCIAL EXCHANGES

The ubiquitous influence of the social other on development cannot be denied. Culture is present throughout the environment of the newborn. Cultural meaning and value are embedded in organization of spaces, objects, attitudes, and patterns of action, toward the infant. It is almost impossible to think about a nonsocial environment. Moreover, the helplessness of the human newborn makes the presence of social exchanges as pervasive as cultural tools. So, a situated or contextual analysis of the process of development must consider social dynamics as a necessary condition for understanding development.

The difficult questions confronting the researcher who wants to investigate the processual nature of development in social context can be summarized as follows: Should the dynamics of social exchange be considered as similar to other types of exchanges that promote development? If so, such dynamics may be like those within organism and physical environment relationships the child must integrate in his or her perception-action system. Or, should the dynamics of social exchange be considered as a distinctive type of organism—environment relationship. If so, how might these characteristics differ from those created by exchanges with a nonsocial environment? What characteristics of meaning and understanding are created by the dialogical character of exchanges with a social other?

In the following pages we highlight two aspects of the social world that suggest the distinctiveness of social exchanges and the necessity of considering this distinctiveness in order to understand the meaning and role of social exchanges for development: (a) the social world as a necessary condition for the existence of processual partners, and (b) the type of mutual adjustment that partners must make to establish a dialogue with the dynamic specificities inherent in patterns of mutual and interdependent human interactions.

## Partners Within Social Interaction

The idea that the newborn has a core sense of self has been supported by several studies. The fundamental intentionality of the action system of the infant demonstrates the existence of a primitive sense of the differentiation of a self from birth, or at least during the first months of life (Bahrick & Watson, 1985; Butterworth & Hopkins, 1993; Castillo & Butterworth, 1981; Kravitz, Goldenberg, & Neyhus, 1978; Meltzoff & Borton, 1979; Meltzoff & Moore, 1977; von Hofsten, 1989). From an ecological point of view, the core sense of personhood is perceived directly from interactions with the environment (e.g., Gibson, 1979). This initial sense is not a reflexive one; that is, there is no consciousness of the self as an object of knowledge (Neisser, 1988). Rather, Butterworth (1994) argued that "the difference between self-awareness and self-consciousness is only a matter of degree" (p. 13). Further, he claimed, "There is no need for a hard and fast distinction between direct perception of physical and social objects. Social objects are physical objects, albeit with additional qualities" (p. 14). What we intend to provide here is a brief analysis of some aspects of those "additional qualities" as they are reflected in the dynamics of the social exchanges.

If we consider only the idea that what we detect in social exchanges are the variant and invariant properties of the social objects as directly perceived from interactions with these objects, then we are assuming that partners in social interaction are reproductive, but not creative (Reed, 1993). The contrast between person as idea of a person as "finder" or as "maker" (Shotter, 1983) captures the distinction between reproductive and creative that we believe is crucial. The requirement of the social other for the existence of the person long has been recognized (e.g., Baldwin, 1902; Mead, 1934). However, from a dynamic point of view, what makes social encounters a necessary condition for the emergence and development of persons? Recognition of a relational and dialogical person requires admitting the creative nature of both relationships and persons. This admission, in turn, requires that social dialogue be co-regulated (Fogel, 1992, 1993, in press).

The pervasiveness of social relationships and the facilitating characteristics of others in highlighting aspects of the environment that are relevant for development do not themselves argue for social exchange patterns as distinct from physical ones. Neither do they suggest much about a possible connection between these specific dynamic characteristics and their consequences to the person that emerges; questions of distinctness of social exchanges must be found elsewhere. We now turn to a brief consideration of properties of social exchange.

## Properties of Social Exchanges

The characteristic dynamics of dialogue with a social other require that both partners are changing simultaneously as a consequence of a mutual co-regulation (Bakhtin, 1988; Fogel, in press; Lyra et al., 1995; Lyra & Rossetti-Ferreira, 1995; Markova, 1990). The changing role of the social other, which is interconnected with our own action, seems to be a part of the embodied cognition of the emergent self in social context (Fogel, 1993, in press). The creative nature of this process of co-regulation means that we cannot predict in advance either the dynamic of the partner's actions or the result of the emergent outcomes that are co-constructed from the interaction.

It seems that, from an early age, the child can separate some dynamic environmental patterns as belonging to social exchanges, as distinct from physical exchanges. The baby can distinguish social from nonsocial exchanges (Legerstee, this volume, chap. 10; Trevarthen, 1980) and appears disturbed if the rhythmic pattern of turn-taking is disrupted. We propose that the mutual interdependence of exchanges that characterizes the dynamics of dialogue allows an amplification of the creative power in social interactions. This happens because the partners, that emerge from the co-regulation of social actions, incorporate a newer and greater degree of uncertainty that is present in the construction of outcomes from social exchanges. We suggest that the nature of emergent shared meaning, which results from a history of mutual co-regulations, carries for each participant a new degree of uncertainty related to the inclusion of the partner's action. Meaning as a dialogical process of possibilities becomes incorporated into the partners as a consequence of the characteristic dynamics of social exchanges. Thus, the interdependent nature of social exchanges includes uncertainty. Uncertainty allows the emergence of novelty, which may, in turn, be constructed as meaning.

## DEVELOPMENT AS TRANSFORMATION OF NOVELTY IN SHARED MEANING WITHIN THE COMMUNICATION PROCESS: DETERMINACY AND INDETERMINACY

Assuming a dialogical or relational point of view, development of communication from birth can be studied as progressive emergence of novelty and transformation of this novelty in shared meaning arising from the dynamics of social exchanges. The role of determinacy and indeterminacy in development can be analyzed by considering the characteristic dynamic of these exchanges through time. Our focus is on how determinacy and indeterminacy are interconnected through the historical nature of the dynamic of social interaction.

We choose to capture this dynamic in terms of some aspects of the forms assumed by partners' exchanges within the dialogues that create shared meaning. Thinking in terms of form of exchange allows us to represent qualitative differences in interactions of a particular kind: in this case, face-to-face interaction. For example, early in an exchange, eye contact may be used to facilitate the establishment of interaction. Later, eye contact of longer duration begins to serve as a background action for the extension of other aspects of interaction. Still later, eye contact may take an abbreviated form, as the partners use it to quickly check with each other about the status of their interaction. Thus, the form of this exchange carries meaning about the partners and about their history of interaction. We propose that the form assumed by dialogical negotiations functions as an analogical description of both the organizational level of the communication process and the organizational level of the partners in the relationship. One heuristic value of descriptions of processes of communication using the changing form assumed by these interactions is that they can be applied to different social exchanges, while still respecting the creativity and uniqueness of each particular construction between partners. This approach has further value because it makes possible the capturing of generalized aspects of the development of this phenomenon.

In this section of the chapter, we analyze face-to-face mother–infant exchanges from weekly videotaped records (30 to 40 min each) of two Brazilian mother–infant (one boy and one girl) dyads interacting at home under natural conditions during the first 6 months of the infants' lives.

## The Dynamic of Establishing Shared Actions: Establishment

All communication starts with a dynamic of establishment of shared elements of communication between the partners. *Establishment* functions as a construction of preliminary agreement about the starting point for further interaction. Working from or against establishment, other exchanges then can be developed. This initial condition is similar to the ideas of a frame and a consensual frame proposed by Fogel (1993). However, when we consider the historical development of this dynamic, it is the action of highlighting some aspect of a partner's action from the total possibilities, in a specific and contextual moment, that characterizes the beginning of the process of communication. Selecting for further attention some, rather than other, aspects of a partner's actions from the interactional flow is integral to subsequent exchange. Consensual frames or shared meanings are products of this dynamic process. The term *establishment* seems to capture this notion, particularly the fundamentally dynamic nature of communication at this initial moment. All aspects of the frame become consensual or shared through a movement of mutual adjustment of the partners, through successive or concomitant actions of highlighting and establishment. However, the dominant characteristic of the dynamic of the first moment of the communication process is the establishment of at least one shared exchange. This we call the *dynamic of establishment*. The defining feature of this movement is that it highlights some aspects of an exchange and moves other possible choices to the background. Highlighting simultaneously closes some avenues for future interaction as it opens others.

In methodological terms, it is important to recognize that the labeling of *the* moment of establishment of a process of communication is an arbitrary decision. Applying a processual conception of communication means keeping in mind that, at any moment, both partners are changing as a result of the dialogue. Thus, it is impossible, in practice, to ascertain where the first moment of an interaction is located. Following this reasoning, the first moment is, in one sense, a theoretical abstraction. However, it is methodologically possible to consider the development of specific organizations or types of frames of communication. We can search for an initial moment when at least one necessary condition for the development of the analyzed organization starts to be included in the communication process. Such establishment enables particular forms of future interaction. For instance, early in life, eye contact, touching, vocalizing, and other actions might serve as a minimal requirement for face-to-face exchanges. Similarly, if we consider interactions that include an object, we can analyze the initial moment when the partners' exchanges begin to include that object. Thus, one contribution of a processual approach is that it allows us to begin to address how communicative exchanges are established. One illustration of such establishment is shown in Table 4.1.

This dynamic of establishment can use other interactional possibilities besides the ones illustrated. The baby can be in the bed, in a supine position, and the mother can change her own position to catch the baby's gaze direction. The mother can move the baby's whole body or can kiss baby's face, turning the baby's face toward her. The mother can talk, make noises or face movements, or stay quiet in order to maintain eye contact. Also, the mother and the baby can engage in vocal exchanges just before the establishment of eye contact.

Regardless of which possibilities are used, the central aspect of this dynamic is to introduce a first element of communication that, when maintained for a short time, seems to acquire the characteristics of an initial shared activity. This dynamic appears to focus on one main component of the partners' exchanges. In face-to-face interaction, eye contact is often the first element chosen, but we can imagine other components of action assuming similar role. For instance, vocal or even tactile exchanges can serve a similar function in cases of impairment of the visual system. Further, it is important to recognize that before the establishment of eye contact, other

TABLE 4.1
Illustration of Establishment

---

Infant: a 5-week-old boy
1. The baby is on the mother's lap, in a supine position.
(Physical contexts and postures can be considered as preconditions for the possibility of initiating a communicative moment between the partners.)
2. The baby has his face turned away from the mother's face.
3. The mother holds the baby's arms, saying: "Hy, hy, my baby?! Hy, hy, my baby?!" and, looking at the baby's face and holding the baby's arms, turns him so that she can see his face, saying: "Where's Mommy's baby?!"
(The mother tries to establish a first element of contact or communication between the partners: eye contact. She changes the position of the baby and uses vocal production in her attempts to establish this eye contact.)
4. The baby moves his head in the direction of the mother's face and eye contact is established.
(The partners establish eye contact.)
5. The mother says: "Where's Mommy's baby!?"
(The mother uses vocal production in her attempts to establish/maintain eye contact.)
6. Baby changes his gaze to another person who has just arrived.
(The baby seems to engage in this exchange of eye contact for short periods and in an unclear way.)

aspects of interaction already are included in the dialogue: adjustments of biological rhythms, nuances of postures and expressions, emotional moods, and so on. Each of these has been or is being established as a shared activity between the partners. However, in the face-to-face organization of interactions, these aspects recede the background when eye contact is highlighted. Thus, eye contact is the primary focus of the dynamic of establishment of dyadic exchanges with very young infants.

Considering the dynamic characteristics of social interaction, the determined and indetermined aspects of this first moment of face-to-face exchange can be analyzed. We can analyze the role of determinism and indeterminism by focusing on three main concepts and their interactional parameters: (a) the initial range of possibilities of the partners' actions, (b) the actual choice of the partners' actions, and (c) the range of possibilities of future partners' actions as a result of the actual choice of the partners' action.

The initial range of possibilities of the partners' actions is determined by biological, cultural, and historical moments of the partners. Examples of these include: the maturational status of the infant (e.g., the baby's control of his or her head and ability to focus attention); the physical-cultural environment (e.g., whether the baby is in a crib or a hammock); the general cultural background of the mother and her personal history, particularly her beliefs and values (e.g., her degree of insistence on keeping the baby awake or leaving him or her quiet); the historical moment of the partners (e.g., the level to which they have developed a mutual understanding about better times for interacting, such as after meals or after baths).

The actual choice of partners' actions contributes to the indeterminism present in social interaction. Indeterminism is present in the actual action of highlighting. This action involves the mother's making a unique choice at a particular contextual moment, and this choice is co-regulated by the infant's actual actions. Because this choice is dependent on the co-regulation of the partners' action, it cannot be determined before it is actualized. For instance, the mother can highlight the baby's gaze by changing his or her position or by changing her own posture in relation to the baby. This choice is dependent on both the mother's highlighting actions and on the baby's response (e.g., the baby's maintenance of a good mood as a precondition for establishment of eye contact).

As a consequence of this characteristic dynamic present in the establishment of the process of communication, including the initial range of possibilities of partners' actions and the actual choice of the partners' actions, the range of possibilities of future actions resulting from the dynamic of establishment closes some possibilities just when it opens new ones. At this moment, future development is determined by the decreased likelihood of some future actions through the establishment of an actual course of interaction. Simultaneously, future development remains indetermined by the increased likelihood of some other future choices and co-regulations that the construction of a first establishment allows. Thus, the seeds of the future are sown. For instance, the establishment of eye contact determines this as a condition for shared exchanges of smiles. At the same time, it opens new possibilities, including different cadences and frequencies within the exchanges of smiles or connections between smiles and vocalizations.

## Exploring Possibilities of the System: Extension

After a first element of communication has been established as a shared action (e.g., eye contact), it may become part of a background. This can give rise to an extended period during which the maintenance of this element allows for the exploration of possibilities for newly negotiated action to be developed as shared by the partners. This is likely to occur if the system, organization, or frame, that is being constructed by the partners is extended in its possibilities. This seems to require *extension* in the duration of exchanges. Consider the possibilities of exchanges in face-to-face conditions. The most frequently realized possibilities are exchanges of smiles, vocalizations, and face movements. However, different rhythms or cadences, different ways of highlighting, additional mutual touching, or movements of the baby's body can be introduced by the mother. An illustration of this process of extension is shown in Table 4.2.

Once eye contact is established, we can see that the initial range of possibilities of the partners' actions now is determined mainly through the maintenance of eye contact as a shared element of communication. It also is clear that the same constraints of biological, cultural, and historical moments of the partners discussed earlier are still in operation. However, now these constraints operate through the possibility of maintaining eye contact and, so, developing new negotiations of actions. For instance, the extension of eye contact can become a routine after meals or after baths, which allows the development of smiles, vocalizations, and movements as shared exchanges. The particular history of the dyad begins to include or assume both biological and cultural constraints, because these constraints are beginning to be written within and through the shared history of the dyadic co-regulations and shared constructions.

However, the actual choice of partners' actions remains indetermined. The examples described include many possibilities that may arise within the extended moment. For instance, eye contact can be maintained through the exchange of smiles, smiles plus vocalizations, temporal cadences, awaiting the baby's turn, physically moving the baby, and so on.

Again, because of the historical development of the dyad, possibilities for future actions become constrained through the closing of alternatives that had been possible at an earlier moment. These actions were possible

TABLE 4.2

Illustrations of Extension

Example 1. Infant: a 12-week-old boy
The baby is lying in the crib, moving his arms and legs, while the mother, sitting beside the crib, leans toward him and they look at each other.
(Eye contact is established immediately.)
  1. Mother vocalizes, smiling: "Aye? Aye, mommy?!"
  2. Baby vocalizes: "Aaaaa-oou."
  3. Mother vocalizes, smiling: "Ha-ha, mommy! Ee, mommy! Ee, mommy, e? E, mommy?!"
  4. Baby vocalizes: "Eeeer-ar."
  5. Mother vocalizes, smiling: "Eeee."
  6. Baby vocalizes: "Haa."
  7. Mother vocalizes, smiling: "E-eee."
  8. Baby vocalizes, smiling: "Haa."
  9. Mother vocalizes: "Eeee."
10. Baby vocalizes: "Ooo-ar."
11. Mother vocalizes, smiling: "Eeee, mommy! I'm talking!"
(Over a longer period, the partners exchange smiles and vocalizations. Mainly the vocalizations, but also the smiles, extend the interaction through a kind of mutual repetition, having as background the maintenance of eye contact.)
Example 2. Infant: a 12-week-old girl
The baby is lying in the crib moving her arms and legs, while the mother is standing beside the crib, leaning toward the baby, buttoning her blouse. They look at each other.
(Eye contact is established immediately.)
1. Mother vocalizes: "Is it right, sweetie? Opa! Hum!"
2. Baby vocalizes during mother's vocalization: "Eeeeern."
3. Mother stops her vocalization and silently looks at the baby's face for a while.
4. Baby is quiet, looking at the mother.
5. Mother vocalizes: "Now?!"
6. Baby vocalizes: "Eern."
7. Mother vocalizes: "E?!"
(In this example, beyond mutual vocal exchanges, the dyad extends the interaction using the rhythmic of the exchanges as well. The mother highlights the baby's vocal production by stopping talking and waiting for the baby to take her turn. All of this exchange has as background the maintenance of eye contact.)
Example 3. Infant: a 13-week-old girl
The baby is moving her arms and legs, while the mother is beside the crib. They look at each other.
(Eye contact is established immediately.)
1. The mother grasps the baby's hands as if she were going to pick her up by them.
2. Baby vocalizes: "Ooon."
3. Mother vocalizes, smiling: "Try!"
4. Baby vocalizes: "Oooor-er."
5. Mother picks the baby up by her hands and vocalizes, smiling: "Try!"
6. Baby vocalizes: "Oooo."
7. Mother lets go of the baby's hands, laying her down in the crib.
8. Baby vocalizes: "Huuum-huuum."
9. Mother vocalizes: "Dear one!"
(In this example, beyond mutual vocal exchanges, the dyad extends the interaction through the mother physically moving the baby, having as background the maintenance of eye contact.)

before the new negotiation that became shared. Once these negotiated actions are actualized, alternative possibilities for that moment become determined. However, this closing again creates a new level of organization that, itself, was not previously available. This new level creates additional alternatives for action and, thus, creates indeterminism for the next moment. Once again, the seeds of the future are sown.

This simultaneous opening and closing of possibilities can be illustrated by comparing alternative pathways. Some dyads extend face-to-face exchanges primarily through variations of vocal exchanges. Other dyads may use some small interruptions of eye contact, through kisses and physical movement of the baby. The possibilities for developing new shared exchanges are now different for these two dyads. One might develop elaborations of vocal exchanges and the other might develop different cadences of turn-taking based on physical movements. Thus, we see the influence of opening and closing possibilities within the history of each dyad.

### Characteristics of Meaning as Process of Possibilities: Abbreviation

Following a period when dyadic negotiations are extended, we can observe a simultaneous movement toward both reducing the duration of exchanges and extending them through successive new explorations. This last aspect can be observed in the reduction of the number of alternating turns during episodes of face-to-face exchanges. We call this movement an *abbreviation* of the form of interaction. Illustrations are shown in Table 4.3.

The main point about abbreviation is that its indeterminacy is related not only to which actions will be highlighted, but also to characteristics of the abbreviated shared activity. This shared activity encapsulates the history of the period of extension and so allows the actual abbreviated exchange to show different combinations of elements that now are shared as abbreviated meaning. However, such abbreviated meaning can never be the same for both partners, and the degree of similarity of meaning can be tested only by the actualization of action in the future. Therefore, the actual choice of the partners' actions is indetermined *in its process*. This choice has acquired a degree of indeterminacy because it belongs, simultaneously, both to the communication process and to each partner. It is as if each partner now knows that the shared exchange of actions carries possibilities of actualization that remain shared though indetermined.

Abbreviation seems to reflect a new level of organization. The initial range of possibilities of the partners' actions, the actual choice of partners' actions, and the range of possibilities of future partners' actions are more closely connected in abbreviation because their determinedness is even more dependent on the history of partner's constructions. The initial range of possi-

TABLE 4.3
Illustration of Abbreviation

---

Example 1. Infant: a 13-week-old girl

1. Mother puts the baby in a supine position after finishing baby's bath and says: "Upa, Hum!" while drying the baby's hand.
2. They look at each other and they smile at each other.
(Eye contact and smiles are immediately established exchanges.)
3. Mother looks away, drying the baby's body.
(These exchanges are not extended; they are short, abbreviated in time.)
Example 2. Infant: a 22-week-old boy
1. The baby is carried by his sister. The mother, looking at the baby's face, stretches out her arms to him while smiling and says: "Come, come Xando."
2. The baby looks at his mother and stretches out his arms to her, while the mother continues looking at him and calling him.
3. The baby stretches out his arms toward his mother and, looking at her face, vocalizes and smiles.
4. The mother continues calling him and stretching her arms toward the baby.
(Eye contact is established immediately. As in the previous example, exchanges of vocalizations and smiles occur in a short period of time, but here those exchanges, including the abbreviated face-to-face exchanges, include an innovation: the mutual stretching of arms toward the partner. This new exchanged element of communication brings us full cycle to a new extension of dyadic interaction.)
5. The baby, looking at mother's hand, touches it, while the mother continues doing the previously described actions.
(Eye contact is interrupted by the baby so that he can explore mother's hand.)
6. For a moment, the baby looks to his mother, vocalizes, and moves his arms and legs.
(Eye contact is established immediately, including exchanges of vocalization in an abbreviated way. This kind of interaction continues until the baby starts a variation of the game.)
7. The baby turns his face away.
8. The mother calls him.
9. The baby turns his face to his mother and again turns away in a novel way, exchanging eye contact, then smiles or vocalizations.
(Abbreviated face-to-face exchanges now include a new game: the baby's turning his face away from and then back to his mother. This new game extends the dyadic interaction again, in a novel direction.)

---

bilities of the partners' actions becomes part of the joint, shared construction. For instance, play routines, the "right" moment for face-to-face exchanges, and other characteristics of abbreviated exchanges (e.g., containing more vocalizations or smiles) all belong now to the co-constructed history of the dyad present in the abbreviated exchange. The actual choice of partners' actions continues to be indetermined, just as before, but this indeterminism now functions at a different level: it includes the external communication process and the uncertainty contained in the abbreviated shared dyadic meaning. Shared abbreviation in face-to-face exchanges can happen, for example, as only brief eye contact, or as eye contact plus smile, or as eye contact plus vocalization, or as eye contact plus vocalization and smile. These alternatives open possibilities for highlighting aspects of actions of partners and self, thus retaining the characteristic uncertainty of abbreviated shared construction at the levels of both communication and partner.

Indeterminacy also remains for new extensions required for the inclusion of, or interconnection with, new actions never before highlighted. This is a natural movement that transforms abbreviation into extension. Uncertainty contained in the actualization of the abbreviated shared construction begins to be part of new exchanges, including actions never before highlighted. For instance, abbreviated face-to-face exchanges may be included as part of a new game of covering and re-covering the baby's face (peek-a-boo), of turning the baby sideways, of asking for the baby's name in order to carry the baby, or as part of dyadic exchanges that include an object. In these ways, the dynamic of abbreviation brings the dyad to a new organization of the dynamic of establishment.

## SUMMARY AND CONCLUSION

We have examined social exchanges and negotiations between partners during face-to-face interaction. We have made use of the interactional dynamics of establishment, extension, and abbreviation to characterize the emergence of meaning and communication from within these interactions. The analysis of the development of communication processes through the description of the form assumed by the interactions through time allows us to suggest that both the determined and indetermined aspects of this development have a historical flow that tends toward increasing the connectedness of these two aspects of development.

The creative power of this process of co-regulated negotiation between the partners enables the co-construction of shared meaning that can become abbreviated. The nature of this abbreviated meaning suggests that indeterminacy emerges at two levels. At one level, uncertainty remains in the actual choice of each partner's actions in order to continue the negotiation process of development. However, at a second level, the creative power becomes a component of abbreviated shared meaning. This characteristic includes the uncertainty of the subject and the uncertainty of the partner. The partner who abbreviates a shared meaning includes in that abbreviation the characteristic dynamics of both partners. Because they are co-regulated, these dynamics change as a function of both partners' actions. The process of abbreviation shows the emergence of a new organizational level that reveals the constructive nature of meanings at the level of symbols, through the expansion or creation of a new level of uncertainty for which the characteristic dynamics of the social other are required. Thus, we conclude that this expanded indeterminacy arises only in the context of social relationships, the natural condition of all human development.

## ACKNOWLEDGMENTS

This work was supported by grants to the first author from the Conselho Nacional de Desenvolvimento Científico e Tecnológico (CNPq), Brazil, and Fundação de Amparo a Ciência e Tecnologia (Facepe), Pernambuco, Brazil. The authors thank Ana Carvalho for her contributing comments on earlier drafts of this chapter.

## REFERENCES

Bahrick, L., & Watson, J. S. (1985). Detection of intermodal proprioceptive-visual contingency as a potential basis of self perception in infancy. *Developmental Psychology, 21*, 963–973.

Bakhtin, M. M. (1988). Discourse in the novel. In N. Mercer (Ed.), *Language and literacy from an educational perspective* (Vol. 1, pp. 47–58). Philadelphia, PA: Open University Press.

Baldwin, J. M. (1902). *Social and ethical interpretations in mental development.* New York: Macmillan.

Bates, E. (1979). *The emergence of symbols: Cognition and communication in infancy.* New York: Academic Press.

Boulding, K. (1956). General systems theory—The skeleton of science. *Management Science, 2*, 197–208.

Bruner, J. S. (1975). The ontogenesis of speech acts. *Journal of Child Language, 2*, 1–19.

Bruner, J. S. (1983). *Child's talk: Learning to use language.* New York: Norton.

Bullowa, M. (1979). *Before speech.* Cambridge, England: Cambridge University Press.

Butterworth, G. E. (1994). An ecological perspective on the origins of self. In J. Bermudez, N. Eilan, & A. Marcel (Eds.), *The body and the self.* Boston: MIT Press.

Butterworth, G. E., & Hopkins, B. N. (1993). Origins of handedness in human infancy. *Developmental Medicine and Child Neurology, 35*, 177–184.

Carter, A. L. (1975). The transformation of sensory-motor morphemes into words: A case study of the development of 'more' and 'mine'. *Journal of Child Language, 2*, 233–250.

Castillo, M., & Butterworth, G. E. (1981). Neonatal localisation of a sound in visual space. *Perception, 10*, 331–338.

Dore, J. (1975). Holophrases, speech acts and language universals. *Journal of Child Language, 2*, 21–40.

Fogel, A. (1990). The process of developmental change in infant communicative action: Using dynamic systems theory to study individual ontogenies. In J. Colombo & J. Fagen (Eds.), *Individual differences in infancy: Reliability, stability and prediction* (pp. 341–358). Hillsdale, NJ: Lawrence Erlbaum Associates.

Fogel, A. (1992). Co-regulation, perception and action. *Human Movement Science, 11*, 505–523.

Fogel, A. (1993). *Developing through relationships.* Chicago: University of Chicago Press.

Fogel, A. (in press). Information, creativity, and culture. In C. Dent-Read & P. Zukow-Goldring (Eds.), *Changing ecological approaches to development: Organism-environment mutualities.* Washington, DC: APA Publications.

Gibson, J. J. (1966). *The senses considered as perceptual systems.* Boston, MA: Houghton Mifflin.

Gibson, J. J. (1979). *The ecological approach to visual perception.* Boston, MA: Houghton Mifflin.

Halliday, M. K. (1975). *Learning how to mean.* London: Edward Arnold.

Howie, C. (1981). *Acquiring language in a conversational context.* London: Academic Press.

Kravitz, H., Goldenberg, D., & Neyhus, A. (1978). Tactual exploration by normal infants. *Developmental Medicine and Child Neurology, 20*, 720–726.

Laszlo, E. (1972). *Introduction to systems philosophy: Toward a new paradigm of contemporary thought.* New York: Harper & Row.

Lyra, M. C. D. P. (1987, July). *A socio-interactionist constructivist approach. Dialogue: can we grasp the construction of the mother-infant dyad?* Proceedings of Chinese Satellite ISSBD Conference, Pequim, China.

Lyra, M. C. D. P., Pantoja, A. P. F., Cabral, E. A., Souza, M., & Moutinho, A. K. (1995). A produção vocal do bebê: construção partilhada pela díade. *Psicologia: Teoria e Pesquisa, 11*(1), 1–6.

Lyra, M. C. D. P., & Rossetti-Ferreira, M. C. (1987, July). *Dialogue and the construction of the mother-infant dyad.* Ninth Biennial Meetings of the ISSBD, Abstracts and Poster Presentations, Tokyo, Japan.

Lyra, M. C. D. P., & Rossetti-Ferreira, M. C. (1995). Transformation and construction in social interaction: A new perspective on analysis of the mother-infant dyad. In J. Valsiner (Ed.), *Child development within cultural environments, Vol. 3. Comparative cultural-constructivist perspective* (pp. 51–77). Norwood, NJ: Ablex.

Markova, I. (1990). Why the dynamics of dialogue? In I. Markova & K. Foppa (Eds.), *The dynamics of dialogue* (pp. 1–22). New York: Springer-Verlag.

Mead, G. H. (1934). *Mind, self and society.* Chicago: University of Chicago Press.

Meltzoff, A., & Borton, R. W. (1979). Intermodal matching by human neonates. *Nature, 282,* 403–404.

Meltzoff, A., & Moore, M. K. (1977). Imitation of facial and manual gestures by human neonates. *Science, 198,* 75–78.

Neisser, U. (1988). Five kinds of self knowledge. *Philosophical Psychology, 1,* 35–59.

Ochs, E., & Schieffelin, B. C. (Eds.). (1979). *Developmental pragmatics.* New York: Academic Press.

Papousek, H., & Papousek, M. (1984). Qualitative transactions in integrative processes during the first trimester of human postpartum life. In F. R. Prechtl (Ed.), *Continuity of neural functions from prenatal to postnatal life* (pp. 220–241). Oxford, England: Blackwell.

Reed, E. S. (1993). The intention of use a specific affordance: A conceptual framework for psychology. In R. H. Wozniak & K. W. Fisher (Eds.), *Development in context: Acts and thinking in speech environments* (pp. 45–76). Hillsdale, NJ: Lawrence Erlbaum Associates.

Sameroff, A. (1982). Development and the dialectic: The need for a systems approach. In W. A. Collins (Ed.), *Minnesota symposium on child psychology* (Vol. 15, pp. 83–103). Hillsdale, NJ: Lawrence Erlbaum Associates.

Schaffer, H. R. (Ed.). (1977). *Studies in mother-infant interaction.* New York: Plenum Press.

Shotter, J. (1983). "Duality of structure" and "intentionality" in an ecological psychology. *Journal for the Theory of Social Behavior, 13,* 19–43.

Snow, C. E., & Ferguson, C. A. (Eds.). (1977). *Talking to children.* Cambridge, England: Cambridge University Press.

Trevarthen, C. (1977). Descriptive analysis of infant communicative behavior. In H. R. Schaffer (Ed.), *Studies in mother-infant interaction* (pp. 227–270). New York: Plenum Press.

Trevarthen, C. (1980). The foundations of intersubjectivity: Development of interpersonal and cooperative understanding. In D. Olson (Ed.), *The social foundation of language and thought: Essays in honor of Jerome Bruner* (pp. 316–342). New York: Norton.

Tronick, E., Als, H., & Brazelton, T. B. (1980). Monadic phases: A structural descriptive analysis of infant–mother face-to-face interaction. *Merrill-Palmer Quarterly, 26,* 3–24.

van Wulfften Palthe, T., & Hopkins, B. (1984). Development of infant's social competence during face-to-face interaction: A longitudinal study from prenatal to postnatal life. In H. F. R. Prechtl (Ed.), *Continuity of neural functions from prenatal to life* (pp. 198–219). Oxford: Blackwell.

von Hofsten, C. (1989). Transition mechanism in sensorimotor development. In A. de Ribaupierre (Ed.), *Transition mechanism in child development* (pp. 233–258). Cambridge, England: Cambridge University Press.

Weiss, P. A. (1969). The living-system: Determinism stratified. In A. Koestler & J. R. Smytjhies (Eds.), *Beyond reductionism: New perspectives in the life sciences* (pp. 3–55). Boston: Beacon Press.

# DETERMINACY AND INDETERMINACY: THEORETICAL AND PHILOSOPHICAL PERSPECTIVES

George Butterworth
University of Sussex

Indeterminism is the doctrine that different future courses of events are equally compatible with the present state of the universe (Bynum, Brown, & Porter, 1981). Indeterminism means that there can be no one-to-one correspondence between antecedent and consequent and thus, it would seem to render prediction and causal explanation of development impossible. The main purpose of the four chapters reviewed here is to demonstrate that partially indeterminate developmental systems can nevertheless be understood and that determinism and indeterminism act in concert to create development.

The doctrine of *indeterminism*, defined as the principled unpredictability of change, receives its greatest support in quantum physics, yet as van Geert very clearly points out in his chapter, physics is actually highly successful in making scientific predictions. For example, even though the behavior of gaseous systems at the quantum level is indeterminate, determinism can be reintroduced at the macroscopic level, given knowledge of the temperature and pressure of the gas. The important point is that at an appropriate level of aggregation indeterminate phenomena become determinate and prediction is, after all, possible. On this view indeterminism and determinism are two sides of the same coin.

Once models of human development are considered from this perspective, it is apparent that explaining complex, self-organizing systems must simultaneously exploit indeterminacy (to account for the emergence of novelty) and determinacy (to allow for the predictable aspects of development). Van Geert distinguishes between factor and process determinism. In *factor determinism*, a statistical link is established between antecedent and consequent to bridge time but does not invoke time as part of the causal explanation. In *process determinism*, the dynamic changes of the developing system over time are intrinsic to the causal explanation. In the former case, much of the variability inherent to development is consigned to an error term, whereas in the latter case, variability is considered to be the unpredictable dynamic driving development along.

Van Geert argues that computer modelling of growth functions enables the psychologist to establish the extent to which a developmental function is truly indeterminate, the extent to which initial states constrain subsequent states of the system, how the developing system unfolds over time, how the degrees of freedom of a system to vary are reduced or how degrees of freedom may actually be created within the dynamics of growth. The essential advance is that computational modelling of iterative growth processes enables mathematical, formal models to be tested. This is a scientific advance over the verbal models of present-day developmental psychology. Dynamical systems theory enables causal explanations to move beyond factor determinism by revealing how development unfolds over time.

Van Geert has indeed made an important contribution to the field in pioneering computer modelling of development. His approach is not restricted to any single theoretical perspective, being equally useful for modelling aspects of Piagetian stage development as for Vygotsky's social coconstructivism, or for contemporary approaches which place much emphasis on the domain-specificity and context sensitivity of development. In each case, the growth model is dependent upon what resources are available, how they are shared among constituent subsystems and the setting conditions. Many examples are reviewed in van Geert (1994) in a convincing exposition of the thesis that modelling iterative growth functions offers novel insights into development. The reader is recommended to consult that source to supplement the material in this chapter.

Thus, the method is promising, but what are the drawbacks? Van Geert (1994) draws attention to four difficulties encountered in modelling developmental processes. The first empirical problem is that a high sampling frequency of longitudinal data is required. Not only are longitudinal studies relatively rare but the time frame for some developmental processes may be so long as to render the approach impractical. The effect is to direct research toward microgenetic processes, especially where rapid change occurs, as during infancy or early language development, that offer a practical framework for developmental modelling. Such studies illustrate the basic principle that development is turbulent rather than smooth and linear.

A connected problem is that statistical techniques for testing developmental transitions are not yet widely available, although it is possible to simply rely on the eye to establish whether growth curves are similar or different.

A third problem concerns the relationship between time as represented on a computer spreadsheet and real, developmental time. Each iteration of the growth process in a computer occupies an equal time interval but, in real life, developmental time may vary from iteration to iteration. Furthermore, the forward transmission of information in the developing system may be less than perfect. Such effects can be modelled by adding random error to the system and discovering how the perturbation affects the growth function.

The final problem is accounting for novelty. Computer modelling illustrates how a gradual iterative process, applied repeatedly, may nevertheless result in a sudden qualitative change in the structure of a system. But what are the processes in real life which engender novelty? In the field of motor development, spontaneous exploratory movements are candidates for introducing basic variability into development which will eventually give rise to new motor patterns. It remains to be seen whether similar principles will apply to the generation of novelty in cognitive development.

Gulerce further elaborates the links between determinacy and indeterminacy. Paradoxically, as the mathematics of chaotic systems is worked out, scientific commitment to determinacy has actually strengthened the desire to gain control over a disorderly world. These advances, according to Gulerce, have had the effect of separating prediction from determinacy. Predictions can be made without determinacy and determined systems can nevertheless be unpredictable (and, just to complete the matrix, it is possible neither to know the cause yet be able to predict an event and also not to know the cause nor to be able to make predictions).

She argues that developmental psychology needs to keep simultaneously a foot in each of three camps: the biological, the social, and the cultural, and there can be little objection to this statement. However, she suggests that within each domain there are different determinate and indeterminate causal relations. She argues that developmental trajectories in the ecological realm may be highly structured if only by survival pressures, whereas in the social realm there are probabilistic links over time which operate rather like seaways and which only loosely constrain developmental trajectories. She claims that at the symbolic–cultural level causality is indeterministic, with development being a matter of constructing meanings which can be quite idiosyncratic. This three-legged unit of analysis serves to carry the organism through biological, social, and personal developmental trajectories. This is a valiant attempt to integrate the many levels at which a developing system must function. However, the thesis suffers a number of drawbacks. First, it is highly dependent on verbal-conceptual analysis and lacks the rigor that a mathematical model may offer, such as van Geert advocates.

Secondly, there is not necessarily a graded shift from a determinate to an indeterminate causal explanation as one moves from biological to personal development. It is equally possible that all three levels are subject to the same determinate or indeterminate causal analysis. Indeed, one challenge would be to account for the emergence of self and identity as the different biological and cultural resources for growth interact. Gulerce does identify an important question which is how indeterminate processes nevertheless give rise to predictable outcomes. Is this a question of greater canalization of biological aspects of the system as she suggests, or is it necessary to consider whether aggregation of biological and cultural influences occurs to yield determinism at the macroscopic level?

The next two chapters report on focused, microanalytic studies of early communication development from a dynamic systems perspective. Fogel and Branco offer an analysis of metacommunication in the formation of personal relationships. Their thesis is that relationships are built out of developing systems of communication which are not strictly determined. The ongoing interaction between partners creates perturbations leading to indeterminate outcomes in particular cases but which come to carry meaning for the dyad. Metacommunication, whereby the participants in an interaction evaluate their own communication, introduces further indeterminacy insofar as the metacommunication is incongruent with meanings already exchanged.

The authors describe clearly how the process of communication depends upon co-action, both simultaneous and successive, between and within the partners in a social encounter. The characteristics of these exchanges can be neatly captured as a self-organizing dynamic system. Metacommunication occurs at critical transition points as the partners move between interactional frameworks. Fogel and Branco offer the novel suggestion that emotional expression and gaze aversion may serve a metacommunicative function in early development. Gaze aversion as a reaction to the intrusions of the mother may serve to regulate the flow of interaction not merely by the physical act of gaze avoidance but also as a metacommunicative signal of how the infant evaluates the interaction. Similar metacommunicative functions may be found in smiles during play which appear to act as comments on the prior action and serve a function in signalling general intentions. If it is the case that metacommunication serves indeterminately to minimize perturbations at transition points in social interaction, this is an important insight. The authors make a convincing case that the dynamic systems perspective offers a new approach to the development of communication. However, their model remains at the verbal-conceptual level. It is not yet a formal model.

Lyra and Winegar address the question of the origins of communication in mother–infant interaction sequences. Their analysis is similar to that of Fogel and Branco (i.e., of the emergence of new symbolic meanings from a shared history of experience). They propose that the interaction between a mother and her infant can be considered as a continuously changing dynamic process. Since this is ongoing, it is difficult to define when a particular episode actually begins; however, it is possible to identify markers, such as eye contact, vocalization or tactile exchanges, which serve to initiate interaction sequences. While such markers are methodologically convenient, they do not determine the onset of an interaction since it is only in actualizing the contact in relation to the infant's own activities that the possibility of communication is opened up. Initiation of communication is therefore coregulated and partially indeterminate. Once established the interaction both extends to new possibilities and closes down alternatives as a history of mutual coregulation of behavior emerges. As the interaction becomes partly predictable, initiation becomes abbreviated, proceeds rapidly and in a more economical (skilled) form relative to earlier development. This economy of initiation frees the subsequent interaction for further extension in novel directions. The whole process of communication is partly indeterminate because it emerges from the coaction of the partners and necessarily incorporates mutual uncertainty. Lyra and Winegar's analysis remains at the verbal conceptual level. Nevertheless, the dynamical approach applied to the detailed observation of the flow of interaction in early development offers an important natural-history of the emergence of meaning.

In conclusion, these four chapters serve well to illustrate the possibilities and problems of dynamical systems explanations in development. The case is well made that indeterminacy enters into development and contributes importantly to the emergence of novel behavior. The application of formal mathematical models to the explanation of development remains the exception rather than the rule though the field has been well prepared for a process-based developmental psychology founded on dynamical systems theory. The particular domain of early communication is well suited to such an analysis. It is clear that the groundwork is done to allow the next steps to be taken toward a formal model. Given the highly personal nature of the basic interactions which serve to establish communication, a formal model which can explain equifinal linguistic outcomes from idiosyncratic origins will present an interesting theoretical challenge. How do the indeterminate emergent processes of early communication eventually yield the syntax and semantics of language? Perhaps this is where indeterminism and determinism will meet.

## REFERENCES

Bynum, W. E., Brown, E. L., & Porter, R. (1981). *Dictionary of the history of science*. Princeton, NJ: Princeton University Press.

van Geert, P. (1994). *Dynamic systems of development*. Hemel Hempstead: Harvester.

# THEORETICAL APPROACHES TO PEER INTERACTION PROCESSES

# 5

# PLAY AND IMAGINATION: THE PSYCHOLOGICAL CONSTRUCTION OF NOVELTY

Zilma de Moraes Ramos de Oliveira
University of São Paulo, Brazil

Jaan Valsiner
University of North Carolina at Chapel Hill

The basic problem of developmental psychology is how to explain the persistent construction of novelty in the context of the relative conservatism of the developmental process. Modern psychological discourse seems to have failed to bring the solution to this problem any closer than the efforts of the leading psychologists a century (e.g., Baldwin, 1895; Groos, 1908; Janet, 1929), or decades (Piaget, 1946; Vygotsky, 1935; Wallon, 1934, 1942) ago. The progress in developmental psychology seems to come via some nonlinear and non-monotonic trajectory, where the research at any time is not necessarily more profound than that occurring at previous times and in differing contexts.

The major complication that developmental psychologists cannot ignore—in clear contrast with their nondevelopmental colleagues—is the philosophical issue that developmental processes are not reversible because they are bound to irreversibility of time. Hence, the fundamental issue of develop-ment is how the actual future organization of the psychological functions of a person is being constructed in the present (with input from the past via memory) on the basis of unknown, but desired, images of the future. The processes of psychological development are constantly in an ephemeral state—at any moment in time, a future state of these processes is being constructed, but because that construction is not yet complete, it is not possible to discern what it is. Undoubtedly, that creates a great methodo-logical difficulty, which may explain the relatively underdeveloped state of affairs in contemporary developmental research practices. Whichever developmentally relevant phenomenon—cognitive, social, or affective—might be investigated by a here-and-now process, its real functions cannot be discovered before the expected future state of affairs becomes actualized in the form of a new actual present. In it, the determination of the developmental phenomena has to be understood.

The simple imperative for developmental research design that follows these constraints is the normative use of prospective studies (see Baldwin, 1906, p. 21, footnotes). Furthermore, any study of the here-and-now observables requires an analysis of their functions in the construction of immediate outcomes within a microgenetic approach.

Our contribution to the discussion of determinism versus indeterminism is in relation to the child's and the adolescent's imagination. For that, we have considered, with Vygotsky (1986), that the development of higher psychological functions occurs through the internalization of social relationships. Vygotsky emphasized the significance of daily social practices, especially those with partners, as the main sources for human development. If we take the imagination as a higher psychological function, semiotically mediated and historically constructed, the study of its development also has to be based on the study of the child's interactions with partners. That study will depend on the definition we give to the interactional phenomena.

For that definition, we have recovered the concept of *role* created by the sociogenetic tradition (Baldwin, 1895; Bergson, 1889; Guillaume, 1925; James, 1890; Janet, 1929; Mead, 1934; Moreno, 1934) and have taken it to refer to a transactional conception of human interactions.

The important point is not the conception that roles exist in human interaction (a point well made in the nondevelopmental tradition of role theory—see Sarbin, 1950), but how they are (microgenetically and ontogenetically) constructed through interpersonal exchanges more or less mediated by internal processes. This latter emphasis was taken from the work of Sherif (1936), Wallon (1942, 1959), and—in the focus on semiotic mediation—Vygotsky (1935).

We conceive human interaction as a dynamic process of expanding or restricting shared semiotically organized conduct fields, occurring through the coordination of the roles—socially modulated forms of all human actions—assumed by the participants in ongoing situations. The starting condition for their construction is the fact that, from birth, the child is involved in social matrices in which meanings are constructed by him or her and his or her caregivers, as they confront their actions in daily situations, playing roles associated to some counter-roles. Thus, the infant is being confronted with the same person (e.g., the mother) acting in diverse ways in different settings: playing with the awake and content baby; changing diapers of a wet and fussing baby; feeding the hungry baby in the middle of the night, herself half-asleep and fussy; and so on. From the experience of these social matrices' heterogeneity follows the possibility of building up semiotic means of reorganizing them, starting from the early forms of gestural protosymbols emerging in mother–infant communication (Bullinger, 1993; Fogel, 1992; Lyra & Rossetti-Ferreira, 1995), and being modified as verbal language increasingly regulates children's actions in the second and third year of life, and beyond.

Taking a role approach, we present an analysis of some ways young children jointly construct their play, coordinating their actions to fulfill a script of an imaginary situation. After that, we present our view of how the peers' role coordination in play evolves to internal intraindividual role playing in the adolescent's fantasy. Finally, we discuss the question of determination in relation to that process.

In spite of the richness of the theme, careful analysis of the subjective worlds of developing children became either extinct or forgotten in the latter half of the 20th century. As a result of the dominance of positivist research in psychology, the sophistication of personological (Stern, 1938), or symbolic (Piaget, 1946; Buhler, 1967) worlds of children and adolescents have received little attention. For example, the function of children's interactions with adults and peers for the construction of imagination and fantasy is far from being clear. Our basic aim here is to restore the relevance of the investigation of imagination as a central constructive vehicle of human development.

## PLAY AND THE CONSTRUCTION OF IMAGINATION

Developmental psychologists (Baldwin, Mead, Sherif, Vygotsky, and others) have seen the creation of imaginary situations by the child as an activity linked with his or her taking of various roles, with their cultural regulations, into play's transformed settings. Since the earlier studies, the process of imagination was related to a special form of functioning in here-and-now contexts, in which the weakness of personal experiences' nonsubjectivity is transferred into a strength of subjectivity:

> The imaginative individual sets up in his consciousness a world of his own which, precisely because he shares it with no one else, informs inner experience as an extension of his individual personality and the time serves as its protective covering; for without it he would be delivered up to the hardness of the objective world. We now perceive that imagination is not a special power, which makes possible a capricious manipulation of any desired ideas, but a mode of inner experience growing out of the depths of personal striving and fed by these depths in both form and substance. A man is what he imagines. (Stern, 1938, p. 327)

The theoretical necessity of conceptualizing the making of future in human ontogeny led Vygotsky (1933/1966) to look at both children's play and adolescents' fantasy as means for social facilitation of developing functions. In doing so, he was building on the rich interest in the issues of play and constructive imagination that already existed in science (Groos, 1908; Ribot, 1926; Sully, 1896). Largely following his contemporary Continental European intellectual traditions (see Van der Veer & Valsiner, 1991), he emphasized that not only under conditions of social assistance by "more experienced" partners, but also when playing alone, the child goes beyond his or her present state of development.

Vygotsky (1990, 1994), elaborating on imagination and fantasy, disagreed with the idea that they should be related only or mainly to emotional life and with the traditional view of fantasy as an exclusively visual, imagistic, and concrete activity. For him, any creation of the imagination always emanates from elements taken from reality and maintained in the person's previous experience. It depends on how rich and varied that previous experience was and occurs through a very lengthy internal process that leads to the dissociation, alteration, and association of sensory impressions.

According to Vygotsky (1933/1966), in play children are above their daily behavior. Through symbolic play or rule-based games, they create self-help, constructively experimenting with a given model and transforming it into a novel form. Hence, play can be seen as a zone of proximal development, a field of joint actions dynamically related one to another, opening a series of activities in which developmental tendencies are condensed. Play does not serve only as an echo of the adults' world according to the child's eyes and ears, but allows room for novelty. In representing and questioning social rules in play, children prepare their own lives as persons and as members of a generation and, at the same time, contribute to cultural change.

Based in Vygotsky's initial statements and theory, researchers (Elbers, 1994; Gaskins & Göncü, 1992; Ortega, 1994; among others) have conducted studies that have illuminated various points about solitary and group play without the direct participation of an adult, calling into question the unidirectional influence of a more competent partner frequently seen studies of adult–child interactions (see Haigt, 1994; Schaffer, 1984; Wertsch & Stone, 1985).

Our role perspective was used to analyze some episodes from video recordings of small groups of young Brazilian children from low-income families attending day-care centers. We intended to apprehend the conditions for the emergence of the fictional roles assumed by the children and their evolution with age, using data taken from: (a) 20 free-play sessions of two day-care groups (A1: five 2-year-old children, and A2: eight 3-year-old children), 10 sessions of 9 min each, filmed in a 2- to 3-week interval over the course of a year (Oliveira & Rossetti-Ferreira, 1993); and (b) 3 play sessions about the theme "school" of three 4- to 6-year-old groups (B1 = 16, B2 = 13, B3 = 23 children), each session of approximately 30 min.

Using a microgenetic approach, which takes gestures and postures, as well as conversations, as indices of meaning construction, we concluded that, in the children's interactions, roles are delineated through the dynamic joint negotiation of the semiotic aspects of the children's actions. In all the groups, the make-believe play resembled a collage of fragments of their experiences in currently constructed activity contexts. In the 2-year-old group, the children's collage of these fragments in a here-and-now frame took some elements—sounds, movements, clothes, and other objects—as external support for their actions. Given the culturally attributed characteristics of these items, they allowed the reproduction of past experiences in the play situation through highly imitative gestures that reproduced quite well the postures, expressions, and verbalizations that occur in the children's social environment.

In order to apprehend the construction of imagination by the children, we describe the evolution of their play.

1. At 2 years of age, very short periods of gestural complementation in a script were observed, where the script was often modified by the new gestures that were used.

*Vania (age 1;9–1 year, 9 months) carefully rubs a wooden block on another block, as if rubbing soap on a sponge, and then rubs it carefully, from the front to the back, in Telma's (1;11) hair, in a gesture similar to combing hair, asking, with her face quite close to Telma's and looking into her eyes: "Bom, né?" [It's good! Isn't it?].*

*Vania (now 2;0) rubs a toy dog's head with a little piece of wood (as if combing it), and puts it in the dog's mouth (as if offering it some food).*

2. At a subsequent moment a better definition of the theme can be noticed and the children are more easily seen participating in the network of meanings circulating in the situation, as they produce successively better approximations of the basic gestures, facial expressions, body postures, and verbalizations that are frequently seen in interpersonal moments, by using various objects symbolically and presenting more aspects of the basic roles:

*Vania (age 2;1), sitting on the floor, uses a spoon like a mixer inside a cup. She stands up and shows the researcher the cup she left on the floor, saying: "Papá, tia, papá!" [That's food, teacher, food!]. She pretends to eat something and exclaims: "Bom!" [Good!]. Looking to the spoon and the cup on the floor, she says, smiling: "Papá, tia, papá!" [Food, teacher, food!]. She picks them up and says: "Qué? Papá!" [. . . want some? Food!]. She sits down, examines the object and looks to the researcher, saying: "Qué?" [. . . want some?]. She makes a gesture of mixing the spoon in the cup, takes it out, then puts it in her mouth and again in the cup. She looks to John (age 2;4), who is playing with a plastic hammer, and says, in an authoritarian tone: "Papa, João, papa!" [Eat it, John, come on, eat!].*

While interacting, the children try, in many ways, to involve a partner in their script, negotiating shared meanings for their symbolic play. The partner to whom the gestures of preparing and offering juice are directed changes during the episode: It is the peer, oneself, or a play dog or doll. Gradations in some attitudes are observed: For instance, the child offers food in many ways, from stimulating the partner to eat to obligating the partner to eat.

3. With the development of the symbolic function, the child detaches his or her action from the existing external circumstances and acts more mediated by images. An increasing thematic amplification is also observed. Besides the play scripts about child care (combing another child's or a doll's hair, offering food to someone else or to a doll, disciplining a doll or putting it in bed) and daily routines (calling someone on the phone, celebrating a birthday) observed in Group A1, Group A2 also performed scripts related to more general aspects of their social world (playing cops and robbers, driving on a road).

Control over coordination processes of roles is initially dominated by the affective sphere, and the children explore lived situations in their make-believe play by emotive-postural channels. Gradually, their actions become more subordinated to the cognitive domain, being increasingly mediated by language.

*Fabio (3;10) pretends to pour the contents of an empty plastic bottle over his head, puts the bottle on the floor, and tells Davi (3;6), standing beside him: "Põe na cabeça! assim!" [Put it on your head! Like this!] while he cups his hands and passes them carefully in his hair.*

4. The amplification of the elements the children include in their scripts appears more clearly in the 4- to 6-year-old groups of Study B. In them, script construction was mediated not only by a canonical use of the available material—pencils, paper—and by an imitation of interactive formats experienced by the children in their day-care activities, but also by the spatial arrangement they prepared as scenery: lining the chairs up one behind the other, for instance. With these elements, they were challenged to enact, in a very ritualistic way, the teacher's and the students' roles in the school script they were invited to play, introducing these constraining systems to canalize their possible actions. Comparing these data with the videotapes we made of the interactions these children had with their caregiver in the day-care instructional activities, we could see how a collective reproduction of the scenes lived by the group in its daily experiences appears in play.

*The girl in the role of a teacher looks at the children in the role of students. They are making a mess. She says: "Silence! Come on, come on, one, two ..." They continue to talk. The girl-teacher takes the scissors she holds with her right hand and tries to get the children's attention by beating it on the table. She says: "Shut up! Shut up! Stop talking now! One, two, three . . ." and passes three fingers of her left hand in front of her mouth, pretending she is closing a zipper. Three of the children repeat her gesture.*

In sum, in their interactions in play, children try to bring up and coordinate a great number of elements into the present situation, mediated by their emerging imagination: the ornaments, postures, and locutions that constitute the situation. They try to enact various roles by imitating present or previous partners and, sometimes, by opposing them, changing the meanings they confront through their actions.

## INTERNALIZATION OF PLAY: THE EMERGENCE OF FANTASY

The internalization of this process of role coordination that occurs in symbolic play leads children to the realm of emerging fantasy in adolescence, as imagination leads play to become organized by semiotic mediating devices. As a result, the aesthetic relatedness of the adolescent's fantasy with the world is predicated on the semiotic organization of the *Einfühlung* ("inner feeling," according to Lipps, 1920) or *empathy* (as it is usually known in psychological terminology), which starts from child's play. In it,

> The child, playing with a doll raises the lifeless thing temporarily to the place of a symbol of life. He lends the doll his own soul whenever he answers a question for it; he lends to it his feelings, conceptions, and aspirations; he gives to it the pretense of mobility by posing it in a manner that implies movement, or by simple fiat when he asserts that it has nodded, or beckoned, or opened its mouth. Here the assemblance to aesthetic sympathy is already strong, and still further augmented by the use of the child's own body as the instrument of his mimic play. His attitudes and positions are then symbolic. (Groos, 1908, p. 327)

One of the essential features of adolescence, according to Vygotsky (1994), is the liberation from purely concrete imagistic features, accompanied by the infiltration of thought by abstract elements. During adolescence, there is a profound transformation of the imagination: its objectivation, promoted by the antagonisms, antitheses, and polarities that characterize that age period. An adolescent's imagination has a less visual character than that of a child, and demonstrates an inner drive for creative expression. It makes an external rapprochement with thinking in concepts and entertains a peculiar relationship between the abstract and the concrete. Released from the concrete situation, the imagination reworks and transforms its elements. Although it appears as a solitary entity, it is influenced by different personalities and groups.

In order to discuss the adolescent's fantasy, let us look carefully into the case of a young girl, Aurore (actually the novelist George Sand), also reported by Sully (1896, pp. 509–512). In her autobiography (Jurgrau, 1991), she elaborated the personal coconstructive processes of adolescence one of us analyzed elsewhere (Lawrence, Benedikt, & Valsiner, 1992).

Aurore grew up in the 19th century, in a devoutly Catholic French community. The social event of her first communion served as the starting point for her personal reconstruction of a religion in her fantasy world and its externalization in her personal environment. Aurore was challenged by the difference between the meaning system of the church ritual and the irreverent set of nonreligious suggestions presented by her grandmother (who, nevertheless, was present at the ceremony):

> It was a hard ordeal. The incongruous appearance of the deistic grandmamma in the place sufficed in itself to throw the girl's thoughts into disorder. She felt the hollowness of the whole thing, and asked herself whether she and her grandmother were not committing an act of hypocrisy. More than once her repugnance reached such a pitch that she thought of getting up and saying to her grandmother, "Enough of this: let us go away!" But relief came in another shape. Going over the scene of the *Last Supper* in her thoughts, she all at once recognized that the words of Jesus "This is my body and my blood" were nothing but a metaphor. He was too holy and too great to have wished to deceive his disciples. The discovery of the symbolism of the rite calmed her by removing all feelings of its grotesqueness. (Sully, 1896, pp. 509–510)

To restore the equilibrium of her religious beliefs, Aurore's imagination became occupied with the construction of a new private religion, into which nobody else could interfere: "Since all religion is fiction, let me create a novel which might be a religion, or a religion which might be a novel" (Jurgrau, 1991, p. 605).

The form of this new religion and of the new deity (Corambé) came to her in a dream. As an imaginary construction, Corambé was made to fit Aurore's personal needs:

> *Corambé was created by itself in my mind. It was as pure and as charitable as Jesus, as shining and handsome as Gabriel; but I needed a little of nymphic grace and Orpheus' poetry. Consequently it took on less austere forms than the Christian God and more spiritual aspects than the gods of Homer. And then, I also had to complement it at times with a woman's garb, because what I had loved best and understood best until then was a woman—my mother. Hence it often appeared to me with female features. . . . I wanted to love it as a friend, as a sister, all the while giving it the reverence of a god. I did not want to fear it, and for that reason, I wished it to have a few of our failings and weaknesses. (Jurgrau, 1991, p. 605)*

The construction of the personage in Aurore's mind was an active and sensible process of modeling its special characteristics. Human cultural traits were combined by her to dress the created God. Yet, the need for external support for her fantasy led to further development: the making of a temple, a task performed with care and detail. A scenery, thus, was created, according to a general script:

> *My imagination transformed a three-foot high mound into a mountain, a few trees into a forest; a footpath which went from the house to the meadow into the road that leads to the end of the world; the pond bordered with ancient willows into a whirlpool or a lake, according to my whim. And I saw my fictional characters moving, running off together, dreamily walking alone, sleeping in the shade, or singing and dancing in this paradise of my idle dreams.* (Jurgrau, 1991, p. 606)

Aurore's imaginary construction also developed in the form of sacred songs and books that she created for her god orally and in her mind. These events made Aurore become self-occupied, even during her social group's activities:

> *At first I was quite conscious of this labor of mine, but after a very short time, perhaps a few days (for a child a day seems like three), I felt possessed by my subject much more than it was possessed by me. The daydream came to be a sort of sweet hallucination, but so frequent and sometimes so perfect, that it left me as if transported out of this world.* (Jurgrau, 1991, p. 606)

*Possession* and *hallucination* are her words to describe her immersion in her fantasy, seeing herself forced to play various of its roles. The sanctuary, however, was discovered one day by a playmate boy who tracked Aurore to her secret place. That violation of her private world put a dramatic end to her imaginary construction. She saw herself from outside of her fantasy, through the eyes of general disapproval:

> *From the moment other feet than mine had tread the sanctuary, Corambé no longer lived there. The dryads and cherubs abandoned it, and my rituals and sacrifices seemed to me no more than a puerility than even I myself had not taken seriously. I destroyed the temple with as much care as I had taken to erect it.* (Jurgrau, 1991, p. 610)

This episode in the life of George Sand provides us with some glimpses into the coordinated construction of the intra-actional (fantasy) and the externalized imaginary (play) worlds. The whole personal construction by the girl was clearly canalized by the religious context within which she grew up. Yet an episode (involving oppositional role construction during the first communion) led the conflicting child to invent Corambé, and to attribute to him new characteristics that fitted the girl's personal world. That imaginary construction was externally supported by the construction of a private shrine (which lasted as long as it was maintained as private; see Simmel, 1906, on the secrecy construction) and rituals, with their fictional personages.

Fantasy allows the imaginative activity to be transformed from action (and interaction) to the intra-personal domain of psychological functioning, thus distancing the reflective domain from the actional. It leads the cognitive and affective aspects of psychological functioning to be interwoven while individual experiences are elaborated. The protective nature of that activity operates in ways that lead the person to transform himself or herself, to recast relations to the world. As the person acts on the world, the latter becomes transformed as well, in accordance with the person's imagination. Life completely free of imagination is not possible for human beings; if it is restricted in the domain of action, it becomes available in the internalized world of fantasy. In the particular case of Aurore, her imaginative experiences gave her a basis for constructing her later role as a writer. Besides giving form to many characters in her novels, she created her own personage, defining a public identity for herself: someone wearing man's clothes and named George.

## THE EMERGENCE OF ROLES IN PRETEND PLAY: A LOOK AT THEIR DETERMINATION

We now analyze one of the play episodes of our young children to discuss the process of role emergence and its (in)determination.

Situation: Five children aged 3;2 to 3;10 are in the room for more than 6 minutes. They play alone with the objects, occasionally exchanging comments.

*At a certain moment, Wellington tries to put a belt around his waist. He is standing near Fernando, who takes a cowboy hat and put it roughly on his head, breaking the leather strap that is used to hold the hat under the chin. Fernando, with a worried face, goes toward the researcher and asks her: "Quebrou?" [Is it broken?], which is observed by Wellington. The researcher, in a friendly tone, replies: "Quebrou? Não faz mal. Põe na cabeça!" [Is it broken? It doesn't matter. Put it on your head!]. Fernando puts the hat on, holding it with one hand and holding the hanging strap with the other, while Wellington synchronically performs the same gesture, holding the belt's extremities with both hands. After that, Wellington raises his right arm holding high the belt, smiling, and says: "Todo mundo vai apanhar! Vai apanhar, o filho!" [Everybody is going to be bitten! The son is going to get it!] He goes to the mattress near which Daniel and Maristela are playing with some toys, and hits the mattress three times with the belt. Daniel cries.*

*Maristela looks at Wellington, raises her right hand toward her face with an expression of fear, bends her body backward, away from the mattress, and says, in a dramatic way: "Papai! Papai!" [Oh, Daddy! Daddy!], looking at Wellington. After that, she turns back to play with her toys with a peaceful expression. At the same time, Daniel, who has a very disturbed expression, moves off the mattress, circling his head with one of his arms, as if to protect himself, and looks at Wellington, who lies down supine on the mattress and smiles. Wellington raises his trunk, sits beside the mattress, hits it twice with the belt, and looks alternatively at Daniel and Maristela. She immediately looks at Wellington and exclaims: "Pa-pai! Pa-pai!" [Dad-dy! Dad-dy!], in a whining voice, stressing the syllable Dad. He asks her: "Quem foi que te bateu? . . . Ele?" [Who hit you? . . . Him?], pointing at Daniel, at the same time that Maristela also points to him, and hits the mattress twice with the belt near Daniel, who looks at Wellington and covers his face with his right arm. Wellington puts the belt around his waist and goes calmly to manipulate some toys together with another girl in another area of the playroom.*

Through the children's actions, certain signs are framed from the many meanings that are being constructed in the situation and are structuring it. In the episode, some historically constructed symbols related to the father–child relationship come to the foreground of the many meanings circulating around the children's interactions.

The role of an authoritarian father is built up by Wellington on the basis of a belt he found on the floor and after observing Fernando interacting with the researcher regarding the broken hat strap. The expectation of a punishment, maybe predictable in his group's culture, but frustrated by the adult's refusal to assume an authoritarian role, can be interpreted to have influenced Wellington, who had observed the scene. As if in an emphatic state with his partner, Wellington raised over his head the belt he was holding by its extremities with both hands, imitating the gesture of putting the hat on that was suggested to Fernando. Performing this action seemed to open new possibilities for meaning construction as shown in the subsequently elaborated make-believe play. Wellington puts his arm down, raised the belt again with one hand, pulled it down, held its two extremities together, smiling with a playful face, and then began to enact an authoritarian's father role, framing the word *son* ("The son is going to be beaten!"). These elements led Maristela to quickly assume the complementary son/daughter role. Her dramatic frightened expression, "Daddy!," acted as a cue to stimulate the continuation of the symbolic play script, while Daniel, beside her, seemed to be genuinely disturbed by Wellington's performance and did not actively enter into the created script. However, his self-protective gestures and annoyed expressions were enough to encourage the other children to attribute the role of aggressor to him.

The children took some aspects of this episode as emerging signs that prompted them to take certain roles related to the background script being collectively constructed. In their interactions, the children's interpretations of the present events became interwoven with their memories of experienced situations. The delayed imitation of various aspects of their experience that characterizes their symbolic play involved the increasing differentiation of the original elements that were brought into the situation. That reproduction was not cognitively predelineated, however, but emerged as the actual elements gave the children new opportunities to deal with socially constructed meaning systems. The children imitated the model by ritualized gestures, using some objects in a symbolic way as substitutes for others. However, that imitation in play did not bind them to already experienced situations, but liberated them from the past, as they controlled it by volitional repetition and images. In this way, they went beyond historical boundaries.

Play demands that children take new roles that recombine and transform their meaning systems, using all their memories and skills. When they do so, the roles involved in the play situation are brought up to date. By recombining the meanings being created, they could make the belt become a semiotic marker of emerging representations. Nevertheless, although it helped Wellington to perform the authoritarian father's role, that role was subsequently transformed, as some of its contradictions were examined in a vivid way through his peers' interactions. The children also found out, for instance, that besides being someone who punishes, "father" is also a person who protects.

The same dialectical opposition between being submitted to social roles and, because of that, transforming them as they have to to fit the always-new aspects of every situation, is seen in Aurore's fantasy. She was committed to both reproduction and novelty. The more she was possessed by cultural roles, the more she developed her capacities to explore their antagonisms and transform them.

## GENERAL CONCLUSIONS

The transformational nature of the internalization process enables social experiences, structured in specific ways, to gradually lead to the construction of the individual's intrapsychological cognitive-affective system. In relation to the construction of imagination and fantasy, it involves the personal reconstruction of suggestions taken from the social world. This kind of personal constructivity of symbolic forms (Cassirer, 1953; Ohnuki-Tierney, 1981) is embedded in a culturally organized context, within which different other people, while interacting with the child, attempt to guide his or her semiotic action constructivity, supporting or constricting it in a goal-oriented way. These social others, however, have expectations, intentions, and objectives in the actions they take while interacting with the child, some of them related with his or her development, but they cannot predict which exact outcome will occur because they have to coordinate their actions with the child's own intentions and objectives.

That elaboration does not occur based only on cognitive-linguistic growing abilities, but also in the cognitive-postural expressions of feelings. These abilities and feelings, on the other hand, are recreated as part of a whole drama, in which the similar, the complementary, and the antagonistic roles that children enact constitute the mechanism they use to confront themselves with their peers, in order to attain their emerging goals. Play gives support for the child's emancipation from situational constraints, leading to abstraction and creativity. Play is an occasion for recreating culture and for rule-learning in an interactional setting, with plenty of conflicts of different positions and inherent negotiations. It allows children to reflect on social rules and to become aware of their roles and their partners' roles in the network of social relationships, as they take their partners' roles and examines them in relation to their own actions (in many cases attributing their own role to a play partner or to a toy).

That process appears clearly in make-believe play, which, creating an "as if" atmosphere, allows the actualization of internalized regulations first built up with adults. Children examine, modify, and internalize these regulations at the same time. In doing so, they become able to internally master certain roles' relationships, taking different points of view to determine how to construct and attain their goals while interacting with other individuals, who have their own, frequently opposite, intentions. The route for innovation is established, once again.

Some of the contents of different fantasy scenarios are suggested within interpersonal (and mass) communication and have fundamental value for human development. However, as with domains of new knowledge, these broad suggestions entail socialization for ignorance in some domains of activity (Moore & Tumin, 1949). For instance, numerous traditions exist in the realm of persuading people to accept predictions of their futures (e.g., fortune-telling, see Aphek & Tobin, 1990), which, of course, are embedded within the general folkloric practices in the society.

At the same time, the future-oriented functioning of psychological processes makes it possible for fantasy to become a powerful internal regulator of actions: enabling, restricting, or dismissing semiotic encodings of its domain. The semiotically mediated nature of the fantasy domain, despite its being a personal creation, maintains the canalizing functions of the social world in a highly unique, intrapersonal and subjective coconstruction process. The person, creating a scenario of an imaginary horror, blocks himself from acting along the lines of such a scenario or makes a fantasy to lead himself in the direction of becoming disengaged from it. Fantasy production, then, is a culturally canalized, semiotically encoded, and personally coconstructed domain of constant subjective innovation.

The construction of the intra-actional sphere (fantasy) and the externalized imaginary world (play) brings some essential transformations in human development. By making the effort to deal with the social masks and roles that constrain and support conduct and being modified by them at the same time, the singularity of each boy and girl, man and woman, is constructed. A future dimension is thus present in human and cultural development, always creating novelty and history.

## ACKNOWLEDGMENTS

The first author was funded by Brazilian agencies FAPESP and CNPQ to develop this research project.

## REFERENCES

Aphek, E., & Tobin, Y. (1990). *The semiotics of fortune-telling*. Amsterdam: John Benjamins.
Baldwin, J. M. (1895). The origin of a "thing" and its nature. *Psychological Review, 2*, 551–572.
Baldwin, J. M. (1906). *Thought and things: A study of the development and meaning of thought, or genetic logic. Vol. 1. Functional logic, or genetic theory of knowledge*. London: Swan Sonnenschein.
Bergson, H. (1889). *Essai sur les données immédiates de la conscience* [Essay on the immediate duration of consciousness]. Paris: PUF. (Reedited in 1948)
Buhler, C. (1967). *Das Seeleleben des Jugendlichen* [The soul-life of the youngsters]. Stuttgart: Gustav Fischer.
Bullinger, A. (1993). Emotion and representation. *Enfance, 1*, 27–32.
Cassirer, E. (1953). *The philosophy of symbolic forms (1925–29)* (3 Vols.). New Haven, CT: Yale University Press.
Elbers, E. (1994). Sociogenesis and children's pretend play: A variation on Vygotskian Themes. In W. DeGraaf & R. Maier (Eds.), *Sociogenesis Reexamined* (pp. 219–241). New York: Springer.
Fogel, A. (1992). Movement and communication in human infancy: The social dynamics of development. *Human Movement Science, 11*, 387–423.
Gaskins, S., & Göncú, A. (1992). Cultural variation in play: A challenge to Piaget and Vygotsky. *The Quarterly Newsletter of the Laboratory of Comparative Human Cognition, 14*(2), 31–35.
Groos, K. (1908). *The play of man*. New York: D. Appleton.
Guillaume, P. (1925). *L'imitation chez l'enfant* [Imitation in childhood]. Paris: Felix Alcan.
Haigt, W. (1994). Pretend play: A cultural and developmental phenomenon. In A. Alvarez & P. Del Rio (Eds.), *Education as cultural construction* (pp. 53–60). Vol. 3 of P. Del Rio, A. Alvarez, & J. Wertsch (General Eds.), Explorations in Socio-cultural Studies. Madrid, Fundación Infancia y Aprendizaje.
Janet, P. (1929). *L'evolution psychologique de la personalité* [Psychological evolution of personality]. Paris: A. Chachine.
James, W. (1890). *Principles of psychology*. New York: Holt.
Jurgrau, T. (Ed.). (1991). *Story of my life: The autobiography of George Sand*. Albany: State University of New York Press.

Lawrence, J. A., Benedikt, R., & Valsiner, J. (1992). Homeless in the mind: A case history of personal life in and out a close orthodox community. *Journal of Social Distress and the Homeless, 1*(2), 157–176.

Lipps, T. (1920). *Aesthetik* (third ed.). Leipzig: Leopold Voss.

Lyra, M. C., & Rossetti-Ferreira, M. C. (1995). Understanding the co-constructive nature of human development: Role coordination in early peer interaction. In J. Valsiner & H. G. Voss (Eds.), *Structure of the learning processes* (pp. 51–77). Norwood, NJ: Ablex.

Mead, G. H. (1934). *Mind, self and society*. Chicago: University of Chicago Press.

Moore, W. E., & Tumin, M. M. (1949). Some social functions of ignorance. *American Sociological Review, 14*, 787–795.

Moreno, J. L. (1934). *Who shall survive?* Reedited in 1952 as *Foundations of sociometry, group psychotherapy and sociodrama*. Boston: Beacon House.

Ohnuki-Tierney, E. (1981). Phases in human perception/conception/symbolization processes: Cognitive anthropology and symbolic classification. *American Ethnologist, 8*, 451–467.

Oliveira, Z. M. R., & Rossetti-Ferreira, M. C. (1993, March). *Can the concept of 'role' help to understand the internalization process?* Paper presented at LX Meeting of SRCD, New Orleans, LA.

Ortega, R. (1994). El juego sociodramático como context para la compreensión social [The sociodramatic game as a social understanding context]. In A. Alvarez & P. Del Rio (Eds.), *Education as cultural construction* (pp. 79–88). Vol. 3 of P. del Rio, A. Alvarez, & J. Wertsch (General Eds.). Explorations in Socio-Cultural Studies. Madrid, Fundación Infancia y Aprendizaje.

Piaget, J. (1946). *La formation du symbole chez l'enfant* [Formation of symbol in the child]. Neuchâtel/Paris: Delachaux/Niestlé.

Ribot, T. (1926). *Essai sul l'imagination creatice* [Essay on creative imagination]. (7th ed.). Paris: Felix Alcan.

Sarbin, T. (1950). Contributions to role-taking theory: I. Hypnotic Behavior. *Psychological Review, 57*(5), 255–270.

Schaffer, H. F. (1984). *The child's entry into a social world*. London: Academic Press.

Sherif, M. (1936). *The psychology of social norms*. New York: Harper & Brothers.

Simmel, G. (1906). The sociology of secrecy and of secret societies. *American Journal of Sociology, 11*(4), 441–498.

Stern, W. (1938). *General psychology*. New York: Macmillan.

Sully, J. (1896). *Studies of childhood*. New York: D. Appleton.

Van Der Veer, R., & Valsiner, J. (1991). *Understanding Vygotsky. A quest for synthesis*. Oxford, England: Blackwell.

Vygotsky, L. S. (1933/1966). Igra i ee rol' v psiknicheskom razvitii rebenka [Play and its role in the psychical development of the child]. *Voprosy Psikhologii, 12*(6), 62–76.

Vygotsky, L. S. (1935). *Osnovy pedologii* [Foundations of paedology]. Leningrad: Gosudarstvennyi Pedagogicheskii Institut im. A. Gertsena.

Vygotsky, L. S. (1986). *Thought and language* (2nd ed.). Cambridge, MA: MIT Press. (First Russian edition in 1934)

Vygotsky, L. S. (1990). Imagination and creativity in childhood. *Soviet Psychology, 28*(1), 84–96.

Vygotsky, L. S. (1994). Imagination and creativity of the adolescence. In R. Van der Veer & J. Valsiner (Eds.), *The Vygotsky reader* (pp. 266–288). Oxford: Blackwell.

Wallon, H. (1934). *Les origines du caractere chez l'enfant* [The origins of child's character]. Paris: Boivin.

Wallon, H. (1942). *De l'acte a la pensée: essai de psychologie camparée* [From the act to thought: Essay on comparative psychology]. Paris: Flammarion.

Wallon, H. (1959). Le role de "l'autre" dans la conscience du "moi." *Enfance, 3–4*, 279–285.

Wertsch, J. V., & Stone, A. C. (1985). The concept of internalization in Vygotski account of the genesis of higher mental functions. In J. V. Wertsch (Ed.), *Culture, communication and cognition: Vygotskian perspectives* (pp. 162–179). Cambridge, England: Cambridge University Press.

# 6

# From Disordered to Ordered Movement: Attractor Configuration and Development

Maria Isabel Pedrosa
Universidade Federal de Pernambuco, Brazil

Ana M. A. Carvalho
Amélia Império-Hamburger
Universidade de São Paulo, Brazil

PEDROSA, CARVALHO, IMPÉRIO-HAMBURGER
In this chapter, we analyze psychological phenomena within the framework of attractor configurations resulting from a self-organization process in a group of children playing in a room. The epistemological framework of Perrin's 1909 analysis of the Brownian movement of small particles in suspension in a fluid as due to the incessant and irregular movements of the molecules in the medium is adopted as an heuristic tool to account for some of the common features in physical and psychological phenomena: indeterministic and deterministic interactions, disordered and ordered movements, coherent and noncoherent movements, and discontinuous and continuous transformations.

A free-play group of young children, ages 2;6 (2 years, 6 months) to 3;0, is considered here as a system whose ordered states are a product of the interactive, coregulating actions of the component individuals. Interactions are sources of group and interindividual actions and, at the same time, constitute the individuals as unique developing systems, evolving in time.

This kind of analysis is already recognized as useful for physical, chemical, and biological systems (Haken, 1978; Prigogine & Nicolis, 1971) and, more recently, in the field of psychological development (Fogel, 1993; Fogel & Thelen, 1987; Vallacher & Nowak, 1994). Fogel (1993) used the concept of *attractor* to refer to repeated patterns that appear in behavioral observational data, and then, from a dynamic systems perspective, derived the model of consensual frames formation in a complex system; he found "*dynamic systems models extremely heuristic for the purpose of understanding relationships development because they suggest that complex systems can converge toward a stable pattern of behavior without a prescription or plan, merely by the mutually constraining influences of the components. The concept of attractor suggests that it is mathematically possible to model a system in which such convergence occurs spontaneously*" (Fogel, 1993, p. 105).

In our analysis, the subjects' actions are construed as being performed in a field of interactions, where information is exchanged and collective configurations emerge through a self-organization process. This perspective allows for the definition of a *space of information* (signification or meaning), a theoretical concept, analogous to the several concepts of space used in Physics, defined as places (loci) where the objects of thought and experience are situated. The space of information has "*the role of a 'medium' to whose existence the individual parts of a system contribute and from which they obtain specific information on how to behave in a coherent, cooperative fashion*" (Haken, 1988, p. 23). In our context, the space of information is a supraindividual or interindividual locus where information is created and exchanged, and shared attributions of meaning take place. It defines the psychological scope of social phenomena, in a line of thought we believe is fruitful to frame the analysis of individual–social relationships (Carvalho, 1992).

Meanings are constructed when two or more individuals share them; with them, a new quality emerges in the system, through a process where there is a compression of the available information, and new information activates more complex collective states. The space of meanings is constituted by linguistic expressions, such as body movements, gestures, sighs, laughs, and other manifestations besides verbal language; it includes cognitive and emotional features (Fogel et al., 1992).

## Freedom and Constraints

The present analysis considers the dynamics between deterministic (causal) laws manifested by the *correlations* that lead to collective wholes through coregulation processes and the indeterministic spontaneous manifestations at the "free" individual level: the deviations from the deterministic law in Epicure's "clinamen" (Serres, 1977).

The concept of correlation is central in our analysis. Correlations are the exercise or actualization, in the form of actions, of a common property or potentiality of the components of the system—in the present case, properties such as "sociability" (Carvalho, 1992) or "attribution of meanings" (Pedrosa, 1989). It may be realized by any interacting agents, and it occurs in such a way that coherent collective states emerge through the abbreviation of the information present in current noncoherent actions. As Haken put it, "*although . . . the exchange of information may initially occur at random, a competition or cooperation between different kinds of signals sets in, and eventually a new collective state is reached which differs qualitatively from the disordered or uncorrelated states present before*" (Haken, 1988, p. 27).

As this *self-organizing* process takes place in the system, correlated actions (actions that actualize common properties of the components) can converge into *quasi*stable configurations or recognizable patterns, the *attractors* (Haken, 1988). The concept of attractor refers to the mathematical properties of curves in a system of equations that allow them to converge at specific points or trajectories as a function of time (Fiedler-Ferrara & Prado, 1994; Fogel, 1993). It is an order parameter that serves a double role: "*It informs the atoms (the systems' components) how to behave, and, in addition, it informs the observer about the macroscopic ordered state of the system*" (Haken, 1988, p. 25).

From this perspective, the tasks of developmental researchers would be: (a) to identify the constraining influences or deterministic correlation laws that are present in the developing system they are focusing on; (b) to develop an understanding of how the chaos, freedom, or uncertainty that are intrinsic to dynamic, open systems can produce ordered or recognizable stable states within the continuous transformation that constitutes the ontogenetic process; and (c) to identify stable states and changes in this process.[1] Each of these tasks implies overcoming strictly causal or deterministic explanations through the exercise of a new type of logical reasoning (Haken, 1988; Império-Hamburger, 1990a), as pointed out by Wallon, as early as 1942: "*The effect is not exterior to the act: it is simultaneously its result and its regulator*" (Wallon, 1979, p. 83).

## Development: Change and Stability

The ontogeny of a system is a process through which functions and temporarily stable states are constituted and transformed. Functions and stable states can be thought of as products that mark the process in the sense of becoming recognizable by the interactants or developing beings (Nadel & Fontaine, 1989). An observer can frame these products as significant events in the flow of observations, create concepts about them, and relate these concepts in theories (Império-Hamburger, 1990b).

In agreement with the evolutionary epistemological perspective that guides our analysis, when a product arises, it doesn't appear as completely

---

[1]For recent literature in the field of social psychology, see, for instance, Nowak and Lewenstein (1994), and Baron, Amazeen, and Beek (1994).

new. It is as if it were already contained in the previous processes—but this doesn't mean it is preformed. When it is methodologically possible to go back in time and analyze how the product emerged, clues or signs of its future realization can sometimes be recognized, although this existence can seldom be predicted beforehand.

A possible metaphor for developmental processes is the behavior of water vapors in the atmosphere: they move randomly, but, under certain conditions, they group together and form clouds—a recognizable product; they can then condense and form rain, or they can also disperse and return to a state of random movement. Clouds and rain are *products, recognizable moments* of a continuous process of transformation. They are not more evolved or more developed than other moments. They are also part of the process, but they have a quality of momentary stability that makes them recognizable.

Everything that happens in a dynamic system is the actualization of possibilities already present in the system: its properties, processes, and available information. The system contains its own future. Development involves transformation and conservation, change and stability, to be and being, product and process. Development can thus be defined as a dialectical process through which the system transforms itself while maintaining its identity as a system.

Human development, as well as other self-organizing systems' development, can be thought of as an intrinsically nonpredictable chain (in a classical sense) of manifested states or functions of species-specific potentialities; of these, the most primary is that development can only happen in a *social environment* (Wallon, 1979; Vygotsky, 1978; Valsiner, 1991). This reciprocally constitutive social–individual relationship appears as a fundamental law of human interaction, a basic rationality expressed, in a mathematical sense, as a ratio between part and whole (Império-Hamburger, 1996). In the following analysis of a play episode involving young children, we try to discern how the social whole constitutes, and is constituted by, individual actions that exhibit both deterministic and indeterministic dynamic aspects.

## DATA AND ANALYSIS

The episode to be analyzed was selected from a videorecording of free-play activities in a group of 2;6- to 3;0-year-old children in a low-income day-care center in São Paulo, Brazil. This record is part of a longitudinal study in which the children were observed weekly over 12 months in the same settings (indoor or outdoor free-play). The episode involves seven children, two boys and five girls, mean age 2;9. The only adult present in the room was the observer. The room was empty, except for the shelves along the

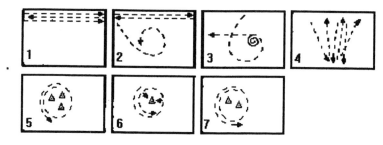

Sequence

| | |
|---|---|
| 1 | Running across the room and falling down |
| 2 | Two groups on different routes: across the room, and along a circular route |
| 3 | Whirling, hand-in-hand |
| 4 | Running to the end of the room and back to the opposite wall |
| 5 | Running around squatting partners ("dogs") |
| 6 | Running around a seated child and patting her head |
| 7 | Running around the "dogs" |

FIG. 6.1. Schematic representation of the group organization along the episode.

walls, where toys and other objects were kept. The total duration of the episode was 6 minutes, 34 seconds; the analysis divides it into seven sequences of variable duration, according to the changes in the interactional dynamics and in the spatial structure of the group. These sequences are depicted in Fig. 6.1, using an abstract drawing intended to represent the group configuration in each sequence. The lines depict the observer's apprehension of the group's configurations, arrows indicating the direction of the trajectories. Triangles represent individual children's positions. A synthesis of the episode is presented next.

## Running in the Room

Previous setting: *Five children enter the room coming from lunch. There are no adult caretakers with them. The children are very excited; they run around randomly, laugh, and vocalize, making a lot of noise. One of them (Dani, a girl, 3;0) is heard calling out: "Eu caí!" ("I fell down!").*

Synthesis of the episode: *The children run across the room with varied rhythms, following routes that are organized and modified along the way: running from one wall to the opposite; falling down; running in circles; two children whirling, hand-in-hand; running in circles around other children who are squatting and pretending to be dogs. There are very few verbal exchanges, but a lot of vocalizations follow the rhythm of the movements. Six other children arrive while the record is made, and two of them engage in the ongoing game. The sequence is interrupted by the arrival of a caretaker, who offers the children a box of toys. The episode reveals dynamic transformations of the group, in which some mo-*

*ments of organization can be recognized through the group's spatial and social configuration; but they cannot be predicted from the prior state of the group or from the individual actions of its members.*

## Group Configuration and the Shared Attribution of Meanings

The identified sequences frame the flow of activities that were recorded. The duration of the sequences varies: some of them last a few seconds (e.g., the first sequence) and others last about 2 minutes (e.g., the fifth). The precise temporal limits of the sequences cannot be established, because the transition from one sequence to the other is a result of the observer's recognition of a pattern or a new configuration. The representation that characterizes a sequence, thus, does not include its whole duration: It is, rather, a scheme of the various related actions of the children.

The configuration is the result of a set of properties of a situation that leads to part of it being perceptually or conceptually highlighted, like a figure against a background. The recognition of a configuration is, in itself, an act of signification. If the attribution of meaning occurred only at the individual level, the process could not be identified, either by the observer or by the play partners; but if the actions of two or more individuals are seen as related through similarity, complementarity, or reciprocity (Camaioni, 1980), a shared act of signification can become recognized and can thus acquire a regulating potential—both for the partners and for the observer whose task is to frame and to build an understanding of the situation.

The shared attributions of meaning originate the correlations that organize the activity in the direction of new meanings—a deterministic aspect of the process. There is, however, an inherent uncertainty in the process of signification. The attributed meaning may not correspond exactly to the other person's attribution; the actions may express correlations in which the correspondence is only partial. This uncertainty and the occurrence of random activities that do not adjust to the configurations constitute a state of disorder that may function as an *activating principle* of the interactional process, because it is a source of potential meanings that can eventually (though not necessarily) be actualized in shared configurations. This potentiality can be considered as an indeterministic aspect of the process, because meanings emerge as novelties regarding the present state of organization of the system, even if their emergence can be related to other levels of organization (e.g., the individual agent's).

In the next item, our analysis is targeted at following the transitions from one sequence to the next in the episode and making explicit the constitution of attractor configurations, that are understood here as manifestations of the property of convergence in the system. We look both for deterministic correlation laws inherent to young children's interactions, and to the aspects of the situation that "escape" the attractors and characterize *disorder* or *chaos* as a moment in which no correlated actions, no organization, and no direction can be discerned.

## Spatial Attractors: Sequences 1 to 4

*Sequence 1. Alex (a boy, 2;9) runs from one side of the room to the other and falls down on all fours when he reaches the wall. Dani (girl, 3;0) follows him and runs back to the opposite wall. Alex joins her and they run together across the room; Dani reaches the wall and bends down as if she were falling, with one of her hands against the wall. From the center of the room, Telma (girl, 2;8) looks at them.*

By running together along the same route, Alex and Dani create a configuration in the previously disordered movement of the group. In this configuration, Alex unexpectedly incorporates a new element: an intentional fall, possibly related to Dani's previous accidental fall, which was highlighted by her verbal comment ("*I fell down!*"). Dani, in her turn, confirms this incorporated element when she enacts a partial fall, which simplifies the movement and reduces its physical cost, but clearly preserves the shared configuration. The facts that a shared activity (running along the same route and falling down) is chosen by the children and that this configuration attracts the attention of a third child (Telma) can be attributed to laws of human sociability, such as recognizing, creating, and sharing information; the particular *form* of this information, however, emerged from accidents of the context, as when Alex chose to incorporate Dani's fall to the game and thus endowed it with a new meaning.

*Sequence 2. Telma runs toward Alex and Dani and joins them in their route across the room. As they reach the wall, they meet Vânia (girl, 2;10) who has been watching them. Telma displays a pretend fall in front of Dani and Vânia, bending her body, and then runs to the center of the room in a circular route. Vânia follows her. From the center of the room, Paola (girl, 2;11) looks at them and slowly introduces herself in the same route.*

Two different sequences are thus formed by the group of five children: Alex and Dani running across the room and "falling down" on reaching the wall; and the three other girls running in circles in the center of the room. Although their paths are different, it can be inferred from the direction of the gazes that the two groups are aware of each other. The cooccurrence of these two attractors is followed by a brief moment of dispersion of the group:

*Dani abandons her route, introduces herself partially to the circular route, then goes to the wall and leans against it with both hands, still looking at the others. The other children stop running. Telma walks around the room; Paola and Vânia walk toward a shelf where a sixth child (Vivi, girl, 2;6) can now be seen playing with pacifiers; Alex joins Dani near the wall.*

Although Dani's action contained elements of the previously shared configurations, as if juxtaposing them (running in the circular route, then back to the wall and touching it as in previous pretend falls), and although the children were mutually oriented, this action was not incorporated to a new shared configuration. Instead, a new fact—Vivi's arrival—interfered in the organization of the group.

**Sequence 3.** *Dani resumes running in a circular route, followed by Alex. They come near Telma, who looks at them and walks away. Dani turns to Alex and puts out her hands, and they start whirling, hand-in-hand. Telma approaches them, followed by João (boy, 2;8) who has just arrived. Telma bends her body. Dani and Alex keep whirling around the room. Other children turn their attention to the whirling dyad. After Dani and Alex stop whirling, Paola puts her hand out to Alex; he falls down near her, then stands up, holds her hand, and offers his other hand to Dani, inviting her: "Vâmo!" ("Let's go!"). Dani ignores him. He holds Paola's hands, and they start whirling. The other children watch them and run around the room randomly. Telma puts her hands out to Vânia, who laughs and does not hold them. Telma runs away. Dani runs in the same direction. Paola and Alex keep whirling, then fall down. Laughing and play noises can be heard throughout the sequence.*

The whirling movement seems to be highlighted and functions as an organizing pole toward a new spatial attractor. It is displayed by two different dyads (although Alex is part of both), which indicates that the configuration belongs to the group and not only to individual members. It is observed and is clearly shared by most of the children, but it is not performed by all, perhaps because it is a difficult motor act at this age. It contains several elements of the previous group organization (running, making a circular route and falling down), but it incorporates an innovation (circular movements holding hands) which is lost further on in the sequence.

**Sequence 4.** *Two girls (Telma and Vivi) run together in a mutually oriented way from one side of the room to the other and touch the wall with both hands on reaching it. This same route is repeated several times with slight changes and increasing synchronization. João runs to the back wall, trying to engage in the same route; the girls refuse his participation, saying "não, João, não!" ("no, John, no!"), and he turns his attention to the other children (Dani, Paola and Alex), who are running in different routes across the room. Dani starts to walk around the room, dangling her head, and Alex imitates her. Paola, João, and Vivi, who has strayed away from her route with Telma, watch them and get closer. Dani sits down and is immediately followed by Vivi, Paola, Alex, and*

*João. Dani, Alex, and Paola stand up and run around João and Vivi, who stay seated.*

Once again, some aspects of a previous form of organization of the group are selected by individual children: Telma and Vivi running from one wall to the other and touching the walls with their hands, their rhythms mutually adjusted, like Dani and Alex in the first sequence. The rest of the group is dispersed and does not engage in this proposal, or in Dani's entirely new activity: walking around dangling her head, which is followed only by Alex. But their mutual attention and their readiness to create a joint activity—a shared meaning—becomes apparent when Dani sits down (which is possibly an elaboration of the previously shared action of falling down) and is instantly followed by the others. A new configuration is beginning at this moment, as is evident from the description of the next sequences of the episode.

## A Symbolic Attractor, and Coupled Attractors: Sequences 5–7

**Sequence 5.** *Vânia approaches the running children. Vivi, still seated, sing-songs and claps her hands. João crouches on all fours and "barks" at the other children, making moves toward them as if he were an attacking dog. Vânia crouches beside him and barks. Vivi crawls on all fours and moves around the room barking, followed by João and Vânia. The three other children laugh and keep running around them. The seventh child, Telma, joins the running group in the circular route around the "dogs." The circle is enlarged in order to include the moving "dogs." The children's movements are rhythmic and are accompanied by loud laughs and cries. Vivi stands up and joins the circular route. The "dogs," Vânia and João, make moves as if attacking the children who come closer to them. An adult caretaker arrives, but does not interfere with the game. Vânia stands up and joins the running group, leaving only João in the dog role. João barks and pretends to attack. The caretaker calls João to change his clothes. As soon as João leaves, Vivi squats on all fours, "barks" and turns her body, following the children who run around her. Then she stands up, and Vânia takes her place.*

**Sequence 6.** *Vânia suddenly stands and "walks" on her knees; she loses her balance and sits on her feet. This new posture seems to modify the perceived configuration: The running group gets closer to her. Dani pats Vânia's head and is imitated by the other children. Vânia leaves her "dog" role and complains, verbally, "Oh, Dani! Oh, Telma! . . ." The children run faster, and touch Vânia's head more frequently, often more than one at the same time. Vânia suddenly gets up on all fours and barks, creating a configuration similar to that in Sequence 5.*

*Sequence 7. The circular route is enlarged to include Vânia, who crawls around and pretends to be a menacing dog. João, his clothes changed, introduces himself into the middle of the circle, goes on all fours, and makes menacing moves. Vivi approaches the two "dogs." Vânia stands up and joins the running group. Vivi looks at João close up, and then runs away. Telma falls down near João. The caretaker offers the children a box full of toys; all the children move toward her, and the game is suspended.*

These three sequences are characterized by correlations in the two groups of children engaged in different activities, but composing a coupled configuration: Some children run around the others, who are squatting and pretending to be dogs. In the preceding sequence (Sequence 4), several actions were performed by different children, casually oriented toward each other. When the children squat together, they create the possibility of a unified direction of action, which is still not predictable. The foregoing description makes clear that some individual actions are integrated in the new configuration, whereas others are discarded. Dani, Alex, and Paola's coordinated running around the squatting children persists as a collective action; the similarity of their individual actions, creating a unity, seems to engender time persistence. On the other hand, the two squatting children take different courses of action: Vivi singsongs and claps her hands, while João stands on all fours and barks. One of these proposals is confirmed as part of the configuration by Vânia's engagement in the game by taking the role of a second "dog."

The sequences described show that the spatial circular attractor configuration frames the inner scenery constituted by the dog representation attractor. The coordinated running of the children sets spatial limits that adjust themselves to the collective movements—as when the circle is enlarged in order to include the moving "dogs." Actions that result from correlations can be identified in both intragroup and intergroup interactions, defining a coupling of the two attractors.

The representations of a dog that each of these children have emerge as meanings that are incorporated by the group as the actions are being performed. The "dog" barks and makes menacing moves toward its "preys," which move away, but not so far as to destroy the spatial configuration that represents a dog surrounded by its prey and/or being teased by them. The menacing posture and the barking, the simulated fear expressed in cries and moves, and the playful mood expressed in laughter, are also components of the configuration and give it an emotional intonation that strongly endorses its symbolic meaning.

The replacement of João by Vivi in the role of dog and the later replacement of Vivi by Vânia indicate that no previous plans were required to maintain the shared configuration. Although many different actions were possible for each child and for the group, *the shared meaning that emerged from the interactional situation seemed to operate as a mutually constraining influence* (Fogel, 1993) that led the group to delimit and select pertinent meanings, and favored certain further actions.

Shared meanings are a result of correlations that tend to reinforce their own actions, that is, tend to create new meanings and strengthen the tendency for other correlations. This defines the process leading to attractor configurations as a dialogue between deterministic and indeterministic aspects of the interactional system, and as a self-organization process presenting moments *"of stability and instability, where new qualities, traits, and characteristics emerge over time"* (Allen, Engelen, & Sanglier, 1984).

## EMERGENT CONCEPTS AND PRINCIPLES

### Field of Interactions—Novelty

It was possible to recognize in this play episode some developments of group organization in a flow of spontaneous individual activities. We can now examine the nature of some principles that lead to the correlation of these activities and potentiate the emergence of collective configurations. *Principles* refer to specific forms (either structural or dynamic) of organization of the system.

It is apparent from the description of the episode that the system we are taking as a unit of analysis is the group, defined by interacting individuals in a delimited spatial setting. At another level of analysis, each individual could be taken as a unit—a system in itself—which would engender other sorts of questions. When individual actions are labeled as spontaneous, we do not imply that they are not subject to correlations, which they probably are—for example, personal history, relationships in the group, and so on. Our question here *is not why* particular actions are performed by particular individuals at particular times, but, rather, *how* the group as a system moves over short time spans from disordered to collectively ordered states constituted by the coordination of spontaneous individual activities without any previous plans or prescriptions.

The micro-transformations in the system are taken as *instances* of the events that constitute the ontogenetic process, at both the group and the individual levels: Development takes place through the concrete moment-to-moment events in a *field of interactions*: self–self, self–other, or self–group interactions.

On a retrospective analysis of the episode, it can be observed that the actions of running and crouching were performed by every member of the group in different forms. João, who came in later and, from Sequence 5 on, performed the "dog" role, had tried to engage in Vivi and Telma's running route in the preceding sequence; and in Sequence 2, Telma did not really crouch, but bent her body as if enacting a fall. The running trajectories created a stable scenery against which other activities could be performed. The whole episode can be framed as variations on the running and crouching actions. The particular nature of each variation could not be anticipated from the analysis of the group as a system. It is a *novelty*: It emerges as a new activity, although, to a certain extent, it can be traced back to previous variations (e.g., squatting from falling down) or can be related to other contexts (e.g., personal history) at the individual level of analysis.

## Disorder as an Activating Principle of Order

In the course of the episode, ordered and disordered moments were identified. Disordered moments are more difficult to frame: Mutual orientation may be present, but the nature and the direction of the activities seem to be disordered or unrelated, and do not allow the observer to highlight a pattern or a configuration. It must be pointed out that children can share a physical environment while engaged in different independent activities and still not configure disorder or disorganization in the system, even if they periodically inspect the surroundings (Carvalho, 1989). It is when new activities of short duration are performed and are accompanied by changing or unstable mutual orientation, that a moment of disorder can be identified. The specific future course of actions in the system cannot be predicted from the analysis of these moments; but, when retrospectively analyzed, *disorder appears as the activating principle of order*. Self-organization requires a situation in which many chaotically manifested possibilities exist, out of which correlations can develop. Correlations occur on the basis of a multiplicity of available choices. Ordered states are reorganizations of random states in which novelties (spontaneous individual actions and surrounding events, such as the arrival of a caretaker) are continuously taking place. Which principles underlie these reorganizations?

## Organizing Principles: Attention, Sharing Meanings, and Meaning Persistence

The first organizing principle is *attention orientation*. This acts as a prelude indicating the children's disposition to engage in the various activities and their monitoring of the other children's actions. Engagement in a particular course of action was always preceded by the orientation of attention in its direction.

It should be noticed that attention orientation does not describe only an individual's action, but also its relationship to a part of the system to which the individual belongs at that particular moment. What constitutes this relationship? In our case, it is two or more children acting jointly, apparently on the basis of shared meanings, that functions as a scaffold and strengthens the activity, which is recognized and accepted as a proposal. There is no need to resort to intentions or plans in order to describe and analyze this process.

This leads us to a second organizing principle: *sharing meanings.* Some of the novel actions initiated by an individual child are "lost" if their performance is isolated from a collective action. An action can acquire a different status in the group when it is confirmed by more than one child—by imitation, by complementary, or by reciprocal actions. A nonshared activity is not strengthened and tends to be replaced: In Sequence 2, Alex abandoned his previous wall-to-wall route and joined Dani, who had changed to the circular route; and Telma stopped running when Paola and Vânia reoriented themselves toward Vivi. In Sequence 3, Alex turned his attention to Dani after she refused to whirl with Paola and him. In Sequence 4, Vivi stopped running when her partner Telma abandoned their common route and joined another group. In a different form, the same sharing principle is exemplified when Vivi instantly resumed João's role as a dog after he left to change his clothes, and when Vânia replaced Vivi in this role shortly after. In both cases, the game required a "dog" role correlated to the running group role in order to maintain its shared meaning.

Shared actions express a consensual meaning, which is achieved through a coregulation process. The individual actions are built jointly through moment-to-moment adjustments. Several parts of our episode offer beautifully clear examples of these adjustments: The nature and rhythm of the actions (running, falling down, squatting, circling) are increasingly synchronized; the spatial relations, the postures, and the expressive actions are kept within limits that preserve and strengthen the shared meaning; and roles are exchanged within the same limits, or *constraining influences.*

Jointly, these two principles—attention and sharing—bring about group cohesion and the identification of which children belong to the collective construction (the four other children present in the room during the episode did not engage in it).

A third organizing principle emerges from the different ways in which the transition to a new sequence occurs. In some cases (Sequences 1 to 2, and 3 to 4), there is a discontinuous transition, where the limits are obscured by chaotic activities, that is, by a disordered moment. But the transition can also occur in a more continuous way, and the elucidating clue in these cases seems to be the symbolic nature of the configuration, as in the transitions from Sequences 5 to 6, and 6 to 7: Vânia's leaving the "dog" role, and then resuming it, and the related changes in the group's running behavior.

It is interesting to notice that in the first case, the discontinuous transition, there is a concurrent activity that at first appears as part of the background against which the already structured activity is a figure. However, as other partners engage in the newly suggested action (sharing principle), the background becomes a figure. It can coexist with the former figure (Sequence 2) or replace it (Sequence 5).

Continuity and discontinuity can be construed as different faces of the system's behavior in recovering and renewing the relations between its constitutive components in unpredictable spans of time. This is what we call the principle of *persistence of meanings*.

The transition from Sequence 4 to Sequence 5 exhibits an interesting feature: Sequence 4's configuration "melts away" while the new configuration is still being delineated. Several activities are tried (running in different routes, running with a dangling head, squatting) before the new configuration is recognized. Sequence 5's configuration is more complex and lasting than any previous one: for the first time, the seven children engage in a single (and complex) activity. Coincidentally, it is in this configuration that a strictly symbolic aspect of the attractor can be clearly seen, although other forms of representations such as the recognition of spatial organizations are already present in earlier sequences.

As a side thought, it seems that a basic principle relates symbolic events and time. Every relation between events occurs in time and has a duration. Due to their potential supraindividual and interindividual nature, symbols allow a *new quality of sharing*, that can overcome the constraints of the immediate situation and acquire regulating properties over a longer span of time and across spatial barriers. It is tempting to suppose that the complexity and the duration of Sequence 5 contain a hint of this time–space freedom that is so characteristic of human interactions in complex social situations.

## SOCIAL INTERACTION AND INDIVIDUALITY

Like a molecule in incessant Brownian movement, a person, as a unique personality, has to submit to continuous changes while preserving individuality. At the same time, this individuality has its inherent constitutive reference in a complementary collective whole. What is usually called the *social environment* should be construed as a *field of interactions*, which is the founder of, and is founded by, the constitutive actions of human beings, and where information (meaning) creation and significant reciprocal communication take place. All the actions in this field appear as transformations at both the individual and the collective levels; they are the explicit expression of realized potentialities in regulated, self-organized states. The social nature of human beings expresses itself not as a sum of the actions of interacting individuals, but as collective, correlated, socially significant actions. Individuality is not opposite of sociability: It is its complementary face.

Human beings establish, and are established in, their individuality in a particular context: their social field of interactions. This *law of human socia-*

*bility* underlies the fact that young children are able to perform collective representations: Their correlated actions balance the indeterministic succession of spontaneous individual actions (which may or may not be meaningful at the individual level).

There is an inherent uncertainty in this interaction process, due both to the random and spontaneous character of individual actions and to the relative freedom that characterizes the attribution of meanings. This uncertainty is the source of innovation in the system: It generates novel actions and unfolded meanings. But the process of collective construction (coconstruction) also requires deterministic organizing principles. Some of these can be construed as properties of the system and/or of its components, such as the law of sociability, the attention, the sharing and the meaning persistence principles. Others are best described as process mechanisms such as coregulation (Fogel, 1993).[2] Free spontaneous action and novelty ensure *availability*; organizing principles ensure the *possibility of correlations and of coregulations* and set constraints, which guide the emergence of previously nonexistent collective states and meanings.

In the enchainment of these states, attractors are configured as privileged states of regulation, that relate individuals with one another and with the whole, expressing a trend toward convergence. Attractors result from communication: the exchange of reciprocally significant information made possible by coregulation processes. They are relatively stable, collective configurations, both in the sense of a sequence of regulated states in one individual, which manifests itself through correlated actions of this individual along time, and as a sequence of correlated actions of different individuals at a particular moment.

The attractor is a mathematical concept that we have used here in a metaphorical sense, aiming at an epistemological understanding. We are left with a methodological question: What sorts of measures and mathematical theories can be profitably used to characterize and to enhance our understanding of the geometry and dynamics of these interactional fields, where social wholes and individualities are simultaneously constructed through ontogeny?

## ACKNOWLEDGMENTS

This work was supported by grants to Isabel Pedrosa and to Ana Carvalho from CNPq (Conselho Nacional de Desenvolvimento Científico e Tecnológico, Brasil). The authors thank M. Clotilde Rossetti-Ferreira, Sylvio Salinas, and

---

[2]The concept of regulation is further discussed in Pedrosa, Carvalho, and Império-Hamburger (in press).

Tânia Thomé for their contributing comments on earlier versions of this chapter.

## REFERENCES

Allen, P. M., Engelen, G., & Sanglier, M. (1984). Self-organizing dynamic models of human systems. In E. Frehland (Ed.), *Synergetics from microscopic to macroscopic order* (pp. 150–171). Berlin: Springer-Verlag.

Baron, R. M., Amazeen, P. G., & Beek, P. J. (1994). Local and global dynamics of social relations. In R. R. Vallacher & A. Nowak (Eds.), *Dynamical systems in social psychology* (pp. 111–138). New York: Academic Press.

Camaioni, L. (1980). *L'interazione tra bambini.* Roma: Armando Armando.

Carvalho, A. M. A. (1989). Brincar juntos: natureza e função da interação entre crianças. In C. Ades (Ed.), *Etologia: de animais e de homens* (pp. 199–210). São Paulo: Edusp/Edicon.

Carvalho, A. M. A. (1992). *Seletividade e vínculo na interação entre crianças.* Postdoctoral thesis. Instituto de Psicologia da USP.

Fiedler-Ferrara, N. F., & Prado, C. P. C. (1994). *Caos: Uma introdução.* São Paulo: Edgar Blucher.

Fogel, A. (1993). *Developing through relationships: Origins of communication, self and culture.* New York: Harvester-Wheatsheaf.

Fogel, A., Nwokah, E., Dedo, J. Y., Messinger, D., Dikson, L. K., Matusov, E., & Holt, S. (1992). Social process theory of emotion: A dynamic system approach. *Social Development, 1*(2), 122–142.

Fogel, A., & Thelen, E. (1987). Development of early expressive and communicative actions: Reinterpreting the evidence from a dynamic systems perspective. *Developmental Psychology, 23*(6), 747–761.

Haken, H. (1978). *Synergetics, an introduction—Non-equilibrium phase transitions and self-organization in physics, chemistry and biology* (2nd ed.). Berlin: Springer-Verlag.

Haken, H. (1988). *Information and self-organization. A macroscopic approach to complex systems.* Berlin: Springer-Verlag.

Império-Hamburger, A. (1990a). Na Física e na Psicologia: Recuperando a ciência da mecânica não mecanicista? *Publicações/ P-849.* São Paulo: IFUSP.

Império-Hamburger, A. (1990b). Epistemological and historical studies of physics concepts for science teaching. In D. E. Hegert (Ed.), *More history and philosophy of science in science teaching. Proceedings of the first International Conference,* May 1989 (pp. 79–85). Tallahassee, Florida: Florida State University.

Império-Hamburger, A. (1996). Comprehension and limits of a theory in natural philosophy: Scientific knowledge in Isaac Newton. *Publicações.* São Paulo: IFUSP.

Nadel, J., & Fontaine, A. (1989). Communicating by imitation: A developmental and comparative approach to transitory social competence. In B. H. Schneider et al. (Eds.), *Social competence in developmental perspective* (pp. 131–144). The Netherlands: Kluwer.

Nowak, A., & Lewenstein, M. (1994). Dynamical systems: A tool for social psychology. In R. R. Vallacher & A. Nowak (Eds.), *Dynamical systems in social psychology* (pp. 17–53). New York: Academic Press.

Pedrosa, M. I. P. C. (1989). *Interação criança-criança: um lugar de construção do sujeito.* Unpublished doctoral dissertation. Instituto de Psicologia da USP.

Pedrosa, M. I., Carvalho, A., & Império-Hamburger, A. (in press). Interaction, regulation and correlation: A conceptual discussion and empirical examples. In M. Lyra & J. Valsiner (Eds.), *Construction of psychological processes in the course of interpersonal communication.* Norwood, NJ: Ablex.

Perrin, J. (1909). Mouvement Brownien et réalité moléculaire. *Annales de Chimie et de Physique, 18*, 1–114.

Prigogine, I., & Nicolis, G. (1971). Theoretical physics and biology. *Quart. Rev. Biophys., 4*, 107.

Serres, M. (1977). *La naissance de la physique dans le texte de Lucrèce.* Paris: Les Éditions de Minuit.

Vallacher, R. R., & Nowak, A. (1994). *Dynamical systems in social psychology.* New York: Academic Press.

Valsiner, J. (1991). Construction of the mental: From the 'cognitive revolution' to the study of development. *Theory & Psychology, 1*(4), 477–494.

Vygotsky, L. S. (1978). *Mind in society* (M. Cole, V. John-Steiner, S. Scribner, & E. Souberman, Eds.). Cambridge, MA: Harvard University Press.

Wallon, H. (1979). *Do acto ao pensamento: Ensaio de psicologia comparada.* Lisboa: Moraes Editores. Translated by J. S. Dinis from Wallon, H. (1942). *De l'acte à la pensée.* Paris: Flamarion.

# 7

# (In)Determinacy and the Semiotic Constitution of Subjectivity

Ana Luiza B. Smolka
Maria Cecilia R. de Góes
Angel Pino
Universidade Estadual de Campinas, Brazil

In this chapter, we contribute to the discussion of (in)determinacy of psychological development by exploring some aspects of the historico-cultural character of development, and by highlighting the role of semiosis in the interpretation of human functioning. We do not directly address the determining conditions and forces. Rather, we unfold some of Vygotsky's ideas concerning sign and drama, as a way of suggesting a shift in emphasis in the current debate on (un)predictable aspects of human actions.

## THE CULTURAL DIMENSION OF PSYCHOLOGICAL DEVELOPMENT

In our approach to the issue of indeterminism in developmental and social processes, we assume that the way we see or inquire about a specific phenomenon, its contours and relevance, how we select units of analysis, the interpretations we make, are closely interwoven threads in the fabric of history and cultural practices. To begin, we briefly address the very concept of *development*, in an attempt to show how the present uses of the term condense different notions that have become part of its meaning in the historical movement of ideas.

One can trace the French origin of the term *develop* to the 10th century, when it primarily meant "to open, to disclose, to take the wraps off," revealing or letting appear what is inside. From the 14th century on—with studies in biology and genetics, and especially with the Darwinian notion of evolution in the 19th century—new meanings infiltrated the term. Questions about biological origins and mutation led to renewed ways of inquiring about the peculiarity of the human species, and its constitution and transformation processes, in both phylogenesis and ontogenesis.

Along with the scientific inquiries of the 19th century came the notion of progress inherited from the philosophical matrix of the Enlightment, which was attached to issues of origin and change as the concept of development became consolidated in the human sciences.

According to progressivism, man, due to his plasticity and incompleteness, would, individually and collectively, gradually improve in an irreversible way. Thus, all men, in all societies would develop through the very same processes—universally similar, continuous, and cumulative—in which the individual would pass from the simpler, undifferentiated forms of behavior to the more complex forms, approaching the ideal configuration: the image of the adult individual of western Europe, considered the highest point of human progress and the reference point of civilization.

In this scenario, the emerging field of developmental psychology approached development basically as a chronological fact, focusing on and studying the evolution of the child in reference to certain adult behaviors. Infancy represented the original state. From there, children's characteristics, as well as their qualitative and quantitative transformations, were described in periods, stages, and phases, and analyzed from the point of view of biological notions, such as growth, or processes inferred from growth, such as maturation. Order and succession in different forms of the child's activities were observed and highlighted.

In this frame of reference, the notion of *growth*, based on particular physiological conditions of the child, implied an increase in quantity that could be measured. The notion of *maturation* described specific behavioral features occurring in sequence or referred to intrinsic regulating mechanisms that might explain equilibria and the progression and direction of observed and anticipated behavioral changes. On such notions—growth, maturation, progression—were based the criteria for evaluating and predicting the child's development and psychological functioning.

Interpreted in such a web of meanings, child development was mainly considered from a naturalistic/idealistic perspective. At the same time, this view provoked, circumscribed, and intensified disputes concerning the prevalent determinants of human actions around the issue of biology versus culture.

Most of the developmental psychology theories of the 20th century adopted the principles and parameters of the biological sciences, and considered cultural aspects to be intervening factors in human development. Among these were Gesell's and Piaget's perspectives, which gave priority to the genetic (i.e., developmental) character and considered culture as an external context in reference to the organism, influencing, but not necessarily constituting, psychological development.

During the debate at the beginning of the 20th century, strong criticism was directed at residual preformism and latent evolutionism, which were contrasted with the notion of development as a complex, dialectical movement. Other genetic approaches also emerged. They questioned the "biologizing" view of development, arguing for the importance and necessity of such an aspect, but also pointing to its insufficiency in characterizing what is specifically human (Janet, 1936; Wallon, 1973).

Among the attempts to overcome these disputes—attempts that tended to reframe the question by placing determination in biological plus cultural factors, or in interacting biological and cultural factors—Vygotsky's theoretical effort was concentrated on the understanding of how phylogenetic, historico-cultural, and ontogenetic development merge into constituting the child's cultural development.

Vygotsky (1981) assumed the "unique nature of the development of higher (human) forms of behavior" (p. 147), and emphasized the social situation of development as

> the initial starting point for all the dynamic changes taking place in development. . . . It defines completely the forms and the path the child follows as he acquires more and more new personality traits, taking them from social activity, the principal source of development. This is the path by which the social becomes the individual. (Davidov & Zinchenko, 1993, p. 99)

Vygotsky took as central for his proposition Marx and Engel's argument that men's modes of (re)producing their means/modes of concrete (physical, social) existence through work represent their *modus vivendi*, which reflects and becomes reflected in what they become. Hence, there is an intrinsic relationship among humans' modes of producing, modes of existing, and the derivative social practices and relationships.

According to this perspective, *mental processes* or *psychological functions* mean internalized social relationships, because as Vygotsky (1981) stated, "We hypothesized that development does not proceed toward socialization, but toward the conversion of social relations into mental functions" (p. 165). Those relationships are, thus, instituted and developed in or through symbolic order, which necessarily implies the social production of signs. For Vygotsky, this unique aspect of the nature of human development is necessarily cultural.

Following Vygotsky's line of reasoning, which supposes that human development is not solely and exclusively inscribed in a biological order, many researchers are now attempting to further elaborate and better specify processes that may account for the child's "cultural development."

As an example of these recent attempts, Rogoff (1990) argued that the development of the child occurs through guided participation, which allows for the sociocultural channeling of individual thinking, abilities, and knowledge. In theoretical terms, the status of the child is that of an apprentice: The child learns what is already (socially) known. Although the participation of others is highlighted in this interpretation, it is assumed on the other hand, that the child appropriates social practices in a creative process. The notion of apprenticeship is used to articulate the roles of the various participants in development: others (guides and providers of support), institutional contexts (frames of knowledge, modes of thinking, technologies, and goals), and the child (an active being, who does not merely reproduce cultural forms of action).

Addressing the issue of sociogenesis, Valsiner (1994) elaborated a coconstructivist model in which development is seen as a joint construction by the child and social others who provide social suggestions, in a collective, culturally preorganized environmental structure. Although this is similar, in broad terms, to Rogoff's approach, there are important distinctions, and different processes are highlighted (Valsiner, 1991). Concerned with the active role of the child and the emergence of novel actions, Valsiner resorted to the notion of *individual resistance*: While handling social suggestions, the subject can display strategies of resistance. Also, the process of development is teleogenetic, and, at any moment, the subject can change his or her goal orientation or strategies of conduct. Hence, development can assume an unexpected and unpredictable direction. Such flexibility in the individual's relations with the cultural surroundings generates novel actions and results in the formation of a personal culture, not necessarily coincident with the collective culture.

Still another line of discussion can be found in Sinha's interpretations of these processes. Sinha (1988) specifically referred to Vygotsky's contributions when the latter sought to explain the socialization of the biological individual (the product of evolution) through nonbiological mediators, such as language and culture. Sinha commented that, in spite of Vygotsky's efforts, his theoretical elaborations reproduce the nature–culture and individual–social dichotomies. Sinha attributed this limitation to Vygotsky's way of treating temporal relations while considering developmental/evolutionary processes, which results in the invoking of a "paleomorphic metaphor" (Sinha, 1992, p. 135) as the explanation of the genesis of higher mental functions.

Sinha derived his arguments from Vygotsky's proposal, assuming that development is anchored in a genetically transmitted biological nucleus, but this basis does not develop through and by itself: "Evolutionary biological processes ... were captured by an emergent cultural process" in such a way that "the biology of human development is a product of the interaction of biological and cultural evolution at the specific site of ontogenesis"

(Sinha, 1992, p. 138). He proposed a reassessment of the notion of representation, characterizing it as more than a cultural/cognitive human capacity, but, instead, as a constitutive property of the involving material environment, which both allows and restricts the activities of the developing organism. The human milieu, built over generations, is made of cultural objects and practices that materialize representational systems that go beyond individual organisms. The plan, design, intentionality, and specificity of objects in their contexts of use—in other words, the objects' structures, functions, forms, and uses—produce enduring artifacts and canonical rules (Sinha, 1992, p. 139).

According to this model, children's cognitive development is channeled by objects and strengthened by teaching relationships in the course of their daily activities. In this process, children appropriate canonical rules, "the fundamental mechanism for the social transmission of the core invariants of culture" (Sinha, 1992, p. 141). Through imitation and symbolic play, they may then violate and innovatively transform such rules, producing novelty.

The three theoretical approaches described so far, suggest that the child learns what is already known, follows social suggestions or appropriates the core invariants of culture, and does not merely reproduce cultural forms of action and knowledge. These are diverse attempts, within the historical-cultural approach, to study instatiations of the unity of biology and culture (Rogoff, 1990, p. 38), attempts to explain how development is constituted, while seeking to overcome strict social determinism or to avoid a return to idealist positions. Yet, despite the advances brought by such interpretations, the Vygotskian argument about the role of sign in intermental and intramental activity, or the essentially semiotic character of psychological functioning, is emphasized in the discussion that follows.

## THE CENTRALITY OF THE SIGN

It is useful, here, to highlight some of Vygotsky's own work, because his analyses explicitly explore or implicitly raise questions that continue to be relevant. "Concrete Human Psychology" (Vygotsky, 1989) is especially pertinent for the debate we are focusing on. This manuscript was composed of personal notes, not elaborated for publication, so it is often schematic, abbreviated, and disjunctive, almost an inner speech, as Puzyrei (1989) suggested in the article's Introduction. Nevertheless, it includes recurrent arguments concerning the problem of determination of human actions and the proposition of a constitutive role of social reality in the interplay of biological and cultural forces.

Arguing against zoopsychology, and in opposition to Pavlov's interpretations, Vygotsky (1989) formulated several strong statements about the role of social processes and the need for viewing psychology as homopsychology. "What is man? . . . For Pavlov, it is a soma, an organism. For us, man is a social person—an aggregate of social relations, embodied in an individual" (Vygotsky, 1989, p. 66). "Man regulates or controls his brain, the brain does not control man (socio!)" (p. 71). "Indeed, one cannot understand the activity of any nervous apparatus without man. This is a man's brain. This is the hand of a man. Herein lies the gist of the matter" (p. 64).

The notes also allude to the comparison made by Pavlov between the nervous system and a telephone network. (These arguments are presented, in brief terms, in the publication of *Mind in Society*; Vygotsky, 1978, p. 52.) Vygotsky corrected this metaphor, asserting that the unique character of human psychology lies in the fact that the telephone and the operator are combined in the same being; a nodal point in the study of man is that he himself is the operator who can produce stimuli and set new connections. However, this capacity does not derive from an internal, spiritual quality; it comes from without, in the sense that it is formed in social reality, organized by the use of signs. The "most basic fact is the fact that man not only develops" individually; "he also constructs himself" socially, through signs (Vygotsky, 1989, p. 63). The sign is not just interposed between the conditions given by the environment and the act as a third element, but it invades and reorganizes the structure of the individual's activity.

Furthermore, Vygotsky argued, "A person acts on another person, necessarily from without, with the aid of signs"; and "a person acts on himself, from without, and with the aid of signs, that is, in a social manner" (p. 72). In man, social functioning is semiotic.

According to these arguments, the *locus* of determination can be found neither exclusively in the realm of external, physical stimuli nor exclusively in internal biological (pre)conditions; and the fundamental *process* by which human actions are performed, is also neither physical nor spiritual. The discussion about locus and process is displaced by the assumption that man is determined by social reality through signs that he necessarily produces with others (for others and for himself). Signifying processes thus emerge in this active production, transforming the individual's activities into meaningful actions.

Social production or construction through signs characterizes historical-cultural development. As Wertsch (1985) stated, "The locus of change shifts from organic evolution governed by natural selection to the stage of mediational means. Mediational means (tools and signs) make possible the transmission of culture, but more important for Vygotsky's approach is the fact that they provide the mechanism for sociocultural change" (p. 56). This semiotic perspective leads us to conceptualize human development in a way that is distinct from both biologizing approaches and cultural, but non-semiotic approaches.

Although biology may account for diversity, heterogeneity, and even individuality and singularity, it does not account for subjectivity, reflexivity, and meaning, which are peculiar and specific aspects of the human condition that are initiated in and through language. Indeed, when Vygotsky said that "the problem of verbalized behavior is the central problem in the whole history of the cultural development of the child" (1987, p. 56), he established the issue of language at the core of psychological investigations.

The importance of language is generally recognized, because it is crucial in the establishing of relationships; it mediates face-to-face interpersonal encounters; and it allows for the communication and transmission of knowledge, values, and social norms. But to acknowledge the importance of language in human development is not equivalent to stating its constitutive role. In the latter case, language is not just a *means* of communication or transmission of knowledge and culture, but it installs and characterizes human cognition and mental functioning. To recognize the relevance of language does not automatically give it the conceptual status as a founding condition of human activity.

To bolster our arguments, we present data that serve as a point of departure for inquiring about theoretical possibilities generated by a distinctive concern with the sign.

In a preschool classroom, groups of 5- to 6-year-old children are involved in different activities. Three girls are playing in the house corner. Alcione decides to be the daughter of Thaís, who immediately takes the role of the mother. Camila is nearby, apparently without an assigned role in the make-believe situation yet. Suddenly, a box and a hat fall off a shelf. Alcione picks up the hat, and puts it on her head.

1. Alc: You were, you were . . . Do you want to play with this hat?
   (Alc. puts the hat on Thaís' head. The latter girl takes it off and puts it aside.)
2. Alc: Then give it to me, give it to me, Thaís!
   (Alcione picks it up again.)
3. Tha: Honey, mom doesn't like hats.
   (Alc. puts the hat on again and looks at Thaís.)
4. Tha: You look pretty!
   (Alc. laughs. Camila takes the hat from Alcione. Thaís is writing.)
5. Tha: Veronica (writing down the name she is assigning to herself)
6. Tha: What is your name? (addressing Alcione)
7. Alc: My name is . . . mine is Bete, Bete Carrera.
8. Cam: Mine is also Bete Carrera.
9. Tha: Ahn, it can't be. Then, I'm called . . . Bete.

10. Alc: I'm called ... I'm called ...
11. Tha: I'm called Bete Carrera!
12. Cam: I'm called Joana ... No, I'm called Síria!
13. Tha: I'm called Bete.
14. Alc: I'm called Raquel.
15. Tha: Síria? Are you called Síria? (addressing Camila)
    (Camila confirms with a head movement and Thaís starts writing down *Síria*.)
16. Alc: Mine is Thaís!
17. Cam: Mine is Laís. No, mine is Siria, mine is Siria!
    (A pen is dropped by Camila, and the children get involved with it. They return to the self-naming game, and Thaís gets involved in writing down the names.)

It seems to us that, taking a historical-cultural perspective, a sign-oriented view requires a different way of looking at and interpreting psychological development and discussing related (in)determinacy issues pertaining to the social constitution of man.

Examining the episode, we can ask about the conceptual and methodological consequences that might follow when we ascribe a central place to semiosis. How do we characterize the expected and unexpected in the children's actions? How do specific, singular modes of acting emerge?

The approaches we have reviewed—Rogoff's creativity, Valsiner's individual resistance, and Sinha's violation of canonical rules through symbolic play—either presuppose or lead to the notion of transformation and novelty. However, we must still ask: In what ways is sign related to the processes that generate or anchor creativity and individual resistance, the power of violating canonical rules?

The organized house corner of the preschool classroom—the table, chairs, bookshelf, small stove, utensils; the pen and out-dated calendar; the hat—are elements in the structured environment where Sinha's canonical rules, inscribed in objects and materials, might function. These can also be interpreted as comprising Valsiner's social suggestions or Rogoff's context of apprenticeship. However, what happens in the scene requires, more essentially, the centrality of the dialogical processes involved.

If we analyze the hat as an artifact with inscribed canonical rules, we can see that, indeed, the children put it on their heads, but why? How? A hat on the head might have many different purposes and meanings: to protect from the sun or rain; to be fashionable or beautiful; it may be just for fun or amusement, and so on. In other words, the children could have used it in a very different way. If we derive from Vygotsky's formulations the idea of the centrality of language, and if we resort to his methological concerns with movement and change (Vygotsky, 1978), and with microgenesis (Wertsch, 1985), then there must be a shift of emphasis.

During the episode, the children did not get to change the canonical rules, but neither was the hat just an artifact. It acquired the status of a sign—something that represents something for somebody—what is quite important in our interpretation. In this situation, the hat made the personage, not just because of the inscribed canonical rules (a certain type of hat is typically used by a certain character), but mainly because of the power of language, which impregnated and transformed the object.

Sinha (1988, 1992) pointed to the fact that imitation and symbolic play might be considered the locus of violation of canonical rules, and stressed the representational materiality pervading objects and artifacts. Although understanding his point of view, we emphasize, the *signi*fying aspect of the (inter)subjective actions, which necessarily implies the inmersion in language and meaning production.

Through language, the children created Bete Carrera (Turn 7), the feminine of Beto Carrero, a cowboy with a typical hat, the main figure of a popular play center called Beto Carrero World. The already seen and the already said got new forms, new contours, and new meanings. In the context of our investigations, the cultural prescription for the use of the hat cannot be approached without considering the many possible meanings of the action that is performed with the object: the act of putting the hat on the head. But the transformation of Beto Carrero to Bete Carrera becomes a strong and meaningful sign, because it leads us to the question of language and subjectivity. Language allows for this specific appropriation, for such a construction and transformation; it allows for a "performance" that synthesizes old and new modes and models of acting. Through language, children assume the name, the role, the place, and the character of the other. Through language, it is possible to become another, to become *Homo duplex* (Vygotsky, 1989, p. 58), or, in fact, *multiplex*. In this consists the dramatic aspect of human experience.

Looking at another aspect of the episode, we observed the children assigning to themselves names of classmates: Siria, Joana, and Raquel. This instance of self-naming implies the common (belonging also to others) and homogeneous (alike in nature), and, at the same time, the distinct (unlike others) and heterogeneous (different in kind, dissimilar).

The children's actions were simultaneously alike and distinct from social models, at once common and peculiar. But the commonness or the uniqueness, the likeness or the difference, were socially recognized, categorized or established through a certain conceptual-discursive framework, depending on the socially attributed meaning, value, relevance, and signification.

Regularity and singularity can be seen, from a biological perspective, in terms of universal patterns or individual differences, considering the individual member of the species; or from a sociocultural perspective, in terms of the proximity to or distancing from social models and norms, considering the member of a social group. When the latter perspective is articulated with a semiotic approach (as illustrated, e.g., by the work of Wertsch, 1985, 1991), the main concern is in the sphere of signifying processes. Therefore, predictable and unpredictable aspects of actions are characterized and discussed in terms of meanings and senses.

Social practices and institutions tend to circumscribe and stabilize meanings and senses, generating regularities and resulting in the expected. However, as Vygotsky (1987) pointed out, "Sense is a dynamic, fluid, and complex formation which has several zones that vary in their stability" (p. 276). This characterizes the polysemic aspect of language, which implies the possibility of multiple meanings. Regularity and singularity can, then, be configurated in the interplay of stabilization and the diversity of senses.

## THE DRAMATIC DIMENSION OF HUMAN EXPERIENCE

Besides pointing to the semiotic-microgenetic approach as a valuable theoretical and methodological means of investigating the social (inter/intra)constitution of man, we return, at this point, to Vygotsky's "Concrete Human Psychology," in which the thesis of semiotic mediation is explored in relation to the idea of the *Homo duplex*—constituted in and through the sign and the other—and to the already-mentioned dramatic character of human experience.

In the discussion of the interactive condition of man, Vygotsky elaborated on Politzer's ideas, according to which the object of psychology should be drama. For Politzer, psychology was oriented to isolated aspects of human functioning, as if they were things. In Politzer's criticism, he stated, "It is impossible for us to recognize ourselves in the narratives of psychology, for they are not narratives of human events" (1977, p. 108, our translation).

The notion of drama was borrowed by Vygotsky to accentuate the specificity of human beings, as a critical argument against the zoologization of human psychology and the neglect of the human's cultural condition.

Nonetheless, if we mention that Vygotsky relied on Politzer's ideas, we also have to acknowledge that neither one deeply explored the concept of drama. For Politzer, the notion of drama did not seem to be sign-oriented, because he did not thematize language or ask about the semiotic dimension; for Vygotsky, although he affirmed that "psychology must be developed in the concepts of drama, not in the concepts of processes" (1989, p. 71), he did not make explicit what he meant by this statement.

So, there is still a need to push forward the relationship between sign and drama and to conceptually elaborate on Vygotsky's suggestions.

Looking for the etymological roots of *drama*, we found in Aristotle's *Poética* the following reference: "It is said that the Dorian people use the verb *dran* meaning to make or to do, while the Athenian use *prattein*" (Aristotle, 1992, p. 25; our translation). The origin of the word allows us to consider drama as related to the possible and multiple forms of human action, not simply in the sense of performance and representation, play and plot, and neither in the strictly literary or common sense; but in a broad, deep, and fundamental sense—which might condense these many others—of meaningful, practiced action in a social system of relationships.

Vygotsky emphasized that homopsychology be taken as the study of drama. At the same time, for him, human actions become distinct and meaningful in and through sign and sense production: Man is a participant in a drama that unfolds within cultural scenarios; hence, he has to be considered as a person in relation to other persons, involved in dramatic roles and composing scenes. For Vygotsky sign permeates all interpersonal relationships; therefore, roles, scenes, and scenarios have to be conceived as semiotically organized.

But this is not all. Indeed, he stated that "All development consists in the fact that the developmental function goes from *me* to *I*" (1989, p. 65), which implies constant movement and changing of positions in relation to others, as well as to oneself. This means that drama does not characterize only an external scenario, but it pervades and characterizes the individual's mental functioning. This involves the possibility of (re)constituting, in a quite singular way, the social drama in the subjective sphere. It seems to be in this sense that Vygotsky stated, "The dynamic of the personality is drama" (p. 67).

Events in the drama are singular, unique, and unrepeatable (even when they occur according to predictions and even when they are consistent with the past or with social models). We can assume that sociocultural circumstances prefigure the scenario and the roles, but in order to study the scenes of drama, the concern should be placed less on conditions of determination, and more on conditions of production and transformation of meanings, in a sort of narrative approach to the understanding of the social constitution of subjective functioning.

In these theoretical-methodological formulations, how, then, do we consider the determining conditions for man's actions? Vygotsky's semiotic mediation and incorporation of the idea of drama seem to induce a displacement: from the effort to establish the locus of determination or the relative prevalence of internal and external forces and sources, to the effort to understand the process of production, reproduction, transformation, and generation of meanings and senses in intersubjective functioning.

# REFERENCES

Aristotle. (1992). *Poética*. São Paulo: Ars Poetica.

Davidov, V. V., & Zinchenko, V. P. (1993). Vygotsky's contribution to the development of psychology. In H. Daniels (Ed.), *Charting the agenda: Educational activity after Vygotsky* (pp. 93–106). New York: Routledge.

Janet, P. (1936). *L'intelligence avant le langage*. Paris: Flamarion.

Rogoff, B. (1990). *Apprenticeship in thinking*. New York: Oxford University Press.

Sinha, C. (1988). *Language and representation—A socio-naturalistic approach to human development*. New York: New York University Press.

Sinha, C. (1992). Vygotsky, internalization and evolution. In R. Maier (Ed.), *Internalization: Conceptual issues and methodological problems* (pp. 125–143). Utrecht: Rijksuniversiteit Utrecht.

Valsiner, J. (1991). Building theoretical bridges over a lagoon of everyday events. *Human Development, 34*, 307–315.

Valsiner, J. (1994). Bidirectional cultural transmission and constructive sociogenesis. In W. de Graaf & R. Maier (Eds.), *Sociogenesis re-examined* (pp. 101–134). New York: Springer-Verlag.

Vygotsky, L. S. (1978). *Mind in society: The development of higher psychological processes*. Cambridge, MA: Harvard University Press.

Vygotsky, L. S. (1981). The genesis of higher mental function. In J. V. Wertsch (Ed.), *The concept of activity in Soviet psychology* (pp. 144–188). New York: M. E. Sharpe.

Vygotsky, L. S. (1987). Thinking and speech. In R. W. Rieber & A. S. Carton (Eds.), *The collected works of L. S. Vygotsky* (pp. 37–285). New York: Plenum.

Vygotsky, L. S. (1989). Concrete human psychology. *Soviet Psychology, 27*(2), 51–64.

Wallon, H. (1973). *Les origines du caractère chez l'enfant*. Paris: PUF.

Wertsch, J. V. (1985). *Vygotsky and the social formation of mind*. Cambridge, MA: Harvard University Press.

Wertsch, J. V. (1991). *Voices of the mind. A sociocultural approach to mediated action*. Cambridge, MA: Harvard University Press.

# Transforming the Canonical Cowboy: Notes on the Determinacy and Indeterminacy of Children's Play and Cultural Development

Cynthia Lightfoot
State University of New York, Plattsburgh

At a certain moment in a Brazilian preschool classroom, a hat falls off a shelf. A little girl, Alcione, picks it up and puts it on her head.

> "What is your name?" asks her friend.
> "My name," says Alcione, "is Bete, Bete Carrera."

Her choice is a significant one. According to Smolka, de Góes, and Pino, "Bete Carrera" is a transformation into feminine form of "Beto Carrero," a popular play figure in Brazilian children's culture, and a cowboy. The episode stands as an example of how children's action—language in this case, and putting off the question of its privileged status for the moment—provides a medium of fluency for the cultural and the personal. When Alcione declares herself Bete Carrera, her drama reveals something about the dialectical process through which novel forms emerge within the "conservatism" of particular, given roles (Oliveira and Valsiner), or, in other terms, how "the system transforms itself while maintaining its identity as a system" (Pedrosa, Carvalho, and Império-Hamburger).

In pulling together in this way certain issues and concerns of the three chapters, I do not mean to diminish their differences, but to define some common ground from which we can then proceed to delineate certain boundaries between them. The common ground, consistent with the theme of this volume, is the authors' efforts to provide some insight into the intractable problem of indeterminism versus determinism. We recognize the issue in a number of other guises and contrastive forms: novel versus normative, flux versus inertia, disorder versus order, freedom versus constraint, chance versus necessity, stochastic versus causal—all come easily to mind. But the problem, in each of these instances, is essentially the same, and it constitutes a core issue for those of us interested in children's development: How do psychological, social, or cultural systems become organized and coherent over time, and once established, how are they reorganized, or perturbed, or supplanted by new psychological, social, or cultural systems?[1]

Despite the abundance of its pseudonyms, or perhaps expressing it, framing the problem of indeterminism versus determinism is a difficult matter, and handled quite differently in the three chapters. The overarching goal of my commentary is to try to get a fix on the various positions from which the authors approach the problem, using, as coordinates, three assumptions regarding the emergence of novel forms of action. The first of these raises questions of *place*; that is, questions regarding the principal location or source of novelty on the one hand, and coherence or stability on the other: How is it that social rules, expectations, or practices stabilize or constrain the vagaries of individual mind, meaning, and action? or, How does the individual organize, order, or compose stable knowledge and understanding from a social environment whose meanings are inherently unstable and incomplete? The second assumption concerns the *direction* of change: How does order emerge from disorder? or, alternatively, How does novelty emerge from system coherence and integrity?[2] The third and final assumption to be treated here concerns attributes of the *medium* of change. Specifically, taking for granted that processes of determinism and indeterminism are manifested in person-environment transactions, what *types* of transactions are considered relevant (social interactional, linguistic, semiotic, etc.), and what is the nature of their *dynamics* (cooperative and co-regulative, or discordant and conflictual).

I realize that posing these sorts of questions is to introduce a particular set of biases, and that the expedient course of action is probably to declare all of them relevant: There is determinism in indeterminism, and this can be written backwards and say precisely the same thing; the source of either can be social or mental life, or both simultaneously; and they work their effects through multiple person-environment media (social, linguistic, psychological)

---

[1]This question applies not only to children's development, but to psychological transformations in general. For example, in a recent extension of chaos theory to the psychoanalytic process, Moran (1991) raises similar issues as they apply to therapeutic change.

[2]Clearly, the issue of "direction" is also one of segmenting. That is, from a bird's-eye view, development proceeds from order to disorder to order to disorder, and so on, in which case "direction" is a matter of where one chooses to cut into its stream.

through which new forms emerge sometimes as a confluence or synchrony of interacting parts, and other times as a dialectical synthesis of opposites. However, the point that I would like to press in this commentary is that these assumptions regarding direction, place, and medium are not so easily resolved, nor are they are independent of one another. I hope to make the case, in particular, that the stand which one takes on these assumptions expresses a more general position on the nature of the relationship between developing individuals and their social environments. One position has it that the individual is part of a social whole; the other, that the individual is an ensemble of social relations. My argument is that the first of these lies at the end of a course charted by classical general systems theory as it is demonstrated in the work presented by Pedrosa, Carvalho, and Império-Hamburger, whereas the latter is the destination of traditional constructivist developmental theories, particularly Vygotsky's, as developed in the chapters by Smolka, de Góes, and Pino, and Oliveira and Valsiner.

## DETERMINISM, INDETERMINISM, AND THE INTEGRITY OF ACTION

General systems theory probably comes closest to providing a common language for most talk of determinism and indeterminism, including that contained in this set of chapters, and its usefulness for illuminating developmental issues is widely recognized in this volume, as elsewhere. According to Jantsch's (1980) account, nineteenth-century advances in thermodynamics marked a significant break from classical, Newtonian physics which had characterized particle movement in terms of the behavior of single, material points, and whose movement was understood to take place along reversible space-time trajectories, as impelled by external forces. The revolutionary insight of thermodynamic theorists was that particles move as populations, not just as individuals.

As captured by Prigogine's well-rehearsed dictum, "order through fluctuation," the distinction between macroscopic and microscopic processes opened a window onto a view of determinism and indeterminism as integral to the same process. From this view, the microscopic is stochastic, time-dependent, in flux, and in transition between old and new structures. The macroscopic, on the other hand, is the deterministic element, the higher-order complexity which constrains the behavior of the component parts. The significance of imposing a hierarchical distinction between macro and micro levels of analysis is nowhere more apparent than in Jantsch's (1980) discussion of finding the "rules of the game" at the higher-order level of semantics:

> A cell contains several thousand biochemical processes in a very small volume, and many of them are interlinked by complex, intermeshing feedback loops.

As Varela (1975) has shown, the microscopic equivalent of following all these individual process interactions would require infinite time. . . . However, if one searches for "rules of the game" for all these processes and for criteria of holistic system behavior—in other words, if the semantic level gets introduced—one may hope for a simple representation. However, this simplicity is then no longer the above-cited "simplicity of the microscopic," but a new "simplicity of the macroscopic" which is yet to be discovered. (p. 41)

The introduction of the "macroscopic order" cleared a path for understanding dynamic processes as irreversible, directed, and self-organizing. The last of these, self-organization, or *autopoiesis* ("self-production," from the Greek), in particular, was seen to occupy a special place in the functioning of evolving systems, as set apart from structure-preserving systems. The principal function of autopoiesis is self-renewal; the expression, Jantsch writes, of "a particular individuality, a particular autonomy from the environment" (1980, p. 44). The internal, self-amplification of autopoiesis is not unlike the *entelechy* described by Aristotle as the inward determination of parts by the whole; the design in all things. Self-organization contrasts with the allopoietic régime of mechanical systems whose functions are determined externally, and whose products exist independently and apart from the systems themselves.

The influence exerted by general systems theory on developmental psychology has been considerable. Sameroff (1989), for example, has laid out the basic principles of systems theory and, point-by-point, their developmental analogs. Chapman (1991) has interpreted Piaget's life work as an "incipient theory of self-organization" on the grounds that it emphasizes dynamic equilibria between the parts and wholes of relational totalities (organic, mental, or social), distinguishes between irreversible knowledge acquired through equilibration, and reversible knowledge gained through learning mechanisms, and sees knowledge as a progression towards increasing order along a trajectory which is inherently probabilistic, indeterminant, and nonteleological.

Although general systems principles have been embraced as a package by many developmentalists, it is the principle of self-organization which has stirred the most interest. As Cairns' (1986) aptly puts it, "there is an integrity to behavior," and the concept of self-organization provides insight into the tendency of organisms to conserve action patterns. In this regard, self-organization contains tremendous heuristic power for understanding the inertia of systems. Specifically, once organized, systems become increasingly resistant to change, and the interrelations among their parts begin to contribute to system stability, coherence, and direction (p. 37). Thelen (1989), in fact, argues that the principle of self-organization—that "*pattern and order can emerge from the process of the interactions of the components of a complex system* without the need for explicit instructions" (p. 79)—holds the solution to a major theoretical impasse which has been dogging the discipline from the outset. In particular, she celebrates the principle as one which can deliver developmental psychology from the infinite regress following strictly unidirectional, causal accounts of person-environment influences.[3]

The work presented in each of the three chapters takes long strides away from such naive conceptions of person-environment relationships. Indeed, I am hard-pressed to deliver a single example of modern scholarship which takes seriously such a simplistic version. However, having called into question the viability of unidirectional causal models, we are left with the difficult task of formulating possible alternatives. As suggested previously, Pedrosa, Carvalho, and Império-Hamburger champion a general systems perspective in which the individual functions as part of a social unit, whereas Smolka, de Góes, and Pino, and Oliveira and Valsiner advance a constructivist perspective which casts the individual as an ensemble of social relations. Each perspective is explicated below, with special attention to the assumptions regarding the *place* or source of determinism and indeterminism, the *direction* of change, and the type and dynamic of the *medium* of change.


## THE INDIVIDUAL AS PART OF A SOCIAL WHOLE

The target of the chapter by Pedrosa, Carvalho, and Império-Hamburger is the free play of 3-year-olds considered as a system which organizes itself not unlike that of the movement of small particles suspended in a fluid. Myself no stranger to preschoolers' capacities for wreaking havoc and mayhem, it was a simple matter to imagine them all as small particles, bouncing off one another chaotically, coming into momentary accord—"attractor configurations" (whirling hands in hands; running around the dogs)—and flying off again in new directions which may or may not settle into new and equally tenuous accords.

In addition to the charm and appeal of the metaphor and the data analysis, the work presented by Pedrosa, Carvalho, and Império-Hamburger is carefully wrought theory, and a fine example of what it means to take seriously the axiom that the individual is a part of a social whole. Thoroughly grounded in a general systems perspective, the authors view children's social groups as dynamic systems whose "ordered states are the product of the interactive, co-regulating actions of the component individuals," and they present a well articulated case for how the interactional complexity of the collective is more than the sum of its constituent parts

---

[3]The logical regress, as formulated by Oyama (1985), among others (see Thelen, 1989), is that if new forms are understood to be induced by factors external to them, then those very forms are by definition preexisting or incipient.

which, in this case, are the actions of the individual children who comprise the play group.

To adopt this particular perspective on the relationship between the individual and the social environment is also to assume a specific stance on the three assumptions introduced earlier. On the issue of *place*, the authors are explicit in locating indeterminism, instability, and innovation in the "spontaneous" or "free" behavior of individual children. Determinism, on the other hand, is manifested at the level of the group, as a "correlation" or "co-regulation" of individual actions, through which stable action patterns are produced. To get the authors' position regarding the *direction* of change, one need go no further than the title of their paper, "From Disordered to Ordered Movement." The emphasis is on the emergence of ordered, collective states from non-coherent, individual actions. Order from disorder. As Pedrosa, Carvalho, and Império-Hamburger insist in several contexts, the current state of disorder—the novel, non-synchronous action of individuals—stands in no particular relationship to other orders, past or present. Its only referent is the ordered state towards which it tends: "Our question here . . . is rather *how* the group as a system moves from disordered to collectively order states constituted by the coordination of spontaneous individual activities, without any previous plans or prescriptions, in short spans of time."

This is apparent not only in the treatment of the data, but (and as it should be) at the theoretical level, and reflects one way of interpreting the self-organization of an autopoeitic system. That is, it need have no other meaning or referent or significance outside of itself. Thus, innovation cannot be anticipated by the action of the group. Individual action is inherently unintelligible. It erupts randomly, and its significance for the emergence of higher-order complex forms is apparent only in retrospect, by working backwards from the determinate form that it has assumed. Thus, in a certain "get behind me Satan" way, novelty is something to overcome, and to configure into regularity, order, pattern, design.

The authors' treatment of the type and dynamic of the medium of change is wholly consistent with their assumptions regarding place and direction. Borrowing from Haken (1988), they describe a "field of interaction" from which individuals receive information on how to behave coherently and cooperatively. In general terms, individuals provide potential, an abundance of chaotic possibilities from which correlations can occur. Action is thus brought to heel, and becomes synchronized, rhythmic, and self-reproducing. Indeed, the evolution of new forms is probably best described as a process of selective extinction: Novel actions are "lost" if they are performed in isolation from collective action. Thus, the type of medium is entirely interactional, and the dynamic is that of agreement, confluence, and synchrony.

In defending their treatment of the individual as a source of spontaneous variation, Pedrosa, Carvalho, and Império-Hamburger make the point that they would proceed differently if the individual, rather than the group, is taken as the principle unit. The individual, they suggest, would then constitute its own self-organizing system which ensures its own continuity through time by co-regulating variations from certain of its component parts (personal history and relations in the group are provided as examples). Indeed, the chapters by Oliveira and Valsiner, and Smolka, de Góes, and Pino focus more fully on the individual, and employ language and arguments which are occasionally strikingly similar to that of Pedrosa, Carvalho, and Império-Hamburger. However, construing the individual as an ensemble of social relations also places them at odds with traditional general systems approaches.

## THE INDIVIDUAL AS ENSEMBLE
## OF SOCIAL RELATIONS

Consistent with an emphasis on the individual, both papers are concerned with the development of subjectivity, reflexivity, and meaning. Despite the intramental focus, there is a certain unity of perspective shared with Pedrosa, Carvalho, and Império-Hamburger, as we might expect given the fact that systems theory is the common denominator for discourse about determinism and indeterminism in development. Both chapters, for example, discuss social practices as processes which stabilize or constrain personal meanings and actions, and to this extent the *location* of determinacy is social process, and that of indeterminacy, individual action. Moreover, Smolka, de Góes, and Pino's sense of drama as "significant action," and Oliveira and Valsiner's concept of "role coordination" as it functions to expand and restrict "semiotically organized conduct fields" is not altogether unlike the "attractors" and "fields of interaction" discussed in the previous chapter. In certain respects, then, there is also overlap with regard to the transactional nature of the *medium* of change. Nevertheless, the assumption that dramatic experience, role coordination, or any other intersubjectively generated meaning is *foundational* to intramental functioning, a mechanism of development rather than a description of it, sets these two chapters apart from the first. In particular, Smolka, de Góes, and Pino, share with Oliveira and Valsiner a desire to recapture the subjectivity that is often eclipsed in social interaction research. As such, the *direction* of change is from determinacy to indeterminacy, that is, from the constraints and regulation of sociocultural processes, to their transformation and internalization by individual actors and agents. Moreover, the *medium* of change in these chapters, is symbolic or semiotic in type, and oppositional or dialectical in dynamic.

Smolka, de Góes, and Pino's contribution to the discussion of determinacy and indeterminacy takes place in two parts. The first is an interesting historical account of how indeterminacy insinuated itself into scientific focus after some centuries of myopic concentration on the deterministic aspects of children's development, including the universality of its stages, sequences, and final endpoints. Coupling this historical transition to the emergence of interest in children's "cultural development," especially as conceived by Vygotsky, the authors overview several contemporary attempts to get beyond a strictly deterministic point of view by actively incorporating the creative, transformative, and unexpected aspects of children's action and development.

The second part of the chapter highlights the centrality of the semiotic function for psychological development, with special reference to its dramatic quality. Setting their perspective apart from other general "cultural" approaches, the authors argue that language is first and finally a mechanism of individual and sociocultural change. It "installs" cognition and mental functioning. This is because language is always in some sense a "performance," and involves the setting up of a show-self, a dramatic synthesis of the personal and canonical: *My name is Beta Carrera.* And because development is taken to move inward, from the worldly me to the subjective I, it is our primary means of reconstructing cultural meanings as personal ones, of being that which we are not. There is a unity of the "common and peculiar," and in this unity is dramatic experience which pervades not only the performance, but mental life itself. Quoting Vygotsky (1989), "the dynamic of the personality is drama" (p. 67). Finally, and also consistent with the view of development's inward movement and the individual as ensemble of social relations, language becomes the source not only of new meanings and dramas, but of subjectivity and reflexivity. On the issue of determinacy and indeterminacy, the authors present what is finally a revisionist agenda, calling for a shift of attention away from determinacy towards dramatic "production, reproduction, transformation and generation of meanings and senses in intersubjective functioning." A shift, that is, towards indeterminacy and the transformation of the canonical.

The work presented by Oliveira and Valsiner is also committed to understanding the dramatic and semiotic character of children's action and development, although their concept of semiosis extends beyond language to include a more general symbolic function, and they go somewhat farther in articulating the longer haul of ontogenesis. On this expanded view, the mediational role and developmental significance of play, imagination, and fantasy are all on a par with that of language by virtue of their transformative power. The unplayed and unsaid are made over into new forms through play and language which detaches the child from external circumstance and liberates the child from the past. In other words, the symbolic function, whether displayed in play, fantasy, or langugage, is the source of innovation, creativity, and novel ways of being.

In their analysis of the pretend play of 2-year-olds, and the fantasy life of an adolescent, Oliveira and Valsiner clarify how imaginary situations become increasingly scripted, well-defined, and thematic over microgenetic time. The fantasy develops into itself, and takes on, in a manner of speaking, a life of its own, a certain autonomy. And this is true not only in the short run of microgenetic time, but across the longer period childhood. Play becomes increasingly detached from the plane of action, that is, increasingly intramental and semiotically mediated as indexed by the transition from the external, pretend play of young children, to the internal imagination and fantasy of adolescents and adults. However, unlike the self-organization discussed by Pedrosa et al., for which the system requires no external referent or plan, the fantastic and the imaginary always have a meaning or significance which extends beyond them. (It should be noted that this applies to Smolka et al.'s position, as well.) The empirical examples juxtapose reproduction and novelty, and are meant to illuminate the dialectical opposition between submitting to social roles, and transforming them. Through play and fantasy, regulations are examined, modified, and internalized, and this leads to mastery of role relationships, and the ability to take different points of view. Thus, the 2-year-olds acted out a frightening episode of being disciplined, which then devolved into a scene of paternal concern and nurturance; and the adolescent, following a period of religious disenchantment, constructed a fantasy religion, sympathetic, and replete with holy places, personages, and ritual—something which she could believe in.

Symbolic action, in contradistinction to social interaction, is always of or about itself, but also of or about something else. One sees, from this perspective, a hierarchical bracketing function, an epistemological distancing at work. By definition it symbolizes, re-presents, signifies, and this lends it an oppositional quality. So whereas the social system of Pedrosa et al. eventuates in harmonious coordination and a confluence of parts, the meaning constructed in play and fantasy is a dialectical synthesis of opposites; and the implication of advancing a truly dialectical perspective is to admit the possibility of critique and reflexivity.

## RESCUING REFLEXIVITY

The difference between the two perspectives introduced here—individual as part of social system, and individual as ensemble of social relations—really turns on the issue of reflexivity. To include it is to permit distinctions between mimicry and mime, identification and emancipation, singularity and subjectivity, whirling hands in hands and ritual dance, and these distinctions are important ones if our aim is to understand not only the reproduction of cultural and canonical forms, but their transformation. However, the role of reflection and critique in children's cultural development remains obscure, despite efforts, here and elsewhere, to illuminate it. The problematic and unfinished task, it seems to me, is to coordinate within the child's experience processes of reflexivity with those of social interaction or cultural identification. For example, when Wellington plays the role of the punitive father who first attacks, and then protects his child, he expresses something about the types of acts (punitive, nurturing, etc.) that can be legitimately included within the role of father, as he understands it. But what needs further explication is Wellington's understanding of the *flexibility* of role itself, which is to say, his understanding of role as role whose relationship to the acts which instantiate it is not one-to-one or direct. This very knowledge, in fact, accounts for the difference between Maristela, who *dramatizes* her fear of the father, and poor Daniel who could not play because he was truly frightened.

If we are to remain faithful to our commitment to explore relations between determinacy and indeterminacy, we need to rescue reflexivity. This would have the effect of introducing a determinacy of meaning at the level of the individual act. Thus, variation and innovation would not be random, but anchored dialectically to role and tradition. A determinacy of meaning at the level of the act is essential for understanding the creativity of thought, as well as its emancipation from social, cultural, and linguistic forms (see also Hirsch, 1976). When the development of a reflecting, critical subject is included in our efforts to understand cultural experience, interactional synchrony becomes dialectical synthesis, temporal rhythm becomes history, and transitory meanings become forms of knowledge which linger long enough to be toyed with.

## REFERENCES

Cairns, R. (1986). A contemporary perspective on social development. In P. S. Strain, M. Guralnic, & H. Walker (Eds.), *Altruism and aggression: Social and biological origins*. Orlando, FL: Academic Press.

Chapman, M. (1991). Self-organization and developmental process: Beyond the organismic and mechanistic models? In P. Van Geert & L. P. Mos (Eds.), *Annals of theoretical psychology* (Vol. 7, pp. 335–348). New York: Plenum.

Haken, H. (1988). *Synergetics, an introduction—Non-equilibrium phase transitions and self-organization in physics, chemistry and biology*. Berlin: Springer-Verlag.

Hirsch, E. (1976). *The aims of interpretation*. Chicago: The University of Chicago Press.

Jantsch, E. (1980). *The self-organizing universe*. Oxford: Pergamon.

Moran, M. (1991). Chaos theory and psychoanalysis: The fluidic nature of the mind. *International Review of Psycho-Analysis, 18*, 211–221.

Oyama, S. (1985). *The ontogeny of information: Developmental systems and evolution*. Cambridge, England: Cambridge University Press.

Sameroff, A. (1989). Commentary: General systems and the regulation of development. In M. Gunnar & E. Thelen (Eds.), *Systems and development: The Minnesota symposia on child psychology, Vol. 22* (pp. 219–235). Hillsdale, NJ: Lawrence Erlbaum Associates.

Thelen, E. (1989). Self-organization in developmental processes: Can systems approaches work? In M. Gunnar & E. Thelen (Eds.), *Systems and development: The Minnesota symposia on child psychology, Vol. 22* (pp. 77–117). Hillsdale, NJ: Lawrence Erlbaum Associates.

Vygotsky, L. (1989). Concrete human psychology. *Soviet Psychology, 27*, 51–64.

# THE SEMIOTIC ARGUMENT FOR INDETERMINISM IN DEVELOPMENT

Gorjana Litvinovic
University of North Carolina at Chapel Hill
and University of Belgrade, Yugoslavia

A number of themes emerge from the reading of the chapters written about the issue of (in)determinism in developmental processes by: Oliveira and Valsiner; Pedrosa, Carvalho, and Império-Hamburger; and Smolka, de Góes, and Pino. All three chapters place the major burden of indeterminism on the shoulders of semiosis, and the inherent flexibility of the symbol. They all place the semiotic process in the context of an individual-social relationship, stressing both the unity and the distinction between these spheres. They recognize a certain relationship between the past, present, and future, which is marked by historicity, a forward lunging motivational impetus, and constrained, yet flexible, potential. Finally, they all talk about ways in which psycho-social reality is structured and processes through which it is restructured, stressing the reversible figure-ground nature of the relationship between order and hierarchy, on one side, and chaos, on the other.

The thematic dimensions of these three chapters are, then: semiosis, individual-social, forward movement, and structure-process. These dimensions stake out a field—the compounded "theory of indeterminism in psychological development," which is implicitly presented by the three chapters. In this commentary, I outline that emergent synthetic view, by clarifying several principles which seem to be in its foundation.

## THE PRINCIPLE OF INTERSUBJECTIVITY

The very first assumption must be that persons facing each other will recognize each other as social partners. This is not an exclusively human property, as anyone will know who has looked into the eyes of a cat. Explanations for it might be sought in lower-level processes or evolution. In psycho-social explanations, however, it is axiomatic. In order for sociocultural interaction to take place and for its mechanisms to have any effect, there first must exist this elementary communicational basis. Pedrosa et al. express this principle in the following way: "The ontogeny of a system is a process through which functions and temporarily stable states are constituted and transformed. Functions and stable states can be thought of as products which mark the process in the sense of becoming *recognizable by the interactants or developing beings*" (p. 137, italics added). In the case of human development, the products, with their "quality of momentary stability which makes them recognizable," can only be formed within a social environment, that is, within a reciprocally constitutive "social-individual" relationship (p. 138). In the example they analyze, the running configurations emerge, and are maintained and transformed out of such mutual awareness. It is in this example that we best see emergent interaction—a collusion of social partners is present, which is not yet quite a full-fledged goal-directed negotiating exchange. Oliveira and Valsiner introduce the concept of role as the chief shaping feature of this initial property of mutual awareness. Thus, "human interaction [is] a dynamic process of expanding or restricting shared semiotically organized conduct fields, occurring through the coordination of the roles ... assumed by the participants in ongoing situations" (p. 120). The most basic implication of the authors' fluid understanding of roles is that the role is, in its basic formulation, simply the orientation, stance, or attitude, that the social partners have with respect to the present-in-awareness other. Semiotic embellishment of the role leads to its transformation into a "relatively stable recognizable state" (as in Pedrosa et al.), which is preserved in memory and becomes the basis for goal-directed negotiation. Smolka et al. also presume this kind of basic intersubjectivity when they cite Vygotsky: "man is a social person—an aggregate of social relations, embodied in an individual" (p. 158). Social reality can be constitutive of man only if there is an a priori open communicational channel between person and other. However, according to Smolka et al., the communication via this channel will necessarily become semiotically articulated as "a person acts on another person, necessarily from without, with the aid of signs [and] a person acts on himself, from without, and with the aid of signs, i.e., in a social manner" (p. 158).

## THE ZONE OF INTERACTION

Primary social awareness is not a static datum, but the underlying assumption of what is, in fact, constant mutually directed activity. A further assumption is that this mutually directed activity is *inter*active, that is, that its flow plays off the preceding and the present context as recognized by each of the partners. In this way, a flow is structured, and possible relatively stable states (i.e., products) are achieved, which surpass the potential of each of the partners individually. In this sense, it may be said that constructive activity takes place at a behavioral, that is, functional, interface. There is an initial tentative separation between the individual and the social realm. Contact is established at the outer behavioral plane, into which partners emit activity. Some of this activity, at least, is socially directed. The contact is interactive, in the sense of a continuing other-awareness and a continuing reactivity of each of the partners to what transpires between them. Given this, new shapes (e.g., of verbal strings, of motion, of meaning) are formed between the interactants, with each of them intersequentially contributing little bits. Novelty thus emerges in interaction. This field of meaningful social exchange, which is external but proximal to the individual, can be called the zone of interaction. The novel products of social interaction affect at the same time the interacting system and the individuals involved in it, who are said to "internalize" these effects. Although the zone of interaction is initially understood and modeled after an individual-social distinction, the same principle of construction at functional interfaces, that is, construction within the zone of interaction, holds true in personal development, where the interacting partners are in fact internalized social voices. The zone of interaction is very clearly described in all three chapters. Pedrosa et al. call it the *space of information* (p. 130). They say: "What is usually called 'the social environment' should be construed as a *field of interactions*, which is the founder of, and is founded by, the constitutive actions of human beings, and where information (meaning) creation and significant reciprocal communication take place" (p. 148). The same point is made by Smolka et al., when they assert that what is of essential importance in understanding the concepts of "creativity," "individual resistance," and "power of violating canonical rules" (proposed by Rogoff, Valsiner, and Sinha, respectively), is the consideration of interlocutory processes involved in examples of meaning-emergence (p. 160). Or, in the words of Oliveira and Valsiner, "we could conclude that in the children's interaction roles are delineated through a dynamic joint negotiation of the semiotic aspects of the children's actions" (p. 123). In their case, the role is the product under analysis.

## THE PRINCIPLE OF SEMIOTIC FLEXIBILITY

The constructive activity in the zone of interaction is assumed to take place, most importantly, through the employment of signs and sign systems. Meaning is assumed to be the key ingredient of human existence, and the use and construction of signs is assumed to be the central property of specifically human functioning. Smolka et al. explicitly equate sign with the word. "If biology may account for diversity, heterogeneity, even for individuality and singularity, it does not account for the question of subjectivity, reflexivity, and meaning, which are peculiar and specific aspects of human condition, inaugurated in/through language" (p. 159). Oliveira and Valsiner take a broader view, including "gestures and postures, besides conversations, as indices of meaning" (p. 125). For Pedrosa et al., "the recognition of a configuration is in itself an act of signification. . . . if the actions of two or more individuals are seen as related through similarity, complementarity or reciprocity . . . a shared act of signification can be recognized and can thus acquire a regulating potential" (p. 140). It follows that what is configured is not an important consideration. This understanding of sign-as-configuration is, in fact, echoed by Smolka et al., when they say: "The sign is not just interposed between the conditions given by the environment and the act, as a third element, but it invades and reorganizes the structure of man's activity" (p. 158).

Novelty, as we have seen, arises in the zone of interaction, because of diverse input into a context which surpasses its elements in space and time. However, an additional and important source of novelty is the "inherent uncertainty in the process of signification" (Pedrosa et al., p. 190). Two complementary characteritics of the semiotic functioning illustrate this uncertainty. One is *polysemy*, that is, the possibility of multiple meanings being associated with a sign. The concrete interpretation at any moment will be open to variations, even if directed by the general context. Polysemy is illustrated by the preschooler Vania rubbing a toy dog's head with a piece of wood as if combing it, and then putting the piece of wood into the dog's mouth, as if feeding it (Oliveria and Valsiner, p. 123). A dramatic (literally) effect of sign polysemy is illustrated by the group of children who, in play, assign to themselves the names of their classmates (Smolka et al., p. 159). The other characteristic of semiotic functioning that contributes to its flexibility is contextuality. The exact meaning attributed to signs depends on the particular context of their appearance. Thus, even an unknown sign will be attributed meaning in a concrete situation, and this meaning will be derived from the context. The precise meaning of the particular sign will, however, remain uncertain. Contextuality is very well exemplified by the unexpected, but definite loss of the symbolic status of Aurore's sanctuary, when it was suddenly placed in a new relationship with (until that moment) independent social elements, that is, when it was "discovered" (Oliveira and Valsiner, pp. 126-127).

## THE PRINCIPLE OF HISTORICITY

The past is assumed to be retained in the present in a way which is cumulative but not additive. Furthermore, the present can be understood only in the light of the past. Any present state of the system has emerged on the basis of possibilities given in the immediately preceding past state of the system, just as the immediate future is given as a possibility in the present state. As the present is being constructed in the zone of interaction, this process draws on elements that have been instituted as relatively permanent forms in the system. This implies that there exist certain systemic structures that preserve the past, allowing it to be selectively drawn upon, its elements selectively recombined in new situations, renegotiated in meaning and form. These vehicles of history are the crystallized but mutable structures of collective culture and personal memory. In other words, they exist on both sides of the personal-alien divide. Smolka et al. stress the framework for development set by the global cultural-historical past. They go along with Sinha in stating that the "human ambiency, built along generations, is made of cultural objects and practices that materialize representational systems which go beyond individual organisms" (p. 157). However, this global framework is placed in motion only in the context of immediate intersubjective action, which draws on individual memory in order to do something with the elements of this framework. In the scene with the Beto Carrero hat, for example, the hat is not "just an artifact. It acquires the status of a sign—something that represents something for somebody" (p. 161). In this example, the past enters the process of future-construction in multiple ways. The collective past is encoded in the assumptions for the use of a hat, in the very shape of this garment. Personal past is encoded in the children's knowledge of the typical use of the hat. History is encoded in the personage of "a cowboy." Personal past is encoded in each child's understanding of this personage. A similar view is held by Oliveira and Valsiner. Thus, "make-believe play occurs through a process of collage of fragments of [the children's] experiences in presently constructed activity contexts" (p. 123), or, "the children's interpretations of present events interweave with their memories of experienced situations" (p. 130). Historically constructed roles, scripts, and canons are encoded both in the environment and in the child's experience. These elements are interpreted and integrated in the flow of immediate interaction, shaping the collective construction of a shared script. Do Pedrosa et al. uphold this principle in their chapter? Strictly speaking, the time relationships which they analyze do not surpass the duration of the concrete segment they are looking at. However, within it, they clearly show that later states emerge out of elements present in previous states. They call this the "principle of persistence of meanings" (p. 148). Although not focused on, personal history, relationships in the group, etc., are assumed to be importantly correlated to action (p. 175).

## THE PRINCIPLE OF CONSTRAINTS

As individuals and social entities are actualized through the developmental process, it is assumed that there are properties of reality which limit possible choices in action and variability in production. In other words, the scope of possibilities for change is limited by the set of properties of the existing system, which may simply not contain the potential for certain kinds of action, or may limit the options on other kinds of action. This set of implicit limitations in a system can be called the *constraining system*. Elements of the constraining system are to be found in universal laws, functional "habits," structural arrangements, and the availability of present resources, as all these affect a particular system. Many of the constraints are a result of past development (e.g., evolutionary, cultural, personal), but some are the primary properties of the human biological and social nature.

In Pedrosa et al., we are introduced in detail to two aspects of the constraining system, which are, in a sense, at opposite ends from each other, at least with respect to their durability. On the one side, there are correlations, which are the stable laws in a system. On the other side, there are attractors, which are ephemeral configurations that emerge from the system's functioning, and which act as constraining influences as long as they are present. There is a motivating quality in the interplay between the long-term and the short-term constraints, the emergence of which is based on some semiotic uncertainty as well as randomness. The authors express this in the following way: "This uncertainty, and the occurrence of random activities which do not adjust to the configurations, constitute a state of disorder which may function as an *activating principle* of the interactional process, because it is a source of potential meanings which can eventually (though not necessarily) be actualized in shared configurations" (p. 146). There are, then, moments in the actual process of interaction which are, at times, more or less constrained, depending on the establishment of temporary attractor configurations. This seems to be exactly what Oliveira and Valsiner are referring to when they say: "We conceive of human interaction as a dynamic process of expanding or restricting shared semiotically organized conduct fields, occurring through the coordination of the roles" (p. 120). The latter authors' analysis, though, draws more explicitly on the encoded structural constraints present in individual memory and environmental structure—role-playing in any situation, namely, is a temporary attractor configuration, which explicitly and constantly draws on the individuals' knowledge about roles as well as the constraining influence of available resources. An example of this is Wellington's use of the belt (a physically available element) in the enactment of the role of authoritarian father (p. 128). A further elaboration of the constraining system introduced by Oliveira and Valsiner is the presence of constructed goals on the part of the participants in interaction. Thus, "personal constructivity of symbolic forms . . . is embedded in a culturally organized context, within which different other people, while interacting with the child, attempt to guide—supporting or constricting—his or her semiotic action constructivity, *in a goal-directed way*. These 'social others,' however . . . have to coordinate their actions with *the child's own intentions and objectives*" (p. 130, italics added). Smolka et al. cement the collective stand on the constraining system by claiming with full force its symbolic quality, so that "the *locus* of determination cannot be found exclusively in the realm of external 'physical' stimuli or of internal biological (pre)conditions," but rather, "man is determined by social reality through signs which he necessarily produces with others (for others, for himself)" (p. 163).


## THE PRINCIPLE OF RECONSTRUCTION

So far, we have seen that developing systems, both individual and social, or private and shared, are formed through interactive processes. A further claim is that the elements of the developing system are not entirely stable, but are transformed by use. So, the process by which elements of social interaction are taken in by the individual changes these elements, both by placing them in a new context and by transforming their configuration to some extent. On the other hand, the relatively permanent contents of individual semiotic systems are continuously altered by recombinations, as well as by new input. In shorthand, the two polygons of reconstructive reformulations are the processes of internalization and internal dialogue. It may be important to note that the accent is on active reformulation (active not necessarily meaning conscious), as opposed to a passive attrition of traces or elements in the system. An essential mechanism involved in this active reformulation is the dissonance inherently involved in recombinations that arise out of interaction. Oliveira and Valsiner give examples of reconstruction in both polygons. On the one hand, children in play, prompted by available material to enact an everyday classroom scene, "in their interactions . . . tried to bring up and to coordinate a great number of elements. . . . They try to enact various roles by imitation of present and previous partners and opposition to them, changing the meanings being confronted throughout their actions" (p. 125). On the other hand, an adolescent is brought to a personal reformulation of her religious beliefs, "challenged by the difference between the meaning system of the church ritual, and the irreverent set of non-religious suggestions presented by her grandmother" (p. 126).

Smolka et al. enhance the understanding of reconstructions by pointing to the essential role of the sign in these processes. The authors think of the role of the sign in terms of three steps of its involvement in interactions (both interindividual and intraindividual). First, it "impregnates and trans-forms the object" (p. 161) with which it is associated. An object used in everyday activity "represents something for somebody" (p. 161), it is imbued with the personal and cultural history of its employment. The particular present use is, however, punctuated by the particular present context, and a selective use of the potential polysemy of the sign (sometimes the poly-semy per se is used, as in puns and irony). Second, the sign allows the appropriation of external reality by the subject. In this way, it is a source of self-constitution, but also a source of novel integration. As Smolka et al. say, "it allows for a 'performance' which synthesizes old and new modes/models of acting" (p. 161). Or, yet, this "instance of self-naming implies the common (belonging also to others) and homogeneous (alike in nature), and, at the same time, the distinct (unlike others) and heterogeneous (different in kind, dissimilar)" (p. 161). Third, signs are always used in the necessarily reconstructive flow of narration. Smolka et al. refer to this aspect of sign use as the "dramatic character of human existence" (p. 162). This touches both on the essential property of reconstruction in the flow of developmen-tal events and on the integration of the various forward-moving levels of the developing system, by way of "meaningful action in a social system of relationships," that is, by way of "significant practice" (p. 163).

Pedrosa et al. give a frame-to-frame analysis of reconstructions in interac-tion, by showing how new attractor configurations arise out of self-regulating processes at the group level. Beside the principle of signification, which was already stressed, they bring an additional awareness of the randomness involved in this process. They say: "self-organization requires a situation where many chaotically manifested possibilities exist, from which correla-tions can occur. Correlations occur on the basis of a multiplicity of available choices; ordered states are re-organizations of random states in which *novel-ties* . . . are continuously taking place" (p. 146).

## THE ZONE OF POTENTIAL CHANGE

All this brings us to a reformulation of the classical Vygotskian concept of zone of proximal development into a zone of potential change. The zone of potential change (ZPC) consists in the set of possibilities open at a given moment to a developing person. The direction and magnitude of change, however, is constrained. In this sense, the ZPC represents a synthesis of the previously explained principles. However, it has an important new dimension. Namely, it is assumed that living systems possess a forward lunge. In this sense, the ZPC is a motivational category. The activity of the system is inherently motivated, and this activity is environment-interactive and self-constructive at the same time. This is illustrated well in Oliveria and Valsiner's analysis of the role of imagination as "a central constructive vehicle of human development" (p. 131). In the context of play, they see the zone of proximal development as a "field of joint actions dynamically related one to each other, opening a series of activities in which developmental tendencies are condensed" (p. 122). The developmental tendencies are forward-moving vectors, but also potentialities, open to various options. Development is not seen as being pulled "up" from the side of a more competent partner in interaction, but as motivated by the contrasts and options created by interactional events (both inter- and intrapsychological). In the case of adolescent fantasy construction, the zone of potential change is bounded by the possible combinations and allowable transformations in the adolescent's existing system of knowledge and values, and is pushed forward by the "antagonisms, antitheses, polarities that characterize that age period" (p. 125). It is this motivational aspect of the ZPC that Pedrosa et al. refer to when they say that "uncertainty is the source of innovation in the system: it generates novel actions and unfolded meanings" (p. 149)—this can only be properly understood, though, with respect to the fact that the "system" they are talking about is a human interactional system, in which socially significant actions are correlated in self-organized states. Similarly, Smolka et al. see human activity as unfolding drama. The possibilities of enactment and identifications are guided by role formulations and the meaningful sequence of the unfolding scenarios in human affairs (so that senseless contributions to the interaction will simply "fall through"). Although human drama is always an improvisation, the next step is always bounded by this demand for meaningful contextualization of actions. At the same time, the next step is always necessary, because the story pushes for its own resolution.

## THE COGNITIVE-EMOTIONAL BASIS OF MOTIVATION

It may be said that the inherent motivation of the intrapsychological system is based on the equal status of conceptual and affective associations to symbolic elements. The sign, then, is the carrier of a cognitive-emotional complex, which draws on its originally biological basis (which may have become functionally dissociated in the course of time). The cognitive-affective synthesis creates a motivational base by projecting (not necessarily, but possibly) goals, and by defining valences of environmental offerings. In

the example previously cited from Oliveira and Valsiner, adolescent symbolic constructions emerge not only as a result of cognitive dissonance, but
as a result of the motivating power of feelings about the horror of "hollow-
ness" and "hypocrisy" (p. 126). Their preschool examples, as well, demonstrate how affective-postural elements are equal in status to cognitive
elements in the unfolding of role-play drama. In the authoritarian-father
scene (p. 128), the meaning of the shared scenario is equally based on
Wellington's conscious employment of a tool (belt), Daniel's authentic expression of fear, and Maristela's dramatized expression of fear. And the
action is moved forward in equal measure by Wellington's cognitive-affective
synthesis: "I know how to set the world straight and I'll do just that (but
not for real)," Daniel's cognitive-affective synthesis: "I must get out of here
(even if it isn't for real)," and Maristela's cognitive-affective synthesis: "I
recognize a fear-provoking situation but I know how to deal with it (even if
not for real)."

## THE PRINCIPLE OF CONFIGURATION

Another important assumption underlies the arguments given in each of the
three chapters. It is that the configuration of elements, in space and in time,
is important, rather than the sum of these elements, or even the precise
nature of the elements themselves. This is, of course, reminscent of the
gestalt principle. It is recognizable in the ready use of field and zone notions.
It is also a consistent ingredient in the conceptualization of contextual
effects, and the perception, reception and transmission of patterns. In Pedrosa et al., for example, the recognition of configurations both by the actors
in interactive situations and by the observer is of critical importance. "The
configuration is the result of a set of properties of a situation which leads
to part of it being perceptually or conceptually highlighted, like a figure
against a background" (p. 140). The recognition of such patterns functions
as "an organizing pole towards a new spatial attractor" (p. 142). This micro-
analysis is readily transferrable to the contexts of the discussions of Smolka
et al., and Oliveira and Valsiner. The latter two chapters, however, take this
principle further, from the realm of perception (*aisthetos*) to the realm of
aesthetics. In that sense, the principle of configuration underlies the possibility for understanding the complex movements of natural art, such as
others' inner feelings or the drama of human life (and this is indeed art,
inasmuch as art is the artificial, that is—created, that is—cultural). Oliveira
and Valsiner, thus, propose that "the aesthetic relatedness of adolescent's
fantasy with the world is predicated upon the semiotic organization of the
'feeling in' " (p. 125). Likewise, they stress the creative nature of the products
of the imagination, the "creative" being not merely new with respect to

previous states, but aesthetically valuable—the aesthetic value being predicated upon both stylization and cathartic worth. This understanding can be glimpsed from the equation between "a novel" and "a religion," which is taken over from Aurore (p. 126). In a very similar vein, Smolka et al., call for a "'narrative' approach to the understanding of social constitution of subjective functioning" (p. 163).

## THE PRINCIPLE OF INCOMPLETE KNOWLEDGE

Finally, it is assumed that no one knows everything. The participants in a situation do not have full awareness or knowledge about all its elements. An individual does not have full knowledge of his individual past, and the known elements are not all held in mind simultaneously. Some elements, both of individual and of social nature, are such that they surpass perceptibility by the individual. When intrapsychological elements are externalized, they can be only selectively reproduced, and their interpretative contexts are always new and artificial.

## DISCUSSION

Von Wright (1971), distinguishes between the concept of determinism in the natural sciences and in the social sciences. In the case of the natural sciences, it refers to the idea that events and states in reality are the result of causal necessity. The "diagnosis" of such a determinism is based on predictability. This kind of determinism is not alien to the social sciences (where it may exist, for example, in the form of probabilistic laws on the macro-plane). However, social sciences also base their judgment about determinism on the understandability of the historical and social process. Von Wright calls this postdetermination. "The understandability of history is determinism *ex post facto*" (p. 209). It is teleological explanation, via intentionality, that is opposed here to causal explanation.

In terms of von Wright's distinction, the chapters we are commenting on apparently take it on themselves to discuss the perspective of the natural sciences with respect to their understanding of the concept of determinism. Their argument against determinism attempts to counter the universal applicability of the notion of causal necessity to psychological phenomena.

The key word here is not "cause" but "necessity." Radonjic (1977) names five levels of the understanding of necessity in psychology (as a natural science). The first, and simplest level, states that certain properties always go together in experience. Necessity is here a psychological habit rather than a logical category. The second level consists in the specification of the necessary, and sometimes sufficient, conditions for some outcome. The understanding is refined here by logical analysis and the discovery of certain patterns in the connection of phenomena. The third level of understanding of necessity includes the prediction of phenomena. The value of this is in the confirmation of hypotheses, which adds a degree of certainty to statements about the regular connection of events. The fourth level of the understanding of necessity introduces the notion of the active production of phenomena into causality. This is a dynamic understanding of causality, opposed to Hume's stand that we can never, by observing the world, discover a power which makes an effect the necessary consequence of a cause. Radonjic relates this level of the understanding of causal necessity to experimentation, where the actual practical manipulation of reality allows us to assert a causal law. The final, fifth level of understanding of necessity involves the knowledge of the "inner mechanisms" which connect the two phenomena in question. It is at this level that "real necessity" is established, by the answer to the question why two phenomena are related. The objective of science is to explain this connection.

The chapters in this book address this final level of understanding of causal necessity. By analyzing the mechanisms involved in psychological microprocess (in imaginative play, day-dreaming, or physical play), the authors show that these mechanisms are open to random or otherwise unnecessary outcomes. In such cases, there is no relationship of causal necessity between antecedent and consequent conditions. This argument is not yet complete, however. The authors do not merely attempt to show that there exist cases of event-evolution in which causal necessity does not play a part. They try to prove that, in these cases, it is necessary to think of the outcome as indeterminate, that is, random in some sense. The argument for this is found in the nature of the sign and the process of semiosis.

However, the demonstration that particular psychological mechanisms in micro-process are not deterministic does not yet tell us everything about the determinism of the developmental macro-process. There are many levels of constraint on the human individual system, and after showing that there is an indeterminate element involved in the production of certain base-level outcomes, we now need to show that this makes a difference in terms of other levels of development.

Markovic (1981) defines the notion of determination in a system in the following way: "To say that the system is *determined* at a certain moment $t'$ means that the set of its conceivable possible states is reduced to a subset of real possibilities, any one of which could occur" (p. 774). In this view, there are degrees of determinacy possible, depending on our knowledge of the properties of the system at the moment $t'$. "The degree of determinacy decreases to the extent to which the system gets more complex, the number of parameters grows and the description and measurement of boundary and initial conditions becomes more difficult. Then the number of really possible future states of the system in $t'$ increases. And yet any one of them is *necessary* in the sense that all those conceivable states which were incompatible with existing constraints (laws) have been excluded."[1]

The principle of historicity, the principle of constraints, the zone of potential change, and the principle of configuration, as portrayed by our compounded theory, all indicate that psychological development involves a basic systemic determinacy in the sense defined above. The fact that the prediction of particular states of the system is difficult or impossible does not counteract the strength of the biological, individual-psychological, and historical constraints. Systemic determinacy is transcended in micro-process, through randomness, on the one hand, and semiotic transformations, on the other. In sum, the answer to determinism as causal necessity must take into account the scope of processes which take place within the system. Although the possible subsequent states of the global system can be said to be determined by its previous states, the particular mechanisms within the functional micro-process, related to semiotic activity, are necessarily indeterministic. The question remains as to the ways in which the novel results of the indeterministic micro-process are related to long-term developmental processes.

We should also briefly comment on the implications of this theory with respect to other notions of determinism. For example, determinism could be understood as social necessity, or as personal determination.

As a statement of social necessity, a deterministic assumption can take two forms. One form of social determinism would hold that human activity is at any moment the inescapable result of influences of the present existing social environmental field. The adoption of a developmental point of view will automatically call this kind of determinism into question, because it would make the isolation of any moment in time, with no reference to what has preceded it, methodologically unacceptable. However, it would still be possible to imagine a psychological system which is the result of developmental progression of some sort (maturation, for example), but which is deterministically guided by social forces in any given situation. From the standpoint of the theory considered here, this view would be untenable. The sign, which is the core ingredient of communication, is multifaceted,

---

[1]It isn't by chance that the definition of determinism which is most understandably applicable to our theory arises out of a Marxist philosophy of science. Markovic (1981) defines the general characteristics of any dialectic method (whether idealist or materialist) to be: (a) the effort to encompass the entire whole to which the problem belongs; (b) the stress on the diachronic, historical dimension of phenomena; (c) the stress on autonomy, self-motion, self-determination; and (d) the method of critical thinking, which points out limitations and the possibilities for their overcoming. Whether deliberately or not, this is the method adopted by the set of authors of the three chapters under commentary.

separately and independently interpreted by each of the participants in communication. Its interpretation is constrained, but the constraining system is arbitrary and the only source of its being shared at all by the partners in communication is the history of negotiation of meaning around that particular sign. This negotiating process is never complete, and the meanings on different sides of the communication channel never fully overlap. Simply put, social influence is not fully interpretable for the individual. This is true of all situational social influences, not only linguistic communication.

The other form of social determinism would impute unidirectional social guidance on the process of development itself. The argument against it is essentially the same as above, but with additional emphasis on the principle of reconstruction. Because of the important socio-political implications, it must be stressed that this theory does not imply the possibility of escaping the bounds or constraints set by social practices and structures. Although every person constructs an inexact view of the world and him or herself in it, and develops creative ways of dealing with that world, employing these tools rather freely as occasions and imagination suggest, he or she must still function within a given social world (carrying with it prejudice, laws, customs, etc.) and can, in the construction of private tools, use only those elements which were somewhere somehow socially given. There is no magical transcendence of one's own being implied in this view. Paradoxically, the fact that the reality of the social world is not in any direct way accessible to a person's knowledge actually exacerbates the potential entrenchment in socially determined behaviors (i.e., modes of functioning which are based on the adoption of un-reconfigured elements of social discourse, or on manipulation by social others), since the unaware is unnegotiable.

Finally, there is the question of personal determination. The denial of absolute causal determination, as well as the denial of absolute social determination, naturally leads us to entertain the question of personal freedom. The philosophical understanding of indeterminism denies any determination of human will, be it external or internal (by purpose, goal, norm, or principle). As noted in Filipovic (1984), both determinism and indeterminism essentially disallow a free will, the former through the concept of causality, and the latter through the concept of absolute randomness. It may be that contemporary scientific psychologists should simply stay out of such debates. Yet, one cannot help but note that very much of what is said about psychological realities is motivated by our beliefs on this issue. Also, once again, the content of such beliefs and what is done with them are things motivated by certain sociopolitical reasons.

The three chapters presented here do not imply a clear answer to the issue of free will. The argument against determinism which is based on the essential possibility for random action does not provide a sufficient basis for the establishment of a free will. Plurality of possibilities does not indicate intentionality of choice. However, I would propose that the theory set forth by these articles provides a useful framework for the consideration of this question. The first element which might be useful in such a discussion is the stress on historicity and emergence of functions. Although it may be difficult to conceive of a nonrandom free will as being simply bestowed upon humans, it is easier to see it in an emerging form. Second, the stress on semiosis provides a polygon for its emergence. Semiotic ability brings the possibility of constructing goals, subsuming actions to them, and even re-defining one's own mental tools in the light of them. Finally, and I suggest this with full force, it is the cognitive-emotional synthesis that may provide the best basis for a psychological doctrine of free will. The simultaneous association of conceptual (meaning related) and affective (experience and motivation related) contents to symbolic subsystems that constitute the mind allows us to think of activity as being goal-directed from within itself, that is, as being future-oriented with a general direction which is clarified as the activity proceeds, as opposed to being elicited and directed by a constructed goal (or even a constructed self-regulatory system) alien to the activity itself.

In conclusion to the discussion, let us return to von Wright's breakdown of the sciences into those concerned with causal explanations and those concerned with explanations based on intentionality ("true" teleologic ex-planations). The developmental psychological science, as represented here, does not seem to fall to either side of the dichotomy. Its stand can be summarized as follows: On the one hand, although the general purpose of causal explanations—which are concerned with the precise description of universal relationships in their sequential (time-bound) aspect—is accepted, the principle of causality, that is, the immutable functioning of causal laws, isn't; on the other hand, although the sense of intentionality is clearly incorporated in the basic assumptions about development, teleological ex-planation ("true" or not) is not considered sufficient. Rather, it is the emer-gence and the mechanisms of intentionality and freedom that are sought.

## CONCLUSION

Each of the chapters in this section puts forward one major argument about (in)determinism in developmental processes. Oliveira and Valsiner point out the unpredictability of the interpretations and reconstructions that take place in the imaginational enactment of social roles—from the case of pre-schoolers in pretend play to the case of internalized interaction in the fantasy of adolescents. Pedrosa, Carvalho, and Império-Hamburger observe the emergence of ordered states out of the disordered movement within a small social group, the maintenance of these states and their transformation, based on the interaction of deterministic and indeterministic principles. Smolka, de Góes, and Pino argue that, since development is irreducibly based on the specifically human property of signification and takes place through the enactment of human drama, the method of choice in its study is interpretive, which makes the classical question of determination an irrelevant one.

Beside these explicit messages about (in)determinism in development, these three chapters project a compounded theory of human development. This theory and its implications have been analyzed with respect to different meanings of determinism.

## REFERENCES

Filipovic, V. (Ed.). (1984). *Filozofijski rjecnik* [Dictionary of philosophy]. Zagreb: Nakladni zavod matice Hrvatske.

Markovic, M. (1981). *Filozofski osnovi nauke* [The philosophical foundations of science]. Beograd: Srpska akademija nauka i umetnosti.

Radonjic, S. (1977). *Uvod u psihologiju: struktura psihologije kao nauke* [Introduction to psychology: The structure of psychology as a science]. Beograd: Zavod za udzbenike i nastavna sredstva.

von Wright, G. H. (1971). *Explanation and understanding*. Ithaca, NY: Cornell University Press.

# THEORETICAL APPROACHES TO INDIVIDUAL DEVELOPMENTAL PROCESSES

# 8

# PERSONALITY SELF-ORGANIZATION: CASCADING CONSTRAINTS ON COGNITION–EMOTION INTERACTION

Marc D. Lewis
Ontario Institute for Studies in Education,
University of Toronto

Developmentalists are beginning to conceptualize human development as a process of self-organization. This trend has been fueled by growing interest in dynamical systems theory in the sciences at large, and by new models of complexity and adaptation in biological and evolutionary studies. *Self-organization* means the emergence and consolidation of novel forms that assemble themselves out of recursive interactions among simpler elements. The nature of such forms is qualitatively distinct from that of their precursors—not only greater than the sum of their parts, but new, different, and unspecified by those parts. The concept of self-organization brings change and novelty back to the foreground of developmental modeling, recapturing intuitions that have motivated developmentalists for years.

As a mechanism of change and growth, self-organization replaces two standard assumptions of conventional psychological theories: that strong innate constraints are responsible for the ultimate form of developmental structures, and that structure is imported from the environment through the process of learning. Moreover, self-organization modeling brings together two long-standing insights from diverse fields within psychology. The first is the "organismic metaphor" of development, according to which comprehensive forms evolve from simpler precursors in the service of adaptation, as detailed by Piaget and further articulated in the systemic accounts of Chapman, Laszlo, Sameroff, and others. The second is the recognition that networks of interacting elements achieve stable structure without prespecification, through the process of iteration or feedback, as observed by cognitive scientists from von Neumann to contemporary neural network investigators (e.g., Bates & Elman, 1993). The amalgamation of these conceptual streams is evident in current dynamic systems approaches to development, pioneered by Fogel, Thelen, van Geert, and others. However, true to the metaphor of emergence, the end result of these efforts has yet to be determined. For now, we require a detailed exploration of the utility of self-organization modeling, and an openness to qualitative change in our understanding of human growth.

Two important premises guide the concept of self-organization. First, complex interactions among system elements have the potential to give rise to many different forms. The end result is never fully specified by its precursors, and small variations or random effects can greatly influence outcomes. Without this provision, the assembly of new forms could simply be said to follow some programmed sequence, making the notion of self-organization trivial and allowing no inroad for true novelty. Second, self-organizing systems tend toward coherence and stability. The variability or uncertainty in the system diminishes over time as coherence crystallizes and recurs. The end result is a stable whole with a particular identity, and, in the domain of living systems, such wholes actively preserve their identity over time (Maturana & Varela, 1980). These premises suggest a definition of developmental process as a shift from indeterminacy to determinacy over time. However, self-organizing systems are never completely indeterminate at any stage of their evolution. Rather, system elements and their initial relations with each other are already highly ordered, as are the environments in which they evolve. These structural and contextual specifications constrain the potentially infinite ways in which new forms can assemble. A challenge for dynamic systems approaches, then, is to sort out the roles of determinism and indeterminism that seem deeply interwoven in developmental processes.

Developmentalists are familiar with the idea of constraints, and this term may help us to think about the role of indeterminism in self-organizing systems. Constraints on self-organization include the initial structure of the elements of the system (including their mechanisms of interaction). For example, neural self-organization is constrained by the connectivity and modularity of the cortex (Skarda & Freeman, 1987). Constraints also include the environment within which the system develops. The physical properties of the world constrain the self-organization of perceptual and cognitive categories (Thelen & Smith, 1994), and morphogenetic fields constrain the differentiation and self-organization of embryonic cells (Goodwin, 1987). These examples identify constraints that are similar for all humans, but some constraints vary across cultures, subcultures, and families, yielding predictable developmental diversity. For example, variations in early social resources guide the self-organization of cognitive-developmental pathways (Keating, 1990). Thus, more or less general sources of order, in the system and its environment, constrain self-organizing processes throughout life, and these constraints steer development within recognizable limits of what it means to be human.

All of the constraints mentioned so far are deterministic in one sense. They are prespecified with respect to the developmental process itself. That is, they exist independently of the developing child, waiting, so to speak, to shape that child's development. There is, however, another set of constraints that reflect indeterminism, and these are the constraints that emerge as a result of developmental self-organization. These constraints are the very forms that self-organize from earlier interactions—forms that go on to influence further self-organization as development ensues. In fact, a sequence of emergent constraints cascades down the developmental stream, each influencing the formation of the next, guiding and narrowing the flow through increasingly refined outcomes. Cognitive activities in early development constrain "habits of mind" which mediate learning and scholastic achievement (Keating, 1990). Social adaptations to parents constrain early interpersonal behaviors which influence subsequent peer relations (Sroufe, 1983). These *cascading constraints* are both product and source of the specificity that crystallizes within individual developmental paths. Because they are partially indeterminate yet guide further growth, cascading constraints reflect one kind of relation between indeterminism and determinism: the using up of indeterminacy as developmental paths consolidate.

Cascading, emergent constraints are the very stuff of developmental self-organization: steps on the path from variability to specificity. What role does this leave for prespecified constraints, including the physical, genetic, and cultural structures that guide development? One answer is that prespecified constraints never act directly on developing forms. Rather, their influence is through the action of emergent constraints. For example, familial or cultural forms affect development through their influence on emergent cognitive structures and emotional dispositions. Even something so apparently uniform as the physical structure of the world affects development by influencing the evolution of perceptual and motor categories (Thelen & Smith, 1994). Moreover, these influences are themselves moderated by the individual's history of emerging constraints. Thus, prespecified constraints act on development by influencing emergent constraints, whereas emergent constraints guide and channel their influence. This interaction continues throughout development, and reflects a second kind of relation between determinism and indeterminism: the ongoing interplay between preexisting and self-organizing forms as individual pathways consolidate. As emphasized by Fogel (1993), indeterminism works hand in hand with determinism to shape every developmental outcome.

Prespecified and cascading constraints interact to shape outcomes in all domains, from motor and perceptual development to cognitive and social acquisitions. In this chapter, however, I describe their role in a domain that epitomizes both individuality and uniformity—that of personality development. Personality and interpersonal behavior provide a rich example of the tendency for developmental self-organization to dig its own idiosyncratic trenches as it moves from indeterminacy to determinacy. At the same time, personality self-organization achieves configurations so familiar that we recognize them in strangers after the briefest of encounters. In the following pages, personality self-organization is modeled in a way that accommodates cascading specificity and preexisting forms, and suggests the means by which they interact.

## THE ROLE OF EMOTION IN PERSONALITY DEVELOPMENT: CONVENTIONAL APPROACHES

The study of personality is sometimes considered orthogonal to the notion of development. Personality forms are identified by stable, continuous characteristics, and even personality theorists who focus on children provide little explanation for how personality gets to be the way it is. On the other hand, recent emphasis on personality change in adolescents and adults brings the study of personality closer to the province of developmental psychology (Helson & Stewart, 1994; McAdams, 1994). This matches an increasingly explicit emphasis on personality development by developmentalists themselves (e.g., Malatesta, 1990; Sroufe, Carlson, & Shulman, 1993). Developmental approaches to personality organization stress the role of emotion, and draw heavily on theories of emotional development. Rapid advances in the field of emotional development have fueled this trend. Specifically, proponents of attachment theory, temperament theory, and biologically-oriented theories of emotional development have all tackled the age-old puzzle of how people get to be the way they are, taking emotional organization as their vantage point. A similar perspective is taken by cognitive developmentalists who include emotions in their analyses (e.g., Case, 1988, 1996; Fischer, Shaver, & Carnochan, 1990; Pascual-Leone, 1990).

Attachment serves as a sort of default personality theory for many developmentalists. Attachment theory highlights the influence of maternal behavior on infants' regulation of their emotions in stressful situations, leading to a particular working model of the relationship with the caregiver. The consolidation of this working model is then reflected in a particular style of social and interpersonal behavior that persists throughout development. In response to criticisms by Lamb (1987) and Thompson and Lamb (1984), attachment theorists have debated the resilience of attachment patterns and their susceptibility to environmental change after infancy. To try to explain the apparent flexibility of attachment styles, multiple working models have been suggested (Bretherton, 1985), and changes in caretaking patterns and social contexts have been accorded the potential to modify attachment outcomes. Nevertheless, the core premise of attachment theory remains a relatively stable personality organization, present by 1 year, that predicts interpersonal relations throughout the life span (Hazan & Shaver, 1987).

Temperament theorists view stable individual forms as the product of neurophysiological differences that are genetically determined and observable from infancy (Fox, 1989; Rothbart & Derryberry, 1981). Despite increasing attention to developmental change and interaction with experiential factors, the explanation for stable forms remains grounded in these differences. Temperament affects personality by virtue of the potency of affects, thresholds to stimulation, novelty and discomfort, and prespecified social and attentional dispositions, all of which moderate the behavioral and self-regulatory repertoire of developing infants. Emotional reactivity and regulation are identified as key vehicles of this developmental process. Although measures of temperament are not particularly reliable early in the life span (except for Kagan's inhibition trait), the eventual socioemotional style of the individual is a product of dispositional structures that are already present at birth.

A third view of personality development comes from emotional developmentalists who view basic emotions as shaping recurrent experiences through which cognitive-affective structures are assembled. These structures provide templates for the organization of social experience throughout the life span. This interpretation is proposed in Tomkins' early work on personality styles and his more recent *script theory* (Tomkins, 1979). It is also articulated in Izard's (1977) model of emotion traits, in which personality structures derive from consistent associations between emotions and cognitive imagery. This view has been developed further by Malatesta and Wilson (1988), who postulated that significant exposure to certain emotion elicitors or contingencies early in life organizes the child's personality around trait-like emotion themes, and predisposes him or her toward particular emotions and interpretations. The common thread among these models is the role of basic emotions as organizers, with personality outcomes viewed as recurrent interpretations arranged around emotion themes.

These three frameworks share the assumption that emotion plays a central role in the organization of personality and social behavior, partly through its influence on cognition. However, each locates the source of this organization in structures independent of the developmental process. For attachment theory, maternal personality and behavior constitute a primary environmental condition that shapes the infant's adaptive response. For temperament theory, the essential structure is in the genetic makeup of the infant and its expression in emotional reactivity and regulation. For basic emotions theorists, the organizational locus resides in the structure of the emotion system and its response to social contingencies. Thus, the constraints on development implicit in these accounts are prespecified, not emergent, and indeterminism has little part to play in the assembly of individual developmental outcomes.

Contemporary theorists often borrow from all three accounts, mapping out interactions among temperament, parental influences, and emotional forms (e.g., Malatesta, Culver, Tesman, & Shepard, 1989; Mangelsdorf, Gunnar, Kestenbaum, Lang, & Andreas, 1990). Nevertheless, an interaction of prespecified influences does not amount to a recognition of the indeterminism inherent in early development; nor does it recognize the unbridgeable gap between preexisting constraints and lived ontogenies. This omission remains invisible as long as developmentalists rely on statistical significance as the main criterion for theoretical explanation. The variance accounted for by developmental predictions is often low. For example, predictions of attachment outcomes from both temperamental and maternal variables reveal consistently weak effect sizes despite statistical significance (Goldsmith & Alansky, 1987). This means that indeterminism really does play a large part in individual outcomes, and needs to be understood rather than ignored.

From a dynamic systems point of view, indeterminism is the necessary starting point for the emergence of structure in development and the emergence of coherent behavior in any given situation. This idea is articulated by Thelen and Smith (1994), who maintain that the variability inherent in the system and its context is the necessary condition for self-organization. Building on Haken's (1977) theory of change at points of instability, they view the complex organization of perceptual, motor, and cognitive processes as a result of variability in the brain as well as behavior—variability that permits the coordination of diverse elements under the influence of recurrent experiences. Fogel (1993) has posited the same variability in the early stages of developing relationships. He notes that relationships converge to specific forms and dispositions from a large number of possibilities, reflecting many degrees of freedom early in their history. This variability can be thought of as the fuel for self-organization, permitting the flexibility necessary to generate novel combinations, and hence to develop at all (Thelen & Smith, 1994). Such an approach contrasts with conventional explanations that posit a highly organized brain or environment as the source of highly organized outcomes.

Theories of personality development seem ideally situated to profit from this metatheoretical shift. It may even be suggested that the relative lack of attention to personality *development* reflects the unavailability of explicit terms for modeling self-organization. In fact, however, notions of branching or shifting individual ontogenies, often embodied in the metaphor of a developmental path, capture the spirit of self-organization without its explicit terminology. Recent papers by Sroufe and Jacobvitz (1989) and Magai and Hunziker (1993) demonstrate the power of this perspective. Personality organization epitomizes the emergence of macroscopic coherence from initial variability. Associations among myriad cognitive, emotional, and social elements contribute to highly coherent and stable forms as development ensues. To understand the convergence of these forms from indeterminate beginnings, and their peculiar blend of novelty and familiarity, some basic mechanisms of self-organization must be introduced.

## FEEDBACK AND COUPLING IN HUMAN SELF-ORGANIZATION

Self-organization is a two-sided coin, one side representing novelty and proliferation and the other representing stability and coherence. Novel forms are generated through recursion or feedback. Although there are many types of feedback, perhaps the most important is the global positive feedback through which effects become amplified over time. Activity in the system produces some sort of change, and this change is fed back into the system's state, providing a new starting point for subsequent activity. In order for this to occur, the change must involve at least two system components or subsystems that affect each other reciprocally, such that activity or change flows back and forth from one to the other, building on itself as it does so. Positive feedback allows small changes to feed on themselves, like autocatalysis in chemistry, moving the system from some initial state to an increasingly articulated end state. Thus, feedback constitutes an engine for growth. The ubiquity of positive feedback means that a complex, developing system does not return to its starting point, like a displaced pendulum, but continues to adjust to its own history by revising its present condition.

When positive feedback takes place, relations among many elements of a system change and reconfigure. Specifically, coactivated elements adjust to each other and become coordinated as they participate in the system's global activity. This reciprocal adjustment is called *coupling* or *entrainment*. Elements that do not participate in this activity drop out of the feedback cycle, so they remain uncoupled with those that remain. Moreover, elements that work against the activity are inhibited or turned off; thus they become coupled with the remaining elements in a negative or competitive sense. Coupled elements contribute to positive feedback by providing the coherence needed for self-perpetuation, as when like-minded individuals work together for a common cause and get it off the ground. By the same token, coupled elements resist the tendency for positive feedback to accelerate or deviate indefinitely by maintaining their coordination; the more they are activated by feedback, the more they hold each other in place. It is through this means that positive feedback cycles eventually stabilize. Negatively coupled elements also contribute to negative feedback, by inhibiting the formation of patterns with which they compete.

Feedback and coupling are inextricably related in self-organization, and their relations can be conceptualized at more than one time scale. Over the course of seconds and minutes, called *real time* or *microdevelopment*, coupling among elements allows feedback to get going, whereas feedback generates and maintains the activity of the cooperative elements. However, coupling on each occasion increases the tendency for the same elements to couple on subsequent occasions. This is because small changes in the structure or connectivity of the elements enhance their communication when they are reactivated in future feedback cycles. As a result, patterns that stabilize in microdevelopment are increasingly likely to recur over occasions, creating stability and predictability in developmental time or *macrodevelopment*. This predictability can be described by two kinds of features in the system's *state space*—the space representing every possible state the system can attain. Recurrent coupling among cooperative elements creates *attractors* in the state space—states that the system prefers and tends toward given a range of starting conditions. Recurrent coupling among competitive elements creates *repellors*—states that the system predictably avoids. Attractors and repellors can be visualized as valleys and hills, respectively, on a flat plane. A ball rolling about on that plane (representing the state of the system from moment to moment) will roll away from the hills and into one of the valleys. Thus, relations of cooperation and competition among elements provide the system with tendencies to organize in particular ways as it develops, and these tendencies are enacted by coupling through feedback on each occasion.

Self-organization can thus be construed at two interacting time scales. The system organizes itself in microdevelopment as elements become coupled, and it stabilizes over seconds or minutes as it reaches one of its potential attractors. In macrodevelopment, new attractors form and old attractors fade as patterns of coupling change. However, many of the system's tendencies do not disappear once they have formed. This is because structural changes in the underlying system elements (e.g., synaptic growth in the brain) can never be entirely reversed. Their participation in particular patterns (their cooperation or competition with other elements) constrains their future behavior, providing a mechanism for cascading constraints. Thus, new attractors (and repellors) form within old ones, or grow up next to them, adding increasing specificity as the state space becomes increasingly articulated (see Killeen, 1989). An analogy is the growth of a farming community over many generations: More and more land gets cultivated, family plots are subdivided into smaller parcels, and diversity and specialization replace undifferentiated land use. The elaboration of the system's state space constitutes developmental crystallization, reflecting self-organization at a developmental scale.

## PERSONALITY SELF-ORGANIZATION THROUGH COGNITION–EMOTION INTERACTIONS

Although feedback and coupling are ubiquitous in self-organization, the nature of the elements or subsystems that participate in these processes varies from one developmental domain to the next. For many theorists, personality development implies change and stabilization in emotional patterns and related cognitive activity. Therefore, an account of personality self-organization should be able to model feedback and coupling among cognitive and emotional elements.

Cognition–emotion feedback is an extension of the idea, endorsed by emotion theorists, that cognitive interpretations elicit particular emotions, whereas emotions focus cognitive activity in accord with their particular aims. Traditional emotion theorists have generally investigated one or the other of these links. Appraisal theorists attend to the cognitive interpretations that precede particular emotions (e.g., Scherer, 1984), whereas investigators such as Bower, Isen, and Oatley report on the cognitive consequences of emotions. My own view is that cognitive "appraisals" both precede and follow from emotions, as observed by Frijda (1993), fulfilling the condition for reciprocal causation or positive feedback (Lewis, 1995, 1996). According to this view, the cognitive appraisal of a situation elicits emotions that then adjust the cognitive system, focusing attention, retrieving memories, and specifying expectancies and plans. This adjustment becomes the condition for further appraisal, eliciting further emotion, and updating cognitive organization once again. As shown in Fig. 8.1, this updating process is a continuous cycle through which cognitive activity gives rise to emotions that simultaneously guide that stream of activity.

The elements that participate in cognition–emotion feedback include cognitive entities, such as images, concepts, script elements, and expectancies, but they also include emotional entities. These may be basic emotions—universal packages of feelings, expressions, and action tendencies (Frijda, 1986; Izard & Malatesta, 1987)—but this view is not essential for the model. Coupling among these cognitive and emotional elements both fuels and stabilizes the feedback process. Two types of coupling can be distinguished: coupling among cognitive elements and coupling between cognitive configurations and emotions.

Coupled cognitive elements reciprocally select each other as feedback with an emotion begins. For example, elements of a familiar script draw

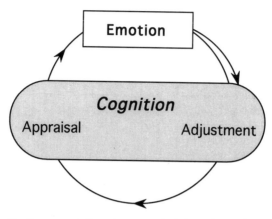

FIG. 8.1. Continuous updating of an appraisal through cognition–emotion feedback. From Lewis (1995). Reproduced by permission of the publisher.

together, or plans begin to assemble from subroutines, with the first trace of a particular emotion in a given situation. As they do, they begin to coalesce into a global interpretation of that situation, providing coherence to the cognitive system. This emergent interpretation invokes an increasingly articulated emotional response, which in turn specifies attention to particular features of the situation or related thoughts and memories. The interpretation becomes increasingly elaborated through the cooperation and adjustment of these additional cognitive elements. This feedback process stabilizes when a fully articulated emotional state holds the elements of an interpretation in place, while that interpretation maintains the emotional state.

A second type of coupling takes place between cognitive interpretations and emotional states themselves. For example, an image of the self as a failure may become linked with anger, sadness, or shame. Links between interpretations and emotions become strengthened over occasions, as feedback processes give rise to similar configurations repeatedly. However, certain cognition–emotion links may be present from birth (Izard & Malatesta, 1987), including species-specific responses of the emotion system to particular classes of situations (e.g., obstruction–anger, loss–sadness). Cognition–emotion coupling fuels the feedback process by guiding reciprocal selection between thoughts and emotions, and it helps stabilize feedback by locking interpretive gestalts into place with emotional states (see Teasdale, 1988). Moreover, coupling among cognitive components is nested within cognition–emotion coupling. Cognitive elements reciprocally select each other under the influence of an emotion that reciprocally selects their totality. This relationship sounds circular, and indeed it is. It exemplifies what Haken (1987) referred to as *circular causality*, the tendency for emergent forms to guide the interaction of the lower-order components from which they arise. This and other forms of nonlinear causation are characteristic of self-organizing systems.

Although these ideas may seem speculative, they are precisely mirrored by a recent model of cognition–emotion interaction in the brain. Based on an aggregation of neuropsychological findings, Tucker (1992) claimed that the layers of the cortex process information in an increasingly integrated fashion, from highly specialized sensory and motor detail at the outer layers to integrated, cross-modal processing at the inner layers. These inner layers happen to be directly adjacent to (and surrounding) the limbic areas where emotion is mediated. Information processing is described as "going into the onion and coming out again" (p. 101), with the integration of input and output pathways occurring in the paralimbic core where emotion exerts its influence. Information from across the senses converges in this region and is sent back outward as an adaptive response consolidates. The perceptual system then funnels the product of this response back down to the paralimbic core, and the cycle repeats itself. This cycling of information is the basis of neural self-organization, resulting in vast changes in the structure of the brain over development (Tucker, 1992). Thus, according to Tucker, emotion is at the center of the brain's self-organizing processes, and individual differences in cognitive organization are shaped by its influence.

Both in Tucker's self-organizing brain and in the present model, information flows in a cycle from cognitive appraisal, to emotion, to adaptive activity, guiding cognition–emotion entrainment in microdevelopment and concept formation in macrodevelopment. Yet the concordance of the two models is most striking with regard to coupling and codeterminacy between cognitive appraisals and corresponding emotions:

> It seems quite possible that . . . the reference frame for cognitive evaluation is the same as that for emotional responses. Cognitive evaluation may occur as paralimbic [emotion-related] networks resonate to emerging neocortical representations, thereby entraining activity . . . [which] may condition not only the person's immediate subjective state, but the endurance of the network states encoding current experience. (Tucker, 1992, p. 106)

To understand personality self-organization, feedback and coupling among cognitive and emotional elements must be considered recurrent processes that influence each other over occasions. On each occasion, the cognitive elements that are drawn together in a particular interpretation become more congruent with each other and with concurrent emotions. For example, images of helplessness, abandonment, and worthlessness become more congruent once they have coassembled on one or more occasions with sadness and shame. This increases the probability that they will converge once again on similar occasions, and, eventually, on not-so-similar occasions, as a depressive constellation consolidates in development. Thus, emotional experiences fall naturally into lineages of recurrent themes, and these themes become enacted in increasingly diverse situations. Most important, however, such themes are not structures that reside in the genes, the mind, the environment, or relationships with others. Rather, they are assemblies that emerge when cognition–emotion feedback activates their component elements in particular situations.

Thus, emotional experiences, and the themes they enact, self-organize on two time scales. They self-organize in microdevelopment with the convergence of a coherent appraisal and a particular emotional state. They self-organize in macrodevelopment as particular appraisal–emotion correspondences become increasingly predictable in given circumstances. The themes that crystallize in personality development are attractors that pull interpretive and emotional activity into stable configurations in real time. These attractors consolidate in developmental time, specifying the behavioral repertoire of the developing individual.

Consider a young child who feels anger and anxiety when his mother is unavailable. An image of the self as helpless or incapable becomes coupled with an image of mother as unresponsive, and these images become organized in a script in which demands for closeness are met by withdrawal and isolation. The coordination of these cognitive elements coemerges with emotions of anger and anxiety, and these in turn maintain attention to failure and helplessness, perpetuating a painful yet coherent conception of the interpersonal world. However, this experience of the self in relation to mother was not inborn, nor was it built into the features of the world. Rather, it coalesced over occasions in which particular elements were coactivated through positive feedback. Temperamental vulnerabilities, maternal behavior, and the logic of particular emotions may all have contributed to this result, but they did not determine it. An illness in the family, a difficult experience with a babysitter, the birth of a sibling, or a premature day-care experience may have played equally important roles in establishing this pattern and getting it going across occasions. The sensitivity of outcomes to chance juxtapositions allows indeterminism to play a powerful role in developing appraisals.

As the child develops and this cognition–emotion attractor consolidates, many situations come to elicit angry, anxious feelings and their accompanying interpretations. However, change does not stop here. New juxtapositions of cognitive and emotional elements give rise to new appraisals in response to cognitive development, new environmental contingencies, interpersonal feedback, and critical emotional events. These appraisals may become new attractors, growing and deepening across occasions. The anxious, angry preschooler may become inhibited, solicitous, vigilant, belligerent, vindictive, or fiercely independent during the early school years. Or, this child may discover new ways to trust others and to expose hidden vulnerabilities. In all probability, a number of these dispositions will emerge, each appearing in different social situations. Personality consolidation does not imply static behavioral structures, nor does it yield predictability across situations (Wright & Mischel, 1987). New patterns, like their precursors, emerge in some situations and not others. Nevertheless, their emergence denotes further crystallization in developmental time, as personality becomes increasingly specified.

Personality and social development can thus be viewed as a branching path, a metaphor used by other personality developmentalists (Kegan, 1982; Magai & Hunziker, 1993; Robins & Rutter, 1990; Sroufe & Jacobvitz, 1989). From the present perspective, new branches emerge when positive feedback activates novel combinations of cognitive and emotional elements, and coupling among these elements consolidates across occasions. As shown in Fig. 8.2, the form of each new branch is constrained by the orderliness already consolidated within the system, while each new branch constrains subsequent branchings. In other words, cascading constraints yield increasingly specified branchings over development. At the descriptive level, this means that attractors, once formed, change more easily in some ways than others. Or, global attractors become regions within which new, more differentiated attractors (or repellors) take shape. At the explanatory level, the cognitive and emotional elements available for new patterns of coordination retain the structural changes they have already undergone through their participation in previous patterns. For example, construals of self, other, need, control, and caring are sculpted through their participation in historical meanings, as embodied in their compatibility with related concepts and accompanying emotions. These elements may reassemble in many ways, but not without some residue of their former meaning. As shown in Fig. 8.2, there are fewer degrees of freedom (in development, not in real time) for each new branching, due to the consolidation of meaning at previous branchings. New cognition–emotion configurations thus converge from the interaction of historical meanings and novel possibilities.

## INTENTION, CONTROL, AND SELF-ORGANIZING DEFENSES

This depiction of personality self-organization echoes other dynamic systems work in developmental psychology in its emphasis on bottom-up, nondirected growth. However, developmental outcomes reflect directed cognitive activities as well, including the intentions, desires, goals, and plans that occupy a central place in traditional cognitive science. Yet the compu-

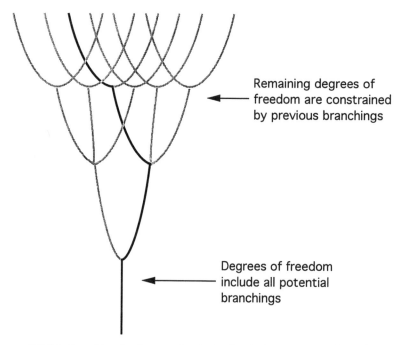

Remaining degrees of
freedom are constrained
by previous branchings

Degrees of freedom
include all potential
branchings

FIG. 8.2. Branching developmental path showing the increasing specificity of personality configurations. Cascading constraints reduce the available degrees of freedom at each successive branching. From Lewis (1995). Reproduced by permission of the publisher.

tational models of cognitive science fail to capture the circuitous, irrational character of intentions and goals in real developmental processes, and this is nowhere more obvious than in the study of social and personality development. A self-organization account has the potential to reinterpret intentional, controlled activities as components of emergent phenomena, in an effort to explain the rational and irrational aspects of mind within a unitary framework.

One of the goals most basic to emotional functioning is the reduction and avoidance of negative emotion, referred to as emotion regulation, coping, or defense. Like many directed activities, coping strategies or defenses evolve from intentional goals to automatic habits (e.g., Bandura, 1986). For example, young children rehearse strategies for overcoming their fears, whereas older children habitually circumvent their fears through self-deception or grandiosity. But how do defenses develop in the first place, and how do the forces of intentionality and self-organization contribute to their formation? To answer these questions, we first need to examine the relationship between intentions and emotions.

Emotion theorists view intentions as products of the action tendencies or aims associated with each emotion (Frijda, 1986; Oatley, 1992). Whereas many emotions motivate approach and engagement, fear and anxiety elicit intentions to withdraw from something aversive (Davidson, 1992) and prevent its recurrence (Stein & Trabasso, 1992). For example, anxiety motivates infants to disengage visually from an aversive mother (Malatesta et al., 1989). However, anxiety may also motivate disengagement within the cognitive system, independent of behavior, by shifting attention to alternative interpretations of potentially painful events (e.g., Case, Hayward, Lewis, & Hurst, 1988; Lazarus & Folkman, 1984). If these alternative interpretations come to replace the original appraisal over time, through the mechanisms of feedback and coupling, then the defensive process may be described as self-organizing in development, while satisfying the goal of reducing negative emotion.

The self-organization of a defense can be traced through three phases: the emergence of a painful appraisal, disengagement from that appraisal, and the move to an alternative appraisal in its place. In the first phase, a painful appraisal of a familiar situation recurs over several occasions, coalescing to an attractor in cognition–emotion state space. As argued by Thelen and Smith (1994), attractors *are* expectancies. That is, movement to the attractor is subjectively experienced as anticipation of a particular state. In the case of painful states, the negative valence of this anticipation is the occasion for anxiety. Thus, to paraphrase psychodynamic theorists since Freud, negatively valenced appraisals coassemble with the additional cognitive and emotional elements of anticipatory anxiety. Now, through more comprehensive coupling, painful interpretations take on the additional character of *core apprehensions*. In the second phase, movement toward a core apprehension motivates intentions to shift attention elsewhere—an expression of the escape tendency intrinsic to anxiety—and this pits a negative feedback condition against ongoing positive feedback. A variety of personality theorists identify negative feedback as the mechanism of emotional control or self-regulation (e.g., Bowlby, 1973; Carver & Scheier, 1990; Higgins, 1987). Unlike positive feedback, whose function is self-enhancement, negative feedback inhibits or terminates processes once they have gotten started. Thus, the positive feedback by which the painful appraisal enhances itself now begins to generate cognitive material incompatible with that appraisal. In the third phase, this competition is resolved when a new cognitive interpretation replaces the first, and the goal of disengagement is satisfied (see Case, 1996, for an example using avoidance). However, this can occur only when the alternative appraisal grows sufficiently to capture and maintain attention. As shown in Fig. 8.3, this necessitates a second positive feedback relation to propagate the coupling of cognitive and emotional elements in a new configuration. Most important, the arrangement of these elements is incompatible with the initial appraisal, so that anxiety is

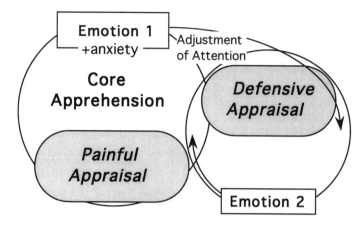

FIG. 8.3. Competition between positive and negative feedback, due to anxiety, increases chaotic cognitive activity until attention shifts to an alternative, defensive appraisal, enhanced by positive feedback. From Lewis (1996). Reproduced by permission of the publisher.

diminished as the system stabilizes, and a new attractor soon emerges in the state space.

The formation of a defensive appraisal and its utility for reducing anxiety depend on two key characteristics of emotional conflict and change. First, the emotion of anxiety is associated with cognitive disorganization (Calvo, Alamo, & Ramos, 1990; Eysenck, 1979; Sarason, 1984). In the present account, the conflict between positive and negative feedback in the vicinity of core apprehensions is responsible for this disorganization. Here, activated elements both enhance and inhibit each other, creating an eruption of discrepancy that is difficult to resolve and that perpetuates further anxiety. Psychological activity now oscillates unpredictably within certain limits, constituting a *chaotic* phase in microdevelopment. This chaotic phase allows for the rapid assembly of alternative appraisals. The capacity for rapid assembly of novel perceptions or interpretations is thought to be an advantage of chaos in cognitive systems (Skarda & Freeman, 1987). Now the system moves through a *bifurcation* or phase shift—a sudden change in its overall organization—such that the alternative appraisal becomes an attractor and the core apprehension becomes, at least for now, a repellor (see Abraham & Shaw, 1988). For example, children who are shamed become intensely vulnerable through attention to their own inadequacies, behave unpredictably for a few moments, and then become angry and belligerent through attention to their parent's faults. Once in an angry state, they are unable to acknowledge their inadequacies further.

The second characteristic of emotional change relevant to defensive appraisals is commonality between incompatible appraisals. Clinical and personality psychologists have long noted similarities between core themes and the defenses pitted against them (e.g., shame and grandiosity, hostility and paranoia, guilt and virtuosity). In the present model, defensive appraisals require such similarities, including shared emotions (e.g., the anger common to failure and blame) and shared conceptualizations (e.g., the attention to status common to shameful and grandiose appraisals). This commonality is necessary so that some of the elements coupled in the core apprehension can retain their coupling in the defense, facilitating a rapid transition between them. One way this might occur is through the rearrangement of script elements in a continuously activated script. For example, in the mind of the abused child, perpetrator and victim may change places in a victimization script, so that the child takes on the role of aggressor—first in fantasy and later in reality (H. White, personal communication, April 1995). The importance of residual activation in real-time cognitive change was recently emphasized by Thelen and Smith (1994). The amplifying properties of emotions might be expected to further augment continuity between successive interpretations of emotion-eliciting events.

It is difficult to assess when and how self-organizing defenses are guided by planning. Core apprehensions certainly generate goals of escape and avoidance, but the earliest emergence of a defensive appraisal may depend on the chance availability of an alternative perspective, epitomizing the role of indeterminacy at developmental junctures. Nevertheless, as defensive appraisals become attractors in their own right, we begin to anticipate them, and guide ourselves toward them, by adopting an inner voice or invoking a particular script to facilitate their convergence. An example can be found in the monologue of 2-year-old Emily, who soothed herself with the words, "babies can cry but—big kids like Emmy don't cry," soon after her father left her in tears at nap time (Dore, 1989, p. 259). We can thus guide the flow of real-time self-organization planfully, by cueing ourselves, thereby tilting the internal landscape toward a preferred attractor, so to speak. This use of self-directed speech is consistent with Fogel's (1993) description of "imaginative cognition" as a means of problem solving and self-comforting. Over time, defensive attractors becomes sufficiently entrenched so that cognitive appraisals gravitate toward them directly, and the core apprehensions against which they were erected become less and less accessible. By this point, the defensive process has moved from intentionality to automaticity, and the original appraisal has become a strong repellor, avoided by the system indefinitely.

The progression from attractor to chaotic bifurcation to repellor may well be recursive over development, tracing a particular lineage of cascading constraints in personality self-organization. New defensive attractors are initially selected because they relieve anxiety, yet moderate amounts of anxiety may remain coupled with defensive interpretations, and may indeed participate in the positive feedback that perpetuates them. Over time, however, these appraisals can elicit increasing amounts of anxiety and become core apprehensions in their own right. This change promotes increasing chaotic activity and the eventual shifting of attention to new, more specialized defensive interpretations. For example, the grandiosity with which young children defend against feelings of incompetence becomes the grounds for shame and anxiety in later childhood. The result may be an emergent style of self-deprecation that extends into adulthood. Over development, straight or circuitous paths from one defensive interpretation to the next reflect increasingly constrained appraisals, each resolving earlier conflicts while paving the way for new ones. These steps can lead to an enormous range of personality characteristics, including those classed as psychopathological, as habits of thinking and feeling become more and more narrowly specified.

An example may help to demonstrate the recursion or layering of self-organizing defenses. In a case study reported by Horowitz (1988), a young woman seeks help because of uncontrolled swings between a painful state of isolation and a numb state of feeling deflated and incompetent. These states are attractors in her present personality landscape: Most of her time is spent in one or the other. The developmental self-organization of this landscape began, according to Horowitz, with a strong, self-assertive script in childhood: an appraisal of herself as triumphing over her critical, aloof father. But this attractor served as a defense against more primitive rage regarding abandonment. It incorporated many of the elements of this previous pattern—including anger and aloneness—within a slightly different configuration: independence rather than abandonment. Eventually, this triumphant attractor came to elicit anxiety, now regarding damage to her father, and became a second chaotic juncture from which her thoughts and feelings migrated. The next attractor in the series is characterized by a sense of helplessness and feelings of incompetence. However, this state also came to elicit anxiety regarding rejection, thus shifting attention to an appraisal of seemingly deserved isolation. It is these last two appraisals that dominate the present state space. Thus, this woman's personality landscape includes at least two alternative appraisals of interpersonally challenging situations, each of which functions as an attractor at certain times and a repellor at other times.

## CASCADING CONSTRAINTS
## AND PREEXISTING FORMS

At the beginning of this chapter, I described the interaction between indeterminism and determinism in human self-organization as a challenge for dynamic systems approaches. The familiar idea of constraints on development was recruited to address this challenge. Two kinds of constraints were stipulated: (a) prespecified constraints, reflecting preexisting sources of order independent of the developmental process, and (b) emergent constraints, described as the progressive outcomes of developmental self-organization. Emergent constraints were shown to cascade in sequences of increasing specificity, each narrowing the possibilities of its successors while fleshing out the individuality of a particular developmental path. Yet these cascading constraints were argued to mediate the effects of preexisting forms as well. In this final section, the interplay between these preexisting and emergent sources of order is explored in more detail.

Cascading constraints in personality formation can be described microscopically, in terms of changes to the structure of cognitive and emotional elements, or macroscopically, in terms of the attractors and repellors that evolve in a developing state space. Microscopically, configurations of cognitive and emotional elements couple with each other through feedback, increasing the likelihood of similar configurations across occasions. The increasing tendency for particular patterns to reconverge reflects the growth of determinacy in personality self-organization. Feedback can be highly sensitive to perturbations, fluctuations, or randomness, because even a small alteration in the configuration of system elements can build on itself with each iteration. However, this sensitivity is reduced as elements couple recurrently over occasions. Coupled elements lose their independence: The activation of one element—a thought, feeling, or expectancy—draws related elements into place when feedback recommences. In this way, coherent appraisals act as constraints on subsequent appraisals, narrowing the range of available interpretations for future events. The net result is the increasing articulation of a developmental path, in which orderliness can be elaborated or modified, but never erased.

Macroscopically, every attractor and repellor constrains further articulation of the state space, including the emergence of subsequent attractors and repellors. We have already seen many examples. First, attractors and repellors constrain development by simple self-enhancement. Self-enhancing attractors constrain subsequent organization by extending the range of situations that invite a particular interpretation. Conversely, growing repellors narrow the range of circumstances that can be interpreted in a particular way—as epitomized by defensive personality organizations. Second, existing attractors and repellors influence the emergence of new ones. As noted earlier, new branches in developmental paths are constrained by meanings already present in the system (see Fig. 8.2). Potential new interpretations are limited by core feelings and beliefs about self and other and about the kind of world we live in. Third, cognition–emotion attractors and repellors influence the behavior of other people. These influences constrain dyadic interactions that feed back to ongoing personality development. Fogel's (1993) consensual frames describe the interpersonal medium in which these influences take shape. Finally, attractors and repellors give rise to one another over developmental self-organization, sometimes in long and convoluted sequences. Repellors in the system emerge from painful attractors that constrain their character and scope. Repellors, in turn, constrain the range of alternate appraisals to which the system can migrate at times of emotional turmoil.

All of these examples of cascading constraints reflect movement from indeterminacy to determinacy in development. But what is the role of pre-specified constraints in the process of self-organization? We know that these constraints are important, because we see the powerful effects of physical structures, phylogenetic structures, culture, familial patterns, and genetic differences on developmental outcomes. Yet, as argued in an earlier section, preexisting forms have no direct contact with the developmental process. In personality self-organization, their impact can only be felt through the emergent constraints—appraisals, anxieties, beliefs, vulnerabilities, defenses—that guide ongoing development. In order to influence development, preexisting forms must forge constraints in the flow of self-organization, yet these constraints are self-organizing configurations in their own right, and cannot be independent of this flow. They belong to the domain of development itself, not to some static, preexisting world.

Preexisting forms influence development through their effects on real-time self-organization. The consolidation of order in the moment is guided by the tendencies for system elements to couple in some ways and not others due to their structure, their modes of interaction, and the contexts in which that interaction takes place. For example, concept formation may be bounded by universal constraints on semantic coherence (Jackendoff, 1994), limiting the potential combinations of units that can participate in the self-organization of semantic categories. These constraints exist in the structure of the language, yet they influence the emergence of idiosyncratic interpretations in the moment. Preexisting social forms constrain the coupling of emotional as well as cognitive elements. Cultures arrange social contingencies in uniform ways, thus constraining the links between events, interpretations, and emotions (Gordon, 1989). For example, certain behaviors occasion social approval or disapproval for members of a culture, promoting the coactivation of similar cognitive and emotional elements for children growing up in that culture. More specifically, familial contexts establish relevance by highlighting particular sequences, thereby shaping the scripts that emerge to make sense of the social world (Nelson, 1986). These preexisting forms do not influence development directly. Rather, they influence the convergence of order in real time. Their effects are always local, in the moment, and codetermined by sources of order that have self-organized within the developing child. Yet the convergence of order over many such moments guides developmental paths.

One preexisting form that is particularly relevant to personality development may be the phylogenetically determined structure of the emotion system. According to many theorists, our emotions reflect a lineage of evolutionary adaptations, as expressed in the links between eliciting conditions, emotional feelings, facial expressions, and particular cognitive tendencies (Izard & Malatesta, 1987). These prespecified links constrain coupling between appraisals and emotions in real time. For example, the perception of a withdrawing object, when that object is valued or exciting, couples easily with sadness, less easily with anger, and not at all easily with joy. Yet even in infancy, such powerful constraints are commingled with individual tendencies. For example, individual differences in emotion responses (anger vs. sadness) to the same stimulus emerge and stabilize between 2 and 8 months (Sullivan, Lewis, & Alessandri, 1992). Whether the stimulus is interpreted as a loss or an obstruction to a goal may already depend on developmental self-organization at this young age. In turn, an angry response moves the infant a step closer to one sort of personality organization, a sad response toward another. Although each microdevelopmental convergence is constrained by the emotional hardware of the species, it is the convergence, not just the hardware, that guides future development. The determinism inherent in preexisting constraints is thus moderated continuously by the indeterminism of individual self-organization.

The nested influence of preexisting and emerging constraints accounts for uniformity in developmental outcomes, and nonlinear interactions among them account for unpredictable variations in phylogenetic, cultural, familial, and even genetic themes. The net result is a sea of attractors in the state space of our species and culture, permitting us to recognize familiar constellations within the spectrum of possible personality patterns. Yet these attractors are themselves broad regions that encompass enormous variability in the expression of general themes.

## CONCLUSION

Individual development flows from indeterminacy to determinacy without ever getting there. This progression reflects a very general characteristic of self-organization: the movement from uncertain beginnings to highly specific outcomes that are never fully predictable, in all processes of change in complex living systems. At the outset, the orderliness of development is inherent in the structure of multiple constituents and the relations among them. These constituents and their possible relations have already self-organized across time scales of centuries and millennia. What is truly novel, then, and so far unspecified, is the individual ontogeny that emerges from the interaction of these constituents. The orderliness of the constituents still permits enormous variability and unpredictability in each developing individual. Personality development captures many of these ideas in a conspicuous way, because of its synthesis of striking idiosyncrasies and familiar typologies. However, all domains of human development demonstrate the emergence of the new in a highly organized world.

## REFERENCES

Abraham, R. H., & Shaw, C. D. (1988). *Dynamics: The geometry of behavior.* Santa Cruz, CA: Aerial.

Bandura, A. (1986). *Social foundations of thought and action: A social cognitive theory.* Englewood Cliffs, NJ: Prentice-Hall.

Bates, E., & Elman, J. (1993). Connectionism and the study of change. In M. H. Johnson (Ed.), *Brain development and cognition* (pp. 623–642). Cambridge, MA: Blackwell.

Bowlby, J. (1973). *Attachment and loss: Vol. 2. Separation: Anxiety and anger.* New York: Basic Books.

Bretherton, I. (1985). Attachment theory: Retrospect and prospect. *Monographs of the Society for Research in Child Development, 50*(1–2, Serial No. 209).

Calvo, M. G., Alamo, L., & Ramos, P. M. (1990). Test anxiety, motor performance and learning: Attentional and somatic interference. *Personality and Individual Differences, 11*, 29–38.

Carver, C. S., & Scheier, M. F. (1990). Origins and functions of positive and negative affect: A control-process view. *Psychological Review, 97*, 19–35.

Case, R. (1988). The whole child: Toward an integrated view of young children's cognitive, social, and emotional development. In A. D. Pellegrini (Ed.), *Psychological bases for early education* (pp. 115–184). New York: Wiley.

Case, R. (1996). The role of psychological defenses in the representation and regulation of close personal relationships across the lifespan. In G. Noam & K. Fischer (Eds.), *The development of close personal relations: Vulnerabilities and opportunities for growth.* Mahwah, NJ: Lawrence Erlbaum Associates.

Case, R., Hayward, S., Lewis, M. D., & Hurst, P. (1988). Toward a neo-Piagetian theory of cognitive and emotional development. *Developmental Review, 8*, 1–51.

Davidson, R. J. (1992). Prolegomenon to the structure of emotion: Gleanings from neuropsychology. *Cognition and Emotion, 6*, 245–268.

Dore, J. (1989). Monologue as reenvoicement of dialogue. In K. Nelson (Ed.), *Narratives from the crib* (pp. 231–260). Cambridge, MA: Harvard University Press.

Eysenck, M. W. (1979). Anxiety, learning, and memory: A reconceptualization. *Journal of Research in Personality, 13*, 363–385.

Fischer, K. W., Shaver, P. R., & Carnochan, P. (1990). How emotions develop and how they organise development. *Cognition and Emotion, 4*, 81–127.

Fogel, A. (1993). *Developing through relationships: Origins of communication, self, and culture.* Chicago: University of Chicago Press.

Fox, N. A. (1989). Physiological correlates of emotional reactivity during the first year of life. *Developmental Psychology, 25*, 364–372.

Frijda, N. H. (1986). *The emotions.* Cambridge, UK: Cambridge University Press.

Frijda, N. H. (1993). The place of appraisal in emotion. *Cognition and Emotion, 7*, 357–387.

Goldsmith, H. H., & Alansky, J. A. (1987). Maternal and infant temperamental predictors of attachment: A meta-analytic review. *Journal of Consulting and Clinical Psychology, 55*, 805–816.

Goodwin, B. C. (1987). Developing organisms as self-organizing fields. In F. E. Yates (Ed.), *Self-organizing systems: The emergence of order* (pp. 167–180). New York: Plenum.

Gordon, S. L. (1989). The socialization of children's emotions: Emotional culture, competence and exposure. In C. Saarni & P. L. Harris (Eds.), *Children's understanding of emotion* (pp. 319–349). Cambridge, UK: Cambridge University Press.

Haken, H. (1977). *Synergetics—An introduction: Nonequilibrium phase transitions and self-organization in physics, chemistry and biology.* Berlin: Springer-Verlag.

Haken, H. (1987). Synergetics: An approach to self-organization. In F. E. Yates (Ed.), *Self-organizing systems: The emergence of order* (pp. 417–434). New York: Plenum.

Hazan, C., & Shaver, P. (1987). Romantic love conceptualized as an attachment process. *Journal of Personality and Social Psychology, 52,* 511–524.

Helson, R., & Stewart, A. (1994). Personality change in adulthood. In T. F. Heatherton & J. L. Weinberger (Eds.), *Can personality change?* (pp. 201–225). Washington, DC: American Psychological Association.

Higgins, E. T. (1987). Self-discrepancy: A theory relating self and affect. *Psychological Review, 94,* 319–340.

Horowitz, M. J. (1988). Unconsciously determined defensive strategies. In M. J. Horowitz (Ed.), *Psychodynamics and cognition* (pp. 49–79). Chicago: University of Chicago Press.

Izard, C. E. (1977). *Human emotions.* New York: Plenum.

Izard, C. E., & Malatesta, C. (1987). Perspectives on emotional development I: Differential emotions theory of early emotional development. In J. D. Osofsky (Ed.), *Handbook of infant development* (pp. 494–554). New York: Wiley.

Jackendoff, R. (1994). Word meanings and what it takes to learn them: Reflections on the Piaget–Chomsky debate. In W. F. Overton & D. S. Palermo (Eds.), *The nature and ontogenesis of meaning* (pp. 129–144). Hillsdale, NJ: Lawrence Erlbaum Associates.

Keating, D. P. (1990). Charting pathways to the development of expertise. *Educational Psychologist, 25,* 243–267.

Kegan, R. (1982). *The evolving self.* Cambridge, MA: Harvard University Press.

Killeen, P. R. (1989). Behavior as a trajectory through a field of attractors. In J. R. Brink & C. R. Haden (Eds.), *The computer and the brain: Perspectives on human and artificial intelligence* (pp. 53–82). Amsterdam: Elsevier.

Lamb, M. E. (1987). Predictive implications of individual differences in attachment. *Journal of Consulting and Clinical Psychology, 55,* 817–824.

Lazarus, R. S., & Folkman, S. (1984). *Stress, appraisal, and coping.* New York: Academic Press.

Lewis, M. D. (1995). Cognition-emotion feedback and the self-organization of developmental paths. *Human Development, 38,* 71–102.

Lewis, M. D. (1996). Self-organising cognitive appraisals. *Cognition and Emotion, 10,* 1–25.

Magai, C., & Hunziker, J. (1993). Tolstoy and the riddle of developmental transformation: A lifespan analysis of the role of emotions in personality development. In M. Lewis & J. M. Haviland (Eds.), *Handbook of emotions* (pp. 247–259). New York: Guilford.

Malatesta, C. Z. (1990). The role of emotions in the development and organization of personality. In R. A. Thompson (Ed.), *Socio-emotional development: Nebraska symposium on motivation* (pp. 1–56). Lincoln: University of Nebraska Press.

Malatesta, C. Z., Culver, C., Tesman, J., & Shepard, B. (1989). The development of emotion expression during the first two years of life. *Monographs of the Society for Research in Child Development, 54*(1–2, Serial No. 219).

Malatesta, C. Z., & Wilson, A. (1988). Emotion/cognition interaction in personality development: A discrete emotions, functionalist analysis. *British Journal of Social Psychology, 27,* 91–112.

Mangelsdorf, S., Gunnar, M., Kestenbaum, R., Lang, S., & Andreas, A. (1990). Infant proneness-to-distress temperament, maternal personality, and mother-infant attachment: Associations and goodness of fit. *Child Development, 61,* 820–831.

Maturana, H. R., & Varela, F. J. (1980). *Autopoiesis and cognition: The realization of the living.* Boston: Reidel.

McAdams, D. P. (1994). Can personality change? Levels of stability and growth in personality across the life span. In T. F. Heatherton & J. W. Weinberger (Eds.), *Can personality change?* (pp. 299–313). Washington, DC: American Psychological Association.

Nelson, K. (1986). Event knowledge and cognitive development. In K. Nelson (Ed.), *Event knowledge: Structure and function in development* (pp. 231–247). Hillsdale, NJ: Lawrence Erlbaum Associates.

Oatley, K. (1992). *Best laid schemes: The psychology of emotion.* Cambridge, UK: Cambridge University Press.

Pascual-Leone, J. (1990). Reflections on life-span intelligence, consciousness and ego development. In C. N. Alexander & E. Langer (Eds.), *Higher stages of human development* (pp. 258–285). Oxford, UK: Oxford University Press.

Robins, L., & Rutter, M. (1990). *Straight and devious pathways from childhood to adulthood.* Cambridge, UK: Cambridge University Press.

Rothbart, M. K., & Derryberry, D. (1981). Development of individual differences in temperament. In M. E. Lamb & A. L. Brown (Eds.), *Advances in developmental psychology* (pp. 37–86). Hillsdale, NJ: Lawrence Erlbaum Associates.

Sarason, I. G. (1984). Stress, anxiety, and cognitive interference: Reactions to tests. *Journal of Personality and Social Psychology, 46,* 929–938.

Scherer, K. R. (1984). On the nature and function of emotions: A component process approach. In K. R. Scherer & P. Ekman (Eds.), *Approaches to emotion* (pp. 293–317). Hillsdale, NJ: Lawrence Erlbaum Associates.

Skarda, C. A., & Freeman, W. J. (1987). How brains make chaos in order to make sense of the world. *Behavioral and Brain Sciences, 10,* 161–195.

Sroufe, L. A. (1983). Infant-caregiver attachment and patterns of adaptation in preschool: The roots of maladaptation and competence. In M. Perlmutter (Ed.), *The Minnesota symposia on child psychology: Vol. 16. Development and policy concerning children with special needs* (pp. 41–83). Hillsdale, NJ: Lawrence Erlbaum Associates.

Sroufe, L. A., Carlson, E., & Shulman, S. (1993). Individuals in relationships: Development from infancy through adolescence. In D. C. Funder, R. D. Parke, C. Tomlinson-Keasey, & K. Widaman (Eds.), *Studying lives through time: Personality and development* (pp. 315–342). Washington, DC: American Psychological Association.

Sroufe, L. A., & Jacobvitz, D. (1989). Diverging pathways, developmental transformations, multiple etiologies, and the problem of continuity in development. *Human Development, 32,* 196–203.

Stein, N. L., & Trabasso, T. (1992). The organization of emotional experience: Creating links among emotion, thinking, language, and intentional action. *Cognition and Emotion, 6,* 225–244.

Sullivan, M. W., Lewis, M., & Alessandri, S. M. (1992). Cross-age stability in emotional expressions during learning and extinction. *Developmental Psychology, 28,* 58–63.

Teasdale, J. D. (1988). Cognitive vulnerability to persistent depression. *Cognition and Emotion, 2,* 247–274.

Thelen, E., & Smith, L. B. (1994). *A dynamic systems approach to the development of cognition and action.* Cambridge, MA: MIT Press.

Thompson, R. A., & Lamb, M. E. (1984). Assessing qualitative dimensions of emotional responsiveness in infants: Separation reactions in the Strange Situation. *Infant Behavior and Development, 7,* 423–445.

Tomkins, S. S. (1979). Script theory: Differential magnification of affects. In H. E. Howe & R. A. Dienstbier (Eds.), *Nebraska symposium on motivation* (Vol. 26, pp. 201–236). Lincoln: University of Nebraska Press.

Tucker, D. M. (1992). Developing emotions and cortical networks. In M. R. Gunnar & C. Nelson (Eds.), *Minnesota symposia on child psychology: Vol. 24. Developmental behavioral neuroscience* (pp. 75–128). Hillsdale, NJ: Lawrence Erlbaum Associates.

Wright, J. C., & Mischel, W. (1987). A conditional approach to dispositional constructs: The local predictability of social behavior. *Journal of Personality and Social Psychology, 53,* 1159–1177.

# 9

# EPISTEMOLOGY OF COGNITIVE DEVELOPMENT THEORY

Antonio Roazzi
Bruno Campello de Souza
Federal University of Pernambuco, Brazil

The adoption of the discourse on determinacy and indeterminacy in the context of modern cognitive science is controversial, but it is of the utmost importance. For instance, at the micro level, some psychological phenomena look indeterminate (i.e., their causes seem to change over time), but at the macro level causation itself may vary at some deterministic pace. If we have a choice, we should prefer to see deterministic causality, because that is the basis of science itself, yet, the nature of psychological phenomena provides us with challenges that undermine the use of deterministic models.

In order to clarify the issues, the present chapter examines the basic concepts and differing perspectives regarding the subject and the epistemology of research on it from the more general standpoint of determining how to discover determinacy or indeterminacy in mental processes. We begin by introducing the purpose of knowledge and the difficulties in its acquisition within the determinism/indeterminism debate. Next, the basic underlying concepts and terminology involved in the topic are presented. Following that, we consider the areas scientific study, especially in terms of the investigation on cognitive development. Finally, a practical example is provided, in which empirical data from a study of mental development of 5- to 7-year-old Brazilian children is shown and analyzed based on all preceding considerations.

## THE PURPOSE OF KNOWLEDGE

Human knowledge is the result of an evolutionary mechanism that allowed relatively weak, slow, and fragile creatures to survive in a hostile world by making them capable of controlling it. Cognitive mechanisms were developed as a response to the need for building models and theories capable of predicting the outcome of events important to human life, and also as a means of identifying procedures capable of interacting with such events in a favorable way and with minimal effort (see Waddington, 1970). To achieve such goals, one must know two things about a given phenomenon: how it happens and why it happens.

Using a depiction of basic control systems theory, such as the one given by Dorf (1980), one can conclude that the answer to the *how* question (in what way, where, and when), that is, the adequate description of a phenomenon, essentially permits predictability. Forecasts and decisions based on such information makes it possible to steer ones actions toward the most favorable aspects of an event and to prepare for, or sidestep, the unfavorable ones. Some sort of primitive or passive control can occur through the use of a "do-this-and-probably-that-will-happen" approach that can be obtained from the predictive models.

The same fundamental control systems tenets also permit one to safely deduce that the *why* question, which addresses the issue of causality, permits effective control. The knowledge of the effect of causal mechanisms and the way in which they work allows one to effectively influence the very core of the event in question, which leads to an active transformation of reality, rather than a passive optimal reaction to unchanged reality that results from a purely descriptive model.

## DIFFICULTIES IN THE ACQUISITION
## OF KNOWLEDGE

Because the answers to *how* help in the sense of prediction and passive control and the answers to *why* lead to transformation and active control, it is quite obvious that the second line of inquiry will yield the best results. Of course, there is the problem that the first things about a phenomenon that come to one's knowledge are that phenomenon's perceptible features, which is why scientists tend to know *how* long before they know *why*. This is due to the level of abstraction and detachment from apparent reality that is required for the apprehension of causality, in contrast with the relatively simple objectivity and pragmatism needed for the observation of events.

One consequence of the difficulty in addressing *why* questions is the controversial debate on determinism versus indeterminism in the causation of cognitive development. This debate arises from the lack of knowledge of the exact nature of the underlying laws responsible for the phenomenon, knowledge that usually has to be inferred indirectly from the observation of *how*. The importance of this issue is related to the need to create developmental theories that are maximally efficacious for applications in education, counseling, therapy, and so on.

## THE DETERMINISM/INDETERMINISM DEBATE

The issue of determinism versus indeterminism is essentially a question of how the law of cause and effect works. It is an abstract and illusive intellectual pursuit, though extremely important for the analysis of practical, even pragmatic, phenomena.

Determinists believe that there are definite, relatively well-behaved, underlying mechanisms that, if fully known, could lead to precise prediction and complete control. So, knowing the past, it would be possible and relatively easy to predict the future. Indeterminists, on the other hand, are those who believe that the vagueness that permeates practically all research on causation is due not to ignorance, but to an intrinsic feature of nature, which makes precise prediction and complete control not only operationally but also theoretically impossible (Schlick, 1925; Stewart, 1989).

It would seem that scientists should be determinists, for they attempt to produce or acquire knowledge that will lead to perfect predictability and control of phenomena, and they try to do so using methods that assume the existence of definite, stable patterns of behavior in the universe. However, seemingly intractable vagueness and insurmountable difficulties in prediction and control are there for all to see, and facts do not cease to exist simply because they contradict our beloved theories. To resolve such a dilemma, one has to analyze the issues of causation, determinism and indeterminism and try to discover how such notions could be applied to satisfy both the utmost purpose of human knowledge and existant empirical findings.

In the context of human development, the answer to the controversy involves answering a series of important questions, such as: Is an individual subject to an active agent of its own development, rather than a passive responder? How can responsibility for actions be maintained if behavior is determined by genetic makeup and environmental experience? If individuals are not in full control of their actions, how can they be held responsible for them?

In order to address these questions adequately, we must briefly consider the notions of causality, determinism and indeterminism and their standing within scientific epistemology. We must then keep such considerations in mind we observe an event of interest (in this case, aspects of human cognitive development) and try to arrive at some useful and reliable conclusions.

## CAUSALITY

### A Definition of Cause

In the study of anything, it is necessary to establish quite clearly and unambiguously what we are investigating, whether we are artists, physical scientists, philosophers, or human scientists. Such a need is especially evident when we deal with such abstract notions as causes. Therefore, for the purposes of this chapter, we proffer the following definition of cause:

> A *cause* is that something that, by itself or in association with other causes, produces a new event, from then on called an "effect," which is a consequence of it. Causes themselves may be the effects of other causes. The existence of a cause means that there necessarily must be an effect, and the existence of an effect means that there necessarily must be a cause, otherwise, the words *cause* and *effect* should not be used.

Applying this definition to the study of cognitive development, a cause of cognitive development is something that, either in isolation or in combination with other causes, brings about in human beings cognitive skills and abilities that previously did not exist.

### A Classification of Causes

Having established exactly what we mean by the word *cause*, it is interesting to analyze causation in terms of how many kinds of cause we can have and how we can classify them. Many systems have been devised to do this, but the one constructed by Aristotle (b. 384, d. 322 BC) stands out for its scope, organization, exactness, simplicity and appeal to common sense.

According to Aristotle, it is possible to classify all causes using four broad categories. These are:

*Material Cause:* The matter out of which the effect is rendered existent in a concrete way.

*Efficient Cause:* The primary source of the effect, that is, the energy which caused change or coming to rest. It is the movement or action which generated the event.

*Formal Cause:* The form or archetype which constitute the "blueprints" for the effect. That is to say, the pattern or "invisible backbone" which defines the event.

*Final Cause:* The purpose behind the effect. It is the end or "that for the sake of which" a thing is done.

Aristotle illustrated the four kinds of causes by using the example of the shoe. The material cause of a shoe is the leather or hide out of which it is made. The efficient causes are the shoemaker's movements and actions. The formal cause is the plan in the shoemaker's mind for the shape and size of the shoe. The final cause is the protection of the foot.

There seems to be a certain continuum and ranking of Aristotelian causes as in the level of philosophical abstraction necessary for their understanding. Material causes are the easiest to deal with, due to their objective and concrete nature. Then come efficient causes, because their understanding stems from the observation of the dynamics of the material causes. After that, are the formal causes, which are more difficult to apprehend due to the need to recognize regularities and patterns in the dynamics of material causes, which requires a certain level of abstraction. The most difficult of all are final causes, because they must be analyzed by hypothesizing the existence of an actual or hypothetical purpose for the regularities and patterns observed.

In any kind of cognitive development also the four kinds of causes are present. The material causes involve the central nervous system and its composition, architecture and organization, as well as all the physical and chemical characteristics of the environment. The efficient causes are the body's general physiological dynamics (especially the biochemical and electrical activity of the nervous system) together with all the physical and social events interacting with them. The formal causes of development are a matter of theoretical taste (e.g., a Piagetian developmentist would consider them assimilation, adaptation, and accommodation, whereas a neurologist would think in terms of genetic blueprints). The final causes are generally seen as survival, well-being, or need satisfaction, and are concerned with motivation.

## The Four Causes and the Study Causation in Science

In science, as in philosophy, one must keep in mind that there are different *kinds* of causes, once an *issue* of causation is chosen in regard to a certain object of study. However, not all kinds of causes can easily be considered legitimate lines of scientific inquiry.

During the Renaissance, there were several attacks on the uses of formal and final causes in scientific inquiry. According to some of the most important thinkers of those days (Bacon, 1620; Descartes, 1629, 1637; Spinoza, 1677), one should exercise skepticism regarding the use of the concepts of formal and final cause in the study of worldly phenomena; because these causes were highly abstract, they were to be used only for inquiries into the transcendental realms of philosophy and religion. Material and efficient causes, on the other hand, could be directly observed and experimented with by physics, biology, medicine, and the like; thus, in effect, guidelines were made for the study of nature.

Later, although the abstract nature of formal and final causes was not denied, the philosophical thinking and ideas generated by them were con-

sidered to be useful for the study of natural phenomena, because they
guided thinking, stimulated the creation of models and theories, and enhanced understanding (Harvey, 1628; Kant, 1781). This line of thought can
be summarized by the following statement by Kant:

> No one has ever questioned the correctness of the principle that, when judging
> a certain thing in nature, namely organisms and their possibility, we must look
> at the conception of final causes. Such a principle is admittedly necessary
> even where we require no more than a guiding-thread for the purpose of
> becoming acquainted with the character of these things by means of obser-
> vation. (Kant, 1781, p. 594)

More recently, Popper (1959) introduced the concept that the intellectual
possibility of falsehood through empirical study is the essential attribute of
scientific knowledge, raising the question of which causes can or cannot be
submitted to that paradigm. Obviously, material and efficient causes apply,
for it is clear that it is at least theoretically possible to verify experimentally
the role of substances, components and elements, as well as of movements,
behaviors, and specific events, in the occurrence of a given phenomenon.
Formal causes also are included since one can experimentally observe the
existence or absence of given hypothetical patterns. With final causes though,
the situation is unclear. Although it is relatively easy to establish hypothetical
purposes for a certain phenomenon and empirically observe whether those
are fulfilled or not during the occurrence of that phenomenon, one can always
create several different purposes that fit the same set of experimental data.

Thus, in the scientific study of causation, material and efficient causes
are fairly pragmatic and undisputed, and are therefore unanimously considered valid lines of inquiry. Formal and final causes, on the other hand,
despite having beneficial epistemological and knowledge-formation implications that are fundamental for the development of scientific theories, by
definition, cannot actually be shown or proven, making their study both an
experimental and a philosophical problem.

## DETERMINISM AND INDETERMINISM

### A Definition of (In)Determinism

*Determinism* is the belief that, for a given set of a priori conditions, identical
causes will yield identical effects. In other words, if one were to flip a coin
several times controlling the coin's mass, shape, and size; the intensity and
direction of the force applied, the temperature, humidity, flux, and dust

particles of the air, the surface where the coin should land, and so forth, a determinist would expect to achieve the same result over and over again.

A determinist would say that a given phenomenon, such as the tossing of a coin, can be predicted if one has exact knowledge about its causal mechanisms and how they act during the time prior to the occurrence of the phenomenon. It considers that any event not only can be traced to a single set of causes, but also that a repetition of such causes will always result in a repetition of the event. According to this view, although it is true that nothing "just happens," that is, everything has a definite cause, it is also true that if certain events occur, others must follow.

*Indeterminism*, on the other hand, is the belief that identical causes, given the same set of a priori conditions, can actually yield different effects. Using the same example, precisely the same throw of a coin might yield either a head or a tail in a series of repetitions. Fully stated, indeterminism is the belief that an event, once it has occurred, can always be traced back to a single specific set of prior conditions of the causal mechanism, but that there are always several different possibilities for the future effect of a present set of causal mechanisms.

## Kinds of Determinism

Determinism can be classified into two distinct categories which differ in the extent they take determinisms epistemological implications.

*Strong determinism* is the belief that, if we knew everything about something's present and past circumstances, we could predict its behavior precisely. The inability to do so, then, necessarily stems from a lack of sufficient data, measurement precision, and/or adequate modeling.

Strong determinism was expressed at the beginning of the 1800s by Pierre Simon Marquis de Laplace. According to Laplace, if it could be possible to know at a precise moment all forces that act on nature and the position of all bodies, in principle it would be possible to predict all subsequent states of the universe. Someone having this knowledge would be able to simultaneously know past, present, and future. This is known as the *Laplacian demon*.

*Weak determinism* is the belief that, within certain bounds or limits, it is possible for one to predict the outcome of a situation based on knowledge of present and past circumstances. In other words, future behavior can be foreseen up to a certain point, if one knows enough about the past. In a way, it is a compromise between deterministic and indeterministic views. Weak determinism seems to be the result of the empirical difficulties encountered in attempts to fulfill the promises made by strong determinism, and tends to be more prevalent in current times.

# THE STUDY OF CAUSATION IN HUMAN COGNITION

## A Gap in the Field of Cognitive Science

Bryant (1986, 1990) argued that, although much is known about how cognitive development takes place, little is known about why such a course of development comes to happen in that particular way instead of in another. One of the reasons that he identified for this is the fact that many researchers use experimental methods that are, by definition, inadequate for the study of causation.

The issue of determination versus indetermination, as stated earlier, is an issue on causation. In cognitive psychology, indeterminism is the continuous alteration of the probabilistic mechanisms that determine cognitive development, which makes it impossible to establish a priori probabilities for cognitive events. At the other extreme, determinism refers to the view that events occur in such an orderly manner that, once given a full description of an antecedent situation, the subsequent one can, in principle, be predicted. It establishes the necessary connection between all phenomena according to the causality principle. Only the acquisition of knowledge of why things happen as they do will settle this debate.

## Problems With the Contemporary Trend Toward Indeterminism

Indeterminism seems to have been quite in evidence in the recent past, as evidenced in Black (1973), Lewis and Hayne (1979), and Popper (1950). In fact, it has become quite fashionable! Some of the reasons for this preference toward indeterministic beliefs are:

- The poor predictive power of deterministic models.
- The advent and dissemination of quantum mechanics, which describes the basic building blocks of all things (subatomic particles) as being essentially indeterminate in their behavior.
- The "political correctness" of indeterministic views that human behavior is too free from the restraints of predictability, causation, and logic to be understood by purely deterministic models.
- The need to break away from behaviorism (perhaps a backlash?).

Of course, most of these reasons cannot be considered valid arguments for choosing indeterminism over determinism.

The uncertainty principle establishes limits to ones knowledge of events at the subatomic level (Heisenberg, 1958); but it does not exclude determinism. There seems indeed to be a paradox between randomness and determinism, because, according to chance theory, it is not possible to foresee events, whereas, according to determinism, that should be possible. According to the French physicist David Ruelle (Ruelle, 1993), the abstract hypothetical domain and the concrete experimental one are not necessarily opposites of one another. According to him, the 100% precise measurement condition, which is absolutely necessary for perfectly accurate forecast, is unattainable, therefore making it impossible to distinguish, in practice, between determinism and indeterminism. In fact, from that point of view the whole discussion seems useless. Italian physicist Bernardini (1993), tends to agree, and added that determinism, as regarded by Laplace, is actually a useless concept (and, if so, then so is indeterminism). Even if one were to accept the idea that there is a fundamental randomness in the configuration of subatomic particles, these random variations would tend to cancel out one another at molecular levels, and would certainly be infinitesimal or null in phenomena as prodigious as biological behavior. Thus, it is not rational do contend that a fundamental uncertainty in the nature and configuration of subatomic particles is a valid reason to suppose that cognitive development in humans is indeterminate.

The belief that determinism is an antihumanistic or even a socially harmful attitude, because it would deny people free will and individual responsibility, is also mistaken. Behaviorist determinists have been described as totalitarian politicians who reserve to the human being the role of automaton (Black, 1973). The fact is that determinism is perhaps even more humanistic than indeterminism, for the former asserts that the nature of behavior can be studied, understood, and controlled, whereas the latter sees us as the victims of the eccentricities of the environment and the caprice of nature (Lewis & Hayne, 1979). In fact, even full-pledged behaviorists, such as Skinner (1973) and Platt (1973), attempted to prove that the acceptance of determinism does not violate the possibility of choice, free will, self-determination and self-control.

Psychology, being (or intending to be) a science, is based on the belief that behavior and development are caused, and that such causes can be empirically discovered and quantitatively measured with adequate enough precision to permit both prediction and control within acceptable limits. If nature proves that belief to be mistaken, then we must dramatically redefine science and its basic tenets. For this reason, no scientist wants to be an indeterminist, if he or she can help it. However, such a stand must never be an excuse for the denial of facts. As Wrightsman and Sanford (1975) pointed out in regard to the determinism/ indeterminism debate:

> But the scientist knows that the problem need not to be finally settled before he can go to work. He knows that there are predictions, even about people,

that he can learn to make. And he follows as a working strategy, but not necessarily as a final truth, the principle of determinism. (p. 542)

## A CAUSAL STUDY OF DEVELOPMENT

### Experimental and Analytical Premises

In the analysis of cognitive development, instead of breaking down cognition into minute, severely restricted components and studying them separately, it seems best to consider an organized set of abilities that have clear implications for observable behavior. Doing otherwise would create the possibility of (a) having an incomplete picture of even the isolated factor being studied (due to the absence of observations as to its interrelations with other factors); (b) attaining knowledge about something difficult to relate to everyday behavior; and/or (c) discovering something that is valid for micro-level phenomena, but not for macro-level ones. Therefore, complex, multifactorial abilities should be investigated in detail to generate a clear, practical understanding of human development.

### The Inadequacy of Simple Correlational Analysis for the Study of Causation

In his review of the subject, Bryant (1990) highlighted the fact that nothing can be inferred about the causes of cognitive development by simply establishing a relationship between two events that occur during the process. First, the relationship can be due to something other than a causal link (e.g., a common cause) and second, even if one were certain that there was a link, it would still be impossible to establish what is cause and what is effect. Therefore, Bryant recommended longitudinal experimental settings for the identification of phenomena that do or do not lead to specific developments.

Although Bryant is correct regarding the adequacy of longitudinal studies and the inadequacy of simple correlational analysis, one must acknowledge that longitudinal studies are usually cumbersome, expensive, and time-consuming; consequently, they are very difficult to be put into practice. Thus, alternative pragmatic, yet valid, methods of investigation must be considered.

### The Use of Structural Analysis Plus Prior Knowledge

Although simple correlations between events are not enough for one to validly infer a causal explanation involving them, the study of structural modifications—that is, the behavior in time of a holistic set of several correlations—together with prior knowledge based on logical reasoning and previous experiments, can lead to reasonable and fairly robust conclusions.

One method for the study of structural modifications is the Similarity Structure Analysis (SSA; formerly known as Smallest Space Analysis; Borg & Lingoes, 1987; Guttman, 1968; Kruskal & Wish, 1978). SSA analyzes similarity data (e.g., correlation coefficients) and provides a geometrical representation of the variables. Each variable is represented by a point in an Euclidean space of one or more dimensions whose location is determined by an algorithm created following an examination of all the associations among all the variables. The distances between the points are directly related to the observed relationships among the variables or items. Specifically, the algorithm maps a given set of variables according to the relative strengths of their correlations, placing those variables with high coefficients between each other closer to one another and those with low correlations further apart. Moreover, the SSA algorithm plots the points in a space of the smallest dimensionality that still preserves the rank order of the relationships.

## THE BEHAVIOR OF THE HUMAN COGNITIVE SYSTEM

### Internal and External Loci and Human Behavior

In the analysis of human behavior, there are two *loci* or places of interest to be considered by the psychologist, one internal and the other external. The *internal locus* is where lie an individual's identity, emotions, feelings, needs, and biology. The *external locus* encompasses all that is not part of the internal locus but tend to create links with it: for instance, the immediate physical-chemical elements surrounding the individual, the biological habitat in which the individual is situated and the sociocultural influences around him. The internal locus is the place where all purely or almost purely subjective phenomena occur. The external locus is where all objective, observable, actions happen. Behavior is something that happens "between worlds," creating a link connecting the two loci. It is born in the internal locus (having a purely intrinsic dimension), and exists in the external locus, as well (presenting itself with an extrinsic character).

This mode of thinking about human mental activity is far from new. Several great philosophers of the past, such as Descartes (1641), Locke (1690), Berkeley (1691), Hume (1739), and Kant (1781), considered the existence of two different worlds, one internal and the other external, that must be considered by any reasoner interested in analyzing the way human beings acquire and manipulate knowledge. It was only through the discovery of what was contained in each of these worlds and of what the relationship between them was that we could ever understand knowledge, the things that can be known, and how we can know them.

Nor is this dual approach something confined to antique philosophy. Vygotsky (1960, 1962) stated that there are two "planes" where cognitive development takes place. The first one he called "the social plane," and it is external to the individual. The second one was called "the psychological plane," and is internal to the individual. Vygotsky understood that any cognitive ability must be developed through the constant dialectic interaction between the two planes. Roazzi (1990) agreed with Vygotsky's statement, adding that the relationship between individual psychological phenomena and social psychological phenomena is quite a complex one, but one that psychologists cannot afford to neglect. According to him, research on behavior is concerned with "the search for the reality that intervenes between the external world and the human mind."

## The Dynamics of the Human Cognitive System

From all that has been presented so far, human intellectual activity seems to be the result of cognitive structures that interact with environmental variables. Motivation appears to play a part in the game as a driving force that animates cognition and other kinds of behavior. And the whole process has an extrinsic dimension and an intrinsic dimension that interact with each other through behavior.

Motivation is the result of intrinsic individual needs of emotional and biological nature that are placed in the internal locus. It generates behavior and is affected by it as well.

The environmental context where behavior will show its extrinsic dimension is in the external locus, influencing behavior as much as it is influenced by it. Behavior itself, as we have already stated, is located between the two loci, having an intrinsic dimension that interacts with internal needs and an extrinsic character that interacts with the situational context.

Cognitive structures come into play as part of an evolutionary mechanism developed to make human behavior more efficient in terms of need satisfaction. Cognitive structures serve as feedback control units for the internal and external dimensions of behavior, so that the individual can act as a dynamic self-organizing system; in the internal locus, they are the interface between behavior and needs. In the external locus, they mediate the interaction between behavior and environmental forces. As a result, when manifesting itself in the external locus, human behavior alters environmental variables and is altered by them, a process that will, in turn, have its bearing on the internal locus, changing the needs that produced the behavior in the first place.

The dialectic and interactive dynamics of the cognitive process as a whole are represented in Fig. 9.1. The global dynamics of the human cogni-

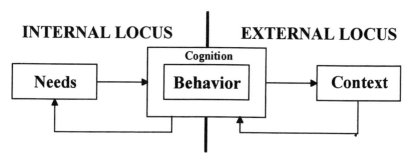

FIG. 9.1. The functional dynamics of the human cognitive system.

tive can be understood as a three-part process with two feedback relationships. The first loop is between need and behavior, and the second one is between behavior and environmental context.

### Cognitive Development

Cognitive development is brought about by motivation, a fundamental factor in any cognitive activity. Emotional and biological needs have an urge to be satisfied, and behavior is a biological response that moves toward the satisfaction of such needs.

Cognition is the key mechanism through which behavior can interact with needs and environmental context to ease that urge. As time passes, biological maturation and changing social influences alter a child's needs, forcing it to acquire new forms of behavior to satisfy those new needs.

Initially, perception, the most simple and vital cognitive structure of all, is the only cognitive structure in existence. It serves as a mechanism that optimizes the occurrence of reflex actions to environmental stimuli, helping to make behavior more effective in terms of need satisfaction. However, ever-changing and continuously interacting internal needs and environmental variables soon render perceptual activity alone an inadequate mental approach to need satisfaction. Unsatisfied needs tend to increase the infant's general level of activity, generating "random" or "exploratory" behavior in the internal locus as well as in the external locus. This process, which depends very much on the environmental context, eventually stumbles on perceptual strategies that tend to maintain perceptions in the mind even after the stimulus that generated them has weakened or disappeared. At first, these strategies are randomly adopted and discharged at a very quick pace, but soon positive feedback and the satisfaction of needs make the infant's behavior converge more and more toward mnemonic strategies. Thus, as a result of a stochastic process, memory develops!

Once memory has emerged, needs and environment motivate still further internal and external exploratory behavior. That activates both perception and memory, as well as reflexive reactions. Then, positive feedback from the satisfaction of needs increases the frequency with which certain combinations of both cognitive structures appear, generating a new mental mechanism: categorization.

Thus, every time needs and environment are altered in a way that lowers the efficiency of the existing cognitive system, a new cognitive structure is developed as the result of a combination of the preceding ones. Each step is more complex than the previous one, until the child experiences the creation of reasoning. Further, every step of the process is marked by the functional integration of all of the existing cognitive structures among themselves.

## A STUDY OF COGNITIVE DEVELOPMENT

Roazzi and Campello (1994) have studied the creative and intellectual development and its structure of 78 Brazilian children. All of the subjects attended school, and they originated from homes of both high and low socioeconomic status (SES).

Creativity was measured through the Wallach and Kogan test (1965), which consists of five different tasks each yielding a measure of fluency and a measure of originality. A brief summary of the tasks and of their stimulus contents, mental operations and so on is given below in Table 9.1.

Intelligence and control locus were measured through the use of Raven's Progressive Matrices Test and the IAR locus of control Scale. A summary of the contents of each of the subtests of these instruments is provided in Tables 9.2 and 9.3.

Using hypothesis tests, regression analysis and facet theory techniques to analyze the data extracted, we obtained results that confirm and illustrate

TABLE 9.1
Summary of the Name, Number of Items, Content, Form of
Presentation, and Mental Procedure Involved for Each of the
Tasks in the Wallach and Kogan Creativity Test (1965)

| Task | Items | Contents | Presentation | Procedure |
|------|-------|----------|--------------|-----------|
| T1—Example | 4 | Generic categories | Verbal | Supply examples |
| T2—Alternative use | 8 | Everyday objects | Verbal | Give alternative uses |
| T3—Line | 9 | Lines in various shapes | Visual | Associate images |
| T4—Similarity | 10 | Pairs of objects and things | Verbal | Point similarities |
| T5—Meaning | 8 + 1* | Composite geometric shapes | Visual | Associate meanings |

*An example is presented before the series of 8 is started (responses are not registered in this case).

TABLE 9.2
Abilities Measured in Subseries A, Ab, and B
of Raven's Progressive Matrices Test

| Series | Abilities |
|---|---|
| R(A) | Perception of size. |
| R(A)/R(Ab) | Spatial orientation in one or two simultaneous directions. |
| | Apprehension of discrete formations spatially related to the whole picture. |
| R(B) | Analysis of the whole through the examination of its constituent elements. |
| | Ability to conceive correlative images. |
| | Eduction of correlations. |

TABLE 9.3
Features Measured by the IAR Control Locus Scale

| | |
|---|---|
| I(+) | - Internal control when in a positive or favorable situation. |
| I(−) | - Internal control when in a negative or unfavorable situation. |
| I(T) | - Total internal control [I(T) = I(+) + I(−)]. |

some of the ideas we have discussed regarding determinism and indeterminism in cognitive development for the specific case of creativity.

## Determinism and Indeterminism in Creative Development

*The Absence of a Pure Age Effect.* If creative development were something completely determinate, then each and every phase of it would be entirely determined by prior conditions. If it were indeterminate, similar conditions should yield different results over the course of time. In dealing with the statistical analysis of a group of individuals, each of whom was of a different age and level of cognitive development, this would mean that determinism should result in a definite relationship between age and level of development, and indeterminism, due to the canceling out of random variations in the causal mechanism, would result in the absence of such a relationship. Thus, age would be the most important individual variable to consider.

A multiple linear regression using the sum of all originality and fluency scores did not show any significant independent effect of age on these two cognitive skills (partial $r = .00$ and $p = .62$ for fluency and partial $r = .00$ and $p = .86$ for Originality). The same results were obtained for the analysis of all individual creativity measures, except for originality on T4 (Similarity). Thus, one comes to the conclusion that there was no observable effect of age per se on the development of creativity. It is interesting to note that, because the mere interpretation of linear correlation coefficients is not enough to infer the presence or lack of a relationship between two or more variables, this analysis of correlation, as well as all of the following, were also checked for nonlinear relationships, through the analysis of scatter-plots and the use of different mathematical transformations.

Because no isolated effect of age could be found, cognitive development, in the case of creativity seems to be indeterminate, at least in terms of determination from the internal locus. As to the external locus determina-tion, if it exists, it would probably be time-independent, which, in a way, is also a form of indeterminism.

## Task Dependency and Creativity

Based on the idea that, at an individual level, the internal causation of a developmental event is associated with the greater possibility of determi-nism and that external causation is the major source of indeterminism (because the environment is something much more complex and subject to variations than an isolated individual), we thought it interesting to analyze the environmental dependency of creative behavior in order to further investigate its determinate and indeterminate aspects.

An analysis of all the intercorrelations between measures of creativity shows that the mean correlation between fluency Scores was $r = .50$, indi-cating that there is a relevant tendency toward the independence of tasks regarding the children's ability to produce numerous responses to a given stimulus. That is, fluency seems to be relatively task-independent. On the other hand, the mean correlation between measures of originality is $r = .17$, indicating that the ability to produce responses that no one has produced before depends greatly on the specific tasks involved. Thus, originality seems to be relatively task-dependent.

So, in spite of the fact that, as has been previously shown, creative abilities in general tend to be indeterminate, fluency is closer to being determinate than is originality, because it is more sensitive to external contingencies.

## Higher and Lower Order Abilities

If the dependency on internal or external factors during cognitive develop-ment is a factor that will help to establish whether development is determi-nistic or indeterministic, we should observe that the most deterministic abilities should also be the most internal, essential, and fundamental ones. In other words, because we have found that fluency is more task-inde-pendent, (i.e., more determinate) and originality is more task-dependent (i.e., more indeterminate) we should find fluency to be a more basic ability and originality a higher order ability.

In order to investigate the structural relationship between fluency and origi-nality empirically, we analyzed the data of children aged 5 to 7 through SSA.

The SSA of item intercorrelations resulted in a two-dimensional solution for each age group, which seemed adequate for interpreting our data (coefficient of alienation < .15; this criterion establishes goodness-of-fit—the smaller the coefficient, the better the fit; Bloombaum, 1970). The projection of the variables on dimensions 1 and 2 for the measures of creativity for each age group is shown in Fig. 9.2. Each of the ten variables that make up our measures of originality and fluency (five variables each) is shown in the map or projection by its name abbreviation.

The partitioning found for each of the three age groups is modular, that is, the space is partitioned into two concentric regions. A modular partitioning of the SSA space reveals a simply (or partly) ordered facet, indicating that fluency and originality have been quantitatively ordered. The inner

### 5 -Year-Olds

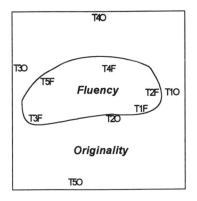

### 6 -Year-Olds

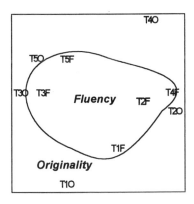

### 7 -Year-Olds

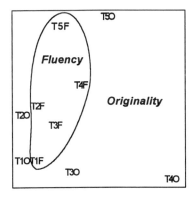

FIG. 9.2. The relationship between fluency and originality from 5 to 7.

region contains the five fluency elements, the outer region contains the five originality elements. This type of configuration makes it clear that fluency is more general, whereas originality is more specific, the former having higher average correlations with all other elements than the latter. So, fluency actually seems to be the more essential creative ability, although originality is the one of highest order. Thus, our experimental findings confirm that determinism/indeterminism and internal/external causation tend to be positively related.

## Fluency Tends to Grow While Originality Tends to Stay Constant

Given that originality has a relatively indeterministic development dependent on uncertain contextual factors, one would expect that, on average, due to the fact that random errors tend to cancel out, originality should oscillate within relatively narrow boundaries. In the case of fluency, however, because it is a relatively context-independent ability, its development should be oriented in a certain specific direction.

From the ages of 5 to 7, fluency scores tend to rise significantly, originality scores stay relatively constant. This is illustrated in Table 9.4. Thus, it is quite clear now that fluency and originality tend to behave as abilities that are, respectively, more and less determinate.

TABLE 9.4
Creativity Scores: Ages of 5 to 7

| Type of Task | | 5-year-olds | | 6-year-olds | | 7-year-olds | | T-Test Comparisons | | |
|---|---|---|---|---|---|---|---|---|---|---|
| | | Mean | SD | Mean | SD | Mean | SD | 5–6 | 6–7 | 5–7 |
| | | | | | Fluency | | | | | | |
| T1-F | Example | 23.9 | 14.02 | 25.6 | 8.79 | 28.2 | 14.12 | - | - | - |
| T2-F | Alt. use | 11.8 | 3.18 | 12.1 | 6.35 | 16.1 | 5.83 | - | ** | ** |
| T3-F | Line | 10.1 | 2.59 | 11.4 | 7.81 | 14.5 | 10.91 | - | - | * |
| T4-F | Similarity | 7.8 | 4.21 | 6.3 | 3.55 | 12.3 | 5.66 | - | ** | ** |
| T5-F | Meaning | 9.1 | 1.59 | 8.6 | 3.95 | 11.9 | 5.34 | - | ** | * |
| TT-F | Total | 62.7 | 18.84 | 64.1 | 21.77 | 83.0 | 37.30 | - | * | * |
| | | | | | Originality | | | | | | |
| T1-O | Example | 2.6 | 2.59 | 2.7 | 2.20 | 3.3 | 3.61 | | - | - |
| T2-O | Alt. use | 0.9 | 1.14 | 1.4 | 2.09 | 1.8 | 1.94 | - | - | * |
| T3-O | Line | 1.3 | 0.64 | 1.5 | 1.64 | 2.0 | 2.90 | - | - | - |
| T4-O | Similarity | 0.8 | 0.82 | 0.4 | 0.50 | 0.6 | 0.82 | * | - | - |
| T5-O | Meaning | 1.0 | 0.59 | 0.7 | 0.84 | 0.9 | 0.97 | - | - | - |
| TT-O | Total | 6.7 | 2.68 | 6.7 | 4.10 | 8.6 | 8.09 | - | - | - |

- Not significant for $p \leq .05$; *significant for $p \leq .05$; **significant for $p \leq .01$.

### Intelligence and Creativity

If originality is more indeterminate than fluency because the latter stems from the former, then the fact that there is no actual effect of age either on fluency or originality suggests that there is a set of cognitive abilities from which fluency stems. Such a set of abilities involve skills that would be basic, dependent on age, and, therefore, closer to being determinate.

The multiple linear regression undertaken with all the cognitive abilities studied shows that there is a significant partial correlation of age with intelligence (partial $r = .13$ and $p = .00$). The three-dimensional SSA for the three age groups is shown in Fig. 9.3.

## 5 -Year-Olds

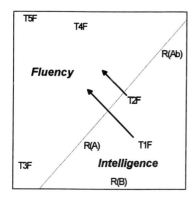

## 6 -Year-Olds

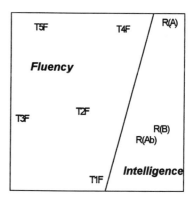

## 7 -Year-Olds

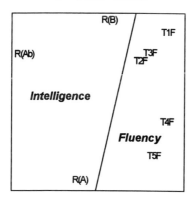

FIG. 9.3. The relationship between intelligence and fluency from 5 to 7.

The plot can be cut into two clear, contiguous, regions, each containing only elements of one particular type (intelligence or fluency) only for the 6- and 7-year-olds. The plot for the 5-year-old group, however, is more difficult to partition because the elements are more intermingled. T2F and T1F do not fit well into the "appropiate" section, because they are more strongly correlated to the three intelligence elements than are to the other fluency elements. Such a structure follows the role of an axial facet (Dancer, 1990). This configuration suggests that intelligence is more related to certain aspects of fluency at an early age, but that the later gradually becomes independent of the former.

We therefore have support for the idea that complex cognitive abilities stem from simpler ones, and that the more sophisticated they become, the more indeterminate they became. However, it is interesting to note that newly formed abilities might be second-order at a certain age, but can, with time, become as rooted as basic abilities.

## The Effect of SES

If creative development is something completely determined, one would expect, in the case of a group of individuals, some kind of a uniform effect of environmental variables, such as SES. In fact, cognitive development seems to be extremely sensitive to SES, as shown by the differences in the test scores of high SES and low SES children (Table 9.5 and Fig. 9.4).

This implies that, in spite of the fact that some abilities observed are more basic and fundamental compared to the others, we have not tapped the really essential abilities, because the effect of an environmental factor still strong. However, such an effect seems to be uniform and homogeneous, meaning that it probably does not affect our previous conclusions regarding determinism and indeterminism.

The notion of basic abilities that arise one from one another, each one more indeterminate than the one before, together with the determinacy/con-textual-sensitivity relationship, should be analyzed through the prism of the

TABLE 9.5
Mean Test Scores for High- and Low-SES Children

| Type of Test | Low SES | | High SES | |
| --- | --- | --- | --- | --- |
| | Mean | SD | Mean | SD |
| TT-F | 46.7 | 11.96 | 76.0 | 26.92 |
| TT-O | 4.1 | 1.79 | 8.2 | 5.52 |
| I(T) | 15.8 | 3.49 | 18.4 | 2.93 |
| R(T) | 16.8 | 5.43 | 20.6 | 5.70 |

All the intergroup differences are significant at the $p \leq .01$ level.

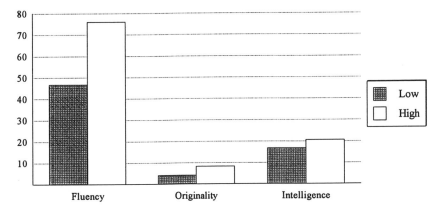

FIG. 9.4. Test scores for children with high and low SES.

environmental effect showing uniform consequences for different abilities and individuals; perhaps, it is due to an effect on one or more very essential abilities).

## Locus of Control Favors Originality but Not Fluency

Perceived locus of control is an attitude that, like any other attitude, is assumed or learned based on an individual's interaction with the environment during the course of his or her life. Therefore, if all the conclusions so far are right, the effect of locus of control on creativity should be greater regarding originality than regarding fluency, because the former is more dependent on environmental factors (i.e., more undetermined) and the latter is brought about more by internal factors.

A multiple linear regression with all the cognitive abilities taken into account resulted in the observation of a definite effect of locus of control on originality (partial $r = .09$ and $p = .01$), but not on fluency (partial $r = .02$ and $p = .23$).

From this one can suppose that locus of control affects originality in a significant way. However, because, due to environmental uncertainty, it is difficult to determine which child will adopt an internal or external locus of control, and to what degree, it is difficult to determine the development of a given individual's originality.

## Analog and Non-Analog Abilities

The differentiation between abilities that are or are not related to the use of analogy seems to be very sharp in all three age groups studied. This factor clearly plays an axial role on dimensions 1 × 2 for the three groups. The structural configurations corresponding to the intercorrelation matrices are depicted in Fig. 9.5.

## 5 -Year-Olds

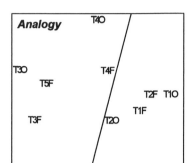

## 6 -Year-Olds

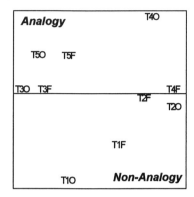

## 7 -Year-Olds

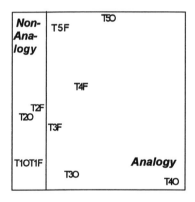

FIG. 9.5. Creative abilities and the ability to make analogies.

This points toward a clear-cut distinction between abilities that could be based on a physiological feature (left- and right-hemisphere differences) and are not altered with time, suggesting a basic criterion responsible for a very deterministic feature of cognitive development.

It is important to stress, also, that the axial role played by this factor in cooperation with the modular role of the fluency/originality facet (see Fig. 9.2), roughly supports a radex configuration.

### Verbal and Visual Abilities

Visual and verbal presentation tasks are clearly independent at ages 5 and 6, but are integrated at 7. This can be seen in Fig. 9.6. This is another piece of evidence in favor of the idea of functional differences in the left and right

## 5 -Year-Olds

## 6 -Year-Olds

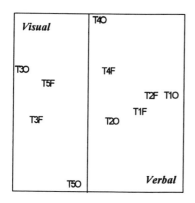
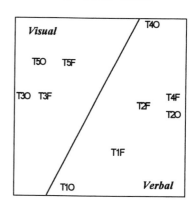

## 7 -Year-Olds

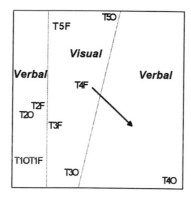

FIG. 9.6.   Verbal and visual abilities.

hemispheres, which should yield results like those at ages 5 and 6. That is, this physiological feature should be responsible for a determinist development of the relationship between visual and verbal abilities. However, the acquisition of literacy certainly can affect such deterministic developments by stimulating greater integration between the two sets of abilities, giving rise to development influenced by uncertain environmental effects (teaching strategies, social values regarding schooling, etc.).

Some of the patterns or results may be related to hemispheric differences in cognition. The left hemisphere is predominantly responsible for verbal abilities and possibly for sequential-analytic processing while the right hemisphere is predominantly responsible for visual-spatial abilities and possibly holistic processing. With the exception of the abilities measured in T4, visual and analogies are always together on one side of the SSA diagram, and verbal and logical are always on the opposite side.

## DISCUSSION AND CONCLUSION

### The Scientific Attitude Toward (In)Determinism

As we have already stated, the utmost purpose of knowledge in human beings is the optimization of behavior in terms of survival and well-being. Human cognitive structures are the result of an evolutionary survival mechanism that maximizes the efficiency of behavior in terms of the satisfaction of vital needs. We have stressed, also, that to know means finding answers to *how* and *why* questions. Furthermore, we have shown that the latter are more important for control and, therefore, for survival and well-being.

In terms of the research on cognitive development, because it is easier to know how than to know why, much more is known about the way in which development occurs than about the reasons it occurs in a particular way. As a result of this ignorance, and also because of theoretical and empirical difficulties with proposed developmental models, there is an ongoing controversy about how the law of cause and effect works in regards to cognitive development. Specifically, there is a debate about whether the process is deterministic (predictable, controllable) or indeterministic (unpredictable, uncontrollable).

There is a certain modern trend toward the preference of indeterminism. The reasons for this are not just theoretical and empirical, but are also ideological. However, most of the idealistic arguments (free-will debates, need to break away from behaviorism, political correctness) are actually fallacious, as well as some of the theoretical ones (Heinsenberg's indeterminacy principle in quantum mechanics, incorrect understanding of the definitions of determinism and indeterminism). The only legitimate reason for a scientist to abandon the idea of determinism (and, therefore, ceasing to be a scientist as we know one) is the occurrence of irrefutable empirical evidence to the contrary.

## EMPIRICAL FINDINGS ON (IN)DETERMINISM AND THEIR THEORETICAL IMPLICATIONS

In the study by Roazzi and Campello previously presented, some evidence was found regarding the indeterminism of cognitive development when it comes to creative abilities. Specifically, it was the lack of a per se age effect on levels of creative skills. However, such evidence is not irrefutable, for not only could we attribute such finding to analytical or theoretical limitations that could very well be removed in the future, but there were also conflicting signs of determinism and indeterminism within the components of a complex ability considered to be, in totum, indeterministic (also of Defays, 1990; Dowker, Flood, Griffiths, Harriss, & Hook, in press; Hofstadter, 1995).

The quantitative development intelligence and fluency has presented itself as relatively determinate, as well as the fluency–originality relationship and some specific interrelations between creative abilities (analog vs. non-analog, verbal vs. visual). On the other hand, originality and, oddly, fluency, have shown elements of indeterminism.

The contradiction in terms of the simultaneously deterministic and indeterministic behavior of fluency is explained considering the causal link age-intelligence-fluency. In other words, age affects intelligence which, in turn, affects fluency, being this indirect relationship, together with the analytical procedures used to access determinism (correlation with age, etc.), the main cause of the paradox. Actually many of such apparent absurdities can be explained in terms of the dynamics of human cognitive development, where primitive, basic, abilities interacting with the environment and with internal motivations tend to form new ones that are more complex, sophisticated and environment-dependent. Of course, one must remember that the environment is considered here as indetermined, but only because its precise variations are unknown for a given particular case (though, in some instances, it can be well-behaved, such as in the case of SES in the study).

## SOME FINAL WORDS

It seems that determinism and indeterminism can appear or disappear depending on the theoretical viewpoint or analytical tools arbitrarily adopted by the scientist. Cognitive models with emphasis on internal or external phenomena as the basis of cognitive development, as well as on micro-level or macro-level phenomena, can make uncertainty become indeterminacy or vice-versa.

In summarizing our conclusions, we hold that, at the micro-level, some psychological phenomena look indeterminate (i.e., their causes seem to change over time), but at the macro-level causation itself may vary at some deterministic pace. If we have a choice, we should prefer to see deterministic causality (as that is the basis of science itself), yet, the nature of psychological phenomena provides us with challenges that undermine the use of deterministic models.

Therefore, we must analyze the different methods and procedures used by psychologists in their research from the more general epistemological standpoint of how these methods allow us to discover determinacy or indeterminacy in mental processes.

## REFERENCES

Bacon, F. (1620). Novum organun. In R. M. Hutchins (Ed.), *Great books of the western world* (Vol. 30). London: Encyclopædia Britannica.

Bernardini, C. (1993). Dove nasce l'incertezza? *Sapere, 59*(6), 49–54.

Black, M. (1973). Some aversive responses to a would be reinforcer. In H. Wheeler (Ed.), *Beyond the punitive society.* San Francisco: W. H. Freeman.

Bloombaum, M. (1970). Doing smallest space analysis. *Journal of Conflict Resolution, 14*, 409–416.

Borg, I., & Lingoes, J. C. (1987). *Multidimensional similarity structure analysis.* New York: Springer.

Bridgman, P. W. (1928). *The logic of modern physics.* New York: Macmillan.

Bryant, P. E. (1986). Theories about the causes of cognitive development. In P. L. C. van Geert (Ed.), *Theory building in developmental psychology.* North Holland: Elsevier Science Publishers.

Bryant, P. E. (1990). Empirical evidence for causes in development. In G. Butterworth & P. E. Bryant (Eds.), *Causes of development: Interdisciplinary perspectives.* London: Harvester Wheatsheaf.

Dancer, L. S. (1990). Introduction to facet theory and its applications. *Applied Psychology: An International Review, 39*(4), 365–377.

Defays, D. (1990). Number: A study in cognition and recognition. *Journal for the Integrated Study of Artificial Intelligence, Cognitive Science, and Applied Epistemology, 7*, 217–243.

Descartes, R. (1629). Rules for the direction of the mind. In R. M. Hutchins (Ed.), *Great books of the western world* (Vol. 30). London: Encyclopædia Britannica.

Descartes, R. (1637). Discourse on method. In R. M. Hutchins (Ed.), *Great books of the western world* (Vol. 31). London: Encyclopædia Britannica.

Dorf, R. C. (1980). *Modern control systems.* Reading, MA: Addison-Wesley.

Dowker, A., Flood, A., Griffith, H., Harriss, L., & Hook, L. (in press). Estimation strategies of four groups. *Mathematical Cognition, 2*(2).

Eccles, J. C. (1951). Hypothesis relating to the brain-mind problem. *Nature, 168*, 53–57.

Eddington, A. S. (1935). *New pathways in science.* Cambridge, England: Cambridge University Press.

Guttman, L. (1968). A general nonmetric technique for finding the smallest coordinate space for a configuration of points. *Psychometrika, 33*, 469–506.

Harvey, W. (1628). An anatomical discussion on the motion of the heart and blood in animals. In R. M. Hutchins (Ed.), *Great books of the western world* (Vol. 28). London: Encyclopædia Britannica.

Heisenberg, W. (1958). *Physics and philosophy.* New York: Harper & Brothers.

Hofstadter, D. (1995). *Fluid concepts and creative analogies.* New York: Basic Books.

Jeans, J. (1933). *The new background of science.* Cambridge, England: Cambridge University Press.

Kant, I. (1781). Critique of pure reason. In R. M. Hutchins (Ed.), *Great books of the western world* (Vol. 42). London: Encyclopædia Britannica.

Kruskal, J. B., & Wish, M. (1978). *Multidimensional scaling.* Beverly Hills, CA: Sage.

Laplace, P. S. (1820). *Théorie analytique des probabilités.* Brussels: Culture Civilization.

Lewis, P. L., & Hayne, W. R. (1979). *Child development.* Glenview, IL: Scott, Foresman.

O'Connor, D. J. (1971). *Free will.* New York: Doubleday.

Pearson, K. (1892). *The grammar of science.* London: Scott.

Platt, J. R. (1973). The Skinnerian revolution. In H. Wheeler (Ed.), *Beyond the punitive society.* San Francisco: W. H. Freeman.

Popper, K. R. (1950). Indeterminism in quantum physics and in classical physics. *British Journal of Philosophical Science, 1*, 117–133, 173–195.

Popper, K. R. (1959). *The logic of scientific discovery.* London: Hutchinson.

Popper, K. R., & Eccles, J. C. (1977). *The self and its brain.* London: Routledge & Kegan Paul.

Roazzi, A. (1990). *Piaget e Vygotsky: Duas teorias do desenvolvimento em confronto*. Recife: Mestrado em Psicologia.

Roazzi, A., & Campello, B. C. (1994). *Criatividade e desenvolvimento*. Facepe Research Report, Recife, UFPE, Brazil.

Ruelle, D. (1993). Un onest'uomo tra caso e determinism. (Interview). *Sapere, 59*(2), 35–36.

Schlick, M. (1925). *Philosophy and nature*. London: Greenwood Press.

Skinner, B. F. (1973). Answers for my critics. In H. Wheeler (Ed.), *Beyond the punitive society*. San Francisco: W. H. Freeman.

Smart, J. J. C. (1968). *Between science and philosophy*. New York: Random House.

Spinoza, B. (1677). Ethics. In R. M. Hutchins (Ed.), *Great books of the western world* (Vol. 31). London: Encyclopædia Britannica.

Stebbing, S. (1937). *Philosophy and the physicists*. London: Methuen.

Stewart, I. (1989). *Does God play dice? The mathematics of chaos*. Oxford: Basic Blackwell

Valentine, E. R. (1982). *Conceptual issues in psychology*. London: George Allen & Unwin.

Waddington, C. H. (1970). Concepts and theories of growth, development, differentiation and morphogenesis. In C. H. Waddington (Ed.), *Towards theoretical biology* (Vol. 1, pp. 1–41). Chicago: Aldine.

Wallach, M. A., & Kogan, N. (1965). *Modes of thinking in young children*. New York: Holt, Rinehart & Winston.

Wrightsman, L. S., & Sanford, (1975). *Psychology: A study of human behavior*. Monterey, CA: Brooks/Cole.

# 10

# CHANGES IN SOCIAL–CONCEPTUAL DEVELOPMENT: DOMAIN-SPECIFIC STRUCTURES, SELF-ORGANIZATION, AND INDETERMINISM

Maria Legerstee
York University, Toronto, Canada

The purpose of this chapter is to provide a general framework for thinking about infant social–conceptual development. The framework presented is a modified structuralist view of the development of infants' understanding of animism, and, in particular, of people. Like other genetic epistemologists, I view the human organism as a complex, self-organizing, open system. It is complex because it has heterogeneous constituents in continuous interaction; it is self-organizing because new structures are formed from the interaction of lower order structures and it is open because the formation of new structures rely on continuous interaction with the external environment. The theory is modified, in that it proposes that infant understanding of people and things is facilitated by domain-specific predispositions that identify and define social and nonsocial domains, rather than by sensory reflexes and the three domain-general processes of assimilation, accommodation, and equilibration. These domain-specific structures are assembled independently within each domain.

Evidence for domain-specific structures is provided by research documenting differential responsiveness to people and objects when perceptual differences of the stimuli are controlled. Subsequent development is viewed as a consequence of how these domain-specific structures deal with experience. In particular, it is suggested that the early structures are neither detailed nor explicit. They become that way through self-organization and through the mediation of social partners. Through their interaction with the environment earlier structures become more specific and detailed, and cross-connect to form higher order structures. Thus, development is viewed as a consequence of subject–environment interactions that together construct knowledge that was not available to either of them alone. In this way, "the domain-specific origins determine the trajectory, the direction of development, but do not pre-determine its end result" (Butterworth, 1990).

## ANIMISM: KNOWING PEOPLE

In 1981, Rochel Gelman and Elisabeth Spelke wrote a fascinating paper in which they gave a detailed account of the mature concepts adults have of animate and inanimate objects, in particular of people and inanimate objects (Gelman & Spelke, 1981). They noted that although people and objects are similar in that both have physical properties (size and shape) and can change over time, the two classes are different because only people communicate, move independently, have feelings, intentions, and thoughts. Not only do people and objects have different properties, but they are perceived differently. When looking at people, we may observe what they wear and how they do their hair, but we focus primarily on their feelings and intentions. Objects do not have inner states and therefore we would only pay attention to the physical characteristics of objects and their functions.

As a consequence of these differences, we interact differently with the two classes. We communicate with people but act on objects. When communicating with people, we expect them to reciprocate verbally or with actions, whereas we do not expect objects to reciprocate. In order to get objects to move or interact we have to manipulate them. Thus we understand that people have inner states and self-generated movement and can communicate. More importantly however, we develop different relationships with people than with objects. Relationships with people are complex, involving emotions and social rules. These emotions can be strong and may enhance or interfere with subsequent cognitive processes. The emotions aroused when interacting with physical objects are usually less intense, and are the result of whether one is successful or not at accomplishing a task (Hoffman, 1981; Legerstee, in press-a). It appears then that knowing what a person is implies not only an understanding of the attributes that constitute a person, but also a knowledge of nonliving things.

## THE DEVELOPMENT OF ANIMISM:
## SOME CONTEMPORARY EVIDENCE

The ability to differentiate people from things is foundational for human development. Theorists as diverse as Piaget (1954), Rheingold (1961), Watson (1972), Bruner (1973), Trevarthen (1979), Gelman and Spelke (1981), and Mandler (1992) have described in detail how infants come to distinguish people from things. According to Piaget (1954) infants do not differentiate between self, other people, and things. In fact, Piaget puts a complete "adualism" between infant and world. The external environment needs to be constructed through action during the infancy period. It is through these actions that mental structures are constructed (at the end of the infancy period) that allow infants to perceive physical and social objects. Piaget's views were supported by empirical reports using traditional *perceptual* methods relying solely on infant gazes to assess infant sensitivity to changes in various configurations of people and objects (e.g., line drawings, pictures, and video recordings of objects and faces (cf. Muir, Cao, & Entremont, 1994). It was hypothesized that the reduction of social information to "simpler" forms would bring out the essential feature cues of "social meaning" thereby making recognition of the meaning easier. However, recent research has suggested that the removal of dynamic and temporal components of social stimuli disadvantaged infants by removing information that is essential for domain-specific perception. In these cases the tasks become more difficult, and may be measuring inferential rather than social perceptual abilities (Moore, Hobson, Lee, & Anderson, 1992). For instance, when measuring various infant responses toward people and objects in naturalistic settings, 2-month-old infants communicate with people but act on objects. They will smile, make prespeech sounds and gesticulate with hand movements when facing responsive people, but are more likely to make hand-and-reach movements when presented with a familiar object that sounds and moves contingently to their eye movements (Legerstee, 1992; 1991a; Legerstee, Corter, & Kienapple, 1990; Legerstee, Pomerleau, Malcuit, & Feider, 1987). Moreover, such differential responsiveness has also been found in infants with Down syndrome, such that it emerges later (at the chronological age of 4–6 months) than it emerges in normal infants but when the subjects have reached approximately the same mental age or level of perceptual-cognitive sophistication (Legerstee & Bowman, 1989; Legerstee, Bowman, & Fels, 1992). This empirical convergence is certainly interesting.

Young infants also expect people to act reciprocally. Infants as young as 5 weeks will imitate mouth opening and tongue protrusions modeled by people, but not react this way to objects simulating these gestures (Legerstee, 1991b). In addition, 3-month-old infants have different relationships with people than with objects. If people are responsive to infants, 3-month-old babies become happy (i.e., coo, smile, etc.) and take in subsequent information faster (i.e., habituate to a multimodal stimulus) than if objects act contingently to the infants' actions. However, if people act in a random way, infants become distressed and fail to habituate to subsequent tasks. In contrast, if objects respond at random to the infants' actions infants behave similarly to when objects act contingently. Infants produce neutral facial expressions, and few vocalizations, while continuing to gaze intensely at the objects (Legerstee, in press-a). Thus, even for very young infants, relationships with people evoke more intense emotions than interactions with objects, and only the relationships with people seem to affect their motivation to learn. It could be argued that this differential responsiveness of infants to people and objects is related to the various perceptual differences between the two classes. But infants also produce differential responsiveness when perceptual differences are minimized (see Legerstee, 1992, for an overview) or when people and objects are absent. For example, in a recent study, 4-month-old infants called for people but reached for toys that were hidden behind a door (Legerstee, 1994b). These results not only suggest that infants were aware that objects had been hidden and that these objects were either animate or inanimate, but they recognized that different procedures were appropriate for the retrieval of, or for interacting with, animate and inanimate objects. This seems to suggest that infants are perceiving more than just surface stimuli in these situations. Piaget (1954) argued that an organism can be said to know something when it uses that knowledge to draw on what it knows to make inferences about properties of events that it cannot perceive (Spelke, 1994, p. 432). By that standard, 4-month-old infants have developed some kind of global understanding of how to interact with people and objects.

Thus, it would appear that information derived from dynamic displays is fundamental for early infant perception and action. These results suggest that "infants use dynamic information in the perception of a world of spatially connected, separately moveable, whole, permanent objects, in the first 5 months of life, long before theories based on static assumptions have led us to believe" (Butterworth, 1990, p. 63).

## MECHANISMS THAT GUIDE DIFFERENTIAL RESPONSIVENESS

What accounts for the manifestation of differential responsiveness to people and objects in such young babies? Hobson (1990) cites Baldwin (1902) as proposing that very early in life, infants respond to "suggestions of personality" in the behavior of others and thereby differentiate people from other things. Thus, for Baldwin, experience of others is grounded in specific ways of "instinctive" communications with others, Watson (1972) would specify the experience with others as containing contingent responses, whereas the experience with inanimate objects do not. This contingency initially defines what is social for infants, while the history of contingency learning from birth creates a difference in young infants' reactions to inanimate objects. Mandler (1992, p. 594) would agree that people "who interact contingently among themselves and who respond from a distance to the infant's actions and vocalizations in a way that inanimate objects do not" will contribute to the concept of animacy in infants. Mandler (1992) suggests that rather than a perceptual learning device (e.g., Watson, 1972), infants have an inborn capacity for perceptual analysis, which is a concept forming mechanism. Infants establish a conceptual core of "animal" around which knowledge accrues later. This initial core may be as simple as a notion of a self-moving (animate or contingently moving) thing. This perception is stored, and in subsequent processes, animate and inanimate objects are compared with this representation. Gradually, other knowledge begins to be added such that animate objects communicate, have feelings and intentions whereas other things do not. Thus, conceptions develop from internal abstractions that are made specific by the perceptual system (Mandler, 1992). However, Mandler (1992) agrees, that in the beginning it would be difficult for very young infants to differentiate between an animate stimulus and a social stimulus, since one would expect them to react to contingent nonsocial objects as if they were social.

If infants use domain-general structures as proposed by Piaget, Watson, and Mandler to sort out the social from the nonsocial, then there would be a time when infants do not make the distinction between people and objects when the two are perceptually similar (either in movement or along stimulus features). However, this argument is not easily supported by data on younger infants showing that: (a) at birth infants have different arm and hand movements to people and objects (Ronquist & Von Hofsten, 1994); (b) at 5 weeks, infants imitate gestures of people but not of objects simulating these gestures (Legerstee, 1991b); and (c) at 7 weeks infants get upset when adults refrain from communicating with them but not when objects remain immobile (Legerstee et al., 1987; Legerstee & Hadden, 1993). These findings would suggest an alternative theoretical interpretation, namely, that infants, rather than possessing a domain-general mechanism (or structures of the whole), instead have domain-specific structures for interacting with the social and physical worlds.

The proposition that infants at birth have domain-specific structures that allow them to interact differently with people and objects is not a new one. Trevarthen (1979) argued that in order for infants to discriminate the behaviors of people before they are able to manipulate objects, thereby to respond so efficiently and appropriately to them, infants must possess "a set of processes in which human stimuli are categorized in emotional and expressive terms," that are different from the set of processes that categorize objects. Trevarthen (1979) proposes that these innate processes allow infants to perceive people to be like them, and expect them to share control in communicative exchanges, each in turn predicting what the other will do. Thus, Trevarthen suggests that domain-specific knowledge guides infants' actions with people and objects. Trevarthen (1980) calls these innate structures human motives, mental structures underlying perception and action that are active at birth. Subjective motives are the mental structures underlying interactions with objects whereas intersubjective motives are those mental structures responsible for interactions with people. These motives would put infants in "a structured state which specifies both forms of action and the affordances which acts anticipate" (Trevarthen, 1980, p. 326).

Bruner (1973) similarly believes that there are innate repertoires of action pattern that are elicited when the infant is presented with a social or non-social object. Thus, skilled interaction suggests that encounters with social and nonsocial objects may provide the infant with a natural fit between action and consequence, as opposed to an arbitrary relationship between the two. According to Bruner, these skilled actions are not just reflexive type of responses to particular social and nonsocial stimulation. Rather, Bruner argues that intention guides skilled activity from the outset.

## STRUCTURES THAT IDENTIFY THE DOMAIN

In order for infants to interact differently with people and objects, they first must be able to perceive valid information of the objects they are acting upon. It has to be more than just the configuration of the eyes, nose and mouth (a mere sketch of three contrast blobs, cf. Johnson & Morton, 1991) that newborns are sensitive to, that draws the 3-month-old infant to the person, since infants differentiate between people and dolls that mimic these facial configurations (Legerstee & Hadden, 1993; Legerstee et al., 1987). What I propose has been borrowed in part from Gelman's (1990) model on the animate-inanimate distinction and from Trevarthen's theory on person-object differentiation. Gelman postulates that infants learn relevant information about the animate–inanimate distinction because they are born with domain-specific perceptual structures that identify people and objects. These structures draw the infant's attention to the various details that distinguish social from nonsocial stimuli, such as causality and surface features. For instance, animate structures specify that people (and other animates) are capable of self-generated movement, and inanimate structures specify that objects need agents to move them. Working with these causal structures is a "domain-general learning mechanism" that allows the infant to learn which cues are predictive of each domain (e.g., hands and legs predict animate objects while wheels predict inanimate objects). However, Gelman does not believe that the distinction between people and objects is made on a perceptual level (e.g., spatio-temporal) since perceptual information is usually ambiguous or incomplete. Rather, the domain-specific structures allow infants to interpret (conceive) the perception of movement of an object differently depending on whether the movement is made by an animate or inanimate object. Thus according to this theory, infants cannot assign a novel object to either the animate or inanimate category simply on the basis of information about whether they see that it moves on its own or not. Rather, infants would differentiate between people and objects soon after birth if the social object moved contingently and had animate features (e.g., legs, feet, mouth), but not if it looked like a thing (no animate features) and acted contingently.

Various studies support Gelman's reasoning. For instance Woodward (1993) showed that 7-month-old infants know that two inanimate objects have to contact each other in order for a causal event to happen but that the same is not true for people. Similar results were obtained by Legerstee (1994b) using a different method. However, these studies do not reveal *how* infants experience human action. Infants may suspend the contact principle because they are aware that animates (people and other animals) can move by themselves but they may not appreciate that humans act according to social rules. Instead they may perceive human actions to be unpredictable (Spelke et al., 1995). What I argue is that, as suggested by Trevarthen (1979), infants have, in addition to causal rules, rules by which they categorize people in social terms. These rules allow infants to perceive people to be like them, and to share control in communicative exchanges. Specifically, when an infant perceives an object that moves toward them and interacts with them their percept is *Will*, which entails not only the knowledge that such objects have internal causation, but also that those objects are social objects and are governed by social rules (see also Trevarthen, 1979, and Premack, 1990, for an elaboration of this point). Thus *Will* is perceived directly through innate predispositions that are different for people and objects. Infants try to communicate with people and not objects because their early domain-specific structures specify not only that different kinds of objects are caused differently, but also *how* they act. This appreciation initiates different actions in infants, an operation on the Will of animate objects and on the physical of inanimate objects.[1]

## DEVELOPMENT OF DOMAIN-SPECIFIC KNOWLEDGE AND SELF-ORGANIZATION

In order to argue for domain-specificity, one not only has to define the sets of thoughts or behaviors that are limited to a particular domain (Sternberg, 1989), but one also has to indicate how the content of each domain changes at each particular developmental level. Social objects are complex, dynamic, ever changing systems. Although domain-specific knowledge helps infants to

---

[1]I am grateful to Loren McMaster, York University, for many insightful discussions regarding the animate–inanimate distinction.

discriminate between people and objects and to interact appropriately with them right from the start, this knowledge is not complete; it is in an infancy state and provides minimal information about the environment for the organism to act upon. Nor is early knowledge explicitly represented so that it can be accessed or verbally reported. Rather, it is internally represented and in procedural form. What this means is that early knowledge allows infants to perform or to act upon the world within domain-specific constraints, but it prevents the infants from using knowledge of one domain in the service of another. For instance, when facing domain-specific stimuli such as the human face (Legerstee, 1991a; Legerstee et al., 1990; Legerstee et al., 1987; Maurer, 1985), and human voice (Legerstee, 1991b; Morse & Cowan, 1982), infants respond with eye contact, vocalizations, smiles, and body orientation. In contrast, if they face a graspable object, these babies may emit prereaches while gazing at the object continuously. Through domain-specific constraints infants remain centered on either the social or nonsocial aspect of the environment. As development proceeds and because of the plasticity of early brain development (Johnson, 1990), domain-specific structures not only become more specific but decentration occurs which allows for cross-connecting of the various domains (Legerstee & Weintraub, in press).

Specification, decentration, and explicit knowledge are made possible through the work of various guiding forces that disrupt the dynamic stability of the organism at various phases in development. In particular, ontogenetic change in domain-specific knowledge becomes possible through dynamic processes of self-organization. Self-organization refers to the construction of novel forms from the interaction of lower order structures of the individual. Self-organization is not only responsible for increasing domain-specification but also for interaction among systems and equilibration. However, despite the organism's achievement of so called "stable states," the organism's sensitivity to the environment results in continuous reorganizations "when environmental perturbations become amplified by recursive, nonlinear interactions among system components" (Lewis, 1995, p. 8). The final product of these reciprocal interactions among systems results in the formation of a new system whose structures were not initially specified.

Although the foregoing account may appear constructivist, since according to Piaget, gene expressions and cognitive development are a function of a self-organizing system that exchanges information with the environment, it departs from that of the conventional epistemologists on two accounts. First, rather than viewing infants as having empty minds and various reflexes to react to the "blooming, buzzing, confusion" out there, in the present state of developmental theorizing, the domain-specific predispositions guide the infants subsequent involvement with social and nonsocial objects in an orderly way. However, development is not determined by these domain-specific structures alone; rather, this model views the environment as a co-determinant in the course of development. Thus the present model uses the infant–environment system as the subject of study and ascribes change and variability to both the infants' cognitive structures and the environmental input. Bremner (1994) views such an interactive system "as a constant interplay between the structure of the infant's knowledge and the structure of the world" (p. 268). At any point in time the infants' maturing cognitive structures determine what will be attended to in the environment. Since at each particular time in development the cognitive structures are more mature than the previous ones, the environment presents the infant with different problems, the solution to which results in the development of more advanced cognitive structures.

Through interacting with people over objects, infants not only construct social and physical concepts, but also functional concepts about how human beings can use the world (Bremner, 1994, p. 266). For instance, Fogel (1990) describes how in simple activities such as transferring an object from infant to mother, the mother's part in the activity continuously adjusts to her infant's activity. Thus, Fogel's words . . . "the action of each individual is organized in part by the action of the other" (p. 77). Within this interaction the infant's responses are given meaning by the mother's as she shows her infant the properties and the functions of the object, thereby modeling culturally appropriate behaviors to her infant.

The second difference between the present model and a more traditional cognitive developmental model (e.g., Piaget, 1954) is that the present model views the social environment not only as a co-determinant in developmental outcomes, but also sees the infant and environment couple in subtle ways leading to the cross-connecting of the domain-specific systems into a single higher system. In other words, new structures emerge and consolidate out of organism–environment interactions that achieve global stability in response to interacting constraints (Fogel, 1993; Sameroff, 1989). The importance of social factors in effecting structural change is emphasized by Chapman (1992) who points out that: "In organism-environment interaction, the other organism is a part of the environment. But once initiated into the human world of symbolic meanings, the knowing subject confronts the objects of knowledge with a repertoire of concepts acquired through interaction with other subjects" (p. 42). Hence, in this model, infants' interactions with people are seen as crucial in effecting structural change and novel forms. That is because people are not simply other objects to be apprehended, but also social agents that serve as guides in the developmental process. This guiding should not be seen as a unilateral didactic approach, but rather as a catalyst that brings about hierarchical changes in infants' understanding of people as well as objects. This coupling between the organism and the environment leads to interaction between the social and physical domains to create a single higher level system. Hence, the system as a whole changes, not only in realtime, when infants are in a specific context, but also in ontogenetic time. The implication is that neither domain-specific structures nor the environment determine development. Rather development gets meaning through continuous interactions and is not proportional to its causes. Thus in this model, development is regarded as a consequence of order that arises out of exchanges with the environment, yet feeds back into the environment, and not, as suggested by Piaget (1954) as a result of assimilation of the environment by the system.

## EPISTEMIC TRIANGLE

Although Piaget emphasized the interactive nature of the infants' social–conceptual development, he often failed to acknowledge the importance of people in some of the epistemological questions he asked (Chapman, 1992; Hamlyn, 1978). One of the questions frequently addressed by Piaget (1954) concerns the developing understanding of the animate and inanimate distinction. As described earlier, infants from birth are confronted with both people and objects. Infants notice while interacting with people that they communicate, act contingently, imitate actions and that objects do none of such things (Legerstee, 1991b, 1992; Legerstee et al., 1987; Watson, 1972). This stimulation of an infant by the social partner has both affective and cognitive consequences. Infants notice people to be independent sources of causality and not objects. Consequently, people are more cognitively motivating to infants than objects, and produce more rapid accommodations than objects (Legerstee, 1994a; Piaget, 1981). As a result, when 6-month-old infants are required to search for hidden people and objects in tasks that are equated on difficulty, more infants search for their mothers than for familiar objects (Legerstee, 1994a). Although Piaget (1981) termed such a difference in performance on tasks that require the same underlying cognitive structure "horizontal decalage," lack of parallelism could also mean uneven knowledge of a particular attribute the two classes have in common, in which case this knowledge must come from separate systems rather than just one.

The domain-specificity of cognitive systems is supported by developmental neuropsychology. For example, infants with Down syndrome show significant and measurable delays on specific-cognitive measures in the early months of life (Legerstee & Bowman, 1989; Ohr & Fagen, 1994). Visual information processing investigations, considered measures of cognitive domain functioning, reveal that infants with Down syndrome aged 1 through 7 months, differed significantly from normally developing infants in terms of their preferences for stimuli. They took longer to habituate and had poorer visual recognition memory than normal infants (Ohr & Fagen, 1994). In contrast, these infants do not show significantly different scores from normal infants when tested on social interaction tasks (Legerstee & Bowman, 1989).

Toward the end of the first half of the year, there is evidence that nondelayed infants begin to integrate person and object domains. The development of intersubjectivity, joint attention and preverbal communication are examples of this integration. For instance, the development of coordinated attention is evident in the furtive glances the infant now directs at the mother's face and the toy in which the baby is interested (Adamson & Bakeman, 1991; Legerstee et al., 1987). Mothers usually seize this opportunity and begin to name the object the infant is gazing at. "The epistemic triangle is constructed from such a coordination of subject–object and intersubjective forms of interaction, and representational thought is the result" (Chapman, 1992). Several months later, infants attempt to coordinate their attention between people and objects for sustained periods. During these episodes we see the beginnings of preverbal gestures, when infants begin to request help from people in obtaining objects, or direct people's attention to interesting objects with nonverbal gestures (Bakeman & Adamson, 1984; Legerstee & Weintraub, in press; Mundy, Sigman, Kasari, & Yirmiya, 1988). It appears that the infant's caretakers are instrumental in establishing this subsequent integration of person and object knowledge. In a recent study, normal infants and mental-age matched infants with Down syndrome were observed in interaction with either their mother, a same-aged peer and the peer's mother (Legerstee & Weintraub, in press). Both groups of infants displayed significantly more behaviors involving the coordination of the social and object domains when they played with their mother or the peer's mother than when they played with a same aged peer. Rather than being involved in a triadic structure consisting of the active subject, the object of knowledge, and a cosubject (the peer) (cf. Chapman, 1992), infants remained focused on either the peer or the object or they remained unengaged.

If there is an impairment in either the social or nonsocial domain, then one would expect a deficit in areas of achievement that depend on the integration of the two domains. In the foregoing study (Legerstee & Weintraub, in press), infants with Down syndrome not only produced less coordinated attention when with the peer, but their overall production of this ability was significantly delayed. Correlational measures showed that differences in coordinated attention were strongly related to differences in language scores in normal infants, but not in the infants with Down syndrome. Other researchers have also reported delays in expressive language skills in infants with Down syndrome and in preverbal communicative behaviors (Mundy et al., 1988; Smith & von Tetchner, 1986). This supports suggestions by Bruner (1973) and others (Bakeman & Adamson, 1984; Tomasello & Farrar, 1986) that the ability to coordinate attention is an important precursor to language development. Hence it appears that the infant's deficit in the nonsocial domain produces deficits in the subsequent interaction phase, and may lead to a deficit in the higher order structures that enable language.

In summary, the development of the ability to coordinate attention relies on both domain-specific structures and environmental factors. In particular, coordinated attention appears to be a product of a triadic structure. This socially constructed state, which has emerged out of the interconnectivity of subsystems under the guidance of social partners, is now free to interconnect with other systems (e.g., linguistic) to form more complex structures that allow for the expression of more advanced behaviors, such as language.

## CONCLUDING REMARKS

As described earlier, the present theory of social–conceptual development adheres to the view that emergent structures consolidate out of organism–environment interactions, where the environment is both physical and social. Specifically, a set of components, some from the individual and some from the context, can be organized in a fluid and task-specific manner so that the resulting behavior is the system's product of all these components (Fogel & Thelen, 1987; Lewis, 1994). Stability and change are fundamental aspects of biological systems. These systems are sensitive to their environment and develop under the influences of domain-specific constraints. As mentioned earlier, the constraints may be organismic but they are also present in the environment. Indeed, Varela, Thompson, and Rosch (1991) proposed that through a history of coupling, the organism and the culture *both* have become specified. For instance, one of the phylogenetic constraints infants possess is their inability to care for themselves. This helplessness ensures parental care and close contact. If infants feel hungry or distressed they may emit differential expressive behaviors to signal their specific discomfort. Parents differentially respond to these signals (e.g., they either play with the baby, or change a diaper, as the case may be). Because parents recognize specific signals, parental responsiveness to these signals must be programmed as well.

The preparedness of parents to interact with their infants allows for the early cooperative activity between parent and infant described above. This cooperative activity often involves objects, but also people. Reorganization in social conceptual development results as a consequence of subject–object interactions, as well as subject and person interactions. This means that interactions with increasingly more complex objects result in the reorganization of knowledge concerning physical knowledge. Increasingly, more complex interactions with people should result in more elaborate human cognition. However, as indicated in the preceding paragraphs, social factors are fundamentally different from nonsocial factors and not simply another form of input. Not only are people more attractive to the child than physical objects (Legerstee, 1994a), but people provide infants with a social interaction that "alters the form of the input and makes it more directly informative to the child" (Fogel, 1992, p. 318). Thus, whereas perception of the physical world is dependent on the infant's actions, perception of the social world is a product of a communicative process where both the infant and the social world co-regulate the input. The problem then is one of knowing what such intersubjective co-regulation consists of and how it leads to changes in social cognition. Piaget (1954) proposed that equilibration in the subject–object relationship resulted from contradictions and lack of information to which the infant has to accommodate in order to gain stability. Similar perturbations are available in the intersubjective interaction. That is, the interaction should not be seen as one where information is shared as discrete messages from sender to receiver, rather, co-regulation should be seen as "a social patterning that results from a negotiated co-construction" (Fogel, 1993, p. 40). However, unlike the object–subject relationship, co-regulation is creative because information is not entirely fixed in advance, "not entirely 'in' the self or 'in' the other" (p. 89). This does not necessarily mean that the subjects have no internal state, rather co-regulation leaves open the possibility that new meaning can be created through the interaction not initially planned by the interactants, nor available to them. Through sharing information that either subject possesses, knowledge can be constructed that neither partner possessed (Chapman, 1992; Oyama, 1985). This cognitive flexibility not only allows for the individual's creativity, but it reveals that the human mind is the consequence as well as the cause of its development.

## ACKNOWLEDGMENTS

This work was supported by a grant from the Social Sciences and Humanities Research Council of Canada (410-94-1743). Many ideas presented in this chapter have been influenced by the writings of: Annette Karmiloff-Smith, Alan Fogel, and Malcolm R. Westcott.

## REFERENCES

Adamson, L., & Bakeman, B. (1991). The development of shared attention during infancy. In R. Vasta (Ed.), *Annals of child development* (Vol. 8, pp. 1–41). London: Kingsley.
Bakeman, R., & Adamson, L. B. (1984). Coordinating attention to people and objects in mother-infant and peer-infant interaction. *Child Development, 55,* 1278–1289.
Bremner, J. G. (1994). *Infancy* (2nd ed.). London: Blackwell.
Bruner, J. S. (1973). Organization of early skilled action. *Child Development, 44,* 1–11.

Butterworth, G. (1990). On reconceptualizing sensorimotor development in dynamic systems theory. In H. Bloch & B. J. Berthenthal (Eds.), *Sensorimotor organizations and development in infancy and early childhood* (pp. 57–73). Dordrecht: Kluwer.

Chapman, M. (1992). Equilibration and the dialectics of organization. In H. Beiling & P. Putfall (Eds.), *Piaget's theory: Prospects and possibilities* (pp. 39–59). Hillsdale, NJ: Lawrence Erlbaum Associates.

Fogel, A. (1990). Sensorimotor factors in communicative development. In H. Bloch & B. Bertenthal (Eds.), *Sensorimotor organization and development in infancy and early childhood* (pp. 75–88). Dordrecht: Kluwer.

Fogel, A. (1992). Movement and communication in human infancy: The social dynamics of development. *Human Movement Science, 11,* 387–423.

Fogel, A. (1993). *Developing through relationships: Origins of communication, self and culture.* Chicago: The University of Chicago Press.

Fogel, A., & Thelen, E. (1987). Development of early expressive and communicative action: Reinterpreting the evidence from a dynamic systems perspective. *Developmental Psychology, 23,* 747–761.

Gelman, R. (1990). First principles organize attention to and learning about relevant data: Number and the animate-inanimate distinction as examples. *Cognitive Science, 14,* 79–106.

Gelman, R., & Spelke, E. (1981). The development of thoughts about animate and inanimate objects: Implications for research on social cognition. In H. Flavell & L. Ross (Eds.), *Social cognitive development: Frontiers and possible futures* (pp. 43–66). New York: Cambridge University Press.

Hamlyn, D. (1978). *Experience and the growth of understanding.* London: Routledge & Kegan Paul.

Hobson, R. P. (1990). On the origins of self and the case of autism. *Development and Psychopathology, 5,* 163–181.

Hoffman, M. (1981). Perspectives on the difference between understanding people and understanding things: The role of affect. In J. Glick & K. A. Clark-Stewart (Eds.), *The development of social understanding* (pp. 67–81). New York: Cambridge University Press.

Johnson, M. (1990). Cortical maturation and the development of visual attention in early infancy. *Journal of Cognitive Neuroscience, 2,* 81–95.

Johnson, M. H., & Morton, J. (1991). *Biology and cognitive development: The case of face recognition.* London: Blackwell.

Legerstee, M. (1991a). Changes in the quality of infant sounds as a function of social and nonsocial stimulation. *First Language, 11,* 327–343.

Legerstee, M. (1991b). The role of person and object in eliciting early imitation. *Journal of Experimental Child Psychology, 51*(3), 423–433.

Legerstee, M. (1992). A review of the animate-inanimate distinction in infancy: Implications for models of social and cognitive knowing. *Early Development and Parenting, 1,* 57–67.

Legerstee, M. (1994a). The role of familiarity and sound in the development of person and object permanence. *British Journal of Developmental Psychology, 12*(4), 455–468.

Legerstee, M. (1994b). Patterns of 4-month-old infant responses to hidden silent and sounding people and objects. *Early Development and Parenting, 3,* 71–80.

Legerstee, M. (in press-a). Contingency effects of people and objects on subsequent cognitive functioning in three-month-old infants. *Social Development.*

Legerstee, M. (in press-b). Domain specificity and the epistemic triangle in the development of animism in infancy. In F. Lacerda, C. von Hofsten, & M. Heimann (Eds.), *Transitions in perception, cognition and action in early infancy.* Mahwah, NJ: Lawrence Erlbaum Associates.

Legerstee, M., & Bowman, T. (1989). The development of responses to people and a toy in infants with Down syndrome. *Infant Behavior and Development, 12*(4), 462–473.

Legerstee, M., Bowman, T. G., & Fels, S. (1992). People and objects affect the quality of vocalizations in infants with Down syndrome. *Early Development and Parenting, 1*(3), 149–156.

Legerstee, M., Corter, C., & Kienapple, K. (1990). Hand, arm and facial actions of young infants to a social and nonsocial stimulus. *Child Development, 61,* 774–784.

Legerstee, M., & Hadden, K. (1993, July). *The development of emotional expression and cognitive behaviors during the first year of life.* Paper presented at the XII biennial meeting of the International Society for the Study of Behavioral Development, Recife, Brazil.

Legerstee, M., Pomerleau, A., Malcuit, G., & Feider, H. (1987). The development of infants' responses to people and a doll: Implications for research in communication. *Infant Behavior and Development, 10,* 81–95.

Legerstee, M., & Weintraub, J. (in press). The integration of person and object attention in infants with and without Down syndrome. *Infant Behavior and Development.*

Lewis, M. (in press). Cognition-Emotion feedback and the self-organization of developmental Paths. *Human Development.*

Lewis, M. D. (1994). Reconciling stage and specificity in neo-Piagetian theory: Self-organizing conceptual structures. *Human Development, 37,* 143–169.

Mandler, J. (1992). How to build a baby: II. Conceptual primitives. *Psychological Review, 99,* 587–604.

Maurer, D. (1985). Infant's perception of Facedness. In T. Field & N. Fox (Eds.), *Social perception in infants* (pp. 73–100). Norwood, NJ: Ablex.

Moore, D. G., Hobson, R. P., Lee, A., & Anderson, M. (1992, September). *IQ-independent person-perception: Evidence from developmental psychopathology.* Paper presented at the meeting of the Fifth European Conference on Developmental Psychology, Seville, Spain.

Morse, P. A., & Cowan, N. (1982). Infant auditory and speech perception. In T. M. Field, A. Huston, H. C. Quay, L. Troll, & G. E. Finley (Eds.), *Review of human development.* New York: Wiley.

Muir, D., Cao, Y., & Entremont, B. (1994, June). Infant social perception revealed during adult–infant face-to-face interaction. *Infant Behavior and Development, 17,* 86.

Mundy, P., Sigman, M., Kasari, C., & Yirmiya, N. (1988). Nonverbal communication skills in Down syndrome children. *Child Development, 59,* 235–249.

Ohr, P. S., & Fagen, J. W. (1994). Contingency learning in 9-month-old infants with Down syndrome. *American Journal of Mental Retardation, 99*(1), 74–84.

Oyama, S. (1985). *The ontogeny of information: Developmental systems and evolution.* Cambridge, England: Cambridge University Press.

Piaget, J. (1954). *The construction of reality in the child* (M. Cook, trans.). New York: Basic Books.

Piaget, J. (1981). *Intelligence and affectivity: Their relationship during child development.* Palo Alto, CA: Annual Reviews.

Premack, D. (1990). The infant's theory of self-propelled objects. *Cognition, 36,* 1–16.

Rheingold, H. (1961). The effect of environmental stimulation upon social and exploratory behavior in the human infant. In B. Foss (Ed.), *Determinants of infant behavior* (Vol. 1). New York: Wiley.

Ronnquist, L., & Hofsten, C. von. (1994). Neonatal finger and arm movements as determined by a social and an object context. *Early Development and Parenting, 3,* 81–93.

Sameroff, A. J. (1989). Developmental systems: Contexts and evolution. In P. H. Mussen (Series Ed.) and W. Kessen (Vol. Ed.), *Handbook of child psychology Vol. 1: History, theory and methods* (4th ed., pp. 237–294). New York: Wiley.

Smith, L., & von Tetchner, S. (1986). Communicative, sensorimotor, and language skills of young children with Down syndrome. *American Journal of Mental Deficiency, 91,* 57–66.

Spelke, E. S. (1994). Initial knowledge: Six suggestions. *Cognition, 50,* 431–445.

Spelke, E. S., Phillips, A. T., & Woodward, A. L. (1995). Infant's knowledge of object motion and human action. In D. Sperber, D. Premack, & A. J. Premack (Eds.), *Causal cognition: A multidisciplinary debate* (pp. 44–78). Oxford: Clarendon Press.

Sternberg, R. (1989). Domain-generality versus domain-specificity: The life and impending death of a false dichotomy, *Merril-Palmer Quarterly, 35,* 115–130.

Tomasello, M., & Farrar, M. J. (1986). Joint attention and early language. *Child Development, 57,* 1454–1463.

Trevarthen, C. (1979). Communication and cooperation in early infancy: A description of primary intersubjectivity. In M. Bullowa (Ed.), *Before speech: The beginning of interpersonal communication* (pp. 321–347). New York: Cambridge University Press.

Trevarthen, C. (1980). The foundations of intersubjectivity: Development of interpersonal and cooperative understanding. In D. Olsen (Ed.), *The social foundation of language and thought: Essays in honor of Jerome Bruner* (pp. 316–342). New York: Norton.

Varela, F. J., Thompson, E., & Rosch, E. (1991). *The embodied mind: Cognitive science and human experience.* Cambridge, MA: MIT Press.

Watson, J. (1972). Smiling, cooing and "the game." *Merrill-Palmer Quarterly, 18,* 323–340.

Woodward, A., Phillips, A. T., & Spelke, E. S. (1993). Infants' expectations about the motion of animate versus inanimate objects. *Proceedings of the Fifteenth Annual Conference of the Cognitive Science Society* (pp. 1087–1091). Hillsdale, NJ: Lawrence Erlbaum Associates.

# Cascades on an Epigenetic River: Indeterminacy in Cognitive and Personality Development

Helena Hurme
Åbo Akademi University, Finland

The three chapters in this section range from the four Aristotelian causes in relation to creativity, through self-organization in personality development, to domain-specificity in infants' social–conceptual structures. My specialization is in none of these areas and I doubt that a person who has specialized in all three areas exists. My task has rather been to comment on and to amplify the themes in these chapters especially from the viewpoint of indeterminism–determinism. I comment first on the terminology used in the chapters, then on some features of each chapter, then look for similarities and differences in them and their relation to the indeterminism debate, and, finally, finish with a proposal for a new metaphor of development.

## COMMENTS ON TERMINOLOGY

It is important that we agree on what terms to use. In my view, indeterminism–determinism refers to schools or views of thinking about the world. Thus we do not see indeterminism or determinism in development, but rather indeterminacy or determinacy and phenomena are either indeterminate or determined. Depending on which view we adhere to, we can be indeterministically or deterministically oriented.

A second comment concerning terminology has to do with the either-or nature of the terms indeterminate versus determined. In a strict sense, the terms are categorical: If something is determined, it is so totally. If not, it is undetermined (a view which Roazzi and de Sousa term "strong determinism"). According to this strict view, a phenomenon cannot be "partly determined." As an example: If the heart stops beating, the individual is dead, not partly dead.

According to Roazzi and de Sousa there is a second meaning of determinism ("weak determinism" in their terms), which is based on predictability. The better the predictability of a phenomenon from some other phenomenon, the more determined the former seems to be by the latter. This meaning of the word *determined* stresses the role of the researcher and the research process without which the probabilities which underlie predictability are hard to define. Such a view of indeterminacy is often based on group means and the empirical work of Roazzi and de Sousa is closest of the three chapters to this meaning of indeterminacy. One could perhaps call it "empirical indeterminacy" because it is established through the empirical observation of multiple co-occurrences. In my view, however, the important distinctive feature is not predictability, but linear causation. A consequence of linear causation is that, from the researcher's point of view, predictability increases and the phenomenon in question seems more determined.

The situation is quite simple when the relation between two variables, especially in the natural sciences, is concerned, as, for instance, the relation between the heart ceasing to beat and death. When a process consists of multiple parameters, however, as in the case of most psychological processes, subprocesses may be determined, but the whole system is more or less indeterminate, partly because of unexpected influences external to the original system, and partly because of self-organization. One also has to take into account that the degree of determination in a complex system depends on what is counted as belonging to the system by the researcher.

The categorical view on determination implies that development is determined only if every aspect of it is determined. There is enough data to show that this is clearly not the case with humans. Therefore, the discussion should be concerned with which subprocesses of development are determined and which are not and which factors determine these processes. This is of course what much of psychology has been about up till now. The new aspect in the indeterminacy discussion is that a large part of development cannot be predicted from external factors or from innate factors because there is self-organization in development or even totally new forms of behavior because of unexpected external influences. In such phenomena, causation is nonlinear. This third meaning of indeterminacy, which perhaps could be called "theoretical indeterminacy," is thought to be in the phenomenon and it is independent of what the researcher does. No researcher could ever predict such a phenomenon, at least not with methods known to us today. This form of indeterminacy is most closely present in Lewis' work and also to some extent in Legerstee's work, which falls somewhere between this group and the previous one in that she besides self-organization is assuming more innate systems than most genetic epistemologists. Thus, she enlarges the area of innate determination and predictability from innate factors at the same time as she assumes indeterminacy of some subprocesses.

In a way, the dividing line between what I have called empirical indeterminacy and theoretical indeterminacy has to do with the researcher's point of view. In empirical indeterminacy, it clearly is more central: The researcher is either able to determine the causes of some phenomenon or is not. In what I have called theoretical indeterminacy, the phenomenon is thought to be indeterminate and no researcher would ever be able to predict it.

A third point in relation to terminology has to do with whose perspective on determination is adopted, the individual's or an outside observer's. The need to make such a distinction becomes especially clear in connection with Roazzi and de Sousa's chapter. From an individual's point of view, internal processes may seem more determined, or determinable, whereas from a researcher's point of view they are at least as undetermined as external processes. There is a danger when different authors speak of different things using the same terms if no decision has been made as to which view to adopt or if each view is not stated clearly in each case.

## SOME FEATURES OF THE THREE CHAPTERS

### Legerstee: Predispositions to React to Humans

Legerstee's main message is that humans have predispositions to react differentially to other humans and to objects but that these reactions are modified by experience. As such, this is perhaps not very surprising, taking into account the very specific innate reaction patterns to different objects in other species. Gottlieb (1991) calls these species-specific perceptions. He says that "usually, these patterns of stimulation are provided by other members of the species" (p. 6).

Legerstee is not alone in presenting thoughts like this. Schaffer (1971) said, almost a quarter of a century ago, "From birth, the infant is equipped with a species-specific cognitive structure which ensures that he is selectively attuned to certain types of environmental stimuli" (p. 37). In later writings, Schaffer (1989) speaks of the infants' "social preadaptation" in referring to "predispositions—certain tendencies, that is, selectively to attend to particular kinds of stimuli and to structure its responses in particular ways" (p. 192). He also says that . . . "on the auditory as on the visual side, infants arrive in the world especially attuned to the kind of stimulation provided by other people" (p. 193). Emde (1989) again states that "the infant comes to the world with a biological preparedness for participating in social interaction" (p. 38) and he also stresses the role of affect in relationship experiences. Astington (1994) observes that "babies seemed to be tuned into people right from the start" (pp. 166–167), but that as such, innateness does not mean that a function is there right from birth.

Legerstee's view is that the predispositions exert their influence through interaction with the environment: "Subsequent development is viewed as a consequence of how these domain-specific structures deal with experience." Very much the same view was espoused by Schaffer in 1971. He says that "Children are not born 'knowing people.' . . . In the early weeks there is no indication that they are able to categorize their environment into its animate and its inanimate constituents and thus differentiate the social from the non-social. Such differentiation comes only as a result of experience, brought about by an environment which provides opportunities to learn, that other human beings as such are, in certain respects, a class apart" (p. 32).

The concept of *experiential canalization* which has become known in developmental psychology through the works of Waddington (e.g., 1957) is also relevant here. Gottlieb (1991, 1992) has modified it to mean that "normal experience helps to achieve species-specific behavioral development . . ." (Gottlieb, 1991, p. 6). He showed that mallard ducklings who were prevented from hearing their own or their sibling's voice did not respond in the "normal," species-specific selective way to their mother's call. With humans, no such experimental manipulation can of course be made. Most humans are reared by adults (with the so-called wild children, who are not, experimental studies are impossible). Therefore it is difficult to say to what extent the differential reactivity of infants to humans versus nonhumans is dependent on experience.

Social partners occupy a central position in Legerstee's model as in the work of other writers. In the conclusions of his 1971 book, Schaffer stresses reciprocity between the infant and his or her mother, observing that "the behavior of each partner gives rise to an increasingly complex response organization in the other partner; the mutual entwining of interaction sequences thus takes place at progressively higher levels" (pp. 172–173). The cross-cultural work of Whiting and Edwards (1988) likewise stresses the importance of innate, reciprocal systems in infants and their caregivers, which ensure survival of the children.

To me, Legerstee's model seems very plausible and her argumentation is very compelling. She has chosen to stress self-organization by mentioning it in the title of her chapter. In the text, she underscores the role of adults as coregulators in the development of the infant. Perhaps she could have stressed it even more by mentioning it in the title as well because it is, after all, one of the factors that differentiate it from the traditional Piagetian view. This would also place her work closer to those writers (e.g., Lightfoot & Valsiner, 1992) who stressed coconstruction of the child's development by the child and the caretaker.

## LEWIS: "WHERE HAS ALL THAT LEARNING GONE"?

Lewis' chapter concerns personality development. The central features of his theory are that emotions are important for personality development and that they interact with cognitions. Through this interaction, new developmental constraints are built.

Speaking of the role of emotions in personality development, he says that "For example, images of helplessness, abandonment, and worthlessness become more congruent once they have coassembled with sadness and shame on one or more occasions. This increases the probability that they will converge once again on similar occasions. . . ." He might as well have said "once they have become associated with. . . ." To me, it is just a question of applying new terminology to an old phenomenon; in this case using "coassemble" for "association" or even for "learning." For a long time I have been wondering what happened to "learning" in writings of developmental psychologists, as this word hardly ever figures in the titles or in the indexes of books on development. It is as if individuals have stopped learning! This is, of course, not the case. Rather, authors present this phenomenon under other labels. Lewis gives one example of this in his article. This is all the more interesting as Lewis at the beginning of his chapter lists as one of the hallmarks of conventional psychological theories that "structure is imported from the environment through the process of learning." It depends on the definition of learning whether also the application of old structures in new combinations and new situations counts as learning or not. To me, it does, and thus Lewis' model contains learning as well.

On a more general level, it is important to analyze which implications of the indeterminism debate are for the concept of learning in developmental psychology and why they have disappeared from the discourse of developmental psychologists.

## ROAZZI AND DE SOUSA: IS CONTEXT-DEPENDENT NECESSARILY INDETERMINATE?

Roazzi and de Sousa look at indeterminacy from the second point of view delineated earlier, that of predictability. Their most central assumption is that which varies in context is less determined than that which is internally determined. On the basis of this central assumption, they then create two classes: task-independent and task-dependent, observing that fluency is more task-independent and determined, whereas originality is more task-dependent and therefore more indeterminate. But do we have to equate context-independent with determined (and therefore predictable)? Could we not think that the individual's degrees of freedom may be greater but, from the researcher's point of view, at least as difficult to predict as factors influenced by the context? Besides, something may depend on the context, but in a predictable manner.

The foregoing discussion boils down to whether one should adopt the researcher's point of view, or, as Roazzi and de Sousa propose at the beginning of the section, "Task dependency and creativity," the individual's point of view, when speaking of indeterminacy–determinacy. Usually, the whole discussion has concerned the researcher's point of view. If this viewpoint is adopted with respect to fluency and creativity, it may well be that, after all, context independent factors seem more indeterminate!

A second point in Roazzi and de Sousa's argument concerns the use of the age variable. They draw, for instance, the conclusion that ". . . age affects intelligence which, in turn, affects fluency. . . ." In my view, age per se cannot affect anything, but is rather an index for something which changes with time. They also make the assumption that ". . . determinism should result in a definite relationship between age or time and level of development." It may, however, be too weak a proof for creativity being indeterminate that there is no correlation with age, especially in a cross-sectional design. Even in a longitudinal design, a high correlation with age could be the consequence of different causal factors in different individuals and as such also not a proof of determination.

A last point concerning Roazzi and de Sousa's chapter has to do with the nature of science. Roazzi and de Sousa say that "*Prima faciem*, scientists should all be determinists, for they attempt to produce or acquire knowledge that will lead to perfect predictability and control of phenomena, and they try to do so using methods that assume the existence of definite, stable, patterns of behavior in the Universe." They also say that "Psychology, being (or intended to be) a Science, is based on the belief that behavior and development are caused, and that such causes can be empirically discovered and quantitatively measured with adequate precision so as to permit both prediction and control within acceptable limits. If nature proves that belief to be misleading, then one must dramatically redefine science and its basic tenets." They do not redefine it, however, but instead continue with presenting their own study which follows precisely the old pattern. There is already now enough information concerning the indeterminate nature of human behavior to permit us to see that we should rethink the goals of a science which studies such behavior and, especially, predictability as a goal of the human sciences.

## SIMILARITIES AND DIFFERENCES
## BETWEEN THE CHAPTERS

One could perhaps say that Legerstee's and Lewis' articles fall into the same category. Lewis gives the general model and Legerstee an exemplification, on the one hand concerned with infant behavior, on the other hand one specific phenomenon, the animistic versus nonanimistic distinction. The model states that there are self-organizing couplings, or cross-connections, of lower-order entities into a higher-order system.

Common also to the two chapters is the centrality of emotion: For Lewis, emotions are central in the development of personality and Legerstee shows that infants react with more intense emotions to people than to objects. The difference between Legerstee's and Lewis' models lies in the fact that Legerstee strongly stresses the role of social partners in this process, a fact which is not explicit in Lewis' chapter. Legerstee mentions, for instance, that "only the relationship with people seem(s) to affect their [the infants'] motivation to learn." Lewis again stresses the role of recurrent couplings in realtime, on the micro level. Perhaps the role of people in these couplings could be stressed even more in Lewis' account.

Indeterminacy is present when development cannot be predicted either from innate or from environmental factors. In this sense, indeterminacy is perhaps most central in Lewis' model. In Legerstee's chapter, determinism versus indeterminism is not mentioned often or at length, but the topic is central to the question. It is as if a greater part of the individual would be "prespecified" (to use Lewis' term) in Legerstee's model than in most current accounts of development. This does not, however, mean a total determination, but it reduces the degrees of freedom for external factors to operate in development.

Where Lewis and Legerstee draw conclusions concerning broad areas of development, cognitive and personality development, Roazzi and de Sousa's chapter concerns a much more narrow subprocess, namely creativity, although their conclusions are intended to concern determinacy–indeterminacy in general. Their argumentation is, however, not as compelling as Lewis' or Legerstee's.

One point in common to both Roazzi and de Sousa's and Lewis' chapters is the question concerning individual versus nonindividual, that is, the question of limits between the individual and his environment. It is especially important for a dynamic systems view to recognize that this boundary is also fluid, that what has been a part of the environment can the next moment be counted as part of the individual, and vice versa. This, of course, is especially clear when physical products (e.g., food) are concerned, but one might also extend this question to concern learning in general and also the self, that is, to what extent the definition of an individual's self is based on factors which might be counted as the environment: clothes, things, drawings or writings by the individual, etc. Where is the dividing line between internal and external? To what extent is it constructed through language and thus through convention? Cross-cultural comparisons and anthropological data might shed light upon this question.

## THE ROLE OF CONSCIOUSNESS OR:
## WHAT IS LACKING IN THE MODELS?

In my view, none of the three chapters gives enough space to the specifically human in human development, to the fact that the individual is capable of totally new ways of thinking and behaving because of consciousness and the possibility of interpreting information and giving it new meaning. This is what causes indeterminacy from the researcher's point of view.

There already exists explanatory models where consciousness has a prominent place and which resemble those of Lewis and Legerstee in that they assume innate structures specific to humans. One is put forward by Bruner (e.g., 1990; Legerstee refers to his earlier writings), and another by Subbotsky (1992). Subbotsky assumes that there are "Fundamental structures of consciousness," namely the notions of object, causality, time, and space. He prefers to use the Kantian term "a priori forms" of these. He says that "Consciousness can perform its specific work—to separate the true from the false, the existing from the seeming, being from non-being—only on the basis of these forms" (p. 127). He refers to the concept of *modularity* put forward by Leslie (1986). A *module* is a formal, innate structure of the mind applied to incoming sensory information. Subbotsky's own experiments concern the causality module, of which he says "The function of the module is to get development off the ground, to set the process of understanding physical causality into motion" (p. 83). In a way, Legerstee assumes a domain-specific module for the identification of animate versus inanimate objects without using the term consciousness or module.

## THE USE OF METAPHORS IN DESCRIBING HUMAN
## DEVELOPMENT

Metaphors are commonly used in science. The behavioral sciences often adopt models from the natural sciences. The advantage of metaphors is that they make complex and abstract phenomena more concrete and often easier to grasp and remember. At the same time, they oversimplify complex phenomena. Still, I do believe in refining metaphors rather than in totally abandoning them.

In the indeterminism debate, there is a danger in taking over new metaphors from the natural sciences and the biosciences which suit the study of human beings as little as the deterministic metaphors we want to abandon. One such source of metaphors is the chaos theory. This is especially clear in Lewis' chapter. He uses such terms as *attractors, repellors, self-organization*, or *cascading*, which all can be found in such popularized books on chaos theory as Gleick's (1987) or Lewis' (1992). The danger is that we start expecting the same type of laws to govern human behavior as those governing, for instance, biological populations or the atmosphere. As an example we could take the cascading constraints which have a prominent place in Lewis' model (see Fig. 8.3 in Lewis' chapter). Whereas Lewis is aptly able to describe the phenomenon known from chaos theory, namely that a small initial change may later lead to massive consequences, yet there is something lacking. Could we not, also, think of cascading opportunities, or even more radically, of a model with totally new branches, either as a result of self-organization (to use Lewis' term) or through unexpected input from the environment?

## AN EPIGENETIC RIVER AS A METAPHOR OF DEVELOPMENT

Lewis says that "All of the constraints mentioned so far are deterministic in one sense: They are prespecified with respect to the developmental process itself. That is, they exist independently of the developing child, so to speak, to shape that child's development." I agree that the constraints are there, at first independent of the child. In a way a part of an individual is there already before birth, as a potential, both in the genes and in the environment. But one could state it in exactly the opposite way: that these constraints (and opportunities) are there, waiting to be shaped by a particular individual. In Lewis' metaphor, the *constraints* cascade down the developmental stream, "influencing the formation of the next, guiding and narrowing the flow through increasingly specific outcomes." I rather propose a riverbed as a metaphor for the prespecified constraints *and* opportunities, waiting for the specific amount of water during a particular year. The riverbed shapes the journey of the water, which in turn shapes the riverbed further down. The flow of water is as irreversible as the development of the individual: Neither can return to the original state. The location of the river determines the end point of the river at large, within certain limits. Humans may cultivate the river: They may straighten it or tame it, but only within the limits set by the riverbeds and the water. The material of the riverbanks determines what the water of the river transports in addition to its original makeup: If there is gold in the soil, it may be found in the water. The borders between "river" and "not-river" are fluid, as are the limits between the individual and the environment. But there are also totally unexpected and unpredictable factors to be found in the water: Pieces of metal from an airplane exploding in the sky landing in the river, a toy dropping in the water, or a rare bird choosing the river as a resting place.

This river metaphor resembles that of the epigenetic landscape of Waddington (e.g., 1957), but is more dynamic than that. There has been some critique against Waddington's model when applied to developmental psychology. Valsiner (1987) has commented on the application of Waddington's concept of canalization to developmental psychology and made the observation that "the constraints are not 'just there' for the child to develop, but are made up by purposefully acting participants . . ." (p. 85), but he has not tried to modify Waddington's model. Gottlieb (1991) says that "Because the epigenetic landscape in which Waddington's developmental pathways are embedded is merely figurative or metaphorical, his concept of canalization is devoid of any empirical content and thus supplies us with no concrete understanding or hypotheses concerning the developmental processes involved" (p. 5). Cairns (1991), in his comment on Gottlieb's assessment of the canalization concept, has given perhaps the harshest critique. He says that "For my money, the biggest flaw of the landscape metaphor is not its genetic basis or its too rigid view of developmental sequences. Rather, it is that the metaphor has been applied to the development of whole organisms and whole systems rather than to particular processes. . . . In buying too much too cheaply, metaphors substitute simple images for the hard-won gains of empirical science" (p. 24).

Despite the earlier critique against Waddington's model, I propose another metaphor, an epigenetic river instead of the more general concept of epigenetic landscape. It involves the same main features as the epigenetic landscape, that is, it sets the main direction of development toward the adult state, but at the same time allows for more interaction with the initial constraints. It is even possible to build in adult guidance in this model, as well as some degree of indeterminism. What it does not contain, though, is human consciousness, neither that of the developing individual, nor that of the interacting partners. My strong belief is that precisely what is most human in human beings will evade every attempt to force it into a metaphor.

## REFERENCES

Astington, J. W. (1994). *The child's discovery of mind.* London: Fontana.

Bruner, J. (1990). *Acts of meaning.* Cambridge, MA: Harvard University Press.

Cairns, R. (1991). Multiple metaphors for a singular idea. *Developmental Psychology, 27*(1), 23–26.

Emde, R. (1989). The infant's relationship experience: Developmental and affective aspects. In A. J. Sameroff & R. N. Emde (Eds.), *Relationship disturbances in early childhood. A developmental approach* (pp. 33–51). New York: Basic Books.

Gleick, J. (1987). *Chaos. Making a new science.* London: Cardinal Books.

Gottlieb, G. (1991). Experiential canalization of behavioral development: Theory. *Developmental Psychology, 27*(1), 4–13.

Gottlieb, G. (1992). *Individual development and evolution. The genesis of novel behavior.* Oxford, England: Oxford University Press.

Leslie, A. (1986). Getting development off the ground. Modularity and infant's perception of causality. In P. L. C. van Geert (Ed.), *Theory building in developmental psychology* (pp. 405–437). Amsterdam: Elsevier.

Lewis, R. (1992). *Complexity. Life at the edge of chaos.* New York: Macmillan.

Lightfoot, C., & Valsiner, J. (1992). Parental belief systems under the influence: Social guidance of the construction of personal cultures. In I. E. Sigel, A. V. McGillicuddy-DeLisi, & J. J. Goodnow (Eds.), *Parental belief systems. The psychological consequences for children* (2nd ed.). Hillsdale, NJ: Lawrence Erlbaum Associates.

Schaffer, R. (1971). *The growth of sociability.* Harmondsworth: Penguin.

Schaffer, R. (1989). Early social development. In A. Slater & G. Bremner (Eds.), *Infant development* (pp. 189–210). Hillsdale, NJ: Lawrence Erlbaum Associates.

Subbotsky, E. V. (1992). *Foundations of the mind. Children's understanding of reality.* New York: Harvester Wheatsheaf.

Valsiner, J. (1987). *Culture and the development of children's action. A cultural-historical theory of developmental psychology.* New York: Wiley.

Waddington, C. H. (1957). *The strategy of the genes.* London: Allen & Unwin.

Whiting, B. B., & Edwards, C. P. (1988). *Children of different worlds. The formation of social behavior.* Cambridge, MA: Harvard University Press.

# LOOKING BACKWARDS AND FORWARD, AND THE PLACE FOR INDETERMINISM

Hideo Kojima
Nagoya University, Japan

## INTRODUCTION AND GENERAL COMMENTS

In the process of reading these three chapters, I became more and more aware of my implicit internal framework as related to determinism versus indeterminism in human development. Some aspects of the framework were evoked or constructed within myself when I tried to deal with these three chapters. Somewhat different aspects would have been evoked if I had read a different set of chapters. In any case, processing and discussing of these chapters where imaginary interactions between the authors and the commentator are involved will certainly modify the latter's framework. In the first section, some general points will be made that were activated in my mind during the initial phase of my reading.

In the second section, I discuss individual chapters, focusing on selected aspects of each chapter and adding concluding remarks in the final section. I begin with some general comments, being interested in how this characterization will be appreciated by the authors as well as by the readers.

***Structural Aspects of Causal Model.*** All the causal models of the three chapters involve multiple and recursive paths. Yet, they are basically combinations of and extensions of linear causal network models, such as cascades or tree structures. The models do not contain weblike networks that are characterized by the crossing of paths at nodal points and a bidirectional stream of influence.

### Former Components in a Developmental System.

Generally speaking, the development is conceptualized as an emergence of something new (i.e., new skills, knowledge, relationships, and so on), actualizing new levels of functioning or psychological structures. For example, the modification of an old habit of mind into a new one, and the replacement of a former structure by the present one in the developmental process, are presumed. What has not been made explicit, however, is how the formerly activated components are still placed or displaced in the current system.

### Mechanical and Organismic Systems to Cope With Perturbations.

As was explained by Peterson (1993), Newtonian equations for the movement of objects were deterministic ones in that once the initial conditions were set, the movement of the objects in a system is determined for good. Thus, what has happened and what will happen in the solar system (e.g., the time of sunrise on a particular day, the time and the place of a particular solar eclipse, and the next return of a comet) are explained and predicted accurately.

We have accepted the deterministic, mechanical model of the celestial motion as a persuasive one. If there were two closed systems with identical sets of initial conditions, a completely identical series of history must have been developed. However, very slight differences in the initial conditions between the two systems may eventually yield quite a big difference in their courses of development. In addition, as Peterson explains, determinism does not guarantee stability of a system. A small perturbation may eventually cause chaotic behavior in a system that has been working on a stable basis for a long period of time. Thus, a generator with built-in self-regulatory devices may get out of control when triggered by a small disruption in the system.

Self-regulatory devices may be contained in mechanical as well as electronic machines, but mechanical machines are generally not self-organizing. In contrast, self-organizing systems can develop monitoring and executing subsystems to respond to internal as well as external perturbations that disturb the stability of the system. These subsystems usually function so as to absorb the influence of the disruption and maintain stability of the system, eventually supporting the development of the system. If it is not possible, however, to maintain the stability of the whole system, some problematic part may be isolated temporarily from the other parts to maintain the functions of the main system. In my view, a certain degree of hierarchical structure needs to be developed in order for this kind of selective switching to occur. In addition, it is theoretically possible that the subsystems may work to disorganize the whole system when a crucial part of the system is endangered. Psychological systems that were dealt with in Part III of this volume generally contain self-organizing functions and try to deal with the dynamic process of maintaining coherence of the whole system. They do not appear, however, to consider the possibility of disorganization. I come back to this problem when I discuss the chapter by Lewis.

***Organizer in Self-Organization.*** On the one hand, the explanation of how self-organization proceeds can be made without posing any locus of agency. On the other hand, the role of the self as agent for intentional endeavor and as monitor and regulator of one's own development is a common concept in the everyday theory of development, as well as in the psychology of adolescents and personality development. The three chapters in Part III deal mainly with development in the early period of life. Still, the self may play an important part in early development. The task is to bridge the gap between the two levels of conceptualization; one involves the self, and the other does not.

## SOME NOTES ON INDIVIDUAL CHAPTERS

### Chapter by Lewis on Personality Self-Organization

The chapter by Lewis is a well-developed and effective presentation of a sound theoretical approach to developmental process. His basic tenet is a bottoms-up organismic model of human development. He neither conceives of developmental changes as dominantly constrained by innate programs nor as imposed by an external, environmental structure. He emphasizes two aspects of self-organization, that is, (a) emergence and consolidation of qualitatively novel forms developed out of recursive interactions among simpler *elements* in the previous states, and (b) self-maintenance in the changing environment.

As the guiding premises for the concept of self-organization, Lewis points out the importance of (a) potential diversity of developmental outcome not completely determined by precursors, and (b) tendency toward coherent and stable system. First, he maintains that though both organism's structural and environmental contextual specifications highly constrain the ways in which new forms develop, there still remains room for an indeterminacy of outcomes. What is not clear here is the source of this indeterminacy. Lewis mentions "small variations or random effects [that] can greatly influence outcomes." These sources are not different from the effects of perturbations referred to earlier that can be dealt with within a mechanical framework.

With regard to Lewis' second point, that is, a system's tendency toward a coherent and stable state, I would like to draw attention to two things: First, I agree with his proposal of the developmental process as a shift from indeterminacy to determinacy over time. Still, changes in some functions within a system may temporarily cause incoherence with other functions, thus making the whole system less stable and giving room for operation of indeterminacy. This phenomenon will be conspicuous especially during the transitional phases. Second, if we look at the foreground sphere of the developmental system, the developing system becomes more coherent through structurization, not necessarily wholly but locally. On the other hand, in the less conspicuous background sphere of the system, it may happen that nonactivated components which are not organized into the foreground phenomenon remain incoherent to each other. I speculate that all of these nonorganized components may not be discarded out of the whole system as waste material in order to make the activated sphere more coherent; a substantial portion of them may be retained in the system. Some of these components may be utilized in later phases of development to construct a new aspect of the system.

One of the most meaningful concepts in Lewis' model is the constraints that emerge as a result of developmental self-organization and that are distinguished from prespecified constraints. According to Lewis, the latter constraints never act directly on developing forms but rather they exert influence through the action of the former constraints.

In this connection, Lewis conceptualizes a sequence of emergent constraints that cascades down the stream of the developmental path of an individual. In my view, however, a figurative representation of this concept (see Fig. 8.2) does not necessarily convey the dynamic nature of his concept. First of all, the figure can be construed as representing a series of progressive specifications of the developmental path whose branching occurs in a largely deterministic way. If all possible outcomes are known and we look back toward the origin, it appears that the degree of freedom for the next-step branching is maximal before the first branching and is minimal in the last branching point. This does not mean, however, that branching or trenching in the earlier phases are less deterministic than that in later ones. It may all be the same. An individual's history of emerging constraints that has been stored in some form within the system may certainly influence its branching at the next point. Still, accumulation of history within an individual and the environment does not necessarily mean the narrowing of the possible paths. It may, on the contrary, enhance the number of alternative paths at the branching point. My view is that all branches are not a completely new creation but partially repeat the processes in the former phases, with accumulated history being projected into the multiple future. The situation is not unlike a young tree that first grows upward without much branching and only later spreads it branches widely, with multiple paths becoming possible at later branching points. Considering these points, the metaphor of a cascade that progressively branches into more specified channels is not the most appropriate one.

Dynamic systems, adaptive self-organization, and emergent constraints that cascade down the stream of a developmental path are key terms in Lewis' model. Certainly it is an organismic model. I can detect, however, a flavor of mechanistic models still lingering. Metaphorically speaking, water is running down through self-dug trenches as guided by prespecified and emergent constraints. Heredity's programs, formative factors of the environment, and psychological structure as the results of the individual's past history of running down the stream, jointly influence, directly or indirectly, the path to be taken by the individual. But are the sources of indeterminacy merely incidental or a random variation of these factors? Can't we think of the individual's self as organizer and agent for self-determination? Now it is due time to look for the answers in Lewis' theoretical model.

Referring to Fogel (1993), Haken (1987), and Thelen and Smith (1994), Lewis takes the position that variability in the developing system and its contexts makes room for diversity among individuals and thus is the necessary condition for the development of novel forms. In other words, out of myriad possibilities of association among cognitive, emotional, and social elements, peculiarly associated, coherent and stable combined forms can emerge. But how are they associated and organized?

Lewis' answer to the foregoing question is the mechanism of feedback and the coupling in human self-organization. First, according to Lewis, a feedback process, especially the global positive feedback that amplifies its effect over time, can generate novel forms. Here gradualism of developmental change is implied. His notion of macrodevelopment as an accumulation of microdevelopment exemplifies this position. Second, coactivated elements in the system reciprocally adjust each other while they participate in the system's global activity, thus being coupled and maintained. On the other hand, elements that do not participate in this activity remain uncoupled, and those that work against the ongoing activity are decoupled from the active elements, sometimes being coupled with each other to form a competitive assembly. Here the notion of a competitive assembly can lead to a dialectical model of development, but it is a different family of model from Lewis'. In addition, Lewis emphasizes reciprocal adjustment among the participating elements and does not pose any higher order regulatory function of the system.

In other words, Lewis' theoretical approach is a bottoms-up construction of highly organized systems out of nested activities of simple subsystems without assuming abstract higher order functions. Hence, the chief source of indeterminacy is assigned to random factors like chance juxtapositions of cognitive and emotional elements. Needless to say, the contents of cognitive and emotional elements change as children develop and their histories of experiences become newly organized. Thus, understandings of self, others, need, control, and so on, change, though they harbor the history of past experiences. It is here where the rooms for the functioning of individual's intentions, desires, goals, and plans develop.

For a bottoms-up developmental theory such as Lewis', the job of taking into account this subjective goal-directedness is not an easy one. What he introduces for this purpose is the formation of an alternative way for dealing with anxiety, that is, a defensive appraisal. The basic assumption is that when a psychological activity oscillates beyond certain limits and constitutes a chaotic phase, this state allows for the rapid assembly of an alternative appraisal of the situation. According to Lewis, when negative feedback caused by anxiety amounts to the degree to induce chaotic activity, it may happen that attention shifts to an alternative appraisal of the situation like defensive appraisal that is maintained by positive feedback. Here again, no higher order monitoring and regulating system are assumed, but the switching function is served mainly by the ordinary cognitive systems.

Though he admits the possible role of intention in the process of self-organization of defense, it is not dealt with systematically. The role of culture for construction of defensive appraisal by the individual beyond uniform effect of a particular culture is also not discussed by Lewis. Still, reference to such terms as inner voice and self-directed speech indicates Lewis' awareness of the need for incorporation of the role of self in the full theory of cognitive, emotional, and personality development. The importance of an individual's appraisal of one's past experience as noticed by Lewis suggests the need for consideration of a narrative nature of one's experiences. Whether this incorporation will be attained by extending the bottoms-up approach, or if it will require self-organization of the basic scheme, is an interesting theme of theory building on human development.

## Chapter by Roazzi and de Souza on Determinism and Indeterminism in Children's Creativity

Along with a systematic review on the concepts of causality, Roazzi and de Souza presented their research findings on cognitive development in Brazilian children between 5 and 7 years of age. I review some of their findings on the creativity dimension, and discuss the interpretation in relation to determinism–indeterminism issues.

What should be questioned first is their logic of connecting determinism versus indeterminism to the presence versus absence of high correlation between the target variables (in this case, fluency and originality scores) and age or time. I accept their definition of complete determinism, that is, "each and every phase of it [creativity] would be entirely determined by prior conditions." But should determinism entail a definite relationship, either linear or nonlinear, between age (or time) and developmental level? Let me here classify the cases in order to make the discussion clearer.

### Case A: Complete Dependence of Competence on Time With No Individual Difference

If we draw age function graphs as a certain index of psychological development for individuals, and then line up the functions, what would the accumulated functions for individuals look like? If they converge to form a single line graph within a range of measurement error, this means that the development of this particular competence depends entirely on age. Of course, this is only a hypothetical case because it presupposes no meaningful individual variation in any age group: a very unlikely case. Still, it is worth examining because it means that for every individual, development of competence depends completely on age, due to the influence of genetic or nongenetic biological factors, culturally defined age-related environmental change, or joint operation of these factors that determine the psychological structure at each level. The parameters of these factors are the same for all individuals from the first set of conditions to the last set. This is a case for determinism. In this case, only the changing level of competence according to age is of chief concern. In addition, because there is no individual difference, group data of age difference obtained cross-sectionally can be used in place of the age change data obtained by the longitudinal method, assuming that no birth-cohort effect is operative.

### Case B: Complete Correlation of Individual's Status Among Time Points

The prerequisite for this case is the existence of variations among the individuals on the target competence at each age level. An individual difference is not to be attributed to random errors but to a theoretically meaningful variation. This is the case of stability of the relative position of each individual within a group. Longitudinal design is required to examine this issue. In this case, line graphs representing individual age functions do not converge into a single graph. Instead, the trajectories move nearly parallel with each other. Though parameters for each individual differ, factors that influence the individual's course of development, including genetic or nongenetic biological factors, environmental factors, and joint operation of these factors are assumed to be the same for all individuals. This is also a case of determinism in the sense that the future place for each individual is highly predictable once we know the parameters for each individual. Note, however, that a high determinacy of developmental trajectories does not necessarily entail a lawful effect of age on the performance.

### Case C: Fluctuating Individuals' Status in a Group Across Times

Instability of relative position across time means that line graphs of age function obtained by a longitudinal method do not take parallel trajectories but rather crossings of lines. These occur everywhere even if we rescale the age dimension to adjust for individual difference in the rate of development. Note that even in this case, a developmental trajectory that is averaged across individuals may show a systematic relation to age. Therefore, a significant age effect does not guarantee the determinacy of an individual's developmental trajectory. Conversely, lack of age effect does not exclude the high predictability of the individual's relative positions across time.

It is unfortunate that the data collection methodology of Roazzi and de Souza does not provide us with the time-to-time correlation data combined with the examination of age effects. Therefore, we cannot conclude that the fluency dimension is more deterministic, whereas the originality dimension is more indeterministic based on the degree of age effect in group data. It is not clear whether Roazzi and de Souza have in mind the degree of departure of the obtained results from Case A due to random factors. With the exception of the unlikely Case A explained earlier, we need cross-time information for individual cases in order to judge whether "each and every phase would be determined by prior conditions." Instead, Roazzi and de Souza report the changing pattern of relations among the variables in the three age groups. Still, these results are based on averaged relations among the variables across children, and they do not provide us with sufficient information to speak of the determinacy versus indeterminacy issue.

### Chapter by Legerstee on Social-Conceptual Development

The main points of Legerstee's chapter can be summarized as follows:

1. Organism-environment interactions are needed in order for an emergent structure in a social-conceptual domain to consolidate, where social as well as physical environments are pertinent. Developmental significance of triadic relations among an organism, another person, and an object (e.g., a plaything) or a third person, is especially emphasized.

2. Development of an organism occurs under the constraints of the organism and the environment.

3. Social factors and nonsocial factors are fundamentally different in an infant's world. The former involves intersubjective coregulation between infants and people. This coregulation is a creative process in that "through

sharing information that either subject possesses, knowledge can be constructed that neither partner possessed."

She characterizes her general framework for the development of infants' understanding of people as a "modified structuralist view." What characterizes her theory most is, in my view, her proposal of domain-specific predispositions whose structures are independently assembled within each domain, that is, social and nonsocial. As the mechanism to explain young infants' differential responsiveness to people and objects, Legerstee postulates the percept of *will* to be applied specifically to people's movements. Still, early structures are neither detailed nor explicit, but they do become more specific and also more general in the sense that they are cross-connected to form higher order structures through the process of self-organization and mediation by social partners.

The self-organizing process of coupling that leads to emergence of a new structure is also conceptualized by Legerstee. Her concept of coupling, however, is described in more abstract terms than is Lewis'. Legerstee notes simply that the subtle ways of coupling of the infant and the environment as a result of interactions leads cross-connecting of the domain-specific systems into a single, stable, higher order system.

Being involved in a triadic structure consisting, for example, of the active subject, the object of knowledge, and cosubject, under the guidance of a social partner is postulated to be an important basis for development of more complex structures, especially representational thought and language. In this connection, the research findings by Legerstee and others on integration of cognitive systems in delayed children are interesting, for they provide us with clues for the process of cross-domain integration.

There are two research directions that should be more clearly explicated in order for Legerstee's model to become a more powerful one in the social-conceptual domain. First, the model should be expanded to deal with multiple social partners. In many cultures it is common for a young child to live in multiple settings (e.g., family and daycare center), and to develop relationships with more than one person (e.g., mother, father, siblings; teachers and peers) in each setting. Thus it is natural for an infant around 1 year of age to develop differentiated cognitive and behavioral systems to deal with interpersonal experience in accordance with the target persons and settings. For example, an infant has different expectations of and shows different behavior patterns to the partner depending on whether the infant is playing with his or her father at home or with a peer in a daycare center. My view is that an infant has developed a common pool of behavioral repertory, out of which the infant constructs an appropriate interaction system in accordance with the conditions of the partner, of self, and of the setting. Through a series of social interactions, contents of the behavioral repertory of the infant may change, for example, by the incorporation of new or modified behavioral patterns, and by the weakening of a behavior pattern that was negatively fed-back in social interaction.

Our exploratory observation of 1-year-olds at both home and daycare centers has revealed that infants often apply a specific behavior pattern consolidated through continuous social interaction in one setting to another. Depending on the sequel at the second setting, the particular behavior pattern is reinforced, modified, or extinguished.

My second point to extend Legerstee's model is concerned with a role of culture in these cross-setting relationships. We have noticed the role of cultural meaning attached to specific behavior patterns. First, at the emergence of such behavior patterns as hand clapping and head patting, Japanese parents and grandparents accompanied sentences or gestures that gave meaning to the infants' behavior. Parents' contingent responses served to consolidate the specific behavior pattern; this interchange developed into a playful interaction. Thus, the parents' gesture and speech served to trigger the infant's specific behavior pattern. In some cases parental speech and model behavior were extended to guide a rather long sequence of the infant's playful behavior. Soon, part of this behavior pattern was elicited at daycare situations that did not necessarily involve direct interpersonal interaction. If people at daycare centers, for example, teachers or other parents, happened to notice the behavior, almost without fail they responded to the infant behavior, and told it to their colleagues or older children there. We have also observed the application of acquired behavior pattern to other settings in the reverse direction, that is, from the daycare to the home. What is crucial was that both family members and staff of daycare centers shared the cultural meaning of a specific behavior pattern. Without their attachment of common meaning to the infant's behavior, it would not be tried again by the infant in the second setting (Kojima, 1995).

I believe that theory of social-conceptual development from an early period of life should certainly become more productive by taking into account the multiperson social network of the developing child and the embedding cultural contexts.

## CONCLUDING REMARKS

### Looking Backwards and Forward in Story-Telling and Searching for Causes

An article that appeared in a popular science magazine (Zimmer, 1995) described an interesting development of story-telling about emergence of tetrapod limbs. A scenario constructed in the 1940s by the Harvard paleontologist Alfred Romer, and long been believed, was that the tetrapod's limbs emerged as a response to the challenge of walking on land. Recent careful analyses of fossil skeletons, inferred locomotive functions based on anatomical structures, and the renewed view of the Devonian environment, have led researchers to construct a new story on the evolution of tetrapod limbs. Two researchers at the University of Cambridge's Museum of Zoology claimed that roughly 360 million years ago, *Acanthostega*, the most primitive tetrapod yet found to have lived underwater, had already developed four limbs and sophisticated, multijointed 8 (not 5!) fingers. These researchers suggested that the limbs of the tetrapods evolved first in the water for use in the water, and it was simply a lucky coincidence that this very feature turned out later to be of better use walking on land. "The first vertebrate that walked onto land did not crawl on fish fins; it had evolved well-turned legs millions of years beforehand" (Zimmer, 1995, p. 120). Therefore, it was not that our ancestors were driven by an imperative to live on land and that they had foresight for their descendants, including us.

The lessons of this story revision testify to the value of good, systematic data for theory building but also the need for careful monitoring of our theory-building process. The phenomenon called preadaptation in evolution is believed to be unpredictable in nature. As was cautioned by Crites (1986), a sequence of events looked at in hindsight has the appearance of causal necessity. We know an outcome and look backwards at the sequences leading up to it in order to construct the story of, say, individual development, from its beginning. Even though we admit the rooms for indeterminacy, a sequence of events being looked at forward tends to have the sense of directionality pulled by something intentional. We, as story-telling beings, tend to construct stories that reflect our ways of thinking in our daily lives.

Builders of dynamic systems theories seem to have been cautious enough to protect themselves from this pitfall. On the other hand, however, they tended to resort to random or incidental small variations in the system as major sources of indeterminacy of the developmental path. As an old Chinese maxim dictates, a very small difference in the beginning may lead to a big difference at the end points. We tend not to be satisfied with the theorem of unpredictability and dynamism mainly triggered by random factors, but seek to know how different we will be and why we are different at the end point of an individual's developmental path. In my view, many aspects of academic activities by developmentalists consist essentially of story-telling. Like theories of evolution or clinical case reports, description of ontogenetic change and causal explanations of the mechanism of change are such stories constructed to be told by researchers. A story cannot be constructed without a mental framework to organize information, and theoretical models of human development represent such mental framework. Models of change and development especially require specification on directionality of change and on causality. In a sense, these scientific models reflect cultural ways of story-telling. I believe that exchanges of ideas of implicit cultural models on human development will certainly be a profitable base for theory development.

## REFERENCES

Crites, S. (1986). Storytime: Recollecting the past and projecting the future. In T. R. Sarbin (Ed.), *Narrative psychology: The storied nature of human conduct* (pp. 152–173). New York: Praeger.

Fogel, A. (1993). *Developing through relationships: Origins of communication, self, and culture.* Chicago: University of Chicago Press.

Haken, H. (1987). Synergetics: An approach to self-organization. In F. E. Yates (Ed.), *Self-organizing systems: The emergence of order* (pp. 417–434). New York: Plenum.

Kojima, H. (1995). Family, children, and culture of the society. In M. Kajita (Ed.), *Interpersonal relationships and human growth* (pp. 80–95). Tokyo: Yuhikaku. (in Japanese)

Peterson, I. (1993). *Newton's clock: Chaos in the solar system.* New York: Freeman.

Thelen, E., & Smith, L. B. (1994). *A dynamic systems approach to the development of cognition and action.* Cambridge, MA: MIT Press.

Zimmer, C. (1995). Coming onto the land. *Discover, 16* (June), pp. 118–127.

# AUTHOR INDEX

## A

Abraham, R. H., 208, 214
Adamson, L., 255, 257
Adler, A., 55, 57, 60
Alamo, L., 208, 214
Alansky, J. A., 198, 214
Alessandri, S. M., 213, 216
Allen, P. M., 145, 150
Als, H., 96, 109
Altman, I., 66, 87, 92
Amazeen, P. G., 137, 150
Anderson, M., 247, 257, 259
Andreas, A., 198, 215
Aphek, E., 131, 132
Aristotle, 163, 164, 168, 220, 261
Astington, J. W., 264, 270
Ayres, J., 74, 87

## B

Bacon, F., 221, 242
Bahrick, L., 97, 108
Bakeman, R., 255, 257
Baker, J., 72, 74, 75, 87
Bakhtin, M. M., 66, 87, 98, 108
Baldwin, J. M., 52, 60, 98, 108, 119, 120, 121, 132
Bandura, A., 206, 214
Baron, R. M., 137, 150
Barriere, M., 83, 91
Bates, E., 95, 108, 194, 214
Bateson, G., 49, 57, 60, 71, 75, 81, 85, 87
Baudonniere, P. M., 83, 90
Baxter, L. A., 66, 67, 72, 87
Beatty, J., 46, 61
Beavin, J. H., 74, 92
Beebe, B., 76, 87
Beek, P. J., 137, 150
Benedikt, R., 126, 133
Berger, C. R., 66, 87
Bergson, H., 61, 67, 87, 120, 132

Bernal, G., 47, 61, 72, 74, 75, 87
Bernardini, C., 225, 242
Berofsky, B., 40, 61
Black, M., 224, 225, 242
Blanck, G., 58, 61
Blanck, R., 58, 61
Bloombaum, M., 233, 242
Bochner, A. P., 74, 88
Bonica, L., 83, 91
Borg, I., 227, 242
Bornstein, M. H., 49, 61
Borton, R. W., 97, 109
Bouchard, T. J., 25, 26, 37
Boulding, K., 95, 108
Bowlby, J., 207, 214
Bowman, T. G., 247, 254, 257, 258
Branco, A. U., 71, 72, 81, 82, 83, 88
Bransford, J. D., 74, 88
Brazleton, T. B., 76, 88, 96, 109
Bremner, J. G., 253, 257, 271
Bretherton, I., 197, 214
Brown, B. B., 66, 87, 92
Brown, E. L., 111, 115
Bruner, J. S., 58, 61, 96, 108, 246, 250, 255, 257, 268, 270
Bryant, P., 224, 226, 242
Buhler, C., 121, 132
Bullinger, A., 121, 132
Bullis, C., 72, 87
Bullowa, M., 96, 108
Butterworth, G. E., 49, 61, 97, 108, 246, 248, 258
Bynum, W. E., 111, 115

## C

Cabral, E. A., 96, 98, 109
Cairns, R., 168, 174, 270
Calvo, M. E., 208, 214
Camaioni, L., 140, 150
Campelo de Souza, B., 230, 240, 242
Canary, D. J., 74, 88

**285**

# SUBJECT INDEX

## A

Abbreviation, 93, 105, 137, 197
  exchange(s), 105, 106
  in time, 106
  face-to-face exchanges, 106
  form, 99
  meaning, 105, 107
  shared activity, 105
  shared construction, 106
  shared dyadic meaning, 106
  shared meaning, 107
Accommodation, 29, 30
Adults, the role of, 264, 270
Age function, 279, 280
Analog, 237
Animate, 76, 245, 246, 248-250, 254
Anxiety, 204, 207-210, 212
Appraisal, 201, 203, 204, 207-213
Arrow of time, 15
Assimilation, 29, 30
Attention, 141-143, 146, 147, 149
  orientation of, 146
Attractor, 135-137, 140-145, 148, 149
  chaotic, 19
  point, 19

## B

Behavioral genetics, 24, 25
Bell curve, 24
  shaped distribution, 16
Brownian movement, 135, 148

## C

Canalization, 264, 270
Catastrophe theory, 33, 34
Cause, 220
  causality, 42, 220-222

development, 226
model, 273
necessity, 185, 186
Central limit theorem, 16, 18
Chance, 45
Chaos, 37, 42, 208-210
  chaotic, 66, 86
  chaotic dynamics, 32
  chaotic model, 19, 20
  chaotic systems, 113
  theory, 269
Cognition-emotion, 193, 201-205, 207, 212
Coherence, 56
Communication, 4, 5, 65, 69, 70-72, 74, 75, 77, 78, 80, 83, 85-87, 94-97, 99-103, 107
Complex order, 21
  complexity, 31, 48
Configuration, 184, 185
Connectionist networks, 34
Consciousness
  the role of, 264, 270
Conservation, 33
Constraints, 180, 181, 193-195, 198, 200, 205, 209-213
Construction, 167, 169, 245-247, 252, 255, 256
Contextual metacommunication, 75
Contingency, 247-249 251, 254
Coupling, 199-203, 205, 207-209, 212, 213
Convergence, 71-73, 78-80, 82-85
Configuration, 135, 136, 139, 140, 142-146, 149
Coregulation, 68, 70, 71, 79, 136, 147, 149
Correlation, 26, 29, 136, 137, 140, 144-146, 148, 149
Coupling, 277, 281
Countertransference, 74

**291**